The Religious and Historical Paintings of Jan Steen

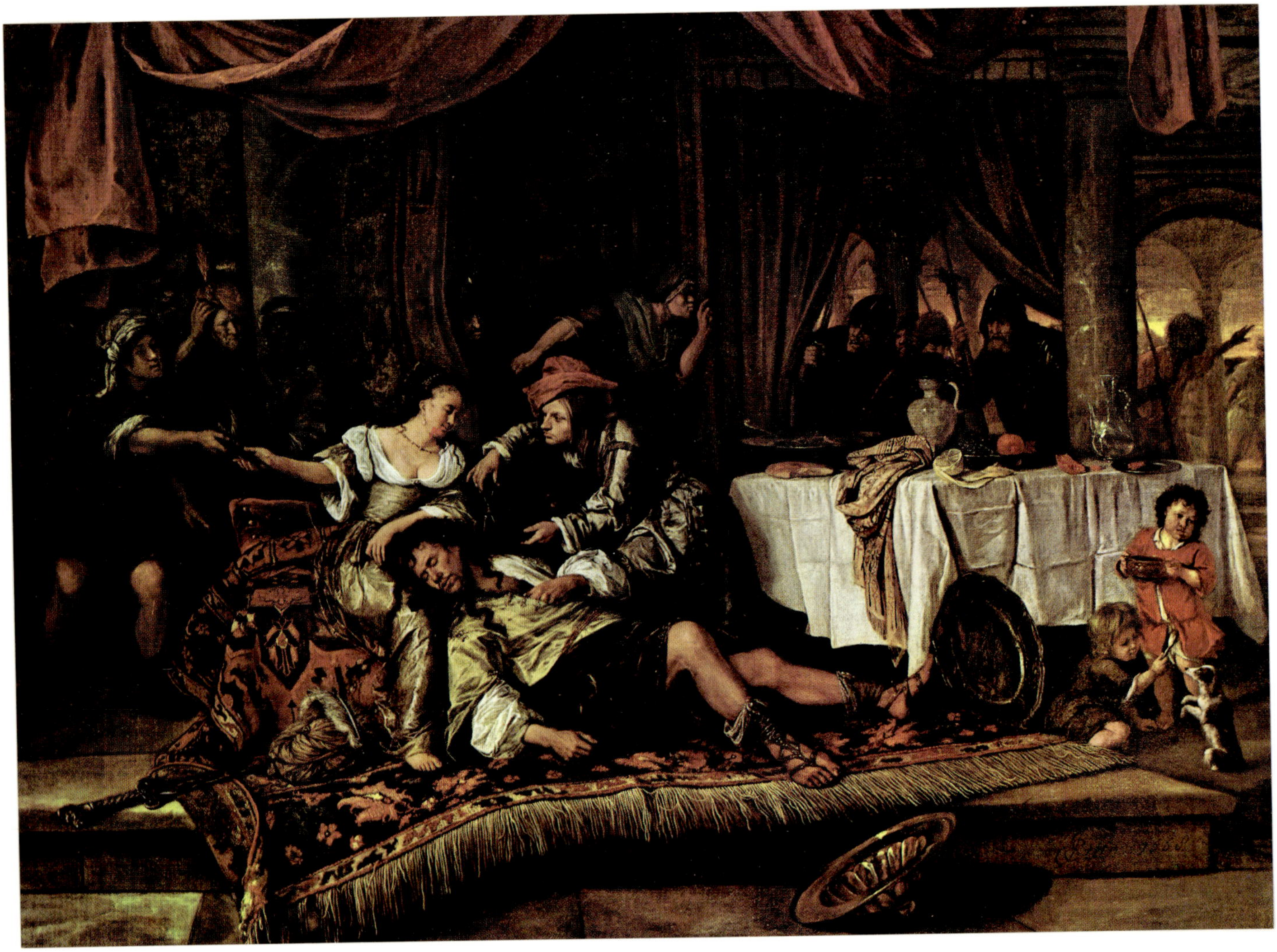

The Religious and Historical Paintings of Jan Steen

Baruch D. Kirschenbaum

ALLANHELD & SCHRAM
New York & Montclair

FRONTISPIECE: *Samson and Delilah,* 1668 (identical with Fig. 67). Private collection, The Netherlands. Photograph by A. Dingjan, The Hague.

ABNER SCHRAM (SCHRAM ENTERPRISES, LTD.)
1860 Broadway, New York, N.Y. 10023

ALLANHELD, OSMUN & CO. PUBLISHERS, INC.
19 Brunswick Road, Montclair, N.J. 07042

Published in the United States of America in 1977
by Abner Schram and by Allanheld, Osmun & Co.
under the imprint *Allanheld & Schram*

LIBRARY OF CONGRESS CATALOGING IN PUBLICATION DATA

Kirschenbaum, Baruch D 1931-
The religious and historical paintings of Jan Steen.

Bibliography: p.
Includes index.
1. Steen, Jan Havickszoon, 1626-1679. 2. Christian art and symbolism—Netherlands. 3. History in art—Netherlands.
I. Steen, Jan Havickszoon, 1626-1679.
II. Title.
ND653.S8K57 759.9492 76-42140
ISBN 0-8390-0170-3

Printed in The United States of America

For Blossom

Preface

My interest in Jan Steen as a painter of Biblical and historical narratives began at the Städelsches Kunstinstitut in Frankfurt. It was there that I saw his early painting of *Moses Striking the Rock* (Fig. 27). Though I had seen others of his Biblical paintings before that, like the great *Sacrifice of Iphigenia* in the Rijksmuseum (Fig. 82), it was this painting that excited my imagination and curiosity. One detail in particular captured my attention—in the family group at the left, a man bending over places his hand gently upon the head of a little girl as he raises a cup to her lips. The girl, seen from the back, drinks eagerly. I was at the time travelling with my wife and small daughter on what was our first and very low-budget trip to Europe. Perhaps it was the painful awareness of our own difficulties that led me to the recognition of that particular motif, and a love of Steen. The interest aroused then, resulted in this study and though I have arrived at a much altered sense of Steen as an interpreter of Biblical and historical themes, something of the quality of that initial response still remains with me. Indeed, that Steen's history paintings should inspire an awareness of contemporary circumstances seems totally fitting. It is precisely such reciprocity between historical and contemporary situations which, as I've tried to show in the chapters that follow, makes up the essential quality of Steen's wonderful and sometimes riotous historical vision.

This study was originally written as my doctoral dissertation for the Department of Fine Arts at Harvard University (1966). I wish to thank all those both here and abroad who helped towards its completion. My very particular appreciation goes to Professor Seymour Slive who, through his teaching and personal warmth, inspired my studies in Dutch painting, and who oversaw with great patience the research and writing of the dissertation.

In the preparation of the material for this study every effort has been made to find the present owners of the paintings catalogued and referred to and to secure proper permissions for their use. I would be most grateful for any information concerning the whereabouts of unlocated pictures.

Difficulty in locating some of the pictures has necessitated in a few cases the use of poor quality reproductions. For this, author and publishers apologize, but with the belief that in a study of this nature some visual reference is better than none.

Table of Contents

List of Illustrations

List of Abbreviations Used

B.	Bredius, *The Paintings of Rembrandt,* 1936
Burlington	Burlington Magazine
FRL	Frick Art Reference Library, New York
GdBA	*Gazette des Beaux-Arts*
Handex	Annotated copy of Hofstede de Groot's *Catalogue Raisonné,* kept at the Rijksbureau voor Kunsthistorische Documentatie at The Hague
HdG	Hofstede de Groot, *Catalogue Raisonné,* I, 1908
J of W&CI	*Journal of the Warburg and Courtauld Institutes*
O-H	*Oud-Holland*
RKHD	Rijksbureau voor Kunsthistorische Documentatie at The Hague
Sm	Smith, *Catalogue Raisonné,* IV, 1833
Sm Supp	Supplement to the above, V, 1842
T-B	*Thieme-Becker Kunstlerlexikon*
W	Van Westrheene, *Jan Steen, étude sur l'art en Hollande,* 1856
Witt	Witt Library, Warburg Institute, London
ZfbK	*Zeitschrift für bildende Kunst*

The Religious and Historical Paintings of Jan Steen

Introduction

> I can easily imagine, that if this extraordinary man had had the good fortune to have been born in Italy instead of Holland, had he lived in Rome instead of Leyden, and been blessed with Michael Angelo and Raffaelle for his masters, instead of Brower and van Gowen; the same sagacity and penetration which distinguishes so accurately the different characters and expressions in his vulgar figures, would, when exerted in the selection and imitation of what was great and elevated in nature, have been equally successful; and he would have ranged with the pillars and supporters of our Art.

So wrote Joshua Reynolds in 1774, in his sixth discourse to the students of the British Royal Academy. With this comment of historical regret, he declared Jan Steen one of Holland's greatest painters—yet, even while extolling, he relegated Steen to the "inferior branches" of art. A particular judgment is implied, and one that had its origins early in the Renaissance and found its most formalized statement in the writings of the French academicians of the seventeenth century. It was André Félibien who made explicit the hierarchy of types within the general category of painting, and when Reynolds, following that critical position, spoke of the natural superiority of the great and elevated in painting and implied Steen's inferior status, he meant that Steen had not a lesser ability but a lesser vision, and therefore ranked lower on the scale of artistic endeavor. For him, Jan Steen was one of the great makers of the "lower class of art," from whom students could learn, but whom they should never imitate if they aspired to true greatness.

As determined by accident of birth, Steen could excel only in that which was rightfully his to paint: family intimacies, tavern jollity, brothel scenes, and the like. To go beyond these limits meant personal failure—and the very degradation of Art. As evidence for his warning, and hence for the exclusiveness of artistic class, Reynolds points to Steen's own occasional sorties into the domain of great themes. In his eighth discourse, delivered in 1786, he is quite specific:

> We often see grave and great subjects by artists of another school [other than the Roman or Florentine]; who, though excellent in the lower class of art, proceeding on the principles which regulate that class, and not recollecting, or not knowing, that they were to address themselves to another faculty of the mind, have become perfectly ridiculous.
>
> The picture which I have at present in my thoughts is a sacrifice of Iphigenia, painted by Jan Steen, a painter of whom I have formerly had occasion to speak with the highest approbation; and even in this picture, the subject of which is by no means adapted to his genius, there is nature and expression; but it is such expression, and the countenances are so familiar and consequently so vulgar, and the whole accompanied with such finery of silks and velvet, that one would be almost tempted to doubt, whether the artist did not purposely intend to burlesque his subject.

Acquaintance with the painting *The Sacrifice of Iphigenia,* now in the Rijksmuseum (Fig. 82, Cat. 74), makes it easier to understand Reynolds' doubt over Steen's intentions. The composition contrasts Agamemnon's excessively dramatic anguish of moral decision with Iphigenia's placid acceptance of fate. Steen has dressed Iphigenia in bridal white; but he has given her a diaphanous silken veil of black. In contrast, her handmaiden, kneeling to pick up a discarded wreath, is brilliant in lemon-yellow satin. The rich textures and light colors of the foreground give way gradually in the middle ground to deeper colors and thicker atmosphere, until there is only faint suggestion of figures before the monochromed landscape in the distance.

However carefully composed and beautifully painted, the picture nevertheless breaks all the rules of classical decorum, which demanded that serious narrative painting be historically appropriate. Steen seems either unaware of or unconcerned with such canons. He has jumbled the costumes anachronistically (none of them can be called truly classical); and, as Reynolds complains, he has hung this finery on radically un-heroic types. This bony-kneed old man with his crown askew, could he be mighty Agamemnon, tamer of horses? Or could this young woman of the seventeenth century be delicate Iphigenia, her father's innocent victim? For Reynolds assuredly they could not be; and so the picture could be viewed only as a travesty. Such humorous incidentals as the crying cupid with his broken arrow or the scolding old wife serve to corroborate Reynolds' view of Steen's lack of historical seriousness, and to provoke censure.

It is difficult to say when the denial of "great subjects" to Steen first began. Houbraken, who in his *Groote Schouburgh* (III, 1721) included the earliest life of Steen, found his paintings spirited and amusing, and testified to Steen's popularity both during and after his lifetime. Houbraken owned *The Marriage of Tobias and Sarah* now in Brunswick (Fig. 66, Cat. 25a/457). He thought highly of it, saying that it was like seeing the actual occurrence.[1] He thought the picture to be simply of a marriage ceremony, however, and did not recognize the Biblical reference. Weyerman in his life of Steen of 1729 indicated that he thought highly of Steen's history pieces. He knew a painting of *Christ at Emmaus* (Fig. 45, Cat. 65) then in the house of Jakob le Beuf at Leiden. He declared that Steen "made that artful piece with the exertion of all the powers of his soul. . . ."[2]

In one instance Houbraken did censure Steen for use of inappropriate detail. He criticized his incorporation of a pickled herring in a presently untraceable painting he called *The Fable of Mithras* (Cat. 75).[3] Had Houbraken been more familiar with Steen's Biblical and historical works, such criticism would probably have occurred more often for he, like Reynolds, believed in the sanctity of the history painting.

From Reynolds late in the eighteenth century, through much of the nineteenth, a prejudicial view prevailed. John Smith in his *Catalogue Raisonné* of 1833 added the following note to the description of Steen's *Marriage at Cana* now in the Beit collection (Fig. 62, Cat. 48/49):

> The total incapacity of Jan Steen to render the necessary dignity of character and expression to his figures, so indispensible in an historical subject, is no less evident in this picture than in every other example of a similar kind; in all other respects the talents and genius of the artist are strikingly evinced.[4]

In his *Treasures of Art in Great Britain* of 1854, Waagen described Steen's *Massacre of the Innocents* (Cat. 42) as "a picture which in its revolting coarseness shows the utter incapability of the artist to comprehend the only legitimate mode of conceiving this subject."[5] And speaking of the *Marriage at Cana,* Waagen found, like Smith, that Steen had degraded the subject "to a level of his sphere of Art."[6] Even Van Westrheene, whose research published in *Jan Steen, étude sur l'art en Hollande* of 1856 was largely responsible for the emancipation of Steen from his image as painter-buffoon, found the subject treatment in the *Marriage at Cana* wanting; he repeated, more mildly, Smith's criticism:

> Quoinque nous comprenions facilement que la dignité exigée pour de tels sujets, fasse défaut dans cette composition, le génie de l'artiste s'y est révélé en plusieurs détails d'expression.[7]

Steen's reputation as a drunkard and a buffoon probably contributed to the moralistic dismissal of especially his religious paintings. Particulars of his life could be adduced as proof of his lack of commitment to Christian values. That raffish reputation had its origin with Arnold Houbraken's anecdotal life of the painter in *De Groote Schouburgh* of 1721, and even more in Campo Weyerman's plagiarized and vulgarized version in *De Levensbeschryving . . .* of 1729. In both works Steen is portrayed as a low-life drunkard whose frolicsome and disreputable personal life, centering around tavern and brewery (both of which he owned at different times), was reflected in the dubious moral quality of many of his popular genre scenes. While stories of Steen's profligacy may have some basis in fact, they came in this case to hide both Steen and his art.

Such obfuscation, as Lyckle De Vries has pointed out in a recent study on Steen's critical acceptance, arose out of the premise found already in Houbraken that the life and work of an artist are an inseparable unity.[8] If Steen was an innkeeper, a brewer and general low-life character, then his art must be equally clownish since that was his natural bent. The French eighteenth-century historian Descamps felt that if Steen painted well it was because his native ability allowed him to rise above the nature of his life.[9] In our time we have learned to do away with the association of life and work. Critically, such dissociation allows us to judge work on its own merit, but it also leads to a narrow view in which art is too often thought of as separable either from life in general or from the life of the person who created it. Because of such separation, our criticism is too often mechanical and bereft of spirit. Our desire must be to discover Steen's vision, and that means a reintegration of his art and his life but without the old moral prejudices.

Van Westrheene in 1856 first swept away many of the old and libelous tales by documenting a juster image of Steen. His monograph not only renovated Steen's image, but opened the way for new research and appreciation. Van der Willigen in *Les artistes de Haarlem* of 1870 and later Bredius in numerous articles continued the work of documentation. Steen emerged from those researches rehabilitated, a serious painter who, though followed and copied even in his own lifetime, was, like so many others of his time, unable to make a living at painting, and was beset by chronic financial problems. Though these problems led him more than once into endeavors outside painting, there can be no doubt that he held himself primarily a painter. His production alone, as listed by Hofstede de Groot in his *Catalogue Raisonné* of 1908,[10] measures Steen's professional dedication. Twice, furthermore, he was foreman and once Dean of the St. Lucas guild in his native Leiden. Over the years since Van Westrheene, Steen has come to be accepted as one of Holland's greatest genre painters. Bredius thought him second only to Rembrandt among the painters of the Golden Age.

Salvage of his personal reputation and the lasting delight in his genre have not, however, made his histories more acceptable. In our century, too, a critical bias prevails, though it differs from that of the nineteenth century. It holds in effect that Steen's themes were merely excuses to paint on a grand scale the joviality and richness which he loved, and we err if we seek in them real religious or historical sentiment. "In general," says H. E. van Gelder, even while recognizing the possibility of deeper meaning, "it does not seem advisable to look for a deep significance in the work of Steen whose realism is almost too childlike."[11] Schmidt-Degener, in a companion article, expressed a similar view:

> Occasionally he [Steen] put a drama on his programme because in his surroundings he found an irresistibly rich choice of fitting "supers," but the tragic spark is immediately quenched in the flood of popular humour.[12]

"The incident," he continues, referring to Samson's capture by the Philistines and the treachery of Delilah (Fig. 63, Cat. 12/10a), "is stripped bare of all its Old Testament quality." He adds that when Steen did attempt a seriously religious work, like *Christ at Emmaus* (Fig. 45, Cat. 65), he failed for lack of true religious depth.[13]

Bredius, who published a monumental collection of plates and commentary on the tricentennial of Steen's birth, maintained that Steen viewed his Biblical and historical scenes with the same humor that pervades his genre. Bredius, like other critics, found that humor light-hearted and palliating *(vergoelijkenden)*, and without serious historical implication.[14]

C. W. de Groot, in his enlightening dissertation on Steen and verbal traditions in the Netherlands, *Jan Steen, Beeld en Woord* of 1952, felt that in the last analysis the religious works left one unsatisfied and disappointed. For Steen, he asserts, the description was more important than the happening. Thus in *The Wrath of Ahasuerus* (Fig. 59, Cat. 18) the opulent still life tumbling to the floor was the main point, and the appropriate spiritual qualities necessary in religious representations were missing. Often when Steen wished to be grandly pathetic he came out only ridiculous, and the tendency is to laugh at him rather than with him.[15]

Willem Martin, who of all Dutch historians has written most on Steen, with studies dating from 1909,[16] still found, in his last book, *Jan Steen* of 1954, the artist's Biblical paintings "important but difficult to grasp." He saw Steen as the great good-humored folk-painter of Old Holland, and felt with Schmidt-Degener that he sometimes failed in recognizing his own limitations:

> It is a great question if Steen always perfectly recognized the limits of his talents and if in some of his allegorical, historical and Biblical representations he did not aim too high. Paintings like his *Christ at Emmaus* and his *Sacrifice of Iphigenia* are rather genre pieces, and the last he borrowed from theater. It appears that he overestimated himself in painting such subjects, for he lacked imagination and historical sense, and was exclusively concerned with daily happenings.[17]

This critical approach to Steen's paintings leaves us with history for genre's sake. It efficiently eliminates the need to consider Steen as a serious painter of religious and historical themes. Being less literary than the older academic criticism, it allows a more joyful appreciation of the formal qualities of Steen's histories, which all agree are among his very richest work. However, in choosing most often to ignore his treatment of the subject, or to pass it off as idiosyncrasy, it no more confronts Steen's historical invention than did the academic attitude which declared the painter misguided and his pictures outrageous.

In his genre painting sometimes he is crude, sometimes banal, sometimes excessively moralistic. Often he burlesques his subjects with clowning and incongruities. These talents and foibles are acceptable, and enthusiastically sought after, in the portrayal of mundane subjects. When, however, he uses some of the same techniques and vocabulary for the great Biblical and classical themes, he creates an apparent clash, both in content and in form, which must be reckoned with and reconciled if we are to understand his works in this area.[18] Steen's very proclivity for genre subjects lies at the heart of his historical invention; but to restrict appreciation of historical scenes to appreciation of genre works is to shirk the task of dealing with the paintings in their entirety.

Steen did mix the vulgar with the elevated, the satirical with the serious, the comic with the tragic; and in so doing, he created an image of historical happening unique in the history of art. It is the intention of this study to re-examine and re-evaluate Steen's work in history in the hope of bringing that uniqueness to better definition and to larger attention.

References

1. Houbraken, *Groote Schouburgh,* III, 1721, p. 16.
2. Weyerman, *Levens-Beschryvingen,* II, 1729, p. 364.
3. Houbraken, *Groote Schouburgh,* II, 1719, pp. 245-246.
4. Smith, IV, p. 32 (No. 100).
5. Waagen, II, p. 138.
6. Waagen, III, p. 207.
7. Westrheene, p. 118.
8. De Vries, *O-H* LXXXVII, 1973, No. 4, pp. 231 ff.
9. Descamps, *La vie des peintres flamands, allemands et hollandais,* v. 3, 1760, pp. 26-31.
10. That number is swelled by the inclusion of sales catalogue references and numerous undetected repetitions. Nevertheless, Steen's *oeuvre* was considerable and Hofstede de Groot's catalogue is an invaluable starting point in any study of his work.
11. Schmidt-Degener and Van Gelder, *Steen,* 1927, p. 35
12. *Ibid.,* p. 17.
13. *Ibid.,* p. 17.
14. Bredius, *Steen,* 1927, pp. 24-25.
15. *Beeld en Woord,* 1952, pp. 168-71.
16. See the Bibliography for a complete listing.
17. "Het is zeer de vraag of Steen de grenzen van zijn talent wel altijd juist heeft ingezien en of hij besefte, dat hij in sommige allegorische, historische en Bijbelse voorstellingen te hoog greep. Schilderijen gelijk zijn *Emmausgangers* en zijn *Offer van Iphigenia* zijn veeler genrestukken, al is het laatste blojkbaar aan het toneel ontleend. Het heeft er alle schijn van, dat hij in zelfoverschatting dergelijke onderwerpen schilderde, terwijl hij de verbeeldingskracht en de historische zin miste en uitsluitend op het dagelijks gebeuren was ingesteld." Martin, *Steen,* 1954, p. 23.
18. In a recent article on Steen's paintings of *The Marriage at Cana,* Wolfgang Stechow has sought to discover some of the deeper significance of Steen's integration of genre and history. *Nederlands Kunsthistorisch Jaarboek,* XXIII, 1972, pp. 73-83.

1

Steen's Development As a History Painter

The Historical Oeuvre

Since the nineteenth century, an increase in the number of historical pictures attributed to Steen has paralleled the increase in his total oeuvre. Smith, in his *Catalogue Raisonné of Dutch Painters* of 1833 and his *Supplement* to that work of 1842, listed about 300 works by Steen, of which 24 represented historical subjects. Van Westrheene, in his catalogue in *Jan Steen, étude sur l'art en Hollande* of 1856, increased the total number to 482, of which 37 were historical. The last catalogue of Steen's oeuvre, compiled by Hofstede de Groot in 1907, *A Catalogue Raisonné of the Works of the Most Eminent Dutch Painters of the Seventeenth Century* (English edition, 1908), listed about 1000 pictures. Of these, 107 were historical.

Both Van Westrheene and Hofstede de Groot included in their listings works reported only in sales catalogues, even when only a single reference was all that was available. Such sparse clues make accurate cross-referencing impossible, and leave many undetected repetitions and unsupportable attributions. This has swelled numbers in both catalogues, though more so in Hofstede de Groot's. However, even based on known works only, a count of the historical oeuvre is still sizeable. Of the 107 historical paintings reported by Hofstede de Groot, he knew personally 44 and could include 22 others on the basis of reliable reports or gathered information: a total of 66. The catalogue of Steen's historical pictures with which this study concludes lists 101 pictures (84 religious subjects and 17 taken from classical mythology or ancient history). Of these, 37 have been personally inspected, 22 others known through photographs, 11 well documented though untraceable, and 31 given as reported from various sources but with little supportable evidence. Hence 70 pictures can actually be credited with good evidence, though that number may include a few doubtful attributions.[1]

These statistics reveal two things. First, the number of historical and non-historical works attributed to Steen has markedly increased over the years. What in Smith was a respectable production comes in Hofstede de Groot to be a formidable output. Steen was born in 1626 and died in 1679 at the age of fifty-three. Considering the shortness of his life, he must have been an indefatigable worker. His earliest dated painting, *The Death of Ananias* (Fig. 1, Cat. 66), comes from 1651; his latest, *The Pastry Seller* in Rouen (HdG 267), is dated 1678. Second, and more to the point here, though his histories are only a small part of his total production—about a tenth—they are more than enough to show a major and lasting concern for such subjects. Seventy pictures (if only the known or well-documented ones are counted) could suffice as a painter's entire corpus; many artists have been judged on far fewer. Further, these seventy historical pictures, coming from all periods of his career, allow the critic range enough to discuss Steen's development as a history painter and to comment about his particular historical vision.

Statistics alone, however, might be misleading, exaggerating only a minor interest. Not so with Steen: his narrative pictures, especially those from his later years, are among the largest and richest, and give ample proof of the effort he lavished upon them. In the Rolzaal in the government buildings at The Hague, for example, hangs a canvas of about 1669 representing *The Banquet of Antony and Cleopatra* (Fig. 60, Cat. 86a/b), in which he created a full 6 × 3½ feet of royal and magnificent company to watch Cleopatra dissolve her pearl in rosy wine while Antony begs surcease.

The consistency with which Steen treated some themes also indicates the depth of his commitment to historical subjects. The miracle at Cana most fascinated him, and he painted the scene at least six times (see Cat. 45–50b). The first was made about 1650; the last, in 1676, some twenty-five years later (Cat. 45 and 50). Judging, then, from the number, quality, and consistency of his effort, Steen's work in history must be seen as a major part of his life's work. His development in that area demands concentrated study.

Chronology

Construction of a chronology for Steen is made difficult by the paucity of dated works. Of his entire production, only fifty-five works are either dated or datable with external evidence, and several of those remain unknown today. Of these dated pictures, none were made before 1651 and only thirteen between 1651 and 1660. This means that while the last two decades of his life are fairly well documented, his early years, and especially those before 1651, yield little material with which to work. The situation with the historical pictures is even more frustrating. Of the possible hundred and one histories painted by Steen, only nine known pictures are clearly dated; two have questionable dates; and one picture was reported sold in 1651, giving it a date of that year or earlier. This last, *The Story of Hagar* (Cat. 2a), is untraceable, but serves to prove Steen's early interest in Biblical subjects. The dated and datable works are as follows:

1651 (or earlier): *The Story of Hagar* (Cat. 2a). As indicated in the catalogue, a work of this subject was purchased in The Hague in 1651 for Field-Marshal Wrangel, the acting Swedish Governor-General of Pomerania. The picture has sometimes been identified with *Hagar and Ishmael* (Cat. 2b), now in New York. But this identification is incorrect; and the picture remains unknown.
1651: *The Death of Ananias* (Fig. 1, Cat. 66).
1667: *The Rich Man and Lazarus* (Fig. 57, Cat. 59).
1667: *Antony and Cleopatra* (Fig. 56, Cat. 86).
1668: *Samson and Delilah* (Fig. 67, Cat. 10).
1671: *David Returning Victorious* (Fig. 83, Cat. 13).
1671: *The Sacrifice of Iphigenia* (Fig. 82, Cat. 74).
1675: *Expulsion from the Temple* (Fig. 94, Cat. 62).
1676: *The Marriage at Cana* (Fig. 95, Cat. 50).

There are two questionably dated pictures. *The Marriage at Cana* (Fig. 30, Cat. 50b), the date of which cannot clearly be deciphered, has been variously dated 1646, 1653, and 1656, and even 1663 (see Catalogue entry). The large painting *Laban Searching for the Idols* (Fig. 89, Cat. 4/652a), now in the Lakenhal in Leiden, has been reported dated both 1660 and 1661; but whichever was correct, the date disappeared with restoration early in this century. The latest opinion, shared here, is that it should have been read 1669 (see Catalogue entry).

The paucity of dated or datable works, especially for the early years, makes it impossible to construct a precise chronology that progresses from year to year. What can be done, however, and perhaps the most that should be attempted in such reconstructions, is to cluster or group the works around the dated ones without forcing a strict order of execution. From the evidence as examined, the following groups emerge on the basis of years:

1. The Early Years—1651 and Earlier
2. Steen and Jacob de Wet—1653
3. Genre and History—1659/60
4. Transition—1665
5. Steen and Baroque Drama—1667/68
6. The New Elegance—1671
7. The Last Years—1675/76

The following parts of this chapter are divided according to this scheme, and it is hoped that as they unfold, Steen's essential development as a history painter will become clear.

Stated most generally, Steen, as a history painter, progresses from the making of small, unpretentious religious pictures such as *Christ Blessing the Little Children* (Fig. 5, Cat. 60) and *The Seven Acts of Mercy* (Fig. 15, Cat. 67) to the making of large, highly dramatic narratives often opulently staged, such as *The Wrath of Ahasuerus* (Fig. 59, Cat. 18) and *The Banquet of Antony and Cleopatra* (Fig. 60, Cat. 86a/b). In this development Steen departs from his unpretentious early efforts to create an ancient world of great luxury and high emotions. In the 1670's, as in *The Sacrifice of Iphigenia* of 1671 (Fig. 82, Cat. 74), his style opens up to become less dramatic, but more elegant. This seems the proper denouement for the climactic statements of the late 1660's.

The Early Years—1651 and Earlier

Steen's earliest dated picture is a religious one, *The Death of Ananias* of 1651 (Fig. 1, Cat. 66). Along with *The Story of Hagar,* a picture reported sold in that year but now lost (see Cat. 2a), it offers evidence that Steen painted religious subjects at the beginning of the 1650's and perhaps before that. Born at Leiden in 1626,[2] Steen was 25 when he painted *The Death of Ananias,* which in seventeenth century terms cannot really be thought of as early in his career. Despite that, judging from a photograph, it is not a strong picture. The action is confined to the foreground area, within which the figures are awkwardly foreshortened and confusingly placed. The body of Ananias is stunted, and it is difficult to tell exactly where Peter stands in relation to the buildings behind him, the steps to the left, and Ananias before him. Steen's intent here seems to be to keep the figures close to the picture plane and to use them to block spatial recession.

Though one must admit the difficulty of working with a single dated picture, and that known only through a photograph, the tendency to adhere to the plane and limit recession by use of the figures confined to the foreground characterizes four undated historical pictures. Grouped here with the *Ananias* as having been made around 1651, they are: *The Marriage at Cana* (Fig. 2, Cat. 45), two versions of *The Adoration of the Shepherds* (Figs. 3 and 4, Cat. 32 and 38) which, though close to one another, are different enough to be variations by Steen himself, and *Christ Blessing the Little Children* (Fig. 5, Cat. 60). As with the *Ananias,* these pictures are all constructed in narrow depth with figures spread across the foreground. In all of them Steen seems somewhat hesitant to delineate space enough within which his figures can work comfortably. In *The Marriage at Cana,* perhaps the earliest of the group, he preferred to organize the space vertically by placing figures on the stairway behind rather than opening up the space, which is effectively blocked by the main group of figures organized horizontally.

The Marriage at Cana and the two versions of *The Adoration* share as well some of the figural distortion found in the *Ananias.* The faces particularly are flattened, as if perspectively misread. The artificial light in the adoration scenes tends to exaggerate this quality by flattening the faces or casting distorting shadows across them. Only in *Christ Blessing the Little Children* is the feeling somewhat alleviated. But even there, particularly in the figures of two old men behind Christ, it can be detected.

Of all the paintings, *Christ Blessing the Little Children* is the most convincing spatially and narratively. In it, though still crossing the foreground with a line of figures, Steen seems more willing to open up the space. The woman in the foreground who strides so purposefully into the picture breaks that restraint. The gestures here are less emphatic than in the *Ananias,* and the narrative more convincing. Christ's almost incidental gesture of blessing and the children's unconcern as they examine a flower make this one of Steen's most pleasing groups.

The probability is that *Christ Blessing the Little Children* is the latest of the group here discussed. It seems to point to the more complicated spatial and narrative construction of *The Village Wedding* of 1653 (Fig. 25, HdG 455), Steen's second dated picture. There, as will be shown in the following section, he integrated his figures within a comfortable spatial environment and divided them into almost independent groups. The colors in *Christ Blessing the Little Children* are mostly browns and red, which form a monochromatic tonality with the whole. In the foreground, touched by an external light, are a few brilliant highlights: the little girl's shoulder, the boy kneeling beside Christ, and the back of the dog. From this it is not possible to generalize the use of color in this group of early pictures, though the adoration scenes seem to be constructed in a similar way with accents of light in a dark interior.

During the time that Steen made the group of pictures discussed above, he was living in The Hague. He arrived there in 1649 and stayed until 1654 or 1655, when he went to live in Warmond.[3] Shortly after his arrival at The Hague in 1649 he married Jan van Goyen's daughter, Margaretha.[4] Their first two children, Thaddaeus and Eva, were born at The Hague in 1651 and 1653, respectively.[5]

Prior to his coming to The Hague, he had been living in Leiden, his native town. In 1644 he signed a document there and in 1646, at the age of twenty, he registered at the University as a student of literature. It is thought that he never seriously studied at the University, but registered to escape the military draft and alcohol taxes.[6] Two years later, in 1648, he joined the newly founded St. Lucas guild in Leiden, having achieved the position of independent artist. It would seem that the years between 1640 and 1648, beginning when he was fourteen or fifteen years old, were his years of training. This means that some ten years of Steen's artistic development, before the first dated work, must be reconstructed on the basis of documentary evidence and stylistic analysis.

Arnold Houbraken published the earliest life of Steen in 1721. Of his early training he mentions only that he studied with Jan van Goyen.[7] Jacob Campo Weyerman, in his *Levens-Beschryvingen* of 1729, reported that Nicolaas Knüpfer of Utrecht was his first master:

> His father's name was Havik Jansze Steen, a brewer from Leiden, who was shown that there was talent in the boy (Havik himself could not see so deeply) so he placed him first with Knüpfer at Utrecht.[8]

Later, according to Weyerman, he studied with Adriaen van Ostade and finally with Van Goyen to learn landscape painting. Of greatest interest here is his relationship to Knüpfer, because the latter was almost exclusively a painter of small historical and allegorical pictures. Hence Martin in 1927 first suggested that Steen may have begun his career as a history painter.[9] Though this premise cannot now be accepted, the question of Knüpfer's influence upon Steen's historical paintings must be studied.

Knüpfer's position within Dutch historical painting is shadowy. He has not yet received monographic treatment, probably because, though well known in his own day (he painted several pictures for the King of Denmark), and often taken notice of in the eighteenth and early nineteenth centuries, he was completely forgotten by the end of the nineteenth.[10] Beginning with Schlie's study of 1896, there has been a small renewal of interest in this minor artist, perhaps because of his connection with Steen. Most recently, V. I. Kuznetsov has completed a study of Knüpfer, complete with the first catalogue of paintings and drawings.[11] His study adds not only to our knowledge of Knüpfer and the themes he chose, but also to our information on the Utrecht school of history painting, to which Knüpfer belonged.

Knüpfer was born in Leipzig, probably in 1603. After studying there with Emanuel Nyssen, and later at Magdeburg, he came in 1630 to Utrecht to work under Abraham Bloemaert.[12] Thereafter Knüpfer is documented as being in Utrecht until his death in 1655.[13] According to Kuznetsov, Knüpfer may have spent some time during the 1640's in The Hague, though this is conjectural and without documentation.

Knüpfer never completely adopted Bloemaert's mannerist style, though he was throughout his life essentially a painter of Biblical, historical, and often obscure allegorical subjects. Sometimes he worked on a large scale, but mostly he made small panels, occasionally even of miniature size, in a loose and almost sketchy manner recalling somewhat the technique of Brouwer. The lightness of his technique can be seen in *The Prayer of Tobias and Sarah,* of 1654 (Fig. 6), in the Centraal Museum in Utrecht. It can also be found in *The Rich Man and Lazarus* (Fig. 7) at the Liège Museum. Sometimes, as in *St. John Preaching in the Wilderness* (location unknown), there are mannerist overtones which do recall Bloemaert. At other times he reveals an orientation towards Rembrandt, as can be seen in some of the faces and the chiaroscuro lighting in *Joseph Interpreting Dreams* (Fig. 8) in Schwerin. The *Absalom and Tamar* in the Hermitage also shows his reliance upon Rembrandtesque types. Though he incorporates many influences, he remains essentially independent in his style as in his choice of subjects.[14]

There seems to be some stylistic affinity between him and Martin Stoop, a painter some fifteen years his junior. *The Seven Acts of Mercy* (Fig. 9) at Cassel, attributed to Knüpfer, has in the past been called Stoop.[15] Stoop worked at some time in Utrecht, and may have been influenced by or even have studied with Knüpfer. Knüpfer's work also recalls somewhat that of the Delft painter Leonard Bramer, who was seven or eight years Knüpfer's senior. Bramer's *Presentation in the Temple* (Fig. 10) in the Johnson collection shows a technique even lighter and more excited with highlights than Knüpfer's, but definitely similar. Similar also is their use of light and slightly mannered figures. In this particular picture Bramer builds an elaborately leveled architectural setting, with steps and galleries, for the historic scene, a means of presentation Knüpfer also favored. He used it in his own version of the subject in Leningrad, as well as in *The Rich Man and Lazarus* (Fig. 7) mentioned above. Despite the similarities that one finds between Bramer, Stoop, and Knüpfer, there is not enough evidence to bind these three artists into a group.

There is even less evidence to support a connection between Steen and Knüpfer in Steen's formative years—unless we assume that by 1651 Steen had forgotten everything he learned from the older master. *The Death of Ananias* of 1651 (Fig. 1) reveals nothing of Knüpfer's influence. As pointed out earlier, the *Ananias* is a weak painting, with little depth and rather unconvincing action. The figures, unlike Knüpfer's graceful ones, seen for example in his *Search After Happiness*[16] (Fig. 11) in Schwerin, are cloddish. Compositionally, Knüpfer almost always placed his figures in a dramatically lighted middle set off by deeply shaded *coulisse* figures. This type of construction can be seen in *The Seven Acts of Mercy* (Fig. 9) in Cassel, and *The Prayer of Tobias and Sarah* (Fig. 6) in Utrecht. He intensified the action by creating an artificial but effective view from below. Steen's picture is seen slightly from above.

These same basic differences in construction and conception are evident in the pictures stylistically grouped around the *Ananias* and assigned here to Steen's early development. In all, the figures are crowded in the foreground and the event witnessed slightly from above. Outside of the use of artificial light in the adoration scenes, Steen did not use the dramatic lighting common in Knüpfer. Steen's pictures are calm, Knüpfer's nervous. If Steen had taken Knüpfer as his first master, as Weyerman asserts, could he possibly have painted religious scenes in 1651, after the completion of his training, showing no hint at all of his master's proclivities? While one must admit this as possible, the probability is slight.

Kuznetsov maintains an opposite position. He feels that Knüpfer was not only Steen's teacher, but his immediate predecessor in what he calls subject-genre pieces. By that he means genre which has specific features of allegory or history—for instance, the wine cellar as a hymn to Bacchus.[17] Kuznetsov is correct in maintaining that Steen shares this tendency, and indeed carried it to brilliance. He did so, it must be added, not so much in his allegorization of genre as in his genre additions to history, which occur mostly in his works of the late 1660's. None of Steen's early works, however, made before Knüpfer's death in 1655, reveal such concerns. Furthermore, as Kuznetsov himself points out, genre of any kind is rare in Knüpfer, who was basically historical in his imagination.[18] If Steen had worked with Knüpfer, it would seem that he should have picked up his master's central interest to some degree, and learned to compose in his manner. Neither is the case.

What makes a negative conclusion on the teacher-pupil relationship between Knüpfer and Steen difficult and problematical is that in the late 1660's two of Steen's pictures, *The Prayer of Tobias and Sarah* (Fig. 65, Cat. 25c) and *The Rich Man and Lazarus* (Fig. 57, Cat. 59), are directly related to known works by Knüpfer. This material will be covered in a later section, but a possible explanation is here offered: that Weyerman was familiar with these later works and assumed that the influence had lasted from Steen's student days. He also had good evidence for connecting the young Steen with Utrecht, for it does appear that he took some of his early training there. What he learned in Utrecht was not figural or historical painting such as Knüpfer would have taught him, but landscape and street-scene painting common also in the Utrecht tradition, and an area to which Knüpfer, as Kuznetsov points out, paid no serious attention.[19]

Two short articles, one by Martin and the other by Gerson, are important in establishing

Steen's early work in landscape painting.[20] Both make the connection with Utrecht painting, though Martin felt also the strong connection with Van Goyen. A painting like *The Ruin on the Hill* (Fig. 12) formerly in the collection of Baron van der Feltz in Brummen (not in HdG) recalled to Martin the work of Herman Saftleven. The ruined castle and the quiet mountains resemble Saftleven's Rhenish landscapes such as the view from Heimbach in the Alte Pinakothek in Munich. The connection with Polenburgh is perhaps even stronger, especially in the way of building up the hills in clear planes and in breaking the landscape with alternations of light and shade.

Another picture (Fig. 13), which was in 1961 in the possession of the dealer Nystad in The Hague, recalls the work of Jan Both. It shows a man and a woman walking through a shallow stream in a wooded landscape. The trees are fine-leafed and pick up a strong sunlight coming from the left, giving an Italianate feeling in the way it strikes the tree-trunk. In the background, on top of a large hill similar to the one in *The Ruin on the Hill,* stands a turreted castle. Though Both's works are richer both in light and foliage, the influence seems present. It is to be found also in another painting called *Gypsies in a Landscape* (Fig. 14) which in 1927 was in the hands of Agnew, the London dealer (HdG 223). The Italianate light here is very strong.

Perhaps another Utrecht painter who influenced Steen's early work was Joost Cornelisz Droochsloot, a painter of village scenes and occasional religious subjects. Born in 1586, he was an old man when Steen came to Utrecht, but still working. In 1665 and again in 1666 he was listed as a member of the painting academy in Utrecht.[21] It was probably under his influence that Steen first began to make street scenes. Martin reproduced a painting by Steen of the Pellenkusserpoort of Utrecht, then in a private collection in Amsterdam which he felt could be mistaken for a mysterious Van Goyen were it not for the figures and the signature. Gerson, however, is more correct in suggesting that it was made under the influence of Droochsloot.[22] Hofstede de Groot had much earlier suggested the elder Droochsloot as one of Steen's true precursors.[23]

The strength of that influence is revealed in Steen's *Seven Acts of Mercy* (Fig. 15, Cat. 67). The scene occurs on a village street of half-ruined stone buildings. To the left of this group of buildings is a shadowed outline of a church, and from between the two buildings sunlight streams in to light the center. Here the small, almost primitive figures gather in groups to receive their charities from stooped old men in monks' robes. All the figures are slightly bent as if physically distorted by humility. There is a similarity of structure between Steen's painting and Droochsloot's own *Seven Acts of Mercy* (Fig. 16) belonging in 1940 to a Rotterdam dealer, and his *Street Scene* (Fig. 17) now in the Boymans/van Beuningen Museum. Though on the whole these paintings are somewhat coarser than Steen's, the placement of the buildings and the lighting are very similar. Droochsloot lights his pictures in areas separated by the shade of buildings, thus making an alternation of sunlight and shade receding into the distance. He repeats this alternation of lights and darks in the faceted articulation of the buildings. The *Street Scene* in Rotterdam is in this respect closer, but the *Acts of Mercy* shows Droochsloot's use of the stony fortress-like architecture used by Steen. Given these similarities, it is not surprising that Steen's picture, monogrammed though it is, was at one time sold as a Droochsloot (see Catalogue entry).

Real and important differences do exist between the Steen and the Droochsloot. The latter tends to organize his figures in depth, making them part of the spatial recession beginning with the corner *repoussoir*. Steen organizes his figures horizontally across the canvas, limiting our entry into the depth of the picture. This tendency of Steen's can be seen in those pictures grouped around *The Death of Ananias* of 1651, Steen's earliest dated picture, studied earlier. The effect is to make the scene a more intimate one.

Despite the differences, the connection of *The Seven Acts of Mercy* with Droochsloot and Utrecht makes it possibly Steen's earliest known religious work, predating by some years *The Death of Ananias* of 1651 (Cat. 66). Though the painting is closely associated with Utrecht, it shows no trace of Knüpfer's influence. It may well be that Steen began his artistic training in Utrecht, as Weyerman says, but as a painter of landscapes and village scenes, which in *The Seven Acts of Mercy* he combines with a religious theme. In 1646, as already pointed out, Steen was registered as a student of literature at the University at Leiden; two years later he joined the newly founded St. Lucas guild there; and in 1649 he went to The Hague to live. It must be, then, that his early training in Utrecht came prior to 1646, or at least prior to 1648, when he joined the guild.

Martin maintains that it was his early interest in landscape which led Steen to study with Van Goyen at The Hague, as was reported by both Houbraken and Weyerman.[24] He adduced proof of the close connection between Steen and Van Goyen by two paintings on which he believed the pupil Steen and the master Van Goyen worked together: *Landscape with the Rijswijk Fair* in a private collection in The Netherlands (HdG 249) and *Landscape with Figures* (Fig. 18) in the Philadelphia Museum. Martin believed that Van Goyen painted the "superb air" in one and a "beautiful gnarled oak tree" in the other. Martin builds a dubious case here, for the fact is that so little of Steen's work comes anywhere near Van Goyen's—even those elements maintained to be by the elder's hand—that it is doubtful if he ever worked under him. Bredius felt that Steen may only have studied with Van Goyen for a while before 1648, but that he had his own way of seeing landscape and did not follow the older master.[25] Even the paintings Martin used to document his assertion have more in common with Utrecht landscapes and street scenes than with Jan van Goyen's open-skyed vistas. As will be seen, the Philadelphia painting better establishes Steen's connection with the Ostades.

Perhaps Steen's marriage to Margaretha van Goyen in 1649 led to the assumption that they met while he was in her father's studio. Houbraken and Weyerman report it so, Weyerman even telling how he followed Van Goyen from Haarlem to The Hague in order to continue the liason with his "Grietje." The dates however do not correspond: Steen would have been eight when Van Goyen came to live in The Hague about 1634, hardly old enough to follow either master or daughter. Steen arrived at The Hague in 1649, at age twenty-three, certainly an age more appropriate to a love affair. Furthermore, it was not from Haarlem that Van Goyen came to The Hague, but from his native town of Leiden, where he had settled in 1618 after his training with Esias van de Velde in Haarlem.[26]

The group of paintings here associated with *The Death of Ananias* must all, if the analysis is correct, have been made around 1651, during which time Steen was living at The Hague and close to the Van Goyen family. These pictures bear as little resemblance to

Van Goyen's work as do his earlier landscapes. *The Village Wedding* of 1653 (Fig. 25, HdG 455), Steen's second dated work, must also have been made while he was at The Hague. The limited landscape in this painting, with its round tower and stone arch, is also closer to Utrecht painting than to Van Goyen's.

The occasional occurrence in Steen's early landscapes or street scenes of bits of Van Goyen-like painting, which Martin has pointed out, in no way proves Steen's place in the studio, but only that he was familiar with Van Goyen's work—as he must have been, being a member of the family. The insignificance of his father-in-law's influence (Martin had to search it out in details) might better lead to the conclusion that precisely because of the relationship Steen avoided imitation in an effort to keep his independence. By and large, the evidence, or the lack of it, points to the conclusion that their relationship was personal, not professional.

Though Steen may have begun his career as a landscapist, it is evident from his work that somewhere quite early he gave up landscape for figural painting. Landscape receded to become a backdrop for human activity. In reverse of Martin's position, it may have been his developing interest in the figure that caused Steen to seek other training. It would not have been to The Hague and Van Goyen that he turned, but almost certainly to Haarlem and the Ostades, who so purposefully combined landscape with dominant figural groups. Weyerman reported that Steen's second master was Adriaen Ostade. Though, as has been demonstrated, Weyerman's word is not always reliable, there exists strong evidence that Steen did study with Adriaen and even more importantly with Isaac Ostade, and that in general he was a scion of Haarlem painting.

The two paintings of *The Adoration of the Shepherds,* one in Aix-en-Provence and the other last reported in a private collection in Italy (Figs. 3 and 4, Cat. 32 and 38), discussed in this section, supply evidence of Steen's early connection with the Ostades. Both paintings, but particularly the smaller one (Fig. 4), create interiors familiar from the peasant pieces of Adriaen Ostade. The peasants have something of the lumpish simplicity of his types, particularly of the 1640's. In these night scenes they are clustered around the madonna and child the way Adriaen's peasants cluster around the table in his etching of a family scene of 1647 (Fig. 19). The mother and child in that etching bear a striking resemblance to Steen's madonna and child in the smaller of the two adoration pictures, even to the way the infant is held on the lap. Adriaen's farmhouse interiors are most often more spacious than Steen's and his figures smaller, but they share the same clutter and warmth of shadowed recesses.

There is evidence also to connect these adoration pictures of Steen's with Isaac Ostade. A wash drawing of the adoration (Fig. 20), formerly in the collection of Frits Lugt, has much in common with the painting at Aix (Fig. 3), especially the kneeling peasant in the foreground, and the structure of light as it plays upon the faces of those gathered around the infant. Lugt attributed the drawing to Isaac Ostade. Van Regteren Altena, however, felt the drawing close enough to Steen to be so attributed, though he readily admitted the difficulty of the judgment.[27] Such closeness establishes between Steen and Isaac a fundamental stylistic affinity. How strong that affinity was can be seen by a comparison with a drawing (Fig. 21) signed by Isaac now in the British Museum. In both cases wash is used in conjunction with light penstrokes to create a slightly nervous and shifting accent. Steen's heavier use of wash in this case results from the adoration being a night scene.

That Steen was affected by Isaac's painting before 1651 was proven by Stechow's discovery in 1928 of the *Winterlandscape* (Fig. 22) in the Baron Rutger von Essen collection at Skokloster, Sweden (HdG 881a).[28] That picture was one of those forming a shipment of Dutch paintings purchased in The Hague for Field-Marshal Wrangel of Sweden in 1651.[29] In that painting, which must have been made in 1651 or earlier, Steen directly imitated winter scenes common in the work of Isaac. Isaac's painting of a similar scene (Fig. 23) in the Alte Pinakothek in Munich reveals the strength of Steen's dependency. Most obviously Steen repeated the white horse trudging across the bridge, the heavy overcast sky, and the bare tree seen against the sky. The conclusion must be that Steen was familiar with Isaac's style before 1651, the date of the sale of the picture.

Another landscape dependency is to be found in a painting already cited, *Landscape with Figures* (Fig. 18) in Philadelphia. As mentioned earlier, Martin felt that the gnarled oak in the left middleground was painted by Van Goyen. The whole, however, more strongly recalls the paintings of travelers in front of inns made by Isaac, even to the hanging inn sign. Isaac's painting in the Kunsthistorisches Museum in Vienna (Fig. 24) shows the same structure as the Steen, only the buildings have been reversed from left to right. There is an equally gnarled oak tree and both artists, following a similar formula, have created an open vista off to one side. Steen, unlike Isaac, has included a genre—perhaps fortune-telling—scene in the foreground, as he did in *Gypsies in a Landscape* (Fig 14, HdG 223), also mentioned earlier. Such an inclusion changes the basic nature of the picture, for our attention is immediately drawn to the activity of the group and the landscape becomes more of a backdrop than it is in the Ostade. Nevertheless, the dependency is clear, even to the shape and feeling of the buildings, and the alternating areas of shadow and light on the ground. If Steen did not know this picture, he must have known others by Isaac similar to it.

A tenuous bit of information exists to prove that Steen knew Isaac Ostade personally. In 1708 a portrait of Isaac purported to be by Steen was sold with the estate of Cornelis Dusart, who, as a close follower, was certainly familiar at least with Adriaen Ostade.[30] If that painting was indeed by Steen (one is tempted to question it because of the paucity of portraits in Steen's oeuvre), and is indeed of Isaac and not posthumous, their association must be pushed back to 1649, the year of Isaac's death, or earlier. The probability is that it occurred prior to 1648 when, as indicated, Steen joined the newly formed guild in Leiden.

In summary, the evidence presented in this section on Steen's early years points to the following conclusions: Steen's period of training probably covered the years 1640–1648. During that time he studied first at Utrecht, largely under the influence of the elder Droochsloot, and later at Haarlem, probably with Adriaen but more significantly with Isaac van Ostade. At Haarlem he learned figural painting of a peasant type, and how to integrate his figures with landscape; earlier he was essentially a landscapist.

No evidence has been found to support the contention that while in Utrecht Steen studied with Knüpfer, or while at The Hague either before or after 1649 with Van Goyen.

His earliest religious painting, *The Seven Acts of Mercy* (Fig. 15, Cat. 67), probably dates from the mid-1640's and shows the influence of Droochsloot. The paintings grouped around *The Death of Ananias* of 1651 (Fig. 1, Cat. 66), the two *The Adoration of the Shepherds* (Figs. 3 and 4, Cat. 32 and 38), *The Marriage at Cana* (Fig. 2, Cat. 45), and *Christ Blessing the Little Children* (Fig. 5, Cat. 60), reveal most strongly his Haarlem background. That background reveals itself again in his relationship to Jacob de Wet, which will be discussed in the following section.

Steen and Jacob de Wet—1653

As concluded in the foregoing section, after leaving Utrecht, it was not to The Hague that Steen went, but to Haarlem.[31] There he learned to deal fundamentally with the figure. Only after this did he return to landscape painting, but this time not to landscape with figures placed within it, but to pictures in which landscape and figures are integrated. Steen's second known dated picture, *The Village Wedding* (Fig. 25, HdG 455) of 1653 in the Boymans/van Beuningen Museum, amply demonstrates his developed skill in this new direction. Integration of figures and village street here is perfect. The people belong to the streets and buildings. They are of the same quality and share the same life. The essential difference can be seen in a comparison with *The Seven Acts of Mercy* (Fig. 15, Cat. 67) or the better known *Fishmarket at Leiden* (Fig. 26, HdG 212) in Frankfurt, in which the little figures seem pasted on the surface.

Martin considered *The Village Wedding* the painting with which Steen came to maturity. There is good reason for his assertion, for in that work the sources of his training are perfectly combined. The tower, the arch, the trees, some of the figures (particularly the seated woman at the left) recall the earlier landscapes; the window scene, the hanging foliage, the warm brown tonality of the whole picture, recall the Ostades. The union of figures and environment seems inspired particularly by Isaac. There is also something new here: the purposeful spotlighting of the major group by a flash of light across the middle ground. Steen did something similar in *The Seven Acts of Mercy* (Fig. 15), but without the same dramatic purposefulness. The only high colors in the wedding picture—whites, yellows, light blues—are in the area of light, and are contrasted with the shaded monochrome background.

Stylistically, four religious works can be grouped around *The Village Wedding* and should be incorporated in a group around 1653. They are: *Moses Striking the Rock* (Fig. 27, Cat. 8); *The Adoration of the Shepherds* (Fig. 28, Cat. 35); *St. John Preaching in the Wilderness* (Fig. 29, Cat. 28); *The Marriage at Cana* (Fig. 30, Cat. 50b). All have in common the small figures within a large but contained environment, and the spotlighting from the left of the main group or action in the middle ground. One, *The Adoration,* is a night scene, which heightens the effect of the lighting. In all these works the figures, small in their surroundings, work beautifully to create a unity of action and space. Light plays an important part in creating the illusion of space, and in the dramatizing of events.

The importance of light in all of these paintings has led to a presumed association with Rembrandt. J. G. van Gelder used *The Marriage at Cana* (Fig. 30), which he erroneously declared to be dated 1646 (see Catalogue entry), to establish a style of the mid-1640's under the tutelage of a Rembrandt disciple, possibly Jacob de Wet.[32] Van Gelder's assertion that this *Marriage at Cana* was Steen's earliest dated work has been disproved, and the half-obliterated date should be read, as Bredius declared, "165(?)."[33] However, Van Gelder's recognition of Rembrandt's influence in this and other related works is correct.

A comparison with the earlier *Marriage at Cana* (Fig. 2, Cat. 45) shows Steen's new use of Rembrandtesque light. In that picture the light enters strongly from the left, giving general illumination to the foreground area while leaving the background in shadow. In the later picture the light also enters from the left, striking across the central area, but leaves most of the large hall in darkness. Out of that darkness, however, shine forth individual vignettes—the man and the woman at the right, the old man in the back—as if each had their own light source. They seem, as in Rembrandt, part of the predominant shadows and one senses a touch of mystery in that large, dimly lighted interior.

Besides the general Rembrandtesque light and sense of mystery in the second *Marriage at Cana,* it contains several distinctly Rembrandtesque types: the white-bearded Jew; the frivolous youth with feather beret; the bearded man in sixteenth century costume. This last, caught between the new wine, magnificent maidservant, coaxing host and nagging wife, appears to be a Rembrandt figure who has suffered a loss of dignity.

The connection with Rembrandt's circle and particularly with Jacob de Wet is strengthened by the painting of *Moses Striking the Rock for Water* (Fig. 27, Cat. 8). In his article on Steen as a landscape painter (mentioned earlier), Gerson found the background of this picture, and particularly the grotto with hanging vines, reminiscent of the mythological works of the Utrecht arcadian landscapist, Abraham van Cuylenburgh.[34] (Compare *Diana and Nymphs* in the Mauritshuis.) That similarity pales when Steen's painting is compared with the one of the same subject by Jacob de Wet (Fig. 31) in the National Museum in Warsaw. The two pictures so closely approximate one another in feeling, types, and structure as to be taken as a case of direct reference. Steen even included the mounted figure seen through the opening of the grotto. Another *Moses Striking the Rock* by de Wet in a sale at Bad Kissingen in 1955, shows that this kind of grotto construction was not an isolated incident in his work.

Bode had some years before Van Gelder suggested that Steen might have studied with de Wet, or at least come in contact with him in Haarlem.[35] On the basis of the above comparison, such an assertion may be made with greater strength. It is not merely isolated motifs that support this contention, but the whole manner of construction. The figures are small and placed within a large but closed environment. The light, as in *The Village Wedding* (Fig. 25), is cast into the center, creating a dramatic nucleus with a predominant shadowed background. Within this environment the figures have a touching smallness, as if huddled in the presence of a greater power.

Jacob de Wet was born in Haarlem around 1610. He was one of Rembrandt's earliest students, possibly even working with him during the master's last year in Leiden.[36] A painting *The Raising of Lazarus,* which in 1947 was in the Hart collection in England, attributed to de Wet, is an interpretation of the Rembrandt etching of 1632, showing the scene as seen from the front of Christ rather than from behind.[37] Another picture, *The Repentant Judas,* which in 1960 belonged to a London dealer, is related in types and feeling to Rembrandt's early painting of the scene in Mulgrave Castle.[38] De Wet lived most of his life in Haarlem where he is often mentioned in the records between 1638 and 1668. In 1645 and again in 1660 he was "hoofdman" of the guild, and in 1661, dean.[39] He was, as shown from a published record book that belonged to him, a highly sought after teacher in Haarlem. In the notations, however, there is no mention of Steen.[40]

It may have been that Steen picked up something of de Wet's manner while in Haarlem in the 1640's, but that seems unlikely since none of it appears in the works prior to 1653. It is best, perhaps, to postulate a contact during the early 1650's while he was living at The Hague, though this cannot be documented. He may simply have been familiar with de Wet's work, with which at the moment he found a real affinity.

Of all the pictures belonging to this chronological group, *St. John Preaching in the Wilderness* (Fig. 29, Cat. 28) is the most historically complex. It is like a compendium of Steen's early training and indicates his eclectic tendencies. The figures in the center grouped around the finely costumed Oriental and the woman at his side come out of Rembrandt's studio at the beginning of the 1630's (compare *The Adoration of the Magi,* B. 541), parasol and all. Such connections support Steen's relationship to de Wet who, as mentioned, was in Rembrandt's studio at the beginning of the 1630's. The figures in the foreground, on the other hand, recall Steen's affinity to Ostade; the landscape is so Italianate, especially the light on foreground trees, that it has been attributed to both Jan Hackaert and Jan Wils[41] (see Catalogue entry).

Utrecht connections have been found in the picture. Gerson, in his article on Steen's landscapes,[42] felt that Jan Both, one of the leaders of the school of Italianate landscape painting in Utrecht, should be considered as a possible influence upon the landscape background. Kurt Simon found the motif of horse and rider at the right similar to that in Knüpfer's *Search After Happiness* of 1651 (Fig. 11), in the Schwerin Museum. While that motif does seem somehow lifted, the direct relation to Knüpfer remains tenuous and can in no way be taken as proof that Steen had already studied with Knüpfer at the time this picture was made.

The other known religious picture belonging to this group is *The Adoration of the Shepherds* (Fig. 28, Cat. 35). It differs markedly from the two earlier works of the same subject (Figs. 3 and 4, Cat. 32 and 38). The figures here are made small in a large space. They emerge from the mist and darkness of the night to celebrate the birth announced by the cherubs above. The movement carried by the light areas is a diagonal one into space. In the earlier works the figures dominate their space and are organized horizontally across the canvas. The chorus of dancing, music-making cherubs afloat in the diaphanous clouds of light creates an external manifestation of the event. Such an inclusion occurs only rarely in Steen's art. The misty light in which they frolic reveals again how much Rembrandt's chiaroscuro affected Steen at this time of his life.

A painting by Steen of *Tobias Healing His Father* (Cat. 24) was destroyed by fire at the Boymans Museum at Rotterdam in 1864. Descriptions of the picture, its early attribution to Dou, and its apparent closeness to Rembrandt's painting of the same subject (formerly in the Arenberg collection—B. 502) give good reason to hypothesize, as Van Gelder did, its inclusion in the present group of paintings. Unfortunately, no reproduction of any kind exists to supply verification. (For description, see Cat. 24.)

In summary, five pictures based on *The Village Wedding* of 1653 (Fig. 25) can be brought together having enough in common to constitute a chronological group. They are *Moses Striking the Rock for Water* (Fig. 27, Cat. 8); *The Marriage at Cana*—dated 165(?) (Fig. 30, Cat. 50b); *St. John Preaching in the Wilderness* (Fig. 29, Cat. 28); *The Adoration of the Shepherds* (Fig. 28, Cat. 35); and possibly the destroyed *Tobias Healing His Father* (Cat. 24). These pictures differ from the earlier group in that they show Steen's strong desire to unite figures in a larger spatial environment. Light plays an important part in the illusion of that space. In this and in numerous motifs, Steen exhibits a powerful affinity to Rembrandt and his school. Jacob de Wet, having studied with Rembrandt in the early 1630's, could very possibly be the major source of the influence.

Genre and History—1659/60

All of the paintings grouped above were made while Steen was living in The Hague, where he stayed until about 1654. In that year his father stood surety for him in the rental of a brewery in Delft called "De Slange." It is not at all sure that Steen and his family ever established themselves in Delft. A bit of evidence that he did is the painting called *The Burgermaster of Delft* (HdG 878) in the collection of Lady Janet Douglas-Pennant in Penrhyn, Wales. It is dated 1655 and shows in the background a view of the Oude Kirk and Prinsenhof of Delft. It can only be stated for sure that he painted in Delft, not that he lived there. In 1656 Steen moved to Warmond, a small town a few miles from his native Leiden, where he stayed until 1660. In that year he moved to Haarlem, where he was to remain for ten years. The years in Warmond are documented by tax receipts[43] and by his painting of 1660 called *The Poultry Yard* (Fig. 32, HdG 330) in the Mauritshuis, which he made for Jan van Wassenaer of Warmond. The latter's ten-year-old daughter, Jacoba Maria Wassenaer, is shown seated on the steps of a courtyard. She is surrounded by birds, domestic and wild, and attended by two servants. Behind her, through an archway, is the family castle "Oud-Teylingen," and above her, embedded in the wall, is the family shield of her grandparents.[44]

In the years between the *Burgermaster of Delft* and *The Poultry Yard,* Steen devoted himself mostly to genre painting. Perhaps this whole side of his art finds completion in *The Morning Toilet* (Fig. 33, HdG 340) of 1663 in Buckingham Palace.[45] In it he developed a tight, clean, almost linear style, sometimes of even miniature fineness. The amorphousness of Rembrandt's illuminated shadows has no place in Steen's middle-class interiors.

Steen's proclivity for genre painting during this period reveals itself strongly even in some of the religious scenes. A picture like *Bathseba Receiving David's Letter* (Fig. 34, Cat. 15) would best be identified as "The Love Letter" were it not for the address of the note which reads: *Alderschonte Barsabe—omdat;* "Most beautiful Bathseba—because." Indeed, at one point the picture was sold as *Le billet-doux*. Steen lavished great care on his adulteress, dressing her in gold and red and white satin, and showing her a lady of class—elegant and vain. She could have stepped out of numerous brothel and "love letter" scenes common to Dutch genre painting of the time, and particularly those of Ter Borch, whose work must have influenced Steen strongly at this period.[46] Ter Borch's use of the letter theme can be seen in his *Refused Letter* of about 1657 in the Alte Pinakothek in Munich, and in *The Curious Servant* of about 1660 in the Metropolitan Museum in New York.[47] For his Bathseba Steen adopted one of Ter Borch's favorite postures for young women. Seen from the side with head turned toward the viewer, their figures have a provocative slouch, and an easy grace carried by the gentle sweep of their satin overskirts. Steen has here interpreted a Biblical theme in terms of contemporary genre, or conversely interpreted a contemporary theme in terms of a Biblical parallel.

Bathseba Receiving David's Letter dates from about 1659, and should be compared to the *Music Lesson* (Fig. 35, HdG 409) in the National Gallery in London. The date of that painting, according to Maclaren, should be read 1659.[48] In each the scene is enframed within a stone archway opening upon a shallow room in which the figures are placed. Off to the right is an arched entry which balances the heavier structure on the left. In the predominantly dark interiors Bathseba and the young woman at her lesson shine forth in their brilliant satin dresses of gold and red, blue and lemon. The music master and the woman servant are played down in color to leave the central accent to the women themselves. In another picture, also dated 1659, *The Musicians* (HdG 438) at one time in the collection of Anthony Rothschild at Ascot near London, Steen displays again his love of draped satin, and uses a similar framing archway, in this case for an outdoor scene.

Two other pictures probably have their origin around this time; both are adorations of the shepherds—one in the Bredius Museum (Fig. 36, Cat. 33/36), the other in the Rijksmuseum (Fig. 37, Cat. 37). The latter is one of Steen's best known religious pictures and has been variously placed in his career. Most recently, in the catalogue of the Steen show at the Mauritshuis in 1958, it is placed around 1670. This dating, given without substantiation, is as much in error as Guldener's and de Jonge's belief that it is an early work showing Italian and Utrecht (Wttewael) connections (see Cat. 37).[49] It is too fine a work to be considered early, as can be seen by a comparison with the two adorations of about 1651 already discussed (Figs. 3 and 4, Cat. 32 and 38). And it is too tight in structure, too humbly undramatic, to be a late work (see *David Returning Victorious* of 1671, Fig. 83, Cat. 13). By "fine" is meant not a quality judgment, but a description of the interest displayed in textures, and in delicate rhythms, as in the swirled cloak of the madonna. This interest makes clear the connection with works like *Bathseba* and *The Musicians,* giving it a date of about 1659/60, though in it Steen reduced the intensity of his colors to conform with the warm red-brown monochrome of the darkened and more humble interior.

Even though the main figures are reversed, the smaller *Adoration* in the Bredius Museum (Fig. 36, Cat. 33/36) shares much with the one in the Rijksmuseum, and should be similarly dated. In this *Adoration,* which is a night scene, Steen uses a hidden candle to pick up the sharp contours of faces and figures, emphasizing Joseph, who holds the candle, most dramatically. The adoration scenes which have been dated earlier are also night scenes. In them, however, Steen used candle and lantern to very different effect. There the light serves not to pick up contours but to contrast large areas of light with the surrounding darkness. The best example of this is the way the light catches the entire under-brim of the hat worn by the woman with the lantern. In the later picture, the light catches only the thin edges or narrow broken areas of objects, spreading the whole with sharp accents. The use of artificial light, especially the lantern, in the adoration scenes is, of course, as Hofstede de Groot mentions, reminiscent of Rembrandt. It is illuminatory and is used here in conjunction with shadow not to obscure outline and image, as in some of his earlier works like *The Adoration of the Shepherds* in Leitmeritz of about 1653 (Fig. 28, Cat. 35), but to bring things to a higher, clearer focus.

Like *The Adoration of the Shepherds,* the painting *The Twelfth Night Feast* of 1662 in Boston (Fig. 38, HdG 509C), also a night scene lighted by a hidden candle, shows Steen's continued interest in this kind of painting. It also shows a similarity of structure. The light is kept within the central area, leaving both foreground and background in shadow. In both cases, also, a figure with back to the picture plane establishes the front plane of the central group.

When Hofstede de Groot mentioned in his Catalogue that these paintings of the adoration were influenced by Rembrandt, he probably had in mind two paintings of the scene by the older master, both of 1646—one in the National Gallery in London (B. 575) and the other in the Alte Pinakothek in Munich (B. 574)—or the etching of the nighttime adoration of 1654 (Münz 226). Steen's and Rembrandt's treatments of the subject, however, differ markedly in concept. Rembrandt painted religiously portentous adoration scenes in which the peasant, in his age-old humble ignorance, is a symbol of the devotion and love of the meek who by this event are saved. They are transformed by love and wonder. Steen's peasants are never thus transformed; they are curious, amused, disinterested, and far more self-involved than Rembrandt's. The seeing God always present in Rembrandt finds little place in Steen, but this does not mean the conception is areligious. Steen's pictures are serious statements, made even more so by their seeming incongruities. Thus the bagpiper and the peasant with the big hat—comic characters both—add a feeling of revelry to the coming of Christ, a touch not often included by Rembrandt but not therefore less true, or less significant.

In another picture made around this time, *The Child Jesus in the Temple* (Fig. 39, Cat. 44), Steen did attempt to depict miraculous spirituality. Under the certain influence again of Rembrandt he has lighted the interior of the synagogue with a cloudburst of illumination, which strikes particularly the face of the young Jesus. The mystery here attempted, however, is not entirely successful. The light remains artificial, not spiritual. The best part of the painting is the group of Jesus, Mary and Joseph; the parents display an awed concern over their son. They seem isolated amidst the rabbinical types, as if they had wandered in from another world. Most strongly they recall the figures from *The Adoration of the Shepherds* in the Rijksmuseum (Fig. 37, Cat. 37).

Also to be associated with *The Child Jesus in the Temple* is *Christ in the House of Mary and Martha* (Fig. 40, Cat. 51). The foreground still life is not convincing as original work by Steen. It blocks entry to the space too completely. Steen sometimes uses a pot or a jug to establish the foreground, but he never restricts entry in this way. Furthermore, he tended to unite still-life elements in compositional groups rather than spread them out individually as is the case here.[50] The group around the table, however, leaves no doubt of the picture's authenticity. Its composition is similar to *The Child Jesus in the Temple* and to the adoration scenes—a horizontal arrangement of figures against which a centrally important group is placed. In both cases also, the right-hand side has been left open, giving a view to another room. Several of the figures have that same Rembrandtesque cast to them and the variegated lighting appears similar. The seriousness with which Steen dealt with this parable—the unworldly quality of Christ, the deep contemplation of Mary—also indicates a time when Steen was concerned with religious mystery.

Another painting which may be included here is *The Dismissal of Hagar* (Fig. 41, Cat. 2). It too shows the influence of Rembrandt, indicating the consistency of Steen's reliance on the older painter. Not only is Abraham a Rembrandt type, but the whole composition is related (in reverse) to the well-known etching of 1637 (Fig. 42, Münz 174).[51] C. W. de Groot suggested that Steen might have reversed the figures to camouflage his borrowing. There is a strong similarity also between Hagar and a small oil sketch of a weeping woman attributed to Rembrandt and now in the Detroit Institute of Art (Fig. 43, B. 366).[52] In terms of religious narrative Steen is more successful here in the broad light than when he tries to capture the religious intensity of Rembrandt—as in *Jesus in the Temple* or in *Christ at Emmaus* in the Rijksmuseum (Fig. 45, Cat. 65), to be discussed below.

It was probably about this time, that is, the early 1660's, when Steen had settled in Haarlem for a second time, that he painted the tender, introverted face of John the Baptist (Fig. 44, Cat. 30a). It too recalls Rembrandt in his studies for the head of Christ, though Steen's portrait is more simply sad than spiritually intense. Though the nose is different, the head is similar to that of the kneeling peasant in the *Adoration* in the Rijksmuseum (Fig. 37, Cat. 37), and also, though more vaguely, to the head of the disappearing Christ in Steen's *Christ at Emmaus* (Fig. 45). This last painting must also have been made in the middle 1660's, as it shows resemblance to such works as *Grace Before Meat* in the Morrison collection (HdG 375) dated 1660 and shares something of the soberness of *The Poultry Yard* (Fig. 32, HdG 330), made in the same year. In it Steen does not work in the same manner as he did in the adoration scenes, but makes his areas less variegated and broader in form. This can be clearly seen in the tunic of the servant passing out the wine.

Christ at Emmaus has been considered Steen's most profound religious painting. It has also been considered a grand failure precisely because in it Steen entered an area which was beyond his scope as a painter.[53] Steen interprets the mystery of Christ's recognition and disappearance at Emmaus as hallucination, as dream. The evening light, of which Steen is such a master, the soft colors, the nebulous atmosphere, the heaviness of the air absorbing all sound, and the remarkable stillness of the figures, create the world of a dream-trance. The boy in red pouring out the wine does not really move, and the servant bringing bread lowers her eyes in response to the miraculous sleep of the two pilgrims. All is still, and Christ disappears in the silence. Whether success or failure, Steen never repeated religious painting of such intensity, and *Christ at Emmaus* in this respect is singular among his works. The direction he took was away from anything intensely personal, private, or mysterious—to the portrayal of events in a more theatrical, and eventually spectacular manner.

Eight religious pictures have been discussed in this section. They are: *Bathseba Receiving David's Letter* (Cat. 15), *Adoration of the Shepherds* (Cat. 37), a second *Adoration of the Shepherds* (Cat. 33/36), *The Child Jesus in the Temple* (Cat. 44), *Christ in the House of Mary and Martha* (Cat. 51), *Dismissal of Hagar* (Cat. 2), *Head of St. John the Baptist* (Cat. 30a), and *Christ at Emmaus* (Cat. 65). As has been indicated, they are less easily unified than the earlier ones. While it is impossible to make them into a coherent group, their inclusion together and at this time seems justified on the basis of comparison with other dated works. It must have been, for Steen, a time of experimentation and change.

As in the earlier works around 1653, Rembrandt proves again to be an important and continuing influence. At this time more than at any other it would seem that Steen was tempted, as in *Christ at Emmaus,* to imitate or, better, to create for himself something of the older master's religious intensity.

Transition—1665

In the group of historical pictures placed under this heading Steen shows a decidedly more dramatic side than has been thus far observed. His technique is looser, and his colors more variegated. Landscapes are dominant and full of mellow evening light, soft foliage, and almost animate trees. The group consists of four pictures: *Erysichthon Selling His Daughter* (Cat. 73), *The Rape of the Sabine Women* (Cat. 76), *Hagar and Ishmael in the Wilderness* (Cat. 2b), and *Lot and His Daughters* (Cat. 1). The pictures have so much in common, both in landscape and figure style, that the grouping is an obvious one. To find an accurate place for them is, however, more difficult.

Hagar and Ishmael in the Wilderness (Fig. 46) has in the past been confused with *The Story of Hagar* (Cat. 2a) which was purchased at The Hague in 1651 (see Catalogue entry). It was therefore thought to be an early work. Such a conclusion, despite awkwardnesses in the picture, is unacceptable. In it there is so much of Steen's developed technique—as comparison with his earliest dated picture, *The Death of Ananias* (Fig. 1, Cat. 66), reveals—as to rule out placing the picture so early. There are connections, especially the tendency to foreshorten the heads; but the figures, the space, the composition of the *Ananias,* are tightly constricted compared to the freedom of the *Hagar and Ishmael.* Further, the *Ananias* has little of that rhythm of narrative and form present in *Hagar and Ishmael* and characteristic of all of Steen's mature works. The landscape also, with its hazy evening light and soft foliage, indicates a mature work. The kind of landscapes Steen made in his early years can be seen in *Gypsies in a Landscape* (Fig. 14, HdG 223), or *Landscape with Figures* in the Philadelphia Museum (Fig. 18, HdG).

The picture, then, as both Bredius and Plietzsch recognized (see Cat. 2b), must be dissociated from *The Story of Hagar* and given a later place in Steen's career. One dated picture, called *Rustic Love* or *Lovers Under a Tree* (HdG 796) of 1659, formerly in the Kann collection at Paris, is close in style. That picture, however, has been shown to be a replica of the one now in "De Lakenhal" at Leiden (Fig. 47, HdG 819), which in its originality is even closer in landscape and figure type to the pictures under discussion. It is, unfortunately, undated; and all evidence points to the possibility that the 1659 date on the replica is an invention of the copyist.

An indication of the later date for the four pictures grouped in this section can be had by a comparison of *Lot and His Daughters* (Fig. 48, Cat. 1) with the background painting in the *Parable of the Rich Man and Lazarus* (Fig. 57, Cat. 59), dated 1667. A similar scene between two women and a drunken man is enacted at the rich man's table. Steen in his mature pictures generally goes from a fine focus in the front plane to diffused painting in the background. In *Lot and His Daughters,* and in the other three pictures associated with it, he seems to have made whole paintings of what was or was to become his background style. Though the connection with *Lazarus* may be tenuous, evidence for a precise dating is not available.

Lot and His Daughters documents the longevity of Steen's attraction to the Rembrandt manner. The general setting and composition, the figures of Lot and the daughter on his left-hand side, are taken from Jan van Vliet's etching of the same subject (Fig. 49), possibly made after a lost painting by Rembrandt, or after a drawing of the subject attributed to him now in the British Museum (see Cat. 1). The etching is inscribed "R-I van Rijn inventor—1631—J. G. van Vliet fecit." It must have been Van Vliet's etching that Steen knew, since both his painting and the etching reverse the British Museum drawing.

The Rape of the Sabine Women (Fig. 50, Cat. 76) and *Erysichthon Selling His Daughter* (Fig. 51, Cat. 73) are, as far as can be determined, Steen's first pictures dealing with classical themes.[54] Even this statement might be incorrect, for it has been suggested that that true subject of the former is *The Benjaminites Carrying Off Shiloh's Daughters,* an obscure incident related in Judges 21:21-24 (see Catalogue entry). There is at the moment no way of correctly identifying the subject. The story of Erysichthon coming from Ovid's *Metamorphoses,* however, leaves no doubt of its classical origins.

Both the paintings form a clearly discernible group with *Hagar and Ishmael in the Wilderness* and *Lot and His Daughters,* and should therefore be similarly dated. C. W. de Groot suggested that the *Erysichthon* be dated about 1670; but this is clearly too late, for by then Steen had opened up his landscapes and moved to cooler tones and more precise lines. It may be that *Erysichthon* is the latest of the group, for it seems to have many fragmented accents. It is a little nervous. This kind of painting is found in several of Steen's dated works of 1667—e.g., *Trick-Track Players* in the Hermitage (Fig. 53, HdG 719), in which the leathered wall-covering shatters the light in a way very similar to the foliage behind the bargaining Erysichthon.

The other dated genre pictures of this period, *Birth Feast* of 1664 in the Wallace collection (Fig. 54, HdG 448) and the *Music Group* of 1666 in Chicago (Fig. 55, HdG 442), show little stylistic similarity to the works being discussed.[55] This fact makes the dating of this group tenuous, but since Steen's work of the late 1650's through early 1660's and late 1660's is well known, the mid-1660's can be hypothesized as a possible time for these pictures. Indeed the whole group can be seen as a transition between the intense religious pictures made around the beginning of the 1660's and the dramatic broadening out which Steen accomplishes in the late 1660's.

Steen and Baroque Drama—1667/68

Steen's return to Rembrandt in *Lot and His Daughters* and to the early Rembrandt, with his exaggerated gesture, motions, and emotions, presages the direction Steen was to go in the historical paintings of the late 1660's. In those last Haarlem years (he was to return to Leiden in 1670) Steen gave up the fine touch for the broad sweep, the delicate encounter for the dramatic confrontation. He became a painter of great mythical and Biblical histories, of events of a greater and more glorious day. It is no wonder, then, that in this new interest the mature Steen turned to the early Rembrandt to find a larger and more dramatic expression. The works of the late 1660's also offer the first reliable evidence of his contact with Knüpfer, which seems also to fit with his growing interest in grander narratives.

Two pictures, *The Banquet of Antony and Cleopatra* (Fig. 56, Cat. 86) and *The Parable of the Rich Man and Lazarus* (Fig. 57, Cat. 59), both dated 1667, show these new affinities. In the first, Antony, dressed in Oriental luxury, hand raised in astonishment and eyes wide with emotion, recalls some of Rembrandt's grandest emotion-wrought potentates, such as Belshazzar rising in fear from his own feast table in the painting in London (Fig. 58, B. 497). Even closer to Belshazzar in feeling is Steen's wrathful Ahasuerus from the painting of Esther's banquet in Birmingham, England (Fig. 59, Cat. 18); though undated, this picture is related, in types and structure, to *Antony and Cleopatra*. Indeed, Antony looks more an Ahasuerus or Belshazzar. Steen will improve the type in the much larger picture at The Hague (Fig. 60, Cat. 86a/b), giving him the youth and trimness of his ardor.

The Rich Man and Lazarus supplies the first really acceptable evidence of the connection between Jan Steen and Nicolas Knüpfer. In 1927 Martin (see Cat. 59) attempted to show that a painting of *Lazarus and the Rich Man* at the Museum at Strasbourg attributed to Metsu (Fig. 61) was really a Steen, and that he had taken the central motif and general setting from Knüpfer's painting of the same subject at the museum in Liège (Fig. 7). There can be no doubt of the connection between the two pictures. However, Martin's attribution of the Strasbourg painting to Steen is dubious and has not found general acceptance.[56] The picture, though signed Metsu, may very well be a second version of the subject by Knüpfer himself.[57] If this is so, as the present author believes, then Steen's reliance on Knüpfer for his own *Lazarus* is even more direct. Steen turned the raised dais around, but kept the servant girl with the peacock-pie on the steps. He kept the balustrade and the relief sculpture on the walls, and the servant shaking the waste from a tablecloth; he kept the main motif of the begging Lazarus.[58] What he did not keep was the view from below, so typical of Knüpfer. Steen's view is about central here, looking slightly downward at the foreground figures and slightly upward at the feast on the dais.

In 1667, when Steen painted this picture, Knüpfer was long dead, and Steen, forty-one years old, was long past his student days. The conclusion then must be that Steen knew the Strasbourg picture, but not necessarily its author. As shown, his earlier painting indicates no direct influence of Knüpfer. Such vague statements as Hofstede de Groot's that he learned effects and the use of architectural motifs from Knüpfer, or Martin's that he learned from him the use of stairways and galleries and brown undertone, or Schmidt-Degener's that his recollection of Knüpfer's historical painting gave compactness and precision to his genre scenes[59] cannot be accepted. All these things he could have just as well learned elsewhere. Most recently I. V. Kuznetsov in his study of Knüpfer has suggested that Steen followed Knüpfer in allegorized genre; however, as pointed out earlier, this tendency is not to be found in Steen's early work.

Steen may have known Knüpfer; he may have met him in his early days in Utrecht; he may even have owned some of his pictures, perhaps the *Lazarus on the Steps;* but there is no indication that he ever studied with him, or was directly influenced by his work earlier than 1667, the date of *Lazarus and the Rich Man.* Thereafter he used the steps and galleries commonly found in Knüpfer in others of his pictures, such as *The Marriage at Cana* in the Beit collection (Fig. 62, Cat. 48) and *Samson Mocked by the Philistines* in Cologne (Fig. 63, Cat. 12/10a). Both are pictures painted at the end of the 1660's and are to be associated with the two works of 1667 and also with *Samson and Delilah* of 1668 (Fig. 67, Cat. 10), yet to be discussed.

One other picture of this time also shows direct reliance upon a work by Knüpfer. Steen took his *Prayer of Tobias and Sarah* (Fig. 65, Cat. 25c) directly from Knüpfer's work of the same subject dated 1654 (Fig. 6). Both pictures are in the Centraal Museum in Utrecht, and their correspondence leaves no doubt of the dependence. Steen even borrowed the fluttering cupids carrying a marriage wreath, a type of motif occurring only rarely in his work. Steen's picture as originally conceived must have been even closer to the Knüpfer, for it included the angel Raphael exorcising the devil who prevented the consummation of Sarah's several earlier marriages. That portion of the painting has been cut, leaving (after cleaning) only the ends of the angel's wings and sword.[60] The association of the two pictures and the 1654 date on the Knüpfer led the writer of the 1952 catalogue of the Centraal Museum to declare the date of the Steen "omsteeks of kort na 1654." Such a date is a clear impossibility when one knows the kind of work Steen did around 1654—for example, *The Village Wedding* of 1653 (Fig. 25, HdG 445). Any date earlier than 1667 or

1668 for *The Prayer of Tobias and Sarah* is unacceptable stylistically. Such a conclusion shows again that direct contact between Knüpfer and Steen can only be found in the late 1660's, that is, after Knüpfer's death, and places in doubt the whole assertion that Steen studied with him formally.

Sarah and Tobias kneeling in fervent prayer on their wedding night are found in a different pose and with only slight variation in dress in another painting by Steen of the signing of their marriage contract (Fig. 66, Cat. 25a/457), now in Brunswick. The similarity between the couples has often been noted. Schlie in his study of Knüpfer of 1896, unaware that Steen painted a prayer scene, marked the similarity between Knüpfer's figures and those in Steen's marriage celebration, thus missing the even closer correspondence. The connection between these two Steens is important because, giving more material, it helps establish the date of both. *The Marriage of Tobias and Sarah* has been reported dated 1667, but this is incorrect, for the canvas is not dated. That date, however, or perhaps better 1667/68, is stylistically accurate, and must because of the recurrence of types and the similarity of conception be accepted for the painting at Utrecht.

Substantiation of 1667/68 as the date for both of these pictures can be had by a comparison of them with *Samson and Delilah* (Fig. 67, Cat. 10) of 1668, the third dated religious picture of these years, and with other pictures of that time, such as the well known *Twelfth Night Feast* at Cassel also dated 1668 (Fig. 68, HdG 494). Stechow, in an article on a *Merry Company* in the museum at Oberlin College,[61] succinctly characterized Steen's manner of composing in the late 1660's as a "vaulting forward" of the main group from the background. This can be seen very clearly in *Samson and Delilah,* where the group of three figures—Delilah, Samson, and the timid barber—stand out in focus, in brilliance of color, and in tightness of structure against the looser, monochromed setting. Steen projects the group forward, making the corner of the carpet upon which they all are placed touch the picture plane. All the other figures, like stage extras, in their lower intensity support the main action.

The Prayer of Tobias and Sarah and *The Marriage of Tobias and Sarah* are both constructed in the same way as the *Merry Company* and *Samson and Delilah.* The marriage picture, being the more diverse, may be the earlier, but in any case the two Tobias and Sarah paintings cannot be very distant from each other. In the marriage scene the group of mother, father, and notary around the carpeted table, though it is not the main group, claims a position similar to that of Samson, Delilah, and the barber. Tobias, Sarah, the angel and the grinning servant form a second group a little deeper in space. Both groups are distinguished from the background and give the picture a bow-like structure. In the scene of the prayer, Tobias and Sarah form the main group, but one can be sure that the missing angel made a strong vertical accent, perhaps somewhat in the manner of the clowning musician in the *Twelfth Night Feast* at Cassel (Fig. 68).

This method of composition differs from anything previously seen in Steen's work, either historical or genre. In the works of the 1650's, as for instance in *Moses Striking the Rock* (Fig. 27, Cat. 8), or even in the earlier *Christ Blessing the Little Children* (Fig. 5, Cat. 60), the fundamental movement of space is inward; the compositions are concave. This remains true of the work of the early and middle 1660's even in pictures with a *repoussoir* figure like the *Twelfth Night Feast* of 1662 (Fig. 38, HdG 509C) or *Christ at Emmaus* (Fig. 45, Cat. 65).

Steen's manner of construction at this time also separates his *Prayer of Tobias and Sarah* from Knüpfer's and accounts for much of the difference between them. Steen moved the couple forward past the foot of the bed, placing them before the background of the chamber. Knüpfer keeps them within the space delineated by the box of the room. In his picture we are led in a semi-circular movement from left to right and thus enter into the experience of the event as we enter the space. Steen, in projecting the couple forward, blocks recession, and allows only a spectator's disinterested view.

The attitude of external observation is part of what is new in Steen's approach to historical subjects in the late 1660's. It rests not only on the projected or vaulted group, but also on the use of strong horizontals in the front plane, and on internal framing devices such as curtains or open views through columns or arches. *Samson and Delilah* of 1668 (Fig. 67, Cat. 10) offers an example of the use of all such devices. So also does *Antony and Cleopatra* (Fig. 60, Cat. 86a/b) and the several paintings of *The Wrath of Ahasuerus* (Figs. 59, 74, 75, 76, Cat. 18–20). In all cases the horizontal formed either by a step or simply by a vacant or near-vacant foreground strip serves to limit active participation within the pictorial space, while the internal framing limits extension beyond the picture itself. Steen creates a kind of forced visual focus. There are no great perspective rushes or sweeping diagonals which carry us kinetically into the space.

In pictures of this time Steen does not attempt to give a sense of continued motion. His paintings are like motion-picture stills. In *The Wrath of Ahasuerus* in Birmingham (Fig. 59, Cat. 18) the great peacock-pie knocked from the table in anger is caught in its fall as though glued to the table, and Haman cringing from the King poses more than moves. Perhaps it is something of this stasis that gives to such paintings their exaggerated theatricality. The pictures are really presentations, performances, and not the simple recreation of occurrences, as were Steen's earlier works like *The Adoration of the Shepherds* (Fig. 37, Cat. 37/31) or even *The Rape of the Sabine Women* (Fig. 50, Cat. 76). There is no humility about the historical works of the late 1660's. They are pretentious and ostentatious, and Steen brought all his ability to create an ancient world of high emotion and princely luxury.

Nowhere in his early work can be found the silks, satins, porcelains, marbles, and bronzes of the dining chamber of Ahasuerus. Steen developed a technique of broken, light-struck surfaces to make all of the textures glow in their richness and variety. At the foot of Ahasuerus' table Steen passes us from feathery peacock-tail, to Ming porcelain, to Turkish carpet, to the satins of Esther's dress, to the fur of the barking dog. In color the range goes from blue-brown, to the deep reds and blues of the carpet, to the salmon and tan/gold of Esther's dress. Ahasuerus' tunic is lemon-yellow, his sash and cuffs light blue silk, and his cape, the center of the composition, the most intense red of the painting. Steen plays all these colors off against the soft monochrome of the background. The very richness here serves in its own way to put us off, as if this is a world not really to enter. The invitation of the picture is not to participate either in action or in space, but to observe with wonder, and enjoy with a certain voyeuristic pleasure, to which Steen often directs us by the inclusion of leering self-images or pranksterish clowns.

In the extravagance of setting and the theatrical externalization of emotions the works of the late 1660's are truly high baroque in their aesthetic. Fundamental to that aesthetic was the direct communication of emotional—or better, emotive—experiences, through narrative. In turn narrative was dependent upon a whole language of easily read gestures and expressions, which in their rhetorical explicitness often seem to us, today, hackneyed and overstated. *The Wrath of Ahasuerus* (Fig. 59, Cat. 18) or *Samson Mocked by the Philistines* (Fig. 63, Cat. 12/10a) can be read without ambiguity through the exaggerated externality of the emotions. Samson's eyes roll as Delilah taunts him with mocking gesture; Haman shrinks in fright as Ahasuerus, wide-eyed and furious, leaps up, his fists clenched in anger. It is not at all surprising that in these late narratives, as already suggested, Steen turned to the early Rembrandt of the 1630's for inspiration. In paintings like *The Sacrifice of Isaac* of 1635 in the Hermitage (B. 498) or *Belshazzar's Feast* in London (Fig. 58, B. 497) of a similar date Rembrandt made use of the same emotional explicitness to be picked up later by Steen. Rembrandt also supplied Steen with the lush orientalism of Biblical trappings and settings. Yet there is an important difference between Steen and Rembrandt, and for that matter, baroque aesthetics in general. The pathetic and heroic emotions of the baroque are true, where Steen is always comically pathetic and mock-heroic. Rembrandt's Samson in the *Blinding of Samson* in Frankfurt (Fig. 64, B.501) is a powerfully heroic figure; Steen's Samson in *Samson Mocked by the Philistines* is, at the moment of his fall, a ludicrous figure stripped of all nobility, the butt of cruel and vulgar jokes. Far from being accidentally ridiculous, as C. W. de Groot suggests,[62] Steen purposefully makes his great heroes and heroines transparent in their emotions and slightly embarrassing to the serious viewer. Such comment, however, anticipates the discussion of Steen's historical vision to be found in Chapter 4, and will be reserved for that place.

The group of pictures centering around the three dated religious works—*The Rich Man and Lazarus* (Fig. 57, Cat. 59), *Antony and Cleopatra* (Fig. 56, Cat. 86) of 1667, and *Samson and Delilah* (Fig. 67, Cat. 10) of 1668—and finding stylistic support in such genre works as *The Twelfth Night Feast* (Fig. 68, HdG 494) of 1668 constitute Steen's largest production of historical paintings. In all, from these last years in Haarlem there are twenty works, only a few of which have found place in the above discussion. A list of the paintings within this group follows:

The Trial of the Infant Moses (Fig. 69, Cat. 6)
Samson and Delilah (Fig. 67, Cat. 10), 1668
Samson Mocked by the Philistines (Fig. 63, Cat. 12/10a)
Bathseba Receiving David's Letter (Fig. 70, Cat. 14)
Bathseba Receiving David's Letter (Fig. 71, Cat. 14b/348)
Tamar and Amnon (Fig. 72, Cat. 16)
Esther Before Ahasuerus (Fig. 73, Cat. 17)

The Wrath of Ahasuerus (Fig. 59, Cat. 18)
The Wrath of Ahasuerus (Fig. 74, Cat. 19a)
The Wrath of Ahasuerus (Fig. 75, Cat. 19)
The Wrath of Ahasuerus (Fig. 76, Cat. 20)
The Marriage of Tobias and Sarah (Fig. 66, Cat. 25a/457)
The Marriage of Tobias and Sarah (Fig. 77, Cat. 25b)
The Prayer of Tobias and Sarah (Fig. 65, Cat. 25c)
The Angel Raphael Casting Out the Devil (Fig. 78, Cat. 25d/69)
The Rest on the Flight to Egypt (Fig. 79, Cat. 39)
The Marriage at Cana (Fig. 62, Cat. 48/49)
The Return of the Prodigal Son (Fig. 80, Cat. 55)
The Parable of the Rich Man and Lazarus (Fig. 57, Cat. 59), 1667
Antiochus and Stratonice (Fig. 81, Cat. 84b/54)
The Banquet of Antony and Cleopatra (Fig. 56, Cat. 86), 1667
The Banquet of Antony and Cleopatra (Fig. 60, Cat. 86a/b)

It should be noted with how few themes Steen dealt during these years, and how he was prone to repeating subjects. A discussion of Steen's choice of themes is reserved for the second chapter. Here it might be pointed out, however, that such scenes as the adoration of the shepherds or the flight to Egypt which made up a large part of his earlier work have been eliminated, in favor mostly of heroic scriptural narratives.

The New Elegance—1671

Though his paintings do not show it, the 1660's did not end happily for Steen. In 1669 Margaretha van Goyen died, leaving him a widower after twenty years of marriage. The following year he buried his father, Havik Steen. Upon his father's death Steen inherited a house in Leiden opposite the Wolsteeg, where he went to live, thus returning to his native city. In 1672 he obtained from the city permission to keep a tavern. Many of the stories of his profligacy found in Houbraken's and Weyerman's biographies may come from this time of his life, since they have their source in his occupation as an innkeeper. Steen married again in 1673, to the widow Maria van Egmont, and the following year she bore him the last of his children, a son called Theodorus. During these years Steen was "hooftman" of the Lucas guild in Leiden. He had been one of the first members in 1648. In 1674 he was named "deken," or dean of the guild.[63]

In the earliest years of the 1670's Steen's historical pictures became even richer than those of the late 1660's. The air clears a little of its haze; the light, though still an evening glow touching things with warmth, sharpens; the lines are harder, and the textures become more delicate. The figures themselves are slighter and taller and move with a more delicate grace. It is as though out of the opulent richness of the pictures of the late 1660's was created a slighter and more aristocratic class, at ease with luxury. *The Sacrifice of Iphigenia* of 1671 (Fig. 82, Cat. 74) displays these changes and even more so does *David Returning Victorious* of the same date (Fig. 83, Cat. 13). A comparison of Michal as she greets David, or of the singing women with mandolins, with any of the women from the paintings of the end of the 1660's, for instance Esther or Tamar or Delilah, shows how Steen has disminished their large beauty for one more delicate and slender. Elegance and elongation go to the extreme in *The Generosity of Scipio* (Fig. 84, Cat. 83), where one wonders how that foppish, moustached cavalier and his tall, thin, languid bride ever found their way into a painting by Jan Steen.

The Sacrifice of Iphigenia and *David Returning Victorious* also show how in the early 1670's Steen opened up his compositions. The tightness of the projected group is gone and the viewer is allowed more freedom within the space of the picture. The background lightens; and though the main groups are still played against its lower intensity, one feels it more as an active force than only a backdrop. *The Worship of the Golden Calf* (Fig. 85, Cat. 7) should be dated around 1671 and perhaps shows the beginnings of Steen's opening up of the composition. Though the group is still tight, the prohibiting foreground horizontal has been eliminated, and we enter the pictorial space through an inverted triangle.

These changes can be most dramatically seen in the contrast between *The Marriage of Tobias and Sarah* in Brunswick (Fig. 66, Cat. 25a/457) of around 1668 and the painting of the same subject in the de Young Museum in San Francisco (Fig. 86, Cat. 25/487),[64] belonging to this later group of pictures. The whole painting is lighter, airier; the figures are slighter and more delicately posed, and the room is more open, breaking the tendency towards limited space of the late 1660's. Even the drama seems to be taken less seriously and less excitedly. Tobias in the earlier picture stands flat-footed. He is a costumed farm-boy, his wife-to-be a shy milkmaid, uncomfortable in her dress. In the San Francisco picture Tobias' elegance and sense of belonging make it hard to believe he just wandered in off the road. He stands in almost an affected classical contrapposto. Sarah, looking down her nose, is completely self-possessed, even haughty.

In the Brunswick picture, as pointed out earlier, we read and react to the groups as convex projections out of the space behind; in the later work Steen forces us to move around an interior semicircle starting with Tobias' traveling bag at the left and ending with the draped table cover at the right. Thus by progression we touch each point of the story. Steen demands the same movement in *The Generosity of Scipio* (Fig. 84, Cat. 83), in the questionable painting of *The Banquet of Antony and Cleopatra* (Fig. 87, Cat. 85) and in *The Sacrifice of Iphigenia* (Fig. 82, Cat. 74). In the latter picture, which is dated 1671, the distribution of elements in a less structured way than in the sixties leaves the two main elements of the story—Iphigenia to the left and Agamemnon to the right—separated by a disturbingly vacant center.

The opening up of space at this time is accompanied by a renewed interest in landscapes. Two paintings, *Moses Striking the Rock for Water* from the Johnson collection in Philadelphia (Fig. 88, Cat. 9) and *Laban Searching for the Idols Hidden by Rachel* in Leiden (Fig. 89, Cat. 4/652a),[65] reveal this new concern. These two paintings represent Steen's only really open landscapes since his very earliest days in Utrecht, and even then he did not create the full and distant vistas of these late paintings. The backdrops which he used throughout his career, giving a sense of warmth and close physical presence, are here lifted and the confinement of his pictorial environment broken.

In summary, the group of pictures around 1671 consists of eight paintings mentioned in the text: *Laban Searching for the Idols* (Fig. 89, Cat. 4/652a); *The Worship of the Golden Calf* (Fig. 85, Cat. 7); *Moses Striking the Rock* (Fig. 88, Cat. 9); *David Returning Victorious* (Fig. 83, Cat. 13); *The Marriage of Tobias and Sarah* (Fig. 86, Cat. 25/487); *The Sacrifice of Iphigenia* (Fig. 82, Cat. 74); *The Generosity of Scipio* (Fig. 84, Cat. 83); and *The Banquet of Antony and Cleopatra* (Fig. 87, Cat. 85). To those discussed should probably be added *Bathseba With David's Letter* (Fig. 90, Cat. 14a/814a), which displays the same sharp satiny elegance found in the *Iphigenia* or *The Marriage of Tobias and Sarah* in San Francisco.

During this time Steen seems to have developed two styles of painting, one reserved mostly for his historical scenes in which he could manifest all his love of delicate stuffs, and the other for his peasant pieces which he painted in a rougher manner and with a looser brush. Proof of this is to be found in *Village Wedding* in the Rijksmuseum of 1672 (Fig. 91, HdG 454), which was painted at approximately the same time as *The Marriage of Tobias and Sarah* in San Francisco (Fig. 86, Cat. 25/487). Two conceptions could hardly be more separate. In one the painting is tight and clear, the palette light and even a little cool. In the other, the figures are almost squat, and the painting is loose, the colors warmer. The same qualities are found in *The Quarrel Over Cards* of 1671 at the Museum in Arnhem (Fig. 92, HdG 774), which might be compared with either *The Sacrifice of Iphigenia* (Fig. 82) or *David Returning Victorious* (Fig. 83) both of the same date. It would seem that in this split Steen discovered an appropriateness of manner dependent upon subject and possibly therefore also upon class.

The Last Years—1675/76

Steen's last years, from 1674 to the end of his life in 1679, are almost as confusing as his earliest years. Many things were going on, and he seems to have continued working in several manners, depending upon the nature of the subject. For this reason it is particularly difficult to discover a coherent group among his late religious or historical pictures. Some tendencies, however, seem to emerge clearly enough to be delineated.

His interest in large spaces, if not always in landscape, seems to have maintained itself with some consistency. It can be seen in the *Rustic Feast in a Large Tavern* of 1674[66] in the Louvre (Fig. 93, HdG 601), in *The Expulsion from the Temple* of 1675 (Fig. 94, Cat. 62), and in *The Marriage at Cana* of 1676 (Fig. 95, Cat. 50). In each, Steen created a large architectural interior for his scene. In all three, as in *Laban Searching for the Idols* (Fig. 89, Cat. 4/652a) and *Moses Striking the Rock* (Fig. 88, Cat. 9), the extended space is formed into a large semicircle by the figures, one group of which cuts across the open space. Essentially the same construction seems to be true for the *Garden Party* of 1677 (Fig. 98, HdG 52/440; see Add. 13), Steen's next-to-last dated picture, and also in the rather puzzling painting of *The Marriage at Cana* which at one time was in the collection of the Duke of Arenberg (Fig. 96, Cat. 46). In this last picture Steen created a large hall, not unlike that in the *Rustic Feast in a Large Tavern* (Fig. 93, HdG 601), but covered half of the space in the large painting by a hanging dust cover. The figures, semi-circularly arranged, are correspondingly small.

The Expulsion from the Temple is of particular interest at this moment in Steen's development, for it seems in so many ways, as does the *Marriage at Cana* just mentioned, to hark back to the kind of small figural work he was doing much earlier—even in the early 1650's. There is also a harking back to Rembrandtesque types, especially in the old Jews grasping the money at the left-hand side. The spotlighting effect on the main group seems also to have its origin in the early 1650's. Here, however, it occurs not in a dimly lighted, cramped interior, but in a large hall. Essentially the painting is a peasant piece, and Steen returned to older techniques to accomplish it. Only the troubled woman at the right surrounded by admirers reflects the flowing softness of his late figures. A very similar motif (the old lecher with the young girl) occurs on the left in the *Garden Party* of 1677 (Fig. 98) just mentioned as Steen's next-to-last dated picture.

The *Garden Party,* often called *The Prodigal Son,* perfectly embodies the second important tendency in Steen's last works. The figures are painted in soft outlines and flowing rhythms and soft light colors as they loll to the music of masquerading players, sport on the lawns, or stroll in the balustraded garden of the villa Paedts on the Rapenburg in Leiden.[67] The picture, most recently in an unknown American collection, might best be called "The Garden of Love" or "Fêtes Galantes," for it fully anticipates French 18th century garden scenes.

Referring to this painting and to another similar scene of a garden party or "concert" in the Hermitage (Fig. 99, HdG 416), Kuznetsov declares Steen's attitude in these pictures to be one of "bitter irony."[68] Bitter, that is, against the growing artificiality of taste affected by the Dutch upper class during the time of the French invasions. Native Dutch dress has been pushed to the rear by imported fashions. Kuznetsov sees a great incongruity between the physical types (still farmerish) and the delicate accessories of French classicistic taste; he suggests that this was Steen's way of commenting on a life of bourgeois pretension against which he stood. The paintings were empty of the old joy and humor because the life was empty. The vitality of Dutch art was drained, for realism depended upon the depiction of the life of ordinary people.

Kuznetsov's interpretation of these last paintings by Steen offers much insight and feeling. He is aware of the implications of values and meanings in the way things and people are depicted. His is an interpretation which finds the brightened elegance of Steen's late pictures false and unacceptable. One must ask, however, whether it is possible to distinguish in Steen "bitter irony" from, for example, humorous irony or satirical irony. Does Steen poke more fun at the antics of these bourgeois celebrants than he does at his peasants wheeling home a drunken companion in a barrow? Or is that to be taken as a sign of the joy and humor of the ordinary people? The point is that Steen was constantly ironical without regard to class. He was much too accepting and much too delighted with human foibles ever really to be biting about behavior, on the basis of class, affected or otherwise. Kuznetsov may well be right that the new tastes, the new delight in luxury and the attendant subversion of indigenous qualities meant the end of significant painting in Holland of the seventeenth century. Steen's reactions to these changes, however, are far from clear.

Some of the feeling, the looseness and the soft flowing rhythms and delicate colors of the *Garden Party,* which can be labeled aristocratic, are to be found in Steen's historical works as well. *The Marriage at Cana* dated 1676 (Fig. 95, Cat. 50), while seemingly associated more with *The Expulsion from the Temple* (Fig. 94, Cat. 62) of a year earlier,[69] incorporates much of this softer manner. The crowd of musicians in the balcony is extremely sketchy and flowing. The figures at the marriage table, especially one with long hair who may be the groom, recall several of the figures in the *Garden Party* and even more strongly one of the young men in a similar scene of garden games formerly in the Spencer Churchill collection in Blockley, Gloucestershire (HdG ?) made at the very end of the 1670's. Another similarity of motif is found in the page bringing a tray to the bride's table in *The Marriage at Cana* and the page pouring wine in the *Garden Party* of 1677 (Fig. 98). They are the same figure seen from different sides. On the whole the looseness of the painting, the openness of the structure, and the light coloring indicate a cross-over of modes between the more aristocratic genre paintings and some of the Biblical subjects.

Another, smaller version of *The Marriage at Cana* in Dresden (Fig. 97, Cat. 47) depicts the scene in a similar hall with arcade at the back, only here it is seen through an enframing archway hung with garlands. Christ, raised on a dais, is clearly visible behind the drunken woman sprawled on the steps. The painting, especially of the background figures and the musicians on the balcony, is very similar to that of the 1676 picture, and even a little freer. It is probably his last treatment of the theme, though verification of that must await study of the original.

Two versions of *Manius Curius Dentatus and the Samnite Ambassadors* (Figs. 100 and 101, Cat. 84 and 84a) possibly belong to this last group of pictures. Though in many ways they are related to the previous group, especially to *Laban Searching for Idols* (Fig. 89, Cat. 4/652a), the looseness of the painting, especially in the former version, requires a later date. Furthermore, the little boy on the ground with a skirt full of turnips looks very much, in both features and in painting, like the boy rolling the cask in *The Marriage at Cana* of 1676 (Fig. 95).

Two other historical paintings belong to this group, *The Banquet of Antony and Cleopatra* reportedly from the Roëll collection (Fig. 102, Cat. 86c) and *The Rich Man and Lazarus* (Fig. 103, Cat. 58). The latter is a particularly clear example of how the form of upper-class genre spread into the historical paintings. The only leftover from Steen's older manner is the turbaned Oriental of a rich man. Otherwise there is here almost a completely new group of figures. Even the children at the left seem a different, less earthy breed. This painting is probably Steen's last historical work.[70] Unlike *The Rich Man and Lazarus* of 1667 (Fig. 57, Cat. 59), Steen has brought the genre elements to the foreground and left both Lazarus and the rich man in the back. Steen here used the parable for a display of the good life—or better, the rich full life, with all its content of sensuality, which he took such pleasure in painting. How ironic that in this of all his historical pictures Steen points a moral; "In weelde ziet toe," "In wealth take care" is inscribed upon the low stone wall. With mocking humor he seated his buxom, purple-clothed singer with vine leaves in her hair immediately above the inscription.

Eight paintings, then, two of them dated, can be grouped together as Steen's last works in narrative painting. They are:

The Marriage at Cana (Fig. 96, Cat. 46)
The Marriage at Cana (Fig. 97, Cat. 47)
The Marriage at Cana (Fig. 95, Cat. 50), 1676
The Parable of the Rich Man and Lazarus (Fig. 103, Cat. 58)
The Expulsion from the Temple (Fig. 94, Cat. 62), 1675
Manius Curius Dentatus and the Samnite Ambassadors (Fig. 100, Cat. 84)
Manius Curius Dentatus and the Samnite Ambassadors (Fig. 101, Cat. 84a)
The Banquet of Antony and Cleopatra (Fig. 102, Cat. 86c)

The grouping is not a tight one. Divergent tendencies prevail, and it is only in detail that a new feeling, a softness of contour and ease of rhythm, emerges. For the most part the figures, even of peasants, seem less earthbound, and more aristocratic in spirit.

General Summary

In summary, Steen's development as a history painter, as seen in the detailed study of seven groups of his paintings, can be stated as follows. He goes from being essentially a folk-painter who tried his hand occasionally at some of the more common religious themes (e.g., the adoration of the shepherds) to being a painter of large, often ostentatious, religious and historical and mythological scenes. His flair for the dramatic comes out most strongly in the late 1660's, after which he pursued a calmer but more elegant manner. His choice of themes reflects this development. In the early years he painted mostly scenes from the New Testament dealing with the life of Christ or John the Baptist. In the 1660's, however, he turned to the great narrative stories of the Old Testament—Esther, Samson, Tamar—and for the first time to stories from classical mythology and history.

The fact that Steen's real interest in narrative painting did not begin until after his student years, and then largely under the influence of Rembrandt, leads to the conclusion that he did not begin his studies with Knüpfer in Utrecht as reported by Weyerman. There is evidence that Steen began in Utrecht, but as a landscape painter and not under the tutelage of a figural painter working in a classical tradition. Much later Steen did make use of at least two of Knüpfer's pictures, which fact may account for the original idea that he studied with the German master.

It is difficult also to accept Steen's father-in-law, Jan van Goyen, as one of his early teachers. Coming from Leiden, Van Goyen lived in The Hague from about 1634 until his death in 1656. Steen, however, did not arrive there until 1649, when he was twenty-three. There is little in the early landscapes which can be directly attributed to his influence, despite Martin's feelings to the contrary. Steen's training may have been first with Droochsloot in Utrecht, then definitely with the Ostades in Haarlem. Isaac Ostade seems to have had the more important place in his training. It may also have been that Steen, while in Haarlem, fell under the spell of Jacob de Wet. That influence, however, did not show itself until the early 1650's, when Steen was already at The Hague.

Steen has a permanent place in history as a painter of peasant and middle-class life. One can hardly damage that image by revising it somewhat. The consistency of his interest in historical painting, and the number and quality of the works, do call for something of a re-evaluation of his reputation. He was not only one of The Netherlands' greatest genre painters, moving as no one else did across the whole breadth of Dutch life, but also one of her most accomplished and prolific painters of narrative histories, an occupation which he took with extreme seriousness. This is not to say that he painted without humor, but only that he was aware of his own purposes, some of which have met with critical disapproval.

His mature historical paintings are like compendia of all that was best in Dutch painting of the mid-seventeenth century. In a work like *The Banquet of Antony and Cleopatra* at The Hague (Fig. 60, Cat. 86a/b) or *The Wrath of Ahasuerus* in Birmingham (Fig. 59, Cat. 18) one can witness Steen's remarkable mixture of the *Fein-malerei* of Leiden still life and genre painting, the religious drama of Rembrandt, and the low humor of Haarlem's peasant painters. Leiden, Amsterdam, Haarlem, Utrecht—the great centers of Dutch painting—are brought together in Steen's narrative imagination.

Out of the union of these elements Steen created a style, or really several styles, of great originality. In truth he was neither the follower of any single master nor the leader of a school. In his mature narrative pictures, Steen shares the opulence and emotional vigor of baroque painting in general. Nevertheless, in one aspect of his historical imagination he stands alone within the whole sweep of Dutch and European painting of his time. What isolates him is his conscious use of incongruous elements and his sense of historical ridiculousness; both these subjects will be pursued in the following chapters.

References

1. Omitted from the present catalogue are eight paintings of *The Satyr and the Peasant "Who Blows Hot and Cold"* listed in the historical section by Hofstede de Groot (Nos. 77–81). Though the story includes a mythological creature, it is essentially legend rather than myth; and Steen treats it as folk-genre. Probably for similar reasons Van Westrheene excludes two such works from his historical listing and places them in the vaguer category "Subjects Divers." Also omitted are two other paintings: HdG 70, *Ascanius and Lucilla,* illustrating a scene from Bredero's *Lucelle,* and HdG 87, *The Story of Pieter Ghijsen,* an unknown painting representing a theme from Dutch history. Neither of these is historical in the strict sense of the word.

2. That date is not documented but is arrived at by the fact that in 1646, at the age of twenty, he registered at the University in Leiden.

3. Bredius, *Steen,* 1927, p. 19.

4. *Ibid.,* p. 90.

5. *Ibid.,* p. 91.

6. Martin, *Steen,* 1954, p. 14.

7. Houbraken, *De Groote Schouburgh,* III, 1721, p. 13.

8. "Zyn vaders naam was Havik Jansze Steen, een Brouwer tot Leyden, die gewaarschouwt zynde dat er geeft stak in den Jongen (zelfs kon Havik zo diep niet zien), zo beftelde hy hem eerst by Knuffer, tot Utrecht." Weyerman, *De Levens-Beschryvingen,* 1729, II, p. 348.

9. Martin, *ZfbK,* LXI, 1927/28, p. 330.

10. Schlie, *Uber Nikolaus Knüpfer,* 1896, p. 6.

11. *Trudy Gosudarstvennogo ermitazha,* VIII, No. 3, n.d., pp. 187–232.

12. This information, as Kuznetsov discovered, is based upon an engraving with a self-portrait and a biographical sketch of Knüpfer published in 1649 when the artist was still alive. It was repeated by Cornelis de Bie in *Het Gulden-Cabinet* of 1661, and later by Sandrart, *Teutsche Academie,* 1675; and by Houbraken, *De Groote Schouburgh,* III, 1719.

13. Schlie, *Uber Nikolaus Knüpfer,* 1896, pp. 3 ff.; Kuznetsov, *Trudy . . . ,* pp. 190 ff.

14. Kuznetsov, *Trudy . . . ,* p. 194.

15. C. Willnau suggested that Knüpfer worked on the picture in collaborative effort with J. B. Weenix, who did the animals, and Jan Both, who did the background; see *O-H,* LXIX, 1952, pp. 210–11. Kuznetsov accepts the painting as a Knüpfer; *Trudy . . . ,* VIII, No. 3, n.d., No. 66; he mentions in his text, however, that Knüpfer worked on occasion with Both and Weenix (p. 203).

16. For a discussion of the iconography of *Search After Happiness,* see J. I. Kuznetsow (V. I. Kuznetsov), *O-H,* LXXIX, 1964, pp. 229–30.

17. Kuznetsov, *Trudy . . . ,* p. 202.

18. *Ibid.,* p. 201.

19. *Ibid.,* p. 203.

20. Martin, "Jan Steen as a Landscape Painter," *Burlington,* LXVII, 1935, pp. 211–12; Gerson, "Landschaapen van Jan Steen," *Kunsthistorische Mededelinging,* III, 1948, pp. 50–56.

21. *T-B,* IX, 1913, p. 274.

22. Martin, *Burlington,* LXVII, 1935, p. 212; Gerson, *Kunsthistorische Mededelinging,* III, 1948, p. 52.

23. *Catalogue Raisonné,* 1908, p. 1.

24. Martin, *Burlington,* LXVII, 1935, p. 212; Martin, *Steen,* 1954, p. 29.

25. See Bredius, *Steen,* 1927, p. 15.

26. Cat., Van Goyen, "De Lakenhal," Leiden, 1960, pp. 8–9; see also Maclaren, *The Dutch School,* National Gallery, London, 1960, p. 34.

27. *O-H,* LX, 1943, p. 140.

28. *ZfbK,* LXII, 1928, p. 174.

29. Also in the purchase was *The Story of Hagar;* for details see Cat. 2a and 2b.

30. Bredius, *Kunstler Inventare,* I, p. 61, No. 363; Martin, *Steen,* 1954, p. 29.

31. There is no documentary evidence as to Steen's early stay in Haarlem, but Weyerman reported that he studied with Adriaen Ostade—which would mean that he was in that city; see *De Levens-Beschryvingen,* 1729, II, p. 348.

32. J. G. van Gelder, *O-H,* XLIII, 1926, p. 206.

33. Bredius, *O-H,* XLIII, 1926, pp. 267–68.

34. Gerson, *Kunsthistorische Mededelinging,* III, 1948, p. 53.

35. *Die Meister der holländischen und flämischen Malerschulen,* 1917, ed. 1958, p. 123.

36. Bauch, *Der frühe Rembrandt und seine Zeit,* 1960, p. 235.

37. J. G. van Gelder thought the picture, which is monogrammed RHL and dated 1624, to be one of Rembrandt's earliest efforts. See *O-H,* LXV, 1947, p. 177. This is not accepted by Bauch, who agrees with the attribution to de Wet.

38. Bauch, *Der frühe Rembrandt und seine Zeit,* 1960, pl. 201.

39. Van der Willigen, *Les artistes de Haarlem,* 1870, pp. 21–22, 324.

40. Bredius, *O-H,* XXXVII, 1919, pp. 215–219.

41. While Hackaert has been dropped as a possible painter of the landscape, Bredius and Martin support the idea that the background may be the work of Wils, who was a Haarlem painter. (See Cat. 28.)

42. *Kunsthistorische Mededelinging,* III, 1948, p. 52.

43. Bredius, *Steen,* 1927, p. 91.

44. See Bijeveld, *Om de Hoenderhof door Jan Steen,* 1950, *passim.*

45. For a discussion of the erotic content of this painting see A. P. de Nirimonde, *GdBA,* Ser. 6. LXVIII, 1966, pp. 265 ff.

46. Gudlaugsson, *Terborch,* 1960, p. 136.

47. *Ibid.,* Nos. 124 and 164.

48. *The Dutch School,* National Gallery, London, 1960, No. 856.

49. Guldener, *Phoenix,* III, 1949, pp. 18–21, de Jonge, *Steen,* n.d., p. 14.

50. Martin, *L'Art flammand et hollandais,* XII, 1909, p. 56.

51. Hamann, *Marburger Jahrbuch für Kunstwissenschaft,* VIII–IX, 1936, pp. 558–59.

52. *Beeld en Woord,* 1952, p. 161.

53. Schmidt-Degener and Van Gelder, *Steen,* 1927, pp. 16, 54.

54. The only possible exception might be *Theseus and Acheloüs* (Fig. 52, Cat. 69b), which might be earlier; because of the poor quality of the photograph available, the dating must remain highly speculative. The place of the original is unknown.

55. *Fight Over a Card Table* dated 1664 in Munich (HdG 773) is too weak and awkward a picture to be accepted as an original.

56. In his 1954 monograph on Steen, Martin does not mention this attribution to Steen; he seems there to have dropped the idea.

57. Kuznetsov in his new catalogue of Knüpfer paintings and drawings does not include this painting; *Treasures of the State Collection,* Hermitage, VIII, 1965.

58. In both cases a vulgar inclusion has been painted out. As Knüpfer painted his picture, the servant was urinating on Lazarus. Steen has the little boy urinating in a mug obviously intended for Lazarus. In the Steen the joke is as much on the little boy as on Lazarus.

59. Martin, *Steen,* 1954, p. 28; Hofstede de Groot, *Art in America,* XVI, 1928, p. 250; Schmidt-Degener, *Steen,* 1927, p. 3.

60. Hofstede de Groot believed that the missing piece was to be found in the figure of the angel Raphael chaining a dragon in the Bredius Museum; *Art in America,* XVI, 1928, p. 250. More recently, J. J. ven Thiel of the Rijksmuseum has attempted a reconstruction of the two pieces into a large painting which could possibly have been a pendant to *The Marriage of Tobias and Sarah* in Brunswick (Cat. 25/457). For his ideas and a photographic reconstruction see *Duits Quarterly,* IX, 1965, pp. 6–9. No matter how the two pieces are fitted together, it is doubtful if they are part of the same picture. Though the dimensions of the picture could correspond, both of them having been cut, the angel is just too large to be accepted as part of the bedroom scene.

61. *Allen Memorial Art Museum Bulletin,* XV, 1958, p. 97.

62. *Beeld en Woord,* 1952, p. 170.

63. For documents see Bredius, *Steen,* 1927, pp. 93–95.

64. The possibility exists that this painting is to be associated with Steen's own second marriage, which would give it a date of 1673; see Chapter IV for a discussion of this possibility. A third, possibly original version now in London may well have a place between the Brunswick and San Francisco pictures (see Cat. 25b).

65. The painting of Laban, being unfinished and worked by another hand, gives a misleading impression of Steen's landscapes at this time. The picture has been reported as dated both 1660 and 1661. The date has disappeared; to begin with it may have been incorrect. Stylistically the picture belongs to this later period; see Catalogue entry for further information and a discussion of the painting's condition and dating.

66. The date of this picture is scarcely legible (Martin, *Steen,* 1954, p. 80). Nevertheless, a date of 1674 is not inconsistent with the style.

67. See Bijleveld, *O-H,* XLIII, 1926, pp. 132 ff. for identification of the house.

68. Kuznetsov, *Ezhegodnik,* Akademiia nauk SSSR, Institut istorii iskusstv, 1957, pp. 410–12.

69. The pictures, being of the same size, and dealing with two acts of Christ, have on occasion been considered pendants, but there is little to justify such a conclusion; see Catalogue entry.

70. In the Rouen Museum there is a small painting called *The Pastry Seller* (HdG 267) which, being dated 1678, is Steen's last dated work. Even in this—an old theme—his more delicate manner of the last years is obvious. The three figures do not seem so earthy as they might had the picture been painted earlier.

2

Religious Orientation and Thematic Concern in Steen's Biblical and Historical Paintings

Steen's Religious Orientation

On good evidence, Jan Steen is believed to have been a Roman Catholic. His parents were married as Catholics,[1] and his own children were baptized in the church.[2] Certain of his genre pieces reveal his familiarity with details of Catholic life. In the Rijksmuseum, for example, is a late painting of the plundering of a village (HdG 785), in which a tonsured monk pleads for mercy from the attackers; on the ground lie his cross and rosary. In a far different mood is a picture at The Hague (HdG 828); here a village priest admonishes with obvious pleasure one of Steen's looser women. Steen also painted the confessional box (HdG 245); and the little girl in *St. Nicolaas Day* at the Rijksmuseum (Fig. 105, HdG 510) holds a haloed image of St. John the Baptist. C. W. de Groot, who lists still other examples of Catholic subjects and details in the genre paintings,[3] adds as further evidence of Steen's Catholic persuasion his iconographic preference for the feast of St. Nicolaas and for the Epiphany, both Catholic celebrations which only later became Dutch national holidays.[4]

Yet, despite the details that can be adduced, evidence of a Catholic orientation in Steen's painting is scant. His pieces generally portray the common life of the populace of both low and middle class, and not of a small and mistrusted minority who for many years could celebrate their masses only in hidden chapels. Though more seventeenth century Dutch painters were Catholic than is generally recognized—Vermeer, S. de Bray, and Steen among others[5]—both Dutch art and Dutch culture by the mid-century were overwhelmingly Protestant.[6] Steen's lasting popularity attests to his place within the Calvinist society.

In some religious pictures Steen reveals his Catholic background directly. In *The Rest on the Flight to Egypt* (Fig. 79, Cat. 39), probably painted in the late 1660's, Steen represents the holy family with the adoring infant St. John holding a reed cross and embracing the holy lamb, a purely Catholic motif. With fluttering cherubs holding crown and scepter for the virgin, diffused haloes over mother and child, ecstatic expressions, and warm brown background, it recalls such works of Murillo as the *Virgin of Seville* in the Louvre. Though there are some later restorations, and the background painting is weak and unconvincing, the figures leave no doubt of its correct attribution to Steen.[7] It may be presumed that he made the painting on commission for one of the Catholic families known to him, or perhaps for a Catholic chapel. Its large size (75 × 54½ inches) supports the latter possibility.[8]

Two early pictures, *The Seven Acts of Mercy* (Fig. 15, Cat. 67) and *The Death of Ananias* (Fig. 1, Cat. 66), also reveal some Catholic content. One depicts monks distributing charities. The other, in dealing with the mission of St. Paul, has a Roman orientation. One lost painting, *The Last Supper* (Cat. 63), might be Catholic in conception, and another, *The Concert of St. Cecilia* (Cat. 68), clearly would be.

Though Catholic overtone or iconography is found in the religious painting as in genre, it is exceptional rather than the rule; essentially Steen's religious paintings are Protestant. There are no saints, except John the Baptist; no martyrdoms; no sacred conversations; and only a single image of Christ and Mary, in *The Rest on the Flight to Egypt* already mentioned (Fig. 79, Cat. 39), that could be called venerative or iconic. From the life of Christ Steen painted the nativity, the flight into Egypt, some of the miracles (especially that at the marriage at Cana), and the blessing of the children; but never scenes from the passion.[9] Protestants would have found such images idolatrous and Roman. Rembrandt's paintings of the passion in Munich, for instance, are, like all his works, pictorial narratives and not iconic statements so central in Catholic imagery.

With Protestantism, the Bible, both Old and New Testaments, became a book of narrative history for all to read. It became the single source of God's authority and word. Luther was the first to translate Scripture into a vernacular tongue, and Calvin, like Luther, believed that its reading enlightened the spirit. Holding prophets and apostles on the same level, Calvin wrote in his *Institutes of the Christian Religion:*

> But since we are not favoured with daily oracles from heaven, and since it is only in the Scripture that the Lord hath been pleased to preserve his truth in perpetual remembrance, it obtains the same complete credit and authority with believers, when they are satisfied of its divine origin, as if they heard the very words pronounced by God himself.[10]

Scripture was the source of righteousness and the well of inspiration. Everyone was to draw from the Bible practical lessons in piety and morality. The stories were *exempla* teaching the individual how to stand before God as had Abraham and Moses. For Calvinism the New Testament offered the spirit, but the Old Testament offered the law and the history.

Religious pictures were not prohibited under Protestantism. The painter might tell a story, be a kind of visual preacher—but never create sacred images for veneration. Calvinism shuns any cult of images. In Old Testament pictures emphasis in image shifts from the creation and the story of Eden, a prefigurative first passion, to the history of the generations of the children of Israel. Rembrandt, by telling with such narrative compassion the stories of the patriarchs and prophets, contributed brilliantly and purposefully to what must be thought of as Protestant iconography.

C. W. de Groot has shown that Steen's choice of Old Testament subjects—Abraham, Jacob, Esther, Tobias—closely follows Rembrandt's.[11] Yet it is not only his choice of religious subjects, common enough in the seventeenth century, which makes Steen's work Protestant. His treatment of those subjects, like Rembrandt's, is free of doctrinal symbolism and allegory. The narrative is direct and self-contained. What symbolism does occur is literary or emblematical. Steen tells Old Testament stories without the fundamental Catholic concern for prefigurative meaning; that is, they stand alone without direct reference to New Testament events. His narratives are events out of the history of God's first chosen people, a position the Calvinists believed had passed to them. In adversity they considered themselves the children of Israel, suffering in righteousness, and they took the history of the actual sons of Israel as their own.[12] The popularity of the story of Esther and her intercession with Ahasuerus for the lives of her people rests, as Madlyn Kahr has pointed out, not with doctrinal association, but with a political and historical identification. The Dutch felt a similarity between their own domination by the Catholic Spanish and the domination of the Jews under Persian rule.[13]

When Steen paints the head of John the Baptist (Fig. 44, Cat. 30a), as when Rembrandt paints the head of Christ, only the introverted spirituality of the face indicates divinity. There is no reliance on external sign. Catholic though he was, Steen made pictures befitting the larger religious environment in which he lived. He was in both iconography and treatment essentially Protestant in his religious paintings.

On another level, however, there is something un-Protestant, un-Calvinist, about his work, and in particular his later work. *Samson Mocked by the Philistines* (Fig. 63, Cat. 12/10a) was for Steen the excuse for an almost joyful romp, and a parade of costly stuffs. Bare-breasted Delilah, about to receive her whore's wages, taunts the anguished Samson, whose shorn weakness is demonstrated by the boy holding the chain around his neck. From the drunken captain, to the summer-soldier brandishing his sword, to the old Jew who clenches his hands in pity, all is exuberance and display even at this moment of Biblical horror. Adding a note of irony, Steen places the barber's bowl and open razor case on the floor beneath the sacks of coin, thus in still life symbolically uniting act and payment.

This abundance, this delight in human foible, this touch of humorous irony, cannot be held as either strictly Protestant or Catholic; but certainly the ability to celebrate, and to find humor in scripture, is more a part of the Catholic spirit than the Protestant. Catholicism, less possessed of guilt, and less troubled by individuality, has generally been more open in its acceptance of human weakness. Something of the largeness of Catholicism, as C. W. de Groot has pointed out,[14] finds its way even into Steen's predominantly Protestant vision. Steen's lasting interest in the marriage at Cana, a subject which Rembrandt never used, and perhaps from a certain point of view Christ's most questionable miracle, itself betrays his more tolerant spirit.

Love as a Major Thematic Unity in Steen's Historical Painting

Steen's interest in the marriage at Cana points directly to a major thematic concern in his work more important than either his Protestant orientation or the possible overtones of a more Catholic spirit. Whether in genre, religious, or historical pictures, one of his major concerns was with themes of love. Contemporary or ancient, he used love to reveal the foibles of men and women when they are both at their most passionate and at their most vulnerable. The genre humor he brings to historical subjects makes us understand the universality of such emotions, and allows a view of historical events perhaps less elevated than usual for his time, but certainly more animated.

In his historical pictures Steen painted the great and heroic episodes of ancient love and gave them a grandeur that befitted their own size and the age in which he lived. His late canvases, opulent in color and lavish in decoration, recall heroic drama. His tableaux of great loves, from David's adulterous love for Bathseba to the formidable devotion of Antony to Cleopatra, cannot be taken as a series; nevertheless they form a compendium of amorous affairs ranging from the humble to the grand.

It is not at all surprising to find that love spurred Steen's historical interest, for it appears strongly as a major theme in his genre work. The subjects touching on the theme are multiple. Proposals, advances, marriage, music lessons, brothel scenes, and above all doctors' visits (to treat lovesickness) make up a major part of his work. This correspondence of love themes is one of the major elements linking his genre and historical concerns.

Steen's interest in historical love affairs seems to have begun in the late '50's or early '60's along with his matured genre style. Except for the marriage at Cana, such love themes do not appear among his early works. His early style was too folk-oriented to accommodate either the trappings or the anguish of ancient love. The early historical works consist of subjects in which the peasant and village people play a large part: *Moses Striking the Rock* (Fig. 27, Cat. 8), *The Adoration of the Shepherds* (Fig. 28, Cat. 35), or *St. John Preaching in the Wilderness* (Fig. 29, Cat. 28). They are painted without pretension, and convey traditional religious feelings.

Development of Steen's style from landscape folk-paintings of simple New Testament scenes to extravagant and costly narratives, as outlined in the first chapter, is accompanied by a change in thematic material. All the subjects of the known early pictures with the exception of *Moses Striking the Rock* come from the New Testament. It is only around the beginning 1660's that Steen starts to use Old Testament subjects such as Bathseba, Lot, Hagar; and only in the late 1660's that he turns to mythology and history. The histories of great and dramatic loves, as that between Antony and Cleopatra, need great and dramatic means for the telling if they are not to be so reduced in size as to lose their force. This is true whether the narrative is literal as in Rubens, or treated with humor as so often in Steen.

The later pictures are the true subject of this chapter. They are the most numerous of Steen's histories and the most exciting. In them Steen discovered a style and historical perspective uniquely his own. In early works he made discoveries important for all he did later. Nevertheless these early works are here placed in a position parenthetical to his later painting in which he turned to themes of love and painted his most significant historical pictures.

Since ancient days, love has been divided most simply between the sacred and the profane, between that which ennobles and that which degrades, or to use Kenneth Clark's analogy, between *Venus Celestis* and *Venus Naturalis.*[15] Certainly the division is artificial. Sacred love may include base desires and, contrariwise, what appears only lustful may yet partake of the divine. Both Venuses are after all immortal. Yet the division has conveniences. Steen painted both sides of love and found within each shades of variation, and within each its touching and often boisterous humor. His works will be discussed as they come within these two broad divisions. Though he himself may not have intended such a division, it seems an appropriate one. Into it fit his diverse lovers: youthful, middle-aged, and elderly; frustrated and fulfilled; virtuous and guilty.

Sacred Love

In the province of sacred love, he delights us with youthful love turned inward, oblivious of everything except the passions of the heart. In his painting of *The Marriage of Tobias and Sarah* in Brunswick (Fig. 66, Cat. 25a/457), young Tobias, his hand upon his heart and eyes raised in rapture, is the young poet composing sweet verse to the joys of love. His shy-eyed betrothed, hands gently folded, regards him with blissful admiration in the moment of his inspiration. They are oblivious to the world around them—to the legalism of the contract and to the lasciviousness of the leering servant about to stick the spigot into the cask of wine.

One might raise the question whether Tobias swoons in fear rather than love, for the story goes (Tobit 7:11–15) that Sarah, the cousin of young Tobias, had taken seven husbands before him, each of whom had perished on the wedding night before they had lain together. Tobias' guardian angel Raphael, who is seen behind Tobias, looking rather more ethereal than the rest of the company, taught Tobias how to exorcise the jealous devil who guarded over Sarah's viriginity.[16] Steen, however, assures us here that Tobias is smitten not by fear but by love. He places a single sprig of myrtle, sacred to Aphrodite, by Tobias' feet, and decorates the chair reserved for the bridegroom with cupid heads and dolphins, also attributes of the goddess of love born of the sea. In no other picture did Steen do so well with the poetic obliviousness of young romantic love, or with the antithetical attitudes of the wedding feast.

In his later version of the subject in San Francisco (Fig. 86, Cat. 25/487) he makes the couple older. There, Tobias' swoon seems sham and Sarah knows very well what is going on. Differences in dress, stance, and the physical separation of the couple convert them into a slightly jaded pair. One might hesitate to label this middle-aged love, but certainly they are not so young as the swain and his girl from Brunswick. In *The Generosity of Scipio* (Fig. 84, Cat. 83), another picture of sacred love, Steen almost repeats in reverse the older Tobias and Sarah; but he places the bridegroom on his knee in gratitude for Scipio's return of the bride. Here, however, Steen has made his lover foppish, and we are mostly convinced of his sentimentality.

Steen portrays sacred and youthful love again in his large painting of 1671, *David Returning Victorious* (Fig. 83, Cat. 13). He lays his scene of welcome and celebration across the long canvas, placing the meeting of David and Michal, Saul's daughter, just slighly off center. As Steen painted it, the meeting in which love glances are exchanged is really the subject—or better, the *raison d'être*—of the picture. For the picture Steen united three stories from I Samuel. David's victory over Goliath occurs in Chapter 17; from Chapter 18:6-7 comes the story of his joyous welcome after another victory over the Philistines. It is only in 18:20 that the love between David and Michal is told and in 18:27 that he receives her in marriage. Steen has made their toes just touch as they stride to meet together in victory and admiration. The inscription, which may have been added later (see Catalogue entry), reads in translation:

Soli Deo gloria
It pleases God
that David dared
to slay Goliath
and hurt Saul to the heart.
Victorious he steps forth
here welcomed by his bride.[17]

David, though the same figure as the young Tobias from the Brunswick picture, finds his love not in dreaminess, but in action; and the couples in the two pictures can be regarded as alternatives of unfolding love. But Steen always finds his amusement. As he made Tobias somewhat silly with his hand upon his heart, he gives David the gigantic sword of Goliath to drag behind him. One cannot help suspecting that Steen intended the sword as a phallic analogy, and placed the hilt accordingly. Such lewdness might be out of place between the Biblical young lovers, but certainly not in the bacchanal which Steen created for David's welcome. Anyway, the sword as symbol is meant to impinge not upon their consciousness, but upon ours. By such device or conceit Steen adroitly mixed the sacred and the profane. He did the same in the paintings of the marriage of Tobias and Sarah with the lascivious gesture of the servant.

In *The Sacrifice of Iphigenia,* also of 1771 (Fig. 82, Cat. 74), Steen shows youthful love unrequited. There, though the theme of Agamemnon's moral choice between his war and his daughter predominates, the story is also told of the false promise of marriage to Achilles that was used to bring Iphigenia to Aulis. A dejected, downcast Iphigenia, dressed in bridal white, with a wreath upon her head, kneels before the altar. The ground is strewn with myrtle, ivy, and drooping roses. As if all this were not evidence enough of her tragic love, a crying cupid with unstrung bow and broken arrow is pushed from the scene by a hoary hag preparing the sacrificial fire. Hard-eyed and helmed, Achilles looks on from behind Agamemnon. Despite technical virtuosity of the painting itself, the representation comes off somewhat overexplicit. This might be because the tale leaves no place for Steen's habitual humor—that humor which in *The Marriage of Tobias and Sarah* and even in *The Generosity of Scipio* saves him from the trap of too-literary descriptions. It is a trap which Schmidt-Degener well recognized as Steen's greatest danger.[18]

No ancient story fits better into Steen's repertoire of love tales than that illustrated in *Antiochus and Stratonice* (Fig. 81, Cat. 84b/54). For a long time the picture, now in the Wetzlar collection, was thought to represent the prodigal son among the harlots. Wolfgang Stechow, who correctly identified the subject, called the story "one of the outstanding moral tales of world literature."[19] It was a natural choice for Steen, telling as it does of lovesickness near to death, and of recovery through a father's magnanimity. The first part of the story forms an ancient counterpart with the popular genre theme of the doctor come to treat the lovesick girl, a subject often treated by Steen (see HdG 129–176). The girl swoons in bed or on a chair, while the doctor, often with a knowing glance to her mother, takes the girl's pulse or writes out a prescription. In the picture from the Northbrook collection now at the Van der Vorm Foundation in Rotterdam (Fig. 118, HdG 136), a boy of the family, one would surmise her younger brother, holds an enema cylinder, and smiles vulgarly.[20] In that same picture the love motif is set by the cupid above the door and the love scene in the painting on the wall.

Though popular for centuries, the story of Antiochus is today little known. Its most ancient source is Valerius Maximus' *Facta et Dicta Memorabilia,* Book Five, Chapter Seven. There it is told how the prince Antiochus, son of the great Seleucus, fell desperately in love with his stepmother, the young and beautiful Stratonice. From that love, which he struggled to conceal, he fell mortally ill, and was on the point of death. The physician Erasistratus, discovering a reviving pulse upon Stratonice's passing the prince's bed, correctly diagnoses the illness. Hearing the doctor's report, Seleucus, out of love for his son, cedes him the fair Stratonice and thus obtains his recovery.

The story, as Stechow has shown, went through numerous changes in both ancient and Renaissance literature. Perhaps the most important change was that making Stratonice an active party, sharing the love of Antiochus. This is seen in Steen's picture, where Stratonice, passing by a balustrade, looks longingly at the very much revived prince, who seems to have lost—if he ever possessed it—the classical restraint generally given to the hero. In general, Steen's representation follows a variant of the story, the source of which is not known. He has left out the doctor, making Antiochus confront his father directly with knowledge of his desires. The old emperor reacts with surprise but good will. It would seem also in Steen's interpretation that the malady has already been diagnosed. The prince has already a fetching but clearly undesired bedmate, no doubt provided by the procuress who holds a wreath of flowers. Antiochus, however, like all obsessed lovers, seems to have found no satisfaction in the substitute. Though Steen added to the scene a coterie of low-life comic figures who poke vulgar fun at the situation, there can be no doubt, because of the intensity of the emotions, that he deals here with a theme of sacred love.

Spiced side-remarks such as appear in this painting are often found in his doctor's visits, which as already mentioned dealt with the same theme of the malaise of love. Unlike Antiochus, however, the young ladies in those works never seem aware of the reason for their sickness and hence Steen has even more tricks to play upon them. Here everybody except old Seleucus seems aware of the difficulty. The story deals with the passions of the young, and Steen has kept the three important elements of the story before us: the bed (as both sickbed and love-bed); the request; and the object.

Less direct in their theme of love are the paintings from the book of Esther (Cat. 17–19a). They present the devoted, mature love of the Persian ruler for his Hebrew queen. Ahasuerus' anger against Haman is in indignation at serious wrong done his queen. That the story of Esther and Ahasuerus is a love story is found in Scripture:

> And the King loved Esther above all the women; and she obtained grace and favour in his sight more than all the virgins; so that he set the royal crown upon her head, and made her queen instead of Vashti. (Esther 2:17)

In these paintings, especially in the two called *The Wrath of Ahasuerus* (Figs. 59 and 74, Cat. 18 and 19a), Esther is a mature, well fleshed woman, with a dignity worthy of her position. Ahasuerus in his exaggerated wrath is grand and almost comical. *Esther Before Ahasuerus* in Leningrad (Fig. 73, Cat. 17) shows a tender Ahasuerus supporting Esther, who in her anguish has swooned before the throne. In all of these pictures Steen has made one feel the closeness between husband and wife of high estate. In the picture in Birmingham (Fig. 59, Cat. 18), which is the most extravagant of the group, he does so by confluence of their gesture across the table. They share the same rhythm, and are united in light as Haman, a moustached villain, recoiling from the wrath of the king, shrinks into the shadows, and the great peacock-pie is knocked to the floor.

All the paintings of Esther and Ahasuerus must have been done with other motives in mind besides that of showing the protective love between king and queen. The story was a very popular one in both literature (especially drama) and painting during the sixteenth and seventeenth centuries in Holland. The origin of the popularity, as has been pointed out, may have been in the Dutch struggle during the sixteenth century for freedom from Spanish rule, in which struggle the Dutch often identified themselves with the oppressed children of Israel. The story of Esther is the story of victory over oppression. Such symbolic associations, common particularly among Protestant people, easily found expression in both literature and art.[22]

Esther is a heroine responsible for the salvation of her people. But she is also, as Madlyn Kahr has pointed out, a love goddess—a Protestant substitute for Venus. The success of her intercession is based upon the love which she inspired in Ahasuerus. After three days of ritual purification she dressed herself in queenly attire before approaching the king. Her beauty was the source of her power.[23] Steen shows her richly garmented and at once beautiful and intense in her expressions. Even where she swoons in the arms of her handmaidens, as in the picture in Leningrad, her beauty and nobility are apparent. In reaction, Ahasuerus leans forward to take her arm.[24]

Like the story of Esther, that of Jacob's long suit for the hand of Rachel deals with mature love. In Steen's single representation of the story (Fig. 89, Cat. 4/652a) he did not deal directly with a scene between the lovers but showed Laban's searching through their luggage in quest of the idols which Rachel had taken with her and hidden under her skirts. While Jacob pleads with his father-in-law, Rachel remains a mass of immobility hiding the riches. The scene is a little indirect to be regarded as a representation of love, but the theme is most certainly present.

If the stories of Esther and Rachel can be taken as examples of devotion and constancy, that of Hagar is one of rejection and dismissal. Like the story of Esther, that of Hagar was very popular in the seventeenth century and particularly so with Rembrandt, upon whose etching of 1637 Steen's painting in Dresden (Fig. 41, Cat. 2) is based. Hagar in the painting stands with such columnar weight and with such heavy feet upon the ground that one wonders if she will have the power to move from the doorway. Her grief, communicated by the wiping of her eyes, is more touchingly expressed by her stolid immobility. Ishmael, conversely, is light and springy. It is hard to resist the idea that the love theme of the story is here symbolized by Ishmael himself, who with quiver and bow has the attributes of Cupid. Steen must have meant the association. He used a similar motif in *The Doctor's Visit* in the Wellington collection (Fig. 122, HdG 137). There a young boy as a thinly disguised cupid is a veiled satire on the effects of love. As Steen has painted her, Hagar is the unhappy heroine of a love story, and his painting of her desperate prayer in the wilderness (Fig 46, Cat. 2b) shows the extremity of her suffering caused by Abraham's rejection.

Profane Love

Within the precinct of sacred love between both young and old, Steen depicts both requited and unrequited love, both devotion and dismissal. This was hardly a conscious program on his part, but rather it must have arisen from his interest in love stories, which were, as will be seen later, popular in his day. Within the area of profane love he may have tried more consciously to present its varied sides, or at least one can say that he touched on more numerous aspects of that kind of desire. The stories themselves are more numerous and generally more exciting. It is no secret that the fall of a great man or a great woman through passion entertains us better and teaches us more of the world's wiles than does success won either by beauty or by luck. The good man fallen is, as Aristotle observed centuries ago, the basis of tragedy. He can also be, when made extravagant, the basis of moral comedy, which was Steen's true forte.

In his painting of the incestuous seduction of Lot by his daughters (Fig. 48, Cat. 1), Steen shows the scene not as a virtuous act to preserve the seed, but as a willful seduction of an old fool by two sirens. The scene might even be taken as a depiction of the foolish old man's lusting after the young girl—a subject Steen often treated, and perhaps nowhere better than in the picture called *The Violinist* (Fig. 106, HdG 429a), which was at one time in the Kohn collection in The Hague. There Steen, in a self-image, makes himself the butt of foolishness and is robbed as he leers. Though the same fate hardly awaits Lot, something of the same atmosphere is present, and Steen has taken an obvious delight in it.

Steen again represented the incest theme some years later in the story of *Tamar and*

Amnon (Fig. 72, Cat. 16). Amnon, one of the sons of King David, desired Tamar, his virgin half-sister and sister of Absalom. By feigning illness, he brought her to his chambers and took her by force, after which his desire turned to hate and he had her dismissed by a servant (I Samuel 13:1-17). Absalom later avenged his sister's honor by killing Amnon. Steen tells the story accurately, dressing Tamar in "garment of divers colours," greens and browns with brilliant white sleeves. He added a tear to her face, a hypocritical helplessness to Amnon's, and a snicker to the servant's who helps the protesting Tamar from the room. She is helped out also by Amnon's insulting languorous foot, a symbol of his depravity. Tamar's protest is against his rude dismissal and denial of love after satisfaction:

> And she said unto him, There is no cause; this evil in sending me away is greater than the other that thou didst unto me. But he would not hearken unto her. (II Samuel 13:16)

The story of Tamar and Amnon tells of the forced taking of one woman by one man; *The Rape of the Sabine Women* (or, as it may be, *The Benjaminites Carrying Off Shiloh's Daughters*), which Steen painted some years earlier (Fig. 50, Cat. 76), portrays mass abduction. He painted the event like an ecstatic dance rather than hot pursuit. The picture is a weak one, for though the landscape has Steen's usual warmth and softness, the figures are unconvincing in their emotions and actions. One of the interesting things about the painting of the Sabine women is that even in a subject which traditionally demanded it, Steen refused to depict nude figures. The subject seems strange so well draped. Despite the extent of Steen's use of historical themes, which so traditionally call for them, there are no nudes in Steen's paintings, except as an occasional piece of symbolic statuary—as in *The Oyster Meal* at Lowther Castle (HdG 856) or its repetition called *Easy Come, Easy Go* in Rotterdam (HdG 854); or in background painting in some of his scenes of the doctor's visit (Fig. 121, HdG 130; Fig. 122, HdG 137).[25] The participating figures in such pictures are, however, invariably draped, though sometimes only loosely. The nude is accepted, in a manner of speaking, only as furniture, the symbolic importance of which is addressed to and known only by the viewer.

Like so much else in his paintings, the absence of nudes separates him from traditional history painting and thereby from his supposed master Nicholas Knüpfer, in whose work the nude has an important place. It also shows how powerfully his historical vision was affected by the genre idea, for genre painting and the traditional nude are mutually exclusive; one attempts an illusion of everyday reality, and the other a heroic or idealized image of past existence. The figures in *The Rape of the Sabine Women,* though classically draped or variously costumed, are essentially "vulgar" (that is, not noble) in type, and the scene is decidedly unheroic.

Thus far, among subjects of profane love, Steen has shown incest, lust, and mass abduction. To these, in his paintings of Samson and Delilah, he adds purchased love, whoredom, and betrayal. In both known pictures (Figs. 67 and 63, Cat. 10 and 12/10a) he makes Delilah the harlot and Samson the victim of her charms and her duplicity. In Figure 67 (in a private collection, in the Netherlands), she has fed Samson a great meal and in a royal hall placed his head upon her lap to rest. The barber works timorously to cut Samson's seven locks, while the hidden Philistines make stage whispers in the background. Samson sleeps through his betrayal.

In the Cologne picture (Fig. 63) we are told even more grandly of what happened after the betrayal. Samson is bound, and the man behind him, pointing to his own eyes and brandishing a knife, indicates the champion's fate. The barber has fled, leaving his implements; and a Philistine, looking surprisingly like a Jewish money-lender, is counting out Delilah's payment to an old woman who must be her procuress. The piles of coin indicate that she did not come cheap. Delilah, one breast bared, taunts the stricken Samson as she accepts the caress of a lustful, fat, old Philistine who bears a likeness to Steen himself.

Though according to Scripture Delilah is not a prostitute, her betraying for money quickly earned her that reputation. She was traditionally thought of as the universal harlot, and her lap, upon which Samson sleeps, was equated with the whore's lap. In his *Emblemata* of 1624 Johann de Brune likened the whore's lap directly to Delilah's. One emblem is entitled "Een hoeren Shoot is Duyvels Boot" and a young man is shown with his head in the lap of a whore in the same way Samson rests with Delilah.[26]

As already mentioned, in the Netherlands painting (Fig. 67) Steen set the still life of barber's bowl, drape, and open razor case directly below the bags of money, thus uniting the act of treachery and its payment. The scissors, however, he left standing on their open points below Delilah, as if dropped in haste. So placed, and so spread, they must have been meant as a symbol of Delilah's sexuality. In the light of Steen's use in other pictures of ordinary objects as sexual symbols—*The Marriage of Tobias and Sarah* (Fig. 66, Cat. 25a/457), *David Returning Victorious* (Fig. 83, Cat. 13), and most particularly *The Worship of the Golden Calf* (Fig. 85, Cat. 7)—such a suspicion is unavoidable. The later his pictures, the more elaborate such analogies. To Steen's treatment of bought love might be added the painting of *Erysichthon Selling His Daughter* (Fig. 51, Cat. 73). Erysichthon sold his only daughter for food to assuage his hunger. He had been made insatiable by Ceres as punishment for having cut down one of her sacred groves. His daughter clutches her breast in anguish at the moment of transaction. She will be taken away in bondage by a stranger.

With his paintings of Bathseba receiving David's letter Steen sets another theme in his treatment of profane love: adultery.[27] Here again he dispensed with the traditional nude figure, which Rembrandt used with such nobility in the subject. In the picture in Sussex (Fig. 34, Cat. 15), Steen painted a love-letter scene. Only the address on the note to Bathseba, and the garden behind, call attention to the Biblical subject. Whatever the purposeful confusion between genre and history in this painting, the open curtain revealing the bed, Bathseba's own engaging stance, and the way she holds the letter as if in decision, make us aware of the sexual implications.

In the Sussex painting and in the one formerly in the Bute collection (Fig. 70, Cat. 14) another theme related to love may also be present. In both, old women bring David's letter to the young and beautiful Bathseba. The confrontation of wizened old age and sensual beauty is traditional in the iconography of *vanitas*. In a sexual context the moral is direct and clear—beauty, youth and sensual pleasure are transitory. By disguising his subject in love-letter genre form, by hinting at a *vanitas* meaning, Steen may well be suggesting that this is what the story of Bathseba is all about and that it is continually repeated throughout human life and not isolated in Scripture.[28]

The character of Bathseba in the Sussex painting (Fig. 34), Steen's earliest treatment of the subject, differs greatly from that in his others, and most particularly from that in his latest treatment, now in the Wetzlar collection (Fig. 90, Cat. 14a/814a). In the former, she is slight of figure and reacts to the proposal of love with a certain unshocked haughtiness. In the later version, almost a portrait, a large-boned, well-fleshed Bathseba reacts with an amused but saddened smile. She seems possessed of both wise tolerance and desire, and more in her way capable of being the mother of Solomon. She will go to David and in so doing destroy her husband, Uriah the Hittite.

Love's destructive powers is the theme of another story from the ancient past painted four times by Steen. The saga of Antony and Cleopatra is the story of a great hero destroyed by the greatness of his passion. It touches so universally because we recognize in ourselves the seductiveness of exotic love and know with compassion why Antony sacrificed all for the beautiful Egyptian. In all four of his paintings (Cat. 85–86c) Steen chose to represent the scene of the banquet at which Cleopatra, teasing Antony, wagers she can spend a fortune on an evening's entertainment—and, dropping one of two priceless pearl earrings in her wine, proceeds to drink. Antony entreats against her rashness.

The banquet of Antony and Cleopatra is the subject of Steen's largest historical picture, now in the Rolzaal at The Hague (Fig. 60, Cat. 86a/b). Over six feet in length, the painting shows an opulent apartment lit with soft evening light and crowded with courtiers and servants watching the passionate exchange raised on a richly carpeted dais. Cleopatra, dressed in powder-blue satin embroidered with gold and a diaphanous blue veil across one naked breast, tilts the glass to her lips, holding it delicately and affectedly by the base. In her right hand she holds the second pearl. Antony, crowned with laurel and in purple robes, has left his throne to kneel before the Egyptian, one hand extended towards her and the other spread upon his breast—an expressive gesture very similar to that which Steen used for Esther in her accusation of Haman (Figs. 59 and 74, Cat. 18 and 19a). The drama can be read in a comparison of the gestures. Cleopatra holds her glass by its foot, her little finger affectedly extended as she taunts the beseeching Antony. With great sincerity, one hand on his heart, the other anxiously extended, he kneels before his queen.

In a smaller painting of the same subject (Fig. 87, Cat. 85), Steen has changed these expressions. He shows Cleopatra drunk from the wine and makes her plead the intercession of a stronger Antony. The Göttingen picture of 1667 (Fig. 56, Cat. 86), earlier than the other two, differs in that it gives a smaller area of the regal environment and makes the scene a more intimate one between the lovers. Antony, a great turbaned Oriental more like the older Ahasuerus than an impassioned lover, throws his hands back in shocked surprise at Cleopatra's dissipated plea for frivolous entertainment. The scene is intimate too in the small version reportedly from the Roëll collection (Fig. 102, Cat. 86c), though it has the openness characteristic of Steen's latest works.

In the large Hague picture particularly (Fig. 60), which can be dated about 1668–1669, the theme of romantic love is symbolized by numerous details. Antony's throne-chair is decorated with a cupid's head and dolphins. A cupid-and-dolphin motif is repeated in the sculptural detail at the lower left. In the smoke from the two burning torches at the back of the room appears a cupid holding a bow in one hand and spreading the other out above the two lovers. Steen has included a still life of fruit, and most particularly a melon cut to expose the meat of its ripe, red center. By it he possibly alludes to the luscious fullness of passionate and mature love. Here too Steen makes an analogy to the theme of love by a sort of sub-plot. He has placed two servants at the right, in positions analogous to those of Antony and Cleopatra. They exchange glances of desire. Within the dramatic structure of the painting this couple in their sincere desire seem to act as a foil to the emperor and empress in their troubled passion. Steen makes no social comment here, but only indicates the universality of love and perhaps its leveling capacity. In the late picture from the Roëll collection (Fig. 102) Steen also included a reiteration of the main theme, in what appears to be an abduction scene outside the hall. The motif here, however, is confused and cannot be read with certainty.

One wonders whether the history of Antony and Cleopatra best belongs to sacred or profane love. In its singleness and devotion that love must be called sacred; yet both were destroyed by their passion. For all he sacrificed in the world Antony lost no more than the beautiful Egyptian. It was not, however, a moment of love's ennoblement that Steen chose to show, but a moment of bored boasting and the testing of love's power in a dissolute act. Cleopatra is neither the harlot nor the adulteress, but she is wanton and Steen's treatment of the subject has its better place in the realm of profane encounters.

Peripheral Love Themes

The artist's most profane couple is found in *The Worship of the Golden Calf* (Fig. 85, Cat. 7). Their presence shows how Steen incorporated and emphasized such themes even where the subject was not directly associated with a couple or with a love story. He used the subject, as Lucas van Leyden had before him, as an occasion for presenting human excesses. Steen based his picture upon the central panel of Lucas' triptych now in the Rijksmuseum (Fig. 107). That painting was owned by Jacob Wuytiers, perhaps of Amsterdam, before 1679[29] and Steen could have known it. The basic structure, some of the individual figures, and the mood of revelry are shared by both. It is as though the dance around the golden idol released man from spiritual considerations and, in the absence of God and of guilt, he indulged all his profane appetites. Scripture says: ". . . and the people sat down to eat and to drink and rose up to play."

Here is a frankly salacious couple. Steen has given the purple-costumed man in the foreground an expression of lewd proposition and a lascivious grin. He has also given him something of his own features, as a comparison with the self-portrait in the Rijksmuseum (Fig. 120, HdG 850) shows, but here incorporated as type rather than as portrait. The woman, the brilliant point of focus in the picture, dressed in sparkling white and blue, accepts his flirtation with a coy superciliousness. The bringing together of these two heads between which sexual currents freely flow—as narrated by expression alone—is the best of Steen's accomplishments in pleasure. In direct allusion to the sexual act, the man places the stick within the triangle he is about to strike. Steen has placed this pun, so obvious and yet so subtle, in the center of the picture. Once recognized, it leaves no doubt of Steen's intention.

The still life reiterates again the eroticism of the picture. The melon is split, spilling seeds out of its red core. The big-bellied vase lies on its side, its narrow mouth and triangular lips making a vaginal shape. The gourd on which Steen signs his name can equally be read as a male symbol. Taken together these objects create, in the fullness of their curves, in their juicy palpability, symbols of sexual ripeness and appetite. There is no better example of Steen's use of still-life groups to state the themes of his pictures. This is true whether he does it with the symbolic myrtle alone, or with more elaborate constructions.

Steen has surrounded his delicious couple with other figures also illustrating gratification or display of the senses. Music and dance dominate. The pipes of Pan have been added to the sensuous still life. A drummer dressed in sixteenth century costume strides dramatically into the picture; a Black, crowned with a wreath, dances to his tambourine; in the middle ground a woman sings to the accompaniment of a flutist; and in the background the Israelites dance ecstatically around the idol raised high on a column. Amidst all this hubbub we anticipate the fragile *ping!* of the triangle.

In one place food is being cooked and in another drink offered in an elaborate shell-like goblet. To the right an old woman offers, with a smile, a coin to a little girl in brilliant pink who clutches flowers in her arms, and smiles back at the woman with an expression not unlike that of her counterpart seated on the ground. The old woman and the payment are traditional to the procuress scene. The flowers so tightly clutched might well symbolize virginity; one cannot escape the notion that Steen has used the old theme to add the titillation of deflowering of innocence. The Dutch use the same word, *deflourerien,* taken from the French, and therefore the concept would not have been foreign to Steen.

On the other side of the picture is a little deep-eyed boy with long golden curls and a sensual mouth. His costume is purple. He wears a feather beret, and on his arm carries a parrot as he engages us directly. He seems somewhat out of the picture or out of the festivities, perhaps because Steen uses him as a symbol of the brevity of sensual gratification—that is, of *vanitas.* In his dissertation on Dutch painting and the theater Gudlaugsson has pointed out that the feather beret itself, as an affectation of dress, had a similar symbolic meaning.[30] The couple, the little girl, and this boy are points of high focus and brilliant color within a pervasive red-brown monochrome. That Steen chose so to emphasize them gives each a particular importance; perhaps he wished to unite the boy and the girl in our minds as he did the man and the woman. If so, the connection does not come off quite so strongly as one might wish, and the shared accent might be merely a compositional device.

Whatever overtones of *vanitas* might be present, it is impossible to take the painting in any way as an object-lesson in human failings or the evanescence of sensual pleasure, which is the moral lesson of *vanitas*. Steen is having much too good a time to be didactic, and the moral might better be taken as Edmund's comment on the world from *King Lear:* "ripeness is all." Still the symbols are there, and the subject itself is an episode that, Biblically, led to God's disapproval. It would seem that Steen, like others before and after him, used God's displeasure over man's profligacy as a transparent excuse for depicting the very sensuality which it warns against. It is an old truth that under the guise of disapproval one can present what otherwise would be disallowed. As mentioned in the last chapter, Steen in his painting *The Rich Man and Lazarus* (Fig. 103, Cat. 58) places his buxom, music-making "Venus" with vine leaves in her hair directly above the inscription "In weelde ziet toe"—In wealth take care. The very presence of the motto or the easily read symbols in *The Worship of the Golden Calf* serve to deepen the sensual appeal of the picture.

As stated earlier, *The Golden Calf* reveals that even where the subject of a painting is not directly concerned with a story of love, Steen would find or emphasize such themes. His series of paintings of the marriage at Cana have this tendency in common (Cat. 45–50a). As can be seen in the Norton Simon picture (Fig. 95, Cat. 50), Steen emphasizes the marriage celebration over the working of the miracle. The bride's table dominates the right side of the canvas, while Christ is hardly noticeable off to the left. Most of the celebrants are unaware of his presence though they indulge freely in the renewed wine. In the center he has placed a robust middle-aged couple perhaps as a counterpart to the newly wedded pair. Even in *The Expulsion from the Temple* (Fig. 94, Cat. 62) Steen included at the right a prostitute fawned over by her elderly and outraged protectors. In the late *Moses Striking the Rock for Water* (Fig. 88, Cat. 9) he couples off his men and women in what seems to be a musical-comedy ending where the entire cast is paired.

Moses Striking the Rock also reveals how Steen could manipulate the mood of his figures by slight changes in position and expression. The woman in reddish-pink satin seated on the ground at the right and taking water from a soldier is almost the same figure as the central woman in *The Worship of the Golden Calf.* This is true as regards her dress, her hat, the position of her arms and head, and the fact that she holds a glass in her right hand. But Steen has modified her position, lowered her leg and curved her spine, so that while the attractiveness remains, the salaciousness is replaced by tenderness and need. She does not reach out for a vase with her left hand, but supports herself upon the ground. This gesture of support alone gives enough of the sense of weakness to set the mood and the theme of the picture. She accepts the drink offered by the soldier in the same shell-cup that is offered with a quite different feeling to that of the woman in *The Worship of the Golden Calf.*

Steen's women outshine the men. They are the focal center of all his narratives. More richly dressed, more exuberantly fleshed, and more seriously historic, they appear maturer than the men they captivate with their largess and their dignity. Esther overshadows both Ahasuerus and Haman, and Delilah in her wantonness arrests us more powerfully than does Samson in his anguish. The men seem caricatures while their robust women have an eternally feminine reality and force. They are dominant in spirit.[31] Though it may seem strange to say so in face of his conventional reputation, Steen in his themes of ancient love becomes a painter of great heroines, and must be counted with such as Tintoretto among the great painters of women. Esther, Delilah, Bathseba, Tamar, Hagar, Iphigenia, Cleopatra —these are his heroines, and they all share a largess and nobility of dramatic proportions. One need not insist that love is Steen's only thematic concern, but it is so abundantly present as to be labeled a major one, and one which touched the spirit of his times.

The artists of the seventeenth century, as Frederick Hartt has shown in his essay on "Love in Baroque Art," "placed love beyond the rational" and akin to religious ecstasy.[32] It was part of the universal order of things, and in its passions, both sacred and profane, revealed man's nature and God's presence. It's love that makes the world go round. Its absence is the absence of all things. When Steen celebrates love he celebrates the human spirit.

References

1. Bredius, *Steen,* 1927, pp. 13, 82.
2. *Ibid.,* pp. 15, 91.
3. *Beeld en Woord,* 1952, p. 152.
4. See Gudlaugsson, *Ikonographische Studien,* 1938, p. 82.
5. See Slive, *Art Quarterly,* XIX, 1956, *passim.*
6. See Larsen, *Akten des 21. Internationalen Kongresses für Kunstgeschichte* (1964), III, 1967, pp. 59 ff.
7. Another *Holy Family* attributed by Hofstede de Groot to Steen (Cat. 43) also includes the lamb and child St. John with a reed cross. In this case, though the work is related to Steen, the attribution is in doubt. See Cat. Addendum 5.
8. For other possible sources of patronage see Chapter 4.
9. The one painting of the betrayal listed by HdG as No. 64, now in Prague, is a faulty attribution (see Cat. Addendum 10); and the *Last Supper* listed as No. 63 is untraceable.
10. Bk I, chap. vii, 1.
11. *Beeld en Woord,* 1952, p. 24.
12. Van der Waal, *Vaderlandsche Geschied-Uitbeelding,* 1952, I, p. 28.
13. Kahr, *O-H,* LXXXI, 1966, pp. 228 and 241.
14. *Beeld en Woord,* 1952, p. 154.
15. Clark, *The Nude,* 1956, p. 109.
16. The exorcising of the devil and the wedding night prayer of the young couple was the subject of another painting now in the Centraal Museum in Utrecht, which Steen based upon N. Knüpfer's version of the same subject also in Utrecht. See note 60, Chapter 1.
17. Soli Deo gloria
    T heeft Godt behaeght
    Dat David t heeft gwaeght
    Als hy Goliat verslogh
    En Saul in t hart wrogh
    Victorieus hy treet voruyt
    Hier verwelkomt van sijn bruyt.
18. Schmidt-Degener, *Steen,* 1927, p. 9.
19. *Art Bulletin,* XXVII, 1945, p. 221.
20. For a discussion of the "remedy" theme, see D. Posner, *Art Bulletin,* LIV, 1972, pp. 383–89.
21. *Art Bulletin,* XXVII, 1945, p. 230.
22. See M. Kahr, *O-H,* LXXXI, 1966, p. 228.
23. *Ibid.,* p. 235.

24. In the Leningrad picture the foreground figure of the old man at the table is to be identified not as Haman, as has been suggested, but as Mordecai (see Cat. 17).

25. The question of Steen's use of background images is discussed in Chapter 4.

26. Johann de Brune, *Emblemata,* Amsterdam, 1624, No. XXXIII; see also Evers, *Rubens,* 1944, p. 160. For an iconographical study of the Samson story and particularly of the lap motif, see M. Kahr, *Art Bulletin,* LIV, 1972, pp. 282-299, and LV, 1973, pp. 240-59.

27. He dealt with the theme also in *Joseph and Potiphar's Wife* (Cat. 5), the whereabouts of which is unknown.

28. For a study of the iconography of Bathseba and the moralistic use of the story in the seventeenth century see Kunoth-Leifels, *Uber die Darstellungen der Bathseba in Bade,* 1962, pp. 73-74, and *passim.*

29. Cat. Rijksmuseum, Amsterdam, 1956, No. 1452-A2. For a more detailed discussion of the dependency see Catalogue entry 7.

30. *Ikonographische Studien,* 1938, pp. 67-68.

31. Even in pictures where love is not the main theme, women seem to dominate Steen's imagination. In *The Adoration of the Shepherds* in the Rijksmuseum (Cat. 37/31) he gives great emphasis to the virgin, and in *Christ Blessing the Little Children* (Cat. 60) he builds the whole left side of the tiny canvas around the monumental figure of the mother seen from the back. In his genre pictures too, women play a dominant role, whether as the flirtatious barmaid in *The Oyster Eater* at The Hague (HdG 853) or the drunken housewife in *The Twelfth Night Feast* at Cassel (HdG 494).

32. Hartt, "Love in Baroque Art," 1964, p. 16.

3

Literary Sources of Steen's Subjects and Motifs

Contemporary Drama

Research by J. B. F. van Gils, S. Gudlaugsson, Albert Heppner, and most recently by C. W. de Groot has shown correspondence between Steen's subjects and those popular in contemporary theater.[1] Heppner established Steen's connection with the players or rhetorician guilds of various Dutch cities. These guilds, to borrow Heppner's apt parallel, were like the group of small tradesmen who performed "Pyramus and Thisbe" in Shakespeare's *Midsummer Night's Dream* and were popular throughout the Lowlands particularly during the sixteenth and seventeenth centuries. Cities and towns boasted of their groups and competitions called "landjuweels (jewel of the land) were held yearly and were the center of both art and learning.[2] Many artists were members of these guilds[3] and performed roles as well as contributed to the decoration. Though there is no evidence of Steen's membership in any one of the many Rederijker groups,[4] there is considerable evidence of his connection with them. His uncle, Dirck Jansz. Steen, was definitely a Rederijker, and left a library which probably was inherited by Steen's father—and may have been a source of Steen's familiarity with the Rederijkers.[5] He was also, according to Heppner, a distant relative of the Leiden jester, Pieter Cornelisz. van der March.[6]

Steen made a number of paintings of rederijker "kamers" (chambers), some of which can be identified with particular cities. In the Bredius Museum is a painting (HdG 234) of a group which shows the motto "In liefde Verwamt" (In love warmed), the blazon of the Kamer of Warmond, where Steen lived in the late 1650's. Another cited by Heppner, which was in the Stokvis collection in Brussels (see also HdG 234) shows a group of Rederijkers at a window under which hangs the sign "De Eglantiers" (The Flowering Eglantines), with the motto "In liefde Bloeiende" (Flourishing in love).[7] The name and saying are of the famous Amsterdam chamber which boasted among its members many of the most important literary men of Holland: de Hooft, Bredero, de Coster. Heppner believed that in the self-portrait playing the lute in the Thyssen collection (Fig. 108, HdG 863), Steen cast himself as the traditional "fool" or "jester" of the Rederijker kamers. The costume and joviality support this contention.

Steen was not necessarily limited in experience to the semi-professional productions of the Rederijkers but knew as well the better equipped and more elaborate professional theater of his day, such as he might have seen at the Schouwburg at Amsterdam.[8] By the middle of the seventeenth century, the popular theater gave way to the professional theater, influenced largely by the French.[9] The Rederijkers, after almost two centuries of great popularity and importance, dispersed into obscurity.[10] Steen's use of interior curtains, architectural settings and stage properties such as are seen in *Samson and Delilah* of 1668 (Fig. 67, Cat. 10) supplies evidence that Steen drew inspiration from the professional theater.

The stage at the Amsterdam Schouwburg (Fig. 109) designed by Jacob van Campen in 1637[11] incorporated many of the elements found in *Samson and Delilah.* It was a modified architectural facade stage set upon a shallow proscenium and included side vistas through open colonnades on either side.[12] Other paintings of the late 1660's, like *The Wrath of Ahasuerus* (Fig. 74, Cat. 19a), show a similar construction,[13] but none can be directly associated with that stage, which was replaced in 1665 by a new one of a later design with a deeper stage and moveable wings.[14] Steen's paintings showing the earlier type of construction all postdate the old theater, and while there are similarities, there are also significant differences, such as his use of arched rather than horizontal structure for the arcades.

The Sacrifice of Iphigenia (Fig. 82, Cat. 74) shows most explicitly of all Steen's works the use of stage construction. The wings coming in from both left and right separate foreground from background, and give the illusion of stage scenery. The picture is dated 1671, and Steen could have become familiar with such scenic structure at the new theater built in Amsterdam in 1665. The figure of the goddess Artemis, who was to receive the sacrifice, might also be another bit of seventeenth century stage equipment—the *deus ex machina*—which he could also have seen in the new theater.[15]

The strongest evidence of Steen's theatrical indebtedness is not, however, to be found in his use of curtains, strong foreground horizontals, or stage-like equipment, all of which have precedents in the history of painting. The strongest evidence is the correspondence of many of his Biblical and historical subjects with those of plays written and produced during his own lifetime. During the seventeenth century, in Holland as in France, Biblical and historical drama flourished.[16] One need only recall that Vondel, still considered today Holland's greatest dramatist, wrote mostly historical dramas. While none of Steen's work corresponds in subject to Vondel's plays,[17] Van Gils and Gudlaugsson and Heppner in the works already cited have shown thematic parallels with other dramatists who wrote for both Rederijker groups and the professional stage.[18]

While attempts have been made to show more direct connections, it has been impossible to prove that Steen saw any of the plays in question.[19] The closest one can come is with the *Iphigenia* discussed above, in which stage construction is evident. Samuel Coster, the founder of the Amsterdam Schouwburg, wrote a play, *Iphigenia,* in 1630,[20] which Steen may have come to know considerably later, though there is no evidence to that effect. On the other hand, there exists considerable evidence (as will be demonstrated below), for concluding that Steen and the dramatists shared common formal and iconographic traditions, and that the paintings could actually have been made without direct reference to theatrical production. A strong enough affinity exists, however, to show, as Heppner does, that the theater did serve Steen as a "bridge between nature and fantasy."[21]

In 1618 Abraham de Koninck published a play called *The Tragedy of Samson,* which tells the whole story of the Biblical hero. Steen painted the story of Samson twice. De Koninck's play has been cited as the possible inspiration for the painting now in a private collection in The Netherlands (Fig. 67, Cat. 10) showing Samson with his head in Delilah's lap. Gudlaugsson points out that the tragicomic climax of de Koninck's play comes when a barber is called to cut the hair of the sleeping Samson.[22] Steen clearly reproduced that scene, and did so in a theatrical setting. However, it must be noted that Rubens in his early painting from the Köser collection in Hamburg, (Fig. 111) also represented the scene with a barber cutting Samson's hair. Van Dyck repeated the motif in his picture now at Dulwich College (Fig. 112). J. Matham made a rather clumsy engraving of the Rubens,[23] which may have become well known. Indeed the iconography of the scene, including the barber, was already well-developed in sixteenth-century prints,[24] and it is not possible to attribute its invention to either seventeenth-century painting or drama.

The great difference between the Flemish pictures and the Steen is that Rubens and Van Dyck, in keeping with the Flemish baroque, have made everything grandly heroic—the barber no less so than Samson—while Steen, though more baroque than often thought, still gives us a comic barber understandably nervous at his task. Neither Rubens nor Van Dyck, it is true, creates the kind of stage space that Steen does. Theirs are fundamentally figural compositions, whereas Steen creates a whole environment, which may indicate a source in theatrical production. Whatever the difference, the motif of play and paintings and earlier prints has a source in common: the Biblical narrative. The lines read:

> She made him sleep upon her knees; and she called a man, and had him shave off the seven locks of his head.
>
> Judges 16:19

Steen's *David Returning Victorious* (Fig. 83, Cat. 13) has also been connected with contemporary theater. Van Gils felt that the picture followed closely the stage and poetic description of the event given in Job van der Wael's poetic drama *David and Goliath,* written in 1619 for the Schiedam guild of rhetoricians.[25] That group was called "Het Rood Roosjen," the Red Roses, and Van Gils felt that Steen paid tribute to their name in the red hair and dress of the woman playing the lute behind David. Further he found a similarity between the damp and smoky atmosphere described by Van der Wael and that painted by Steen. Such correspondences are too vague to be taken as real evidence of a dependence.

The subject matter supplies better evidence. Both play and painting fuse episodes from I Samuel 17 and 18. Painter and poet have done a little editing for the sake of romance. David did eventually marry Michal, but at the time of his victory over Goliath there is no mention of it, and what is more he was first betrothed to Merab, Michal's elder sister (I Samuel 18:18–19). The story uniting David and Michal, however, was a familiar one, and appears elsewhere in earlier painting. A painting by Frans Franken II in the museum at Mainz also unites the two episodes. Better known is Poussin's large painting at Dulwich (Fig. 113) made about 1633/34,[26] in which Michal, surrounded by her handmaidens on a classical porch, watches David's triumphant arrival. Though it is possible for all three painters to have known Van der Wael's play, it is very unlikely that such was the fact. A common source or tradition in the imagery again seems the better possibility.[27]

With the picture *Esther Before Ahasuerus* (Fig. 73, Cat. 17) the problem is similar. Very popular in seventeenth century Holland,[28] the Biblical story was dramatized in at least two plays: Nicolaes Fonteyn's *Esther, or the Picture of Obedience* of 1638, and Joannes Serwouter's *Hester, or the Deliverance of the Jews,* first published in 1654 and with numerous later editions.[29] The latter (in the 1659 edition) was introduced by an engraved frontispiece (Fig. 114) perhaps, according to Heppner, by Peter Quast. Heppner accurately points out the similarity between the engraving and Steen's painting of the subject.[30] In both cases Esther swoons before the throne of Ahasuerus and is assisted by her handmaidens as Ahasuerus, scepter in hand, leans toward her in concern.

The similarity of form, however, in no way proves Steen's familiarity with the play or the engraving as Heppner suggests, but only a common tradition having its source again in the Biblical narrative:

> . . . She fell at his feet and besought him with tears to avert the evil designs of Haman the Agagite and the plot which he had devised against the Jews. And the King held out his golden scepter to Esther . . .
>
> Esther 8:3–4

A drawing by Solomon de Bray of 1646 in the Berlin Print Room, and another from the early sixteenth century by Engelbrechtsz, prove that the pictorial tradition, probably based on the Biblical narrative, pre-dates the plays cited. Both are structured similarly, with Esther swooning before the king, who rises from the throne. Lucas van Leyden's 1518 engraving of the subject (Fig. 115) shows the same scene in the same way and is closer in spirit to Steen than is the Quast. In both, Esther and her handmaidens share a delicate fragility.

Heppner believed also that Steen's paintings of *The Wrath of Ahasuerus* (Cat. 18–20) illustrated lines from Serwouter's play:

> —Shame on thee, Haman, now curse the hour of thy birth.
> —Where shall I hide myself, I dare not look upon the face of the king.

Esther's accusation, the fearful wrath of the king, Haman's cowering, and the whole richly dramatic environment of Steen's Birmingham picture (Fig. 59, Cat. 18) seem to support

Heppner's contention. Again we find, however, that traditions within painting itself, in this case particularly around Rembrandt, could have supplied Steen with all the elements of the picture. In the National Gallery in Warsaw is a painting by Lastman which, while differing slightly in subject—*Haman Pleading for His Life*—has the same irate Ahasuerus in turban with a feather, royal cloak, and clenched fist. That sumptuous banquet, like Steen's, centers around a grand peacock pie. In Cologne there is a painting of the same subject either by Bol or by Flinck (Fig. 116) composed around the table. The painting of the subject attributed to Rembrandt in Raleigh, North Carolina (Fig. 117, B. 631) shows the same moment in the story, and parallels Steen's in the dress of Haman, the fantastic orientalism of Ahasuerus, and the bombastic gestures. The influence of early Rembrandt on late Steen can be seen too from Rembrandt's painting of *Belshazzar's Feast* (Fig. 58, B. 497), which is similar in costume and in the manner of noting dramatic emotion, in this case fear rather than anger.

Wolfgang Stechow has shown in an article, "The Love of Antiochus with Faire Stratonice,"[31] how very popular that theme was throughout the sixteenth and seventeenth centuries in drama, opera, and painting. Steen's painting (Fig. 81, Cat. 84b/54) does not follow any of the known versions of the story as described by Stechow, who traces the story back to the *Facta et Dicta Memorabilia* of Valerius Maximum. Steen's version is closest to the French poet Quinault's drama of 1660, which according to Heppner was probably performed in Holland. Both Steen and Quinault eliminate the doctor who diagnoses Antiochus' illness, and make the love reciprocal between Antiochus and Stratonice. Though Quinault's play, according to Stechow, was not translated into Dutch until 1694, there is no reason to limit Steen's knowledge of the theme to that source. A play by Corneille was published in Amsterdam in 1666 and could possibly have been responsible for Rederijker parodies, which would have been closer to the more comic treatment of Steen.[32] Evidence, supporting such a conclusion, however, seems scanty.

Stechow makes it clear that the literary tradition of the story of Antiochus is both stronger and more interesting than the visual one; nevertheless, Steen followed the traditional iconography of the subject in painting. The type, as far as Stechow could unveil it, traces back to Andrea Celesti's painting now in Cassel; he in turn took it in part from Pietro da Cortona's ceiling of the Sala di Venere in the Pitti Palace, decorated in 1641/42. In Celesti's painting are found the canopied bed, the girls in the retinue of Stratonice, the grand antique architecture with large niche figure, all of which are found also in Steen's picture. Though Steen deals more humorously with the story, it appears again that the theater cannot be isolated as the single inspiration behind his handling of the subject.

In other instances, too, Steen's subjects parallel those of contemporary drama. In 1642, J. C. Mayvogel wrote a play called *The Seduction of Tamar* or *Amnon's Aberrant Love,* and Heppner gives evidence that it was played in Amsterdam in 1659. No doubt there was in the play the dramatic scene of dismissal which Steen painted (Fig. 72, Cat. 16), but that this implies a dependence or even a source of inspiration is difficult to prove. Samuel Coster wrote a play, *The Rich Man and Lazarus,* published in 1615. Steen painted the subject twice. One treatment (Fig. 57, Cat. 59) was definitely inspired not by theater but by another painting, possibly by Knüpfer or possibly by Metsu, in the Museum in Strasbourg (Fig. 6).[33] In the other (Fig. 103, Cat. 58) he is more concerned with the humorous comment on the proverb, *in Weelde ziet toe,* "in wealth take care," than in dramatic action. The play can hardly account for Steen's interest in the subject. The popular story of Tobias which Steen used several times found dramatic expression in Elizabeth Hartloop's play *Tobias* published in 1688. In this case also at least one of Steen's paintings, *The Prayer of Tobias and Sarah* (Fig. 65, Cat. 25c), is based upon a Knüpfer painting of the same subject now at the Centraal Museum in Utrecht.

The marriage at Cana, which Steen painted at least six times, presents a more intricate problem as regards its connections with contemporary drama. Some critics have found the kind of colonnaded and terraced structure used in the Beit and Norton Simon pictures (Figs. 62 and 95, Cat. 48/49, 50) a clear reminder of stage setting. Gudlaugsson contradicts this by pointing out that a decree of the Synod of Dordrecht in 1617 forbade the showing of episodes from the life of Christ upon the stage.[34] While it is not here known how long the decree was enforced, none of the plays cited deal with Christ, his life, or his miracles. The marriage at Cana may, however, have been performed. Heppner explains:

> The frequent occurrence of this subject requires some explanation. It seems that at the time when prosperity and luxury had reached their height among the bourgeoisie of Holland, the Rederijkers or theatrical companies were called upon to give performances of the "Marriage at Cana" at the weddings of the wealthier families. These pictures by Jan Steen would then have served to commemorate wedding-celebrations; . . . .[35]

While Stechow challenges Heppner's assertions as being without evidence,[36] Bax makes something of the same point when he says that the group of Orientals found in Steen's paintings may represent a group of players in a Tafelspelen, common at seventeenth century wedding parties.[37] Steen's wedding scene at the Boymans/van Beuningen Museum (Fig. 25, HdG 455) shows the employment of Rederijkers at a wedding. Raised on a balcony, they contribute their music to the celebration and perhaps give a dramatic reading of a poem for the occasion—whatever it is they are doing seems to inspire the groom to a mock gallantry. It is not demonstrable, however, in this picture that the entertainers are giving a dramatic rendering of Christ's miracle.

The Marriage at Cana had long been popular in painting, but certainly Heppner's assertion would explain its popularity with Steen, who was so much a recorder of contemporary life. The question is whether Steen's paintings of the marriage at Cana represent a contemporary event with actors anachronistically costumed and mixing with the guests, as Heppner would have, or are depictions of the ancient event of the wedding and miracle into which Steen has projected elements of his own time and place. This important question will find further discussion in a later section dealing with Steen's particular historical vision.

From the evidence presented thus far, the conclusion follows that Steen's dramatic pictures of the 1660's and 1670's, while paralleling theatrical themes, show a strong reliance upon a well-established pictorial tradition. The point is not that Steen was ignorant of the theater of his day—his clear connections with Rederijkers disproves such a contention—but that his pictures do not rely so heavily upon theatrical sources as has sometimes been maintained or implied. The subjects for the most part were popular in both arts, and some of the similarity of treatment, as has been shown, depends upon common sources which may have been either literary or visual. The probability is that theater and painting shared influences back and forth.[38]

Theater and history painting—one should really say tragic or history theater and history painting—have always had something in common. Both seek to present costumed spatial illusions of specific events, most often inspired by Biblical, historical, or mythological stories. It is not surprising, then, that they shared many iconographic and formal means. Certainly this is true of costumes[39] and background scenic structure. It is even more important in regard to the elaborated vocabulary of gestures and expressions which became part of both baroque theater and painting. Both had the responsibility of creating directly readable dramatic or narrative action. They shared in common the whole necessity of the enframed historical or allegorical presentation. The proscenium stage is the theatrical equivalent of the picture frame, separating as it does the dramatic action from external reality.[40]

The major difference between theater and painting is that in one the action continues through time and can be developed, while in the other it is held basically to a single moment. However, both proscenium theater and narrative painting create an action centered in a continuous space. This is the great change from medieval drama and painting and has its source primarily in the two-dimensional arts.[41] It is not at all surprising that illusionistic stage settings had their beginnings in Italy, where systematic perspective was first developed in painting.[42] Such associations strengthen the argument of a common purpose between theater and narrative pictures. Steen was certainly familiar with the stage and with theatrical types, but his paintings are involved in the formal and iconographic traditions of his own art. The similarities between them were based on influences that passed in both directions.

Commedia dell' Arte

Besides the Rederijker and professional theater, Steen was familiar also with the Italian theater of improvisation. S. J. Gudlaugsson devoted a short study to demonstrating that certain of Steen's repeated figures, both in genre and history, have their source in commedia dell' arte.[43] He also stated that Steen, in his use of such figures out of comedy, adumbrated their use in the eighteenth century, particularly by Watteau.

That Italian comedy was familiar in Holland in the seventeenth century finds proof in Steen's own work. In the *Country Fair* in the Mauritshuis (HdG 625) a group of players on an improvised stage perform before a crowd of curious peasants. It is not, however, only in actual performance that such characters appear. Steen took them from the stage and placed them within his genre scenes. As Gudlaugsson shows, the doctor in high black hat and tunic with white collar who appears in so many of the lovesick or quack scenes (see Fig.

118) has his origin in "dottore," where he is taken both as a medical doctor and a man of mock learning.

In several of his historical scenes Steen introduced among the gathered participants a grotesquely distorted dwarf, usually dressed in theatrical costume. He is found in *The Banquet of Antony and Cleopatra* (Fig. 87, Cat. 85) prancing around with a meaty bone in one hand and a knife in the other; in *Esther Before Ahasuerus* (Fig. 73, Cat. 17) as a laughing soldier with a toy windmill;[44] in the *Marriage at Cana* (Fig. 62, Cat. 48/49) lugging a wine jug; in *Lazarus and the Rich Man* (Fig. 57, Cat. 59) again as an inappropriate soldier. The source for the figure, who appears in genre scenes as well—see the *Egg-Dance* in the Wellington Museum (HdG 600) and the *Wedding Feast* in the same museum (HdG 462), in which he is not made into a dwarf—is, as Gudlaugsson maintains, "Policinelle," from commedia dell' arte, a character whom Steen almost certainly knew from Callot's etchings.[45]

In *Samson Mocked by the Philistines* (Fig. 63, Cat. 12/10a) there is yet another inclusion of a stock comic type. The drunken soldier, his hat askew, at the right behind the bickering money-lender, is modeled upon "Capitano," also from the Italian comedy. The Dutch transformed that figure into a comic representation of the traditional enemy: the Spanish soldier. He was often the butt of political jokes.[46] Steen has made him appropriately ridiculous.

Steen's reliance upon stock comic types marks his approach to narrative as well as genre painting, and may well explain his affinity for commedia dell' arte. Constantly he works with types, whether borrowed from other sources or of his own invention. The painting of Samson's betrayal just mentioned reveals this tendency most strongly. There gathered together to watch and participate in the capture are the Oriental, the Roman, the Jew, the procuress, the money-lender. This band of stock types even incorporates an ensign or captain, who holds a banner and looks nobly distracted. All are recognizable; all are predictable in their behavior, and in their predictability create a kind of stock comedy.

Of all the stock figures that Steen uses, there is none more ubiquitous than himself. He places himself, the jovial, fat man, in so many of his pictures that his face has become immediately recognizable. He is the grinning "Capitano" in the taking of Samson; he is the parting guest in the *Marriage at Cana* (Fig. 62, Cat. 48/49). In *The Banquet of Antony and Cleopatra* (Fig. 60, Cat. 86a/b) he reserved the right-hand side again for his own bemused features. There, not participating in the main scene but purposefully capturing our attention, he transfers his own levity to the viewer, and helps set the mood of the picture. Perhaps the best example of Steen's playful use of his own features is *The Marriage of Tobias and Sarah* in San Francisco (Fig. 86, Cat. 25/487), in which he included himself three times as servant, as notary and as groom. These images cannot really be called self-portraits. He has made himself into a type, a stock character used again and again. Under thin disguise the artist participates in his own narrative and generally in some compromising role. It is as if Steen could not leave himself out of the flow of human life he depicted. He is at once participant and observer.

His penchant for stock types and predictable reactions can be witnessed again in the paintings of the wrath of Ahasuerus, particularly the one in Birmingham (Fig. 59, Cat. 18). Ahasuerus, his eyes rolling with anger, not unlike Samson's in his agony, springs to his feet and with fearful ire threatens the cowering Haman at the moment of righteous accusation. Turbaned and resplendent in his oriental finery, Ahasuerus is a great monarch. Esther in her ripe beauty and nobility is a true queen. And Haman, with feather beret, curling moustache, and shifty eyes, is the traditional villain. Gestures are perfectly and humorously explicit: accusation, wrath, fear—a perfect pantomime. Meanwhile, the little dog yaps, the servants shrink in wonder, and the great peacock-pie is caught midway in its fall to the floor where already a beautiful Ming[47] vase lies broken.

One way to excuse such exaggeratedly stock representations is to say, as does C. W. de Groot, that Steen's primary interest here lies in the details—the falling peacock-pie, the richness of the carpet—and that the description overshadows the event.[48] To say this, however, ignores the primary narrative purpose of the painting, and equally ignores Steen's delight in human behavior and his love of stock situations in which people react in predictable ways. He is not concerned with individual personalities, with the souls or psyches of his characters, but with types reacting to given situations. Because they are so predictable and because they come through in their predictability they are, like the doctor and his lovesick patient, broadly humorous. It is Steen's way of communicating a basic insight into human behavior. As suggested, such an interest may well lie behind his attraction to the Italian comedy, based as it was upon stock characters and situations.

Van der Waal, in his study of historical representations in the Netherlands, comments that to the Renaissance civilization (which for his purposes included the seventeenth century), history was seen essentially as the confrontation of a limited number of types in recognizable situations. The history of the world, he says, was a sort of commedia dell' arte.[49] The difference between most historical painting and Steen's is that he saw even heroic confrontations with the humor inherent to situation comedy. Love and its effects has always been the butt of such humor. It is not therefore surprising that Steen chose love themes so frequently for expression of his basically farcical humor.

For all the connections that can be drawn between Steen and various kinds of theater, he is a history painter and not a theatrical illustrator. The difference is important. In one case the desire is to represent a historical action; in the other the desire is to represent a performance, an imitation of an imitation. The comment is not then upon history, but upon the theater. Steen's desire was clearly to comment on history, even where he may have relied upon the stage. His figures are not actors, but historical personages engaged in historical actions in ways which fulfill our anticipations.

The Didactic Poetry of Jacob Cats

Steen's involvement with love stories connects him with another possible literary source of subject matter. The didactic or moralistic literature of his day from emblem books to copious narrative poems was often concerned with the history and problems of love. Moralizing literature was deeply embedded in the character and culture of the Dutch people. J. C. de Groot holds that the penchant to moralize is one of the basic passions of Netherlanders.[50] Therein lies the immense popularity of Jacob Cats, who even today among the Dutch is known as *Vader* Cats. He was not the only writer of didactic literature, but certainly he was the most productive and is still the most loved.

Cats was lawyer, statesman, agricultural speculator and, above all, moralist. In his poems he deals with every aspect of life: hygiene, poetry, family obligations, economy, sickness, old age and death. But most of all his emblems and poems deal with love. He wrote for instance a long poem called *Houwelick* (Marriage), directed to women, in which he traces the developments of love through six stages: *Maeght, Vryster, Bruyt, Vrouwe, Moeder, Weduwe* (Maid, Sweetheart, Bride, Wife, Mother, Widow), pointing moral lessons for each stage, for example urging maidens to remain pure—that is, not to be "spoilt."

For our purposes the most important of Cats' works is the didactic poem commonly called *Trou-Ringh* ("Marriage Ring"), the whole title of which is *'s Weerelts Begin, Midden, Eijnde Besloten in dem Trou-Ringh met Proef-Steen van den Selvan* ("The World's Beginning, Middle, and End Contained in the Marriage-Ring with Touch-Stone of the Same"). Published in 1637 as a guide to bachelors contemplating marriage, the poem describes and draws morals from great historical love affairs and unions, both fortunate and unfortunate. It begins with the basic wedding, or *gront-Houwelick* between Adam and Eve in the garden. The poem is resolved with the *Lof Sangh op het Geestelick Houwelick van Godes Soon* ("Love Song of the Spiritual Marriage of God's Son"), in which is described Christ's marriage to the Church.

Within *Trou-Ringh* can be found many of the themes that Steen used, and all presenting love in which the heroine plays a dominant role. In the poem the following stories appear: Lot and his daughters; the dismissal of Hagar; Jacob and Rachel; Joseph and Potiphar's wife; the return of David victorious; David and Bathseba; the marriage of Tobias and Sarah.[51] We even find within the rather confused structure of the poem a lengthy description of *De prachtige en dertele Liefkoserije van Marcus Antonius, Veldoverste der Romeijnen en Cleopatra Koninginne van Aegypten* ("The Magnificent and Lascivious Love-Banquet of Mark Antony, General of the Romans, and Cleopatra Queen of Egypt"), in which Cats describes the famous banquet as a luxurious display which fits with Steen's opulent conception of the scene.

The Marriage of Tobias and Sarah in Brunswick (Fig. 66, Cat. 25a/457) supplies some more direct proof of Steen's familiarity with the *Trou-Ringh.* August Fink, who first identified the subject of this picture correctly, mentions that Cats termed the creation of Eve the first genuine marriage.[52] At the left background of the picture Steen included a painting of the creation of Eve. In his notes *(Aenmerckingen)* on Adam's marriage Cats observed that the marriage contract mentioned in the Book of Tobit was the only one to be found either in the Old or the New Testament.

> —and they took a book and wrote an instrument and sealed it.
>
> (Tobit 7:14)

Thus there is established a link between Cats and Steen in that both united two rather disparate themes.[53]

Steen and Cats used other parallel subjects. In 1620 Cats published a dialogue between Joseph and Sephyra, Potiphar's wife, called *Self-Stryt—dat is Krachtige Beweginze Vleese en Spirit,* in which the victory of goodness over lust is attributed to self-restraint. Steen's painting of the subject is lost (Cat. 5), but it clearly is the kind of confrontation that would have attracted him.[54] In the introduction to the dialogue between Joseph and Sephyra, the story of Scipio returning the bride to the bridegroom is cited as another example of virtue gained by self-restraint. Steen's late painting of the theme (Fig. 84, Cat. 83) shows more the magnanimity of the general than his self-restraint; or perhaps in this case the two were the same.

In the section in *Houwelick* given to the *vryster* (sweetheart) is a dialogue between Sibille, the newly married young woman, and Rosette, the young sweetheart. Reference is made to the story of Amnon and Tamar as the older woman cautions the younger about her virginity. In the edition of *De Wercken* of 1655, Volume I, the warning and reference are accompanied by an engraving (Fig. 119) which is close enough to Steen's painting of the late 60's (Fig. 72, Cat. 16) to indicate that Steen knew the engraving either from that or from another edition of Cats' work.

The above citations bear out a real correspondence between the themes in Cats and those chosen by Steen for his historical pictures. That correspondence however is not systematic enough to make one think that Steen set out to illustrate the *Trou-Ringh* or the other poems. Over all, what connects them is their common concern with love, both grand and vulgar.[55] The probability is that Cats served as a general inspiration for Steen's approach to the literary subject, including the moralistic content.

Cats is, to be sure, didactic. He constantly points morals to be learned from the lessons of history. The great love affairs serve both as guides and as warnings for our own behavior. The emblem books on love which Cats compiled[56] are collections of visual proverbs with didactic meanings most often regarding personal behavior. However, in a dialogue like that between Joseph and Sephyra in *Self-Strijt* or that between Sibille and Rosette in *Houwelick* the moral purpose seems somehow subverted by the obvious delight the author takes in dealing publicly with what would otherwise be private. Two women, one eager and the other cautioning, discussing the virtues of virginity, can possibly be didactic, but will surely be amusing, even titillating.

> —There's danger too strictly to confine
> Either young wenches or new wine.

So speaks Rosette (the flower), indicating of course that they both (young women and new wine) need tapping.[57] Cats always preaches the good of humanity and the fear of God, but in so doing thoroughly exploits his stories' licentious resources.[58] Gudlaugsson, in his study of Dutch iconography and the theater,[59] mentions that the seriously didactic literature of the sixteenth century became a means of entertainment in the seventeenth. Such a change permitted the mixing of elevated themes with low comedy. Steen's tendency in this direction, shared with Cats, is the source of his particular historical insight.

References

1. Van Gils, *O-H,* LII, 1935, pp. 130–33; *Op de Hoogte,* XXXIV, 1937, pp. 92–93; *O-H,* LIX, 1942, pp. 57–63; Gudlaugsson, *Ikonographische Studien,* 1938, p. 6 ff.; Gudlaugsson, *De Komedianten,* 1945, *passim;* Heppner, J of W&CI, III, 1939/40, pp. 22–48; de Groot, *Beeld en Woord,* 1952, pp. 34–37.

2. For a description of the festivals see Kernodle, *From Art to Theater,* 1944, pp. 112–16.

3. Frans and Dirk Hals, Brouwer, Wynants, Gerrit Berckheyder, and others were members of the Haarlem chamber "Liefde bovenal"—Heppner, *J of W&CI,* III. 1939/40, p. 24.

4. See Bredius, *Steen,* 1927, p. 83; Heppner, *J of W&CI,* III, 1939/40, p. 24.

5. Bredius, *Steen,* 1927, p. 13; de Groot, *Beeld en Woord,* 1952, p. 57, note 4.

6. Heppner, *J of W&CI,* III, 1939/40, p. 24.

7. *Ibid.,* p. 29.

8. It is not possible to document Steen's presence in Amsterdam on the basis of the painting, *A View of the Dam,* at the Koninklijk Oudheidkundig Genootschaap in Amsterdam (HdG 880). Though the picture is signed, its attribution to Steen is questionable. Throughout the 1660's Steen was resident in Haarlem, only twelve miles from Amsterdam, and visits there, though undocumented, seem plausible.

9. For a listing of French plays given in Holland during the seventeenth century see Fransen, *Les comédiens français en Hollande au XVIIe et XVIIIe siècle,* 1925, and Bauwen, *La tragedie française et le théatre hollandais au dix-septième siècle,* 1921, pp. 261–67.

10. Heppner, *J of W&CI,* III, 1939/40, p. 22; Kernodle, *From Art to Theater,* 1944, p. 114.

11. Already by 1632 the idea of a new theater had been raised; and Cornelis van Campen, Jacob's uncle, a leader in the movement, had begun the plans for the new building before his death in 1636. Nicolaas van Campen, Jacob's grandnephew, was instrumental in the commissioning of the building. See Swillens, *Jacob van Campen,* 1961, p. 64.

12. Worp, *Amsterdamschen Schouwburg,* 1920, pp. 82–83.

13. Laurie, *Bulletin,* Cleveland Museum of Art, LII, 1965, No. 4, p. 98.

14. Worp, *Amsterdamschen Schouwburg,* 1920, pp. 131–32, and plate on p. 128.

15. *Ibid.,* p. 131.

16. The most important reference for history of the Dutch theatrical literature is J. A. Worp, *Geschiedenis van het Drama en van het Toneel in Nederland,* 2 vols., 1904/08.

17. Vondel did in 1666 translate Euripides' *Iphigenia in Tauris,* which tells of the sacrifice though it does not present it on stage.

18. C. W. de Groot has summarized the information on this subject with complete bibliography: *Beeld en Woord,* pp. 34–37. Further, the present Catalogue supplies exact references for each picture.

19. De Groot, *Beeld en Woord,* 1952, p. 69. A painting reported in the Bute collection in 1850 simply called *The Lute Player* (Fig. 110, HdG 70/408; see Addendum 14) has been identified with a scene between Ascanius and Lucelle from Bredero's comedy *Lucelle.* Another painting from the Henzel collection in Paris (HdG 415) with similar figures in different arrangement may represent the same scene. See Gudlaugsson, *Nederlandsche Kunsthistorische Jaarboek,* I, 1947, p. 78.

20. Van Gils, *Op de Hoogte,* XXXIV, 1937, pp. 92–93.

21. *J of W&CI,* III, 1939/40, p. 25.

22. *Ikonographische Studien,* 1938, p. 68.

23. See Evers, *Rubens,* 1944, pl. 55.

24. See Kahr, *Art Bulletin,* LIV, 1972, pp. 290–91.

25. *O-H,* LII, 1935, pp. 130–33.

26. Blunt, *Exposition Nicolas Poussin,* 1960, No. 9; Friedlander, *Nicolas Poussin,* 1964, p. 31, fig. 18.

27. See C. W. de Groot, *Beeld en Woord,* p. 57, note 4. The original text can be found in the Catalogue entry.

28. See Kahr, *O-H,* LXXX, 1966, p. 228.

29. Heppner, *J of W&CI,* III, 1939/40, pp. 41–42; de Groot, *Beeld en Woord,* 1952, p. 35.

30. *J of W&CI,* III, 1939/40, pp. 41–42.

31. *Art Bulletin,* XXVII, 1945, p. 221.

32. *Ibid.*

33. Though the painting is signed Metsu, the attribution has been questioned. Martin believed it to be a Steen (*ZfbK,* LXI, 1927/28, p. 329); and the present author thinks it possibly a Knüpfer, though this attribution is not supported by Kuznetsov in his new catalogue of Knüpfer's painting (*Treasures of the State Collection,* Hermitage, VIII, 1965). For further details see Cat. 59.

34. *De Komedianten,* 1945, p. 6.

35. Heppner, *J of W&CI,* III, 1939/40, p. 44.

36. Stechow, *Nederlands Kunsthistorisch Jaarboek,* XXIII, 1972, p. 74.

37. Bax, *Skilders wat Vertel,* 1951, p. 17.

38. For the connection between theater design and painting in the sixteenth century, see David Rosand, "Theater and Structure in the Art of Paolo Veronese," *Art Bulletin,* LV, 1973, pp. 217 ff.

39. It has been suggested that the Caravaggesque costume used especially for musicians by the Dutch Caravaggesti, for instance, had its source in the Burgundian theater. This tradition was to find its way even into Steen's works; see Judson, *Honthorst,* 1959, pp. 64–65. Friedlander, however, believed that such dress had its source in the livery of pages in the noble households of Rome; see *Caravaggio Studies,* 1955, p. 108.

40. See Rosand, *Art Bulletin,* LV, 1973, p. 221.

41. Kernodle, *From Art to Theater,* 1944, p. 175.

42. See Rosand on Veronese and Theater, *Art Bulletin,* LX, 1973, pp. 217 *passim.*

43. Gudlaugsson, *De Komedianten,* 1945, p. 8 ff.

44. Ripa, in his *Iconologia* of 1593, shows Folly (No. 238) as a man riding a hobby-horse and holding a toy windmill as he plays the fool for the children. Ripa holds this action to be contrary to decorum and therefore foolish. The connection indicates how traditional were some of the devices with which Steen worked.

45. Gudlaugsson, *De Komedianten,* 1945, pp. 52–53.

46. *Ibid.,* p. 34.

47. Hobson, *Country Life,* LXV, 1929, p. 244.

48. *Beeld en Woord,* 1952, p. 168.

49. Van der Waal, *Drie Eeuwen Vaderlandsche Geschied-Uitbeelding,* 1952, p. 15.

50. *Beeld en Woord,* 1952, p. 27.

51. There are other themes from the New Testament, which however do not concern us here. See *Beeld en Woord,* 1952, p. 33.

52. *ZfbK,* LX, 1926/27, p. 231.

53. The popularity of the Tobias story in Holland points up the moralizing penchant mentioned earlier. Van Gils, in a discussion of Steen's fragment of the angel Raphael (see Cat. 25d/69), cites the following Bible book for Catholic children published in Amsterdam in 1617, 1621, and 1647 as a possible source: *Die Historie van den Ouden Tobias ende sijnen Sone den jongen Tobias: inhoudende veel schoone leeringen, hoe een vader sijnen Zoone oderwijsen Sol ende hoe een Godvreesende Kunt zijnen Vader onderdanick zijn sol. enz. . . . .* The very title shows the didactic cast which was given to Biblical narratives. The story found its acceptance and its popularity among both Catholics and Protestants after the Reformation. Of particular moralistic interest was the whole idea of the guardian angel (see Knipping, *De Iconografie,* Vol. I, pp. 173–74).

54. The Metropolitan Museum in New York owns a copy or imitation of a Steen called *The Surprise on the Birth of Twins* in which a wall painting shows Joseph fleeing the bed of Potiphar's wife. The scene is a gay one except for the bewildered father and it is hard to say just what the moral is here. Perhaps it is that the father should have practiced some of young Joseph's self-restraint.

55. J. C. de Groot shows that even Steen's oft repeated *Lovesick Maiden* or *The Doctor's Visit* also has a source in Cats; *Beeld en Woord,* 1952, p. 33, n. 35.

56. For a detailed description of Cats' emblem books see Anne de Vries, *De Nederlandsche Emblemata, Geschiedenis en Bibliographie tot de 18de eeuw . . .* , Amsterdam, 1899; for a general discussion and description of love emblems (some of which will enter the present discussion later on) see Mario Praz, *Studies in Seventeenth-Century Imagery,* 1947.

57. Steen makes use of that epigram in the figure of the servant tapping the wine keg in his paintings of *The Marriage of Tobias and Sarah.* That incorporation is discussed in the next chapter.

58. Briere-Misme, *GdBA,* XLII, 1953, p. 295; see also De Jongh, *Simiolus,* III, 1968–69, pp. 62 ff.

59. *Ikonographische Studien,* 1938, p. 72; see also Keyszelitz, *Clavis Interpretandi,* 1956, p. 53.

4

Steen's Historical Vision

The Synthesis of Genre and History

The mixing of elevated themes with low-comedy or genre details accounts for Jan Steen's particular historical vision. His means to this end in history painting is to unite the past with the present. His pictures for the most part present a strange confluence of the historical and the contemporary. Resultant incongruities form the basis of humorous or comic perspective on ancient events. At times this tendency in Steen is so strong as to disguise completely Biblical or classical themes under the overlay of genre. Even today a number of his pictures have not received their correct titles.

Prime examples of such confusion are his paintings of Bathseba, particularly the one in Sussex where she is shown standing in a contemporary Dutch interior receiving David's letter (Fig. 34, Cat. 15). The picture for a long time was known simply as *The Love Letter* and was exhibited in London in 1878 as *Le billet-doux,* with no mention of its Biblical associations. The love-letter theme was popular in the genre painting of Steen's contemporaries—Vermeer, ter Borch, Metsu—and Steen, it would seem, kept the real subject obscure. Identification rests wholly upon the address of the letter she holds: *Alderschonte Barsabe—omdat,* "Most beautiful Bathseba—because." Here is a confusion of time and place. Bathseba is neither draped in mock-Biblical dress, as she is in the two other paintings of the subject (Figs. 70 and 71, Cat. 14 and 14b/348), nor is she placed within a historical setting. She wears a contemporary fashion of the end of the 1650's or 1660's, and receives her invitation to adulterous dalliance in a leather-lined room. Steen has assimilated a Biblical reference almost as a quotation within a contemporary event, using one to deepen the implications of the other. The same is true for the later painting of Bathseba in the Wetzlar collection (Fig. 90, Cat. 14a/814a). There, likewise, only the address of the letter indicates the true subject of the painting, which in the end might really be this woman's deep reverie.

Very different is another case of confusion in subject-matter in Steen's work. *The Marriage of Tobias and Sara* in Brunswick (Fig. 66, Cat. 25a/457) had since the eighteenth century been thought of as a genre representation of a marriage contract scene. Houbraken, who owned the picture, described it as such:

> I cannot forgo to mention the contents of a large piece (which had been for a long time at my home, and since was sold to the prince of Wolfenbuttel) in which representation stand a Bridegroom and Bride, two old people, and a Notary. These figures were each so natural in their execution as if one were seeing the actual occurrence . . . .[1]

Hofstede de Groot almost two hundred years later lists it also as simply *The Marriage Contract*. Today it is often still so referred to, although in 1926 August Fink identified the subject correctly.[2]

The confusion is easily understood. Except upon very close inspection of the canvas, or familiarity with Biblical themes, the picture would naturally be taken as a scene from everyday life. Servants prepare the wedding feast, parents draw up an "instrument" with a notary, while bride and bridegroom stand lost in their own self-involvement. The hints of the Biblical subject are obscure but indubitably present. The androgynous figure behind the couple can only be Raphael, Tobias' guardian angel. The angel saved Tobias from the fate of Sarah's earlier suitors all of whom met death before the union was consummated. The painting on the wall to the left shows the creation of Eve, which as pointed out already, was thematically linked by Jacob Cats with marriage, and specifically with the marriage of Tobias and Sarah.

The bridegroom's masquerade does not immediately reveal him as Tobias; one important attribute, the traveling bag, is missing and may have been removed by cutting the painting, thus further confusing the subject. (It is present, though, in the later version now in San Francisco.) In context, though, and in the clear relation of this work to *The Prayer of Tobias and Sarah* (Fig. 65, Cat. 25c), about the subject of which there can be no dispute, we know that the bridegroom is indeed the young Tobias.

One can speculate about why the painter has so disguised his subject. It is not the case here as with Bathseba of the use of a popular genre theme. Nor is it the use of a Biblical or classical theme to explicate a veiled meaning placed within a contemporary action. Here we have an ancient action seen in contemporary terms. Steen has more than freely mixed his narratives. He has made a Scriptural love story into a wedding-day spoof and abstracted it out of Biblical time. Love is eternal and the actions that surround it are typically human and for Steen typically humorous. If the dramatic marriage between Tobias and Sarah was on his mind, so also was the contrast between the poetic self-possession of the couple, the cool practicality of the parents, and the eagerness for lustful celebration of the servant. History is here interpreted in terms of repeated human foibles. In many ways the painting is aptly called *The Marriage Contract*—not, however, in ignorance of its real subject, but in appreciation of this unique Biblical mention of the written contract.

Study of Steen's later and somewhat grander version of the subject in San Francisco (Fig. 86, Cat. 25/487) substantiates and amplifies what has been said. Though the positions of the figures are reversed, and the atmosphere has been lightened, the structure of the pictures is essentially the same and Steen has used many of the same motifs and props. The true subject is not quite so hidden. The angel is a little more apparent between the lovers, and the oriental dress of the father and several of the guests is a more overt clue to the historical subject. Also, in the foreground is a traveling bag, the traditional attribute of Tobias.

How daring Steen can be in his anachronism and therefore how confusing he can be in narrative meaning is seen in the costuming of the figures. He costumes the father, as said, in oriental dress, but the mother (who reads the contract) remains essentially contemporary in her clothing. What kind of a match is that? The lawyer, it might be added, is costumed neither in the oriental style popular in Biblical subjects nor in contemporary fashion, but as a "dottore" from commedia dell' arte.[3]

Unlike the Brunswick piece with its single sprig of myrtle on the floor, this painting is filled with contemporary emblems and symbols referring to love and marriage. The wreath of sunflowers over the couple's heads symbolizes constancy, as that flower is constant in its following of the sun.[4] Such wreaths were common in wedding ceremonies during Steen's time, as can be seen in his painting *The Wedding Feast* in the Wellington Museum (HdG 600). The bird in the cage may be read as an emblem signifying happiness found in love's bondage. Such an inclusion establishes another important link between Steen and Cats, who gave to the bird-cage emblem in his collection of love emblems *Sinne en Minnebeelden* this precise meaning: *Bly, door slavernij*—Bliss through slavery.[5] It may also have other meanings as De Jongh has pointed out in his fine article on double meanings in genre subjects, "Erotica in Vogel Perspective." The bird can stand for virginity and the cage for female genitals. Bird (vogel) as in English, can also be used as a reference to the penis. To bird (vogelen) is to copulate. Steen uses the bird cage as a symbol for sexual union quite directly in his painting called *Rustic Love* in the "Lahenhal" in Leiden (Fig. 47).[6]

The frying pan on the floor in the *Marriage of Tobias and Sarah* also has a place in the emblematic literature on love and marriage. In another set of emblems called *Emblemata Moralia et Oeconomica*[7] a frying pan is held over the fire, full with bubbling grease. The suggestion is that it is safer to stay home—*non te quaesiveris extra*—that is, within the frying pan rather than be burnt by the fire. In Steen's painting it may be taken as an allusion to the story—Sarah and Tobias were cousins—or to the general domesticity of marriage. In the same group of emblems just mentioned we find a tree covered with clinging vines and to the left a cupid.[8] The moral here is that one should choose friends carefully, a warning which here comes a little late. The sprigs on the ground are myrtle, a plant sacred to Aphrodite; it also enters into the symbolic iconography of love.[9]

Besides the direct emblematic reference, peripheral motifs in the picture relate humorously to the wedding night. The boy displaying the oranges makes a possible reference to the fruits of marriage. Such a device is used in the emblem page of Cat's poem *Houwelick* discussed earlier. The leering servant (who occurs in all versions of the picture) tapping the keg of wine in anticipation of the coming celebration may illustrate the proverb "There's danger too strictly to confine/Either young wenches or new wine," which, as mentioned earlier, is spoken by the virgin Rosette in that same poem. The servant holds the tap, point up, ready to insert it when the cork is pulled. The reference is direct. A third peripheral motif is that of the maidservant at the steps to the right. She probably has just finished preparing the bedchamber, as she indicates to the couple below. Steen's fondness for such suggestive motifs is shown in *Rustic Feast in a Large Tavern* in the Louvre (Fig. 93, HdG 601), where the motif is repeated. The maid's jocosity may be dampened by her knowledge of the usual outcome of this particular first night.

Something more besides all of these references to love and marriage is going on within the painting. Steen took it as an opportunity for playing with his own features and personality. He shows himself at three stages of life: first the swooning young Tobias, then as the shrewd-faced notary, and lastly as an old Falstaffian reprobate eager to enjoy himself. The likenesses here, and especially that of young Tobias, are confirmed by Steen's self-portrait in the Rijksmuseum (Fig. 120, HdG 850). Further confirmation can be found in the painting *The Twelfth Night Feast* at Cassel (Fig. 68, HdG 494) of 1668, where the older Steen sings behind the table. As we have seen, Steen in using his own features repeatedly turns himself into a stock character or type who can fit into many circumstances. Nevertheless he is always recognizable, and where we may hesitate to call the inclusions in *The Marriage of Tobias and Sarah* self-portraits, they are surely self-images.

There is something serious, even touching, in the way he uses his image as participant in all three aspects of the event: the intimate, the official, and the social. That he is able to see himself at so many ages within one event, and in so many roles befitting those ages, denotes a rare objectivity. And as usual Steen exaggerates gesture and type, making out of what could be melodrama, a comedy of situation: that is, farce. That he could so freely deal with himself within such a context bespeaks Steen's greatness as the observer, for his position in regard to the action is non-participatory, even though he includes himself.

The multiple self-images in this picture generate the impression that there is something special about it. As mentioned, Steen includes himself in other paintings, but not with such repetition or emphasis. It may be that he made this one in celebration of his own second marriage, to Maria van Egmont in 1673. The date would accord well with the style of the painting. He did not choose to include himself at all in the earlier Brunswick picture. Nor did he fill the earlier work with so many symbols of love and constancy. Their presence here, and in such abundance, may indicate a more personal meaning and may substantiate the hypothesis that it is his own marriage picture.

The difference in the mood of the pictures and particularly of the couple seems also to substantiate such an idea. In the earlier version Tobias and Sarah are youngsters, hardly out of their teens. They are star-struck, innocent. Here, while they are certainly not of the ages at which Steen and Maria married (he was forty-seven), they are more middle-aged, and Sarah slightly jaded. What remains unexplained, if this is a painting Steen made for his own wedding, is why he used this particular Biblical subject. Possibly his familiarity with the subject prompted him to try it again in a different mood and with personal associations. The fact that Steen married a widow when he himself was getting on in years may underlie his inclination for a subject in which the bridegroom's predecessors did not survive, in which a guardian angel appears, and in which there is a triumphant finale. It may, of course, simply have been the marriage contract reference that attracted him.

If this painting does indeed relate to Steen's own marriage, it serves here to demonstrate most strongly the intimacy Steen built between contemporary and historical events. Within his pictures there seems to be a wholly individual, even idiosyncratic, conception of time. He consistently integrated contemporary elements, motifs, and meanings within historical occasions, blending the two into a single timeless action. The current and the historical are revealed through each other, and Steen disregarded the incongruity and anachronism thereby created.

In his paintings of the marriage at Cana he pushed this tendency to the extreme. Of all his subjects, this is the one he treated most often (six versions are known: Cat. 45–50a). Steen refuses to treat the miracle directly. Though it is not entirely obscured, he loses it in a welter of genre episodes which in their lowness seem to compromise the sacredness of the event.[10] Christ's presence is hardly noticeable. In all but the early picture (Fig. 2, Cat. 45) he is lost amidst actions relating to the scene not as the enactment of a miracle, but as a wedding celebration. In the best known of the pictures now in the Beit collection (Fig. 62, Cat. 48/49), Steen has given the central foreground to a drunken old peasant sprawled on the steps. His wife, carrying a chicken in a napkin, urges him home. They distract our attention from Christ who, recognized by only a few of his followers, works the miracle quietly in the middle ground.[11]

The paintings of the miracle actually revolve around the act of drinking in celebration of love. People hold up glasses in a toast, raise them to their lips, or offer them to others. In the Norton Simon picture (Fig. 95, Cat. 50) Steen even included, at the right, a child being given to drink; and in the center, an infant is being suckled. In the picture also is included another Biblical reference to the sustenance of drink. At the far left, as a fountain sculpture, appears the figure of Moses who holds a rod. Placed above the flowing fountain the allusion must be to the story of the striking of the rock. In the Dresden picture (Fig. 97, Cat. 47) a drunken woman lies across the entrance steps and leans on a wine-keg while a small boy drinks from her glass. Here is total participation in the act of drinking, and the departing guest is urged to stay now that the wine has been renewed. The toasts drunk solemnize the marriage. Thus in these pictures love and drink, or rather love and the act of drinking, are united and sanctified by miracle. The wedding, as Steen understood it, was not more important than the miracle but the ground of its being. The celebration goes on even as the miracle is enacted.

In the Beit picture (Fig. 62, Cat. 48/49) Steen has carried off a perfectly fitting pun. He monogrammed the picture IHS on the empty wine-barrel being rolled along by a small boy. Such a signature is rare in his late years (he had used it earlier in the 1640's and 1650's); and Schmidt-Degener's suggestion that he used it to correspond with *In Hoc Signo* [Vinces] too neatly fits the case to be ignored.[12] How appropriate not only for the subject, but for Steen's life as well. Wine and beer must have been important for him. He was first a brewer and later a tavern-owner. Many of his genre pictures center around the pleasures and consequence of drink. This in itself might explain Steen's love of the subject of the marriage at Cana, for it constitutes a Biblical sanction for purveyance as well as consumption. The "*In Hoc Signo*" pun would indicate that Steen was well aware of the sanction, and used it to his advantage. If this is so, it is yet another indication that through the use of genre vignettes Steen spiced historical subjects with personal concerns, and the reverse as well. That is to say, he used historical events to dramatize personal and contemporary affairs.

Another possible meaning for the monogram is suggested by Stechow in his study of Steen's paintings of the marriage at Cana. He suggests that the monogram IHS corresponds to the monogram of Christ (IHS = Jesus), and its appearance on the wine barrel constitutes a reference to the Eucharist. He also feels that the young man on the right, who while looking at Christ points to the fountain and the evidence of the miracle, established a prefigurative theme in the painting.[13] If such prefiguration is present it adds another and more Catholic meaning to the picture and to Steen's own understanding of this first miracle. Even as the party goes on, supplied by the new wine, the coming passion of Christ is revealed. That not everybody is aware of the miracle and its possible meanings does not, however, indicate, as Stechow maintains, that Steen is drawing a moral lesson between the way things are and the way they should be. He is simply saying, as Van Gelder saw, that in the living of life miracles and their meanings often go unnoticed and uncomprehended, even as their effects permeate the world.[14]

Steen's interest in drink and drinking and divine sanction is found also in the story of Moses striking the rock which he painted twice and incorporated in one of his paintings of the marriage at Cana (Fig. 95, Cat. 50). In the foreground of the Philadelphia picture (Fig. 88, Cat. 9), Steen placed a deep-eyed, sensuous-mouthed boy with vine leaves in his hair. He is so like Bacchus, as he holds the cup to drink, that one wonders if Steen has not added a classical allusion to the traditional Biblical theme. If so, this union of drink and divinity would parallel that found in his paintings of the miracle at Cana. Is it possible that such pictures were made to be placed in drinking halls and taverns? Even without any proof except the subject-matter and Steen's treatment of them, such an idea seems plausible. Very little is known about patronage for seventeenth-century Dutch pictures, and the suggestion supplies hints at a possible source for commissions. It is known from other paintings by Steen—e.g. *Rustic Feast in a Large Tavern* in the Louvre (Fig. 93, HdG 601)—that paintings were hung in taverns.

Dirk Bax, in his study of Dutch and Flemish pictures in South African museums,[15] offers another explanation of the boisterousness of Steen's Cana celebrations. In the Catholic calendar the memorial day of the miracle at Cana coincides with Twelfth Night, that is the sixth of January. Throughout the sixteenth and seventeenth centuries Twelfth Night was notorious for its celebrations and licentiousness. Thus by inference the church calendar itself made possible the uniting of the pure and the impure, of the elevated and the low. Implied also is the anachronistic jumbling of historical and exotic types with contemporary ones, and the irreverent confusion of historical and present time.[16]

The Use of Genre Vignettes

It may be obvious that in his treatment of the marriage of Tobias and Sarah or the miracle at Cana Steen linked historical and contemporary realities to allegorize and deepen meanings in both. It is less obvious in some of his other late pictures in which genre-vignettes or types obtrude themselves in ancient settings. By genre-vignettes is meant not the use of peasants merely, as in scenes of the adoration of the shepherds or the nativity; this was common practice. The term refers rather to the incorporation of individuals or small groups, peripheral to the major action, and out of historical context.

In Steen's *The Parable of the Rich Man and Lazarus* (Fig. 57, Cat. 59), for instance, at the lower right a servant girl cooks pancakes to grace the table of the rich man, but at the same time a child, napkin wrapped around his neck, holds his plate in readiness. Similarly in the paintings of Manius Curius (Figs. 100 and 101, Cat. 84 and 84a) a servant girl cooks turnips at the fire as the emissaries plead their case. The turnips are an important part of the story, but a girl cooking them is not. While Laban searches for the stolen images among Jacob's possessions (Fig. 89, Cat. 4/652a), three children play marbles in the foreground unaware of the drama of the confrontation. In *Samson and Delilah* (Fig. 67, Cat. 10) two still younger children play with the dog while the barber gingerly snips away. *Samson Mocked by the Philistines* (Fig. 63, Cat. 12/10a) is a collection of types or stock characters coming from a multitude of sources without regard for consistency or historical allusion. The same is true of *The Worship of the Golden Calf* (Fig. 85, Cat. 7), also discussed earlier.

Some of Steen's most touching details are found in the small drinking scenes in both the early and late versions of *Moses Striking the Rock* (Figs. 27 and 88, Cat. 8 and 9). A father gives drink to his little girl, a soldier holds a goblet to the lips of a woman; both are unaware of the force which Moses exerts to create the miracle. In the early *St. John Preaching in the Wilderness* (Fig. 29, Cat. 28), Steen creates in those listening a small drama between the converted and the unconverted. It focuses around the decision of the woman caught between the warning prophecy of John and the angry inveigling of the boorish jokesters at the left who, indifferent to the words of the preacher, enjoy themselves at her distress. In the center, by contrast, a peasant kneels at the moment of his conversion; he will soon join those behind St. John, already enjoying a new peace.

In the early paintings such as *St. John Preaching,* genre inclusions serve a narrative function; that is, they elucidate the occurrence through a diversity of reactions, some humorous, some not. In the later paintings for the most part, though some of this is present, as in the late *Moses Striking the Rock,* they serve little narrative purpose. Often they direct their awareness elsewhere than to the main action. They serve rather as the context of general humanity in which Steen's historical events occur. In their anachronism they symbolize the remarkable continuity and persistence of common life even in the face of great or significant events.

Steen is not alone in the use of such inclusions. In his etching *Christ Preaching ("La petite tombe")* Rembrandt gave the center foreground to a little boy playing aimlessly on the ground. In the "Hundred Guilder Print" another boy tugs at his mother's skirt. Steen is alone, however, in using such side-motifs as humorous anecdotes within great events. Rembrandt's children deepen the spiritual experience by their innocence, as if they "wit not to ask." Steen's vignettes tend to deflate by their incongruity or their purposeful detachment. Thus in *The Marriage at Cana* in the Beit collection (Fig. 62, Cat. 48/49), a peasant woman walks off with a chicken wrapped in a napkin and squabbles with her husband to come home. In *Antiochus and Stratonice* (Fig. 81, Cat. 84b/54) a crude and guffawing ruffian drinks to the occasion. In *The Wrath of Ahasuerus* (Fig. 74, Cat. 19a) a grinning fool engages the viewer from the right-hand corner and by his own humorous detachment makes the scene, with all of its high emotions, somewhat ridiculous.

An interesting sidelight of Steen's use of genre in history is his use of historical scenes in genre. In many of his paintings of the doctor's visit, which are really humorous variations on the theme of the lovesick maiden, the paintings he places on the walls indicate by their subject the true concern of the pictures. In *The Doctor's Visit* in the Mauritshuis (Fig. 121, HdG 130) above the canopied bed of the swooning girl hangs a large picture representing either the battle of the Centaurs and Lapiths or another classical theme including a centaur and an abduction. In *The Doctor's Visit* in the Wellington Museum in London (Fig. 122, HdG 137) the lovesick girl sits weakened and ill before her bed while a disreputable looking doctor takes her pulse. He talks with mock professional concern to the mother, who holds a beaker of urine for analysis in her hand. On the wall also above the bed is a large painting of Venus and Adonis seated on the ground in an embrace before their parting. As if this blatant analogy of the girl's malady were not enough, Steen has given a little boy seated on the floor the attributes of Cupid. In another *Doctor's Visit* now in the Taft Museum in Cincinnati (Fig. 123, HdG 175), Steen included the same Venus and Adonis wall picture, only much reduced in size.

There occur many other such inclusions. Indeed, a whole study could profitably be made of Steen's use of indirect allegory and allusion.[17] Though such a study cannot be undertaken here, several comments are in order. Steen's pictures of such scenes operate on at least two levels. There is the action in which the figures are involved. They are aware of their own desires and their own motives, and act upon them. They remain, however, unaware that they are in an environment which symbolically alludes to their desires and motives. That level of the picture conveyed by symbolic allusions is directed specifically to the viewer. Largely it is this second level which, as comment upon human action, makes the point and defines the meaning. We are faced in Steen's genre pictures with the peculiar combination of realism and symbolism—that is, illusion of reality (the scene as it might have happened, with certain humorous exaggeration, the figures acting without self-consciousness) and yet the whole symbolically directed toward what is often a literary theme. Our attention is directed not only to the actions of people, but to a whole culture founded upon common anecdotes, emblematic devices, and proverbs.[18]

Surprisingly, it is only in his wall paintings, most often of classical themes, that Steen paints the nude which he so consistently avoided in his own historical works, even where the subject might traditionally demand it. It could not have been any general restriction on the use of nudes that affected Steen. Rembrandt used them consistently for paintings of Danae, Susanna and Bathseba. The nude, however, is antithetical to genre painting which seeks to create an illusion of common reality and not of the heroic or the ideal. It may have been Steen's intense commitment to the idea of genre scenes, even in history, that led him to his avoidance of the nude. In his paintings on the walls of his domestic interiors they could be added as part of the daily environment, symbolic though they were in meaning.

In genre, then, as in history, Steen thematically united apparently incongruous elements, and hinted at love's universal presences and persistence. His *miniziek meisjes* may be ridiculous, even laughable, but in their emotions they are in good company. The inclusion of such indirect historical elucidations of contemporary themes can in no way, however, be called anachronistic. They serve the reverse function of the genre elements in history, which are so blatantly transferred from their original milieu.

Anachronism was rife in both sixteenth and seventeenth-century painting. Many ancient events were thought of as allegorical of contemporary happenings. William of Orange, the Protestant, for instance, was welcomed to Brussels in 1577 with *tableaux vivants* showing Moses, Joseph, and David saving the Israelites.[19] The allegorical allusions were perfectly clear. Besides this tendency to cut through time by allegorization, the knowledge of ancient dress was relatively limited and the tendency was to regard what was outmoded, old-fashioned, or Oriental as being of great antiquity.[20] Often sixteenth-century or older dress was used for ancient costume in Biblical scenes as well as those from local history. Steen for instance used the *lansquenet* of the Swiss soldiers with the traditional slashes across the arms, thighs, and chest in *The Worship of the Golden Calf* (Fig. 85, Cat. 7); and Rembrandt in his painting *Jacob Blessing the Sons of Joseph* at Cassel used the *hennin,* fifteenth-century woman's headdress, for Asnath.[21] It would be difficult to cite any Dutch seventeenth-century Biblical or historical painting which could be called archeologically correct. They are jumbles of types and costumes and even architecture arising out of a multitude of varied traditions and notions of antiquity.

It is not then Steen's use of anachronistic costume and elements that sets him apart in his historical painting, but his conscious inclusion in historical scenes of clearly incongruous types and vignettes from contemporary life. His pictures, as pointed out in Chapter 3, are often collections of stock types or characters drawn from many sources and acting in predictable ways. This joining together of incongruities is his means of uniting the high and the low, or better, the elevated and the mundane. Through that union he makes a profound historical statement. History becomes genre in the sense that it is about common human behavior, and genre becomes history in that it is present throughout historical time. To drink when one is thirsty is an act of the spirit, for as in the miracle at Cana, that which is to drink is given.

The Mixture of the High and the Low

Steen chose as a major theme for his historical pictures that passion most open to the mixture of high tragedy and low comedy, and most revealing of human seriousness and folly. Love as the exposure of what is private, love with its titillation of sexual desire, love with its extravagance, love which makes us slaves to our passions and oblivious to the world—love is both elevating and degrading, both poetic and lustful. Steen reveals these contradictions with a warm though sometimes salacious humor, drawn from his work in genre.

For Steen, the lover was always disarmed, revealed by his behavior, open to public jest, and the butt of low humor, even when the love itself might be tragic or destructive. By so placing the great loves in the same context that he might a lovesick girl, or a tavern solicitation, he has put them in a perspective of a universal comedy in which the contemporary and the historical are inextricably united. The fools in Steen's paintings are suffered gladly because of the intensity of their passions.

Samson betrayed (Fig. 63, Cat. 12/10a) is pitiful, but he is also slightly ridiculous. His gigantic turban, and the exaggerated curls lying on the ground, help inflate the vision to proportions of bombast. Delilah acted with gross duplicity, but Samson was a fool before his passions. Antony was also the victim of overwrought emotion. On his knees before his beautiful Egyptian (Fig. 60, Cat. 86a/b), his hand upon his heart, he cuts just as ludicrous a figure as Samson. His mature passion is not far distant from that of the young Tobias caught in the ardor of his love for Sarah (Fig. 66, Cat. 25a/457). The behavior of his heroines, for all their amplitude, is no better. Delilah is a wanton whore without compassion; Cleopatra a strumpet playing with her power over Antony; Sarah a young innocent unaware of the image she presents. What more pitiful yet silly figure is there than the spurned Tamar (Fig 72, Cat. 16), so hurt by her rejection and mocked by both Amnon and his servant.

In poking fun at human behavior Steen cannot be called a moralist preaching right behavior by examples of folly. His historical figures, like his genre figures, are presented for their own sake, and for our recognition and amusement. Steen's laughter overflows with a joy and delight over life. He must have found excess a basic human quality. Heine, in seeking a more joyous Christianity, sang his praises:

> In the house I lodged at in Leyden there once lived Jan Steen, the great Jan Steen, whom I hold to be as great as Raphael. Even as a sacred painter Jan was as great, and that will be clearly seen when the religion of sorrow has passed away, and the religion of joy has torn off the thick veil that covers the rose-bushes of the earth, and the nightingales dare at last to sing joyously out their long concealed raptures.[22]

It is not in his humorous paintings that Steen failed as a religious painter, but in those few works in which he attempted to make direct spiritual statements. In *Christ at Emmaus* in the Rijksmuseum (Fig. 45, Cat. 65) he made one of his rare attempts to deal with religious mystery. For all its beautiful calm, and soft glowing light, it is static and unconvincing, and borders on the seriously sentimental. The same holds true for his painting *The Child Jesus in the Temple* (Fig. 39, Cat. 44), where he tried to create a Rembrandtesque vision of a synagogue filled with divine light. The young Jesus there looks like the over-sweet figures found in popular icons. *The Return of the Prodigal Son* (Fig. 80, Cat. 55) also seems to be more pathetic than spiritual. In *The Rest on the Flight to Egypt* in Dunkirk (Fig. 79, Cat. 39), Steen's most iconic image, he juxtaposes a Murillo-esque madonna with infant, St. John and lamb, with peasant-like Joseph, Joachim, and

Anna. All the expressions are unconvincing, and the holy image surmounted by a group of cherubs is disturbingly sweet.

It is only in his earlier religious paintings that he achieves a convincing image of direct spirituality. As essentially a folk-painter he chose themes around which he could group the Dutch peasants. All his paintings of the adoration of the shepherds, and particularly the one in the Rijksmuseum (Fig. 37, Cat. 37/31), are convincing images of the scene. The peasants bring to the infant adoration and curiosity, and a desire to celebrate the birth. In this we have something of the same mixture of the high and the low that characterizes the later works, only here the vulgar is a natural and traditional inclusion. The same can be said for his touching representation of *Christ Blessing the Little Children* (Fig. 5, Cat. 60). Collected in the evening light, the children come to Christ, who blesses them with tenderness and warmth. *Moses Striking the Rock* in Frankfurt (Fig. 27, Cat. 8) and *St. John the Baptist Preaching in the Wilderness* (Fig. 29, Cat. 28) share these same qualities of directness without pretension to religious mystery. These paintings compare strikingly in their folk reverence to the purposeful irreverence of the paintings from the 1660's and 1670's with which this chapter has been mostly concerned.

That irreverence is not, however, directed against religion, but against the traditional concept of history and history painting. Steen refused to take history seriously or to give his figures the dignity usually accorded them. In so doing he ridiculed both classical and contemporary baroque aesthetics. By breaking the rules of correctness and decorum, by intentionally including sequences out of time and out of place, and by boisterously laughing over the ludicrousness of great actions, he revealed the pompous self-seriousness of high baroque histories. He makes us understand, whether purposefully or not, the artificiality and inhumanness of the grand heroics of much of the history painting of his day. Of all the critics who have written on Steen, Stechow and Schmidt-Degener particularly recognized that his humor and irreverence had a serious purpose. About the painting of *Erysichthon Selling His Daughter* (Fig. 51, Cat. 73) Schmidt-Degener says the following:

> He knew by heart the story of Erysichthon's hunger and of the sacrifice of Hypermnestra, but he obtained his amusing effect by giving what might be called a literal translation of these stories into Dutch. Here was a man of learned Leiden who administered the death blow to pedantry! Unconcerned about verisimilitude, he parodied merrily away: Erysichthon, that good Leiden burgher, "swaps" his daughter for a herring and a loaf of white bread in a forest filled with gathering darkness. . . .[23]

In other cases also Schmidt-Degener finds a sense of liberation in Steen's works, liberation from the seriousness of history painting, and one must assert also of the imagination:

> Consider Steen's pointed paraphrase of the story of Cincinnatus [here called *Manius Curius Dentatus* (Fig. 100, Cat. 84)] and the famous plate of turnips. There is a moralizing inscription: "Natura paucis contenta." But every nook and cranny is filled with turnips, onions, and pumpkins. The grey dictator wallows in them. The whole scene seems to rock with laughter at the silly wisdom of the old Romans. Steen's lavishness with his globular vegetables would have met with the approval of Molière.[24]

The uniqueness of Steen's historical vision is in the transference of the comic spirit of low-genre to traditionally serious subjects. In so doing he poked fun both at the characters in his stories, and at the whole structure of history painting. With Hogarth, who owed something to him, he is one of the few successful comic painters. Unlike Hogarth's, however, his paintings are not wicked satires on contemporary social behavior. They are expositions of the silly propensities of human beings without regard to time, location, or class. His is a humor of overstatement and out of it comes the abundance of things and of people that overflows his canvases. His heroes and heroines possessed by love, whether sacred or profane, join in the great masquerade of history.

References

1. "Ik kan niet voorbygaag te melden den inhoud van een groot stuk ('t geen lang aan myn huis gestaan hebbende, naderhand aan den Vorst van Wolfenbuttel berkogt is) waar in afgebeld stond een Bruidegom en Bruid, twee oude Luiden en een Notaris. Deze beelden waren elk zoo natuurlyk in hunne verrigtingen afgebeeld, als of men 't zelve vezentlyk gebeuren zag . . ." Houbraken, *De Groote Schouburgh,* III, 1721, pp. 16–17 (Swillen's ed., 1953, pp. 12–13).

2. *ZfbK,* LX, 1926/27, p. 230 ff. A later version (Cat. 25/487) now in San Francisco is still called by the genre title.

3. Gudlaugsson, *Komedianten,* 1945, p. 8 ff.

4. See J. Bruyn and J. A. Emmens, *Burlington,* LXXXXIX, 1957, p. 96. See also R. R. Wark, *Burlington,* LXXXXVIII, 1956, p. 53 ff.; he discusses the symbolism of the sunflower in Van Dyck's self-portrait in the Westminster collection.

5. Cats, *Alle de Werken,* I, p. 28.

6. De Jonge, *Simiolus,* III, 1968–69, pp. 22–52 *passim.*

7. Cats, *Alle de Werken,* I, p. 157.

8. *Ibid.,* I, p. 164.

9. In all cases of emblems it is difficult to say that Steen got them and their meaning from one source in particular. Mario Praz in his work on the subject, *Studies in Seventeenth-Century Imagery,* 1947, shows that emblematic devices have a long history of interdependency, many tracing their origin to poetic images in Petrarch's sonnets and others even to antiquity. (For Cats, see particularly pp. 113–14.) Other Dutch and Flemish emblem writers, Daniel Heinsius, Otho Vaenius (Otto van Veen), and the poet Pieter Cornelisz Hooft, compiled *Emblemata Amatoria* prior to Cats and as would be expected some correspondence can be noted. Cats, however, is one of the best and most prolific of emblem-writers.

10. For their lack of spiritual seriousness these pictures were the targets of the most adverse criticism against Steen. Waagen declared that in the Beit picture (Cat. 48/49) Steen reduced the subject "to a level of his sphere of art"; *Treasures of Art in Great Britain,* IV (Suppl.), 1857, p. 296. Another author called the Dresden painting ". . . one of the least attractive pictures by a dissipated character"; Furst, *Apollo,* XXX, 1939, pp. 217–18.

11. In establishing the middle ground as the zone of the sacred Steen may be following a structure which can be traced back to Veronese's *Marriage at Cana* in the Louvre and *The Last Supper* in the Academia in Venice. The latter picture he retitled *Feast in the House of Levi* after he was censured for inappropriate and irreverent inclusions. See Rosand, *Art Bulletin,* LV, 1973, p. 229.

12. Schmidt-Degener, *Steen,* 1927, p. 11.

13. Stechow, *Nederlands Kunsthistorisch Jaarback* XXIII, 1972, pp. 79–80.

14. Van Gelder, *Steen,* 1927, p. 35.

15. *Skilders wat Vertel,* pp. 19–20.

16. Bosch's picture of the marriage at Cana in the Boymans/van Beuningen Museum deploys the same mixture of elements, revealing that Steen's vision has roots within a much older tradition.

17. For a general treatment of the subject through Picasso see Chastel, *Akten des 21. Internationalen Kongresses für Kunstgeschichte* (1964), I, 1967, pp. 15–29.

18. C. de Groot, *Beeld en Woord,* 1952, p. 56 ff.

19. Kernodle, *From Art to Theater,* 1943, p. 69.
20. Van der Waal, *Vaderlandsche Geschied Uitbeelding,* 1952, p. 60; see also Goltz, *Burlington,* LXXIII, 1938, p. 50.
21. *Ibid.,* p. 61.
22. Heine, fragment on Jan Steen taken from *Memoirn des Herrn von Schnabelwopski,* 1831.
23. Schmidt-Degener and van Gelder, *Steen,* 1927, p. 10.
24. *Ibid.,* p. 11.

CATALOGUE
of Religious and Historical Paintings by Jan Steen

The numbering of Hofstede de Groot's *A Catalogue Raisonné of the Works of the Most Eminent Dutch Painters of the Seventeenth Century,* Volume I (1908), and the annotated copy of that catalogue called the Handex (now in the Rijksbureau voor Kunsthistorische Documentatie at The Hague) has been followed in this catalogue. In 1937 E. Trautscholdt compiled a supplement to Hofstede de Groot's catalogue in his article on Jan Steen in Volume XXXI of the *Thieme-Becker Kunstlerlexikon.* He followed the same numbering system. Since the supplements have somewhat complicated the original listings, an attempt has been made to clarify the numbering while at the same time integrating new material. Where numbers have been changed, the old number preceded by "HdG" has been listed immediately below. In the Addendum to the catalogue, Hofstede de Groot's numbers follow the new numbering, separated by a slash.

For the sake of consistency, where integrated material has been indicated by letter designation such as "39A" or "31a," all letters have been given in the lower case and that change noted. Where a picture has more than one Hofstede de Groot number, all numbers are given separated by slashes. Numbers added by the Handex are followed by one asterisk; those added by Trautscholdt, by two; and those added by the present writer, by three. Where pictures have been seen by the author, an asterisk follows the *title.*

The corresponding numbers in John Smith's *Catalogue Raisonné of the Works of the Most Eminent Dutch, Flemish, and French Painters,* IV, of 1833, and his own supplement to that work of 1842, upon which Hofstede de Groot based his catalogue, and those in Van Westrheene's catalogue from his *Jan Steen, étude sur l'art en Hollande* of 1856, have not been given in the listings except where there is error or inconsistency. In that case mention of that fact with the appropriate numbers is made in the text of the entry. Smith and Van Westrheene numbers are listed in Hofstede de Groot.

Titles as given by Hofstede de Groot have been mostly kept except where changes are necessary to bring them in line with the actual subject or in cases where the subject has been reinterpreted. Occasionally a title has been changed for the sake of brevity or for more accurate wording.

Hofstede de Groot is responsible for most of the provenance of the paintings up through 1908. His information has been amended and where possible the later history of the pictures completed. Where no change has taken place his initials (HdG) appear in parentheses at the end of each reference. Where changes have been made or material added, the source is likewise indicated in parentheses at the end of the reference, either as an abbreviation—i.e., Handex—or as a bibliographical reference.

Bibliographical references within the text are indicated by numbers in parentheses. The numbers refer to the abbreviated bibliography that follows each catalogue entry. The bibliographies include works of both direct and related importance, and are listed chronologically. For complete references the reader may consult the general listings at the end of the study.

Within the catalogue the chronological place of the pictures within Steen's career is mentioned briefly. For a detailed study justifying the position given any painting, the reader is referred to Chapter 1, in which Steen's development as a history painter is followed.

RELIGIOUS WORKS

1] LOT AND HIS DAUGHTERS*

Fig. 48

Canvas; 32 x 27 inches; signed in full on rock at lower right.

Wessenbergische Gemäldegalerie, Constance, West Germany.

Provenance: Sale, J. H. van Heemskerck, The Hague, 29 March 1770, No. 107 (HdG); sale, The Hague, 25 May 1772, No. 2 (HdG); sale, Cardinal Fesch collection, Rome, 17 March 1845, No. 739 (HdG); sale, Freiherr von Münchhausen, F. Reichardt, J. P. Weyer, *et al.*, Herberle, Cologne, 28 Oct. 1887, No. 135 (HdG); at this last sale the picture was bought by Dr. Koppe of Constance (1). It may have passed from his possession to the Wessenberg collection which became the property of the city of Constance.

Exhibition: Constance, Alte Kunst aus Konstanzer Besitz, 1945, No. 9.

The Biblical source for the subject is Genesis 19:31-38. Though the subject is quite obvious, the picture was described in the 1770 sales catalogue as "Twee vrouwspersoonen zich vermaakende met een vrolyk oud Man, die beschonken is." I note this because it indicates the reluctance to assign Biblical themes to Jan Steen. Steen's historical works have never been as popular as his genre pieces, being thought of as atypical. Bredius praised this painting, but felt that it would have brought a higher price at the 1887 sale had the subject been different (1).

The picture links Jan Steen with Rembrandt and his school. General setting and composition, and the figures of Lot and of his daughter to the left, are taken from Jan van Vliet's etching of the same subject, possibly made after a lost painting by Rembrandt, or after the drawing *Lot and His Daughters* now in the British Museum (Fig. 49). The drawing has been attributed to Rembrandt by Hind (3) and Valentiner (4), though Benesch calls it a copy after the lost painting (5). The etching is inscribed "R-I van Rijn inventor—1631—J. G. van Vliet fecit" (2), but from this one can still not judge if the "invention" was a painting or a drawing. It must have been van Vliet's etching that Steen knew, since both his painting and the etching reverse the British Museum drawing.

The picture shows certain stylistic affinities with the background painting in *The Parable of the Rich Man and Lazarus* (Cat. 59) dated 1667. A similar scene takes place at the rich man's table, painted with a similar looseness. The probability is that the painting predates the *Lazarus* and should be dated about 1665.

Bibliography: (1) Bredius, *Kunstchronik*, XXIII, 1887, p. 91; (2) Rovinski, *L'oeuvre gravé des élèves de Rembrandt . . .*, Vol. I, 1894, pp. 69-70, Nos. 173, 174; (3) Hind, *Drawings, British Museum*, Vol. I, 1915, No. 115; (4) Valentiner, *Handzeichnungen*, Vol. I, 1925, No. 41; (5) Benesch, *Drawings*, Vol. I, 1954, No. 82; (6) Cat., Alte Kunst aus Konstanzer Besitz, Constance, 1954, No. 9.

2] THE DISMISSAL OF HAGAR

Fig. 41

Canvas; 54 x 43½ inches; signed in full on cornerstone of archway.

Gemäldegalerie—Alte Meister, Dresden, East Germany.

Provenance: Sale, D. C. F. Linkers, Rotterdam, 18 Oct. 1857, No. 48 (Handex). Acquired by the Dresden Gallery from the dealer Ernst, of Dresden, in 1876.

The Biblical source for the subject is Genesis 19:14. Like *Lot and His Daughters* (Cat. 1, Fig. 48), this picture demonstrates Steen's connection with Rembrandt and his school. Richard Hamann (4) has shown that the figural arrangement, the setting, and to a degree the types used by Steen had their origin in Rembrandt's famous etching of 1637 (6). Similarities are numerous: the courtyard with the archway entrance to the house; the steps upon which Abraham stands; Sarah and Isaac within the safety of the house; the sad gesture of Abraham and the weeping of Hagar. C. W. de Groot suggested that Steen's reversal of the figures might have been a means of camouflaging the borrowing (5).

The figure in Rembrandt's chalk study of a weeping woman (7) made as a study for his painting *The Woman Taken in Adultery* of 1644 in the National Gallery, London (3) (10), is similar to Steen's Hagar. There is even stronger similarity between Hagar and a small oil sketch of a weeping woman attributed to Rembrandt and now at the Detroit Institute of Arts (8). Correspondence between this head and Steen's head of Hagar seems undeniable (Fig. 43).

Bredius believed the picture to be a mature work from about 1660 (1). That dating is here concurred with. Bredius correctly maintains that, because of the date, this could not be the painting *The Dismissal of Hagar* that was purchased in The Hague in 1651 by an agent for Field-Marshal Wrangel, the acting Governor-General of Pomerania (1). This opinion is shared by Eduard Plietzsch in his annotations to the 1958 edition of Bode (9). For a discussion of the Wrangel picture see Cat. 2a and 2b.

Bibliography: (1) Bredius, *Steen*, 1927, pp. 27–28, pl. 3; (2) Cat., Staatlichen Gemäldegalerie zw. Dresden, 1930, No. 1727; (3) Bredius, *Paintings of Rembrandt*, 1936, Nos. 566, 366; (4) Hamann, *Marburger Jahrbuch für Kunstwissenschaft*, VIII–IX, 1936, pp. 558–59; (5) de Groot, *Beeld en Woord*, 1952, pp. 161, 178; (6) Münz, *Etchings*, 1952, No. 174; (7) Benesch, *Drawings*, Vol. III, 1955, No. 535; (8) Richardson, *Bull., Detroit Inst. of Arts*, XXXVI, 1956/57, pp. 58–59; (9) Bode, *Malerschulen*, ed. 1958, p. 156, note 1; (10) Maclaren, *Dutch School*, 1960, No. 45, n. 8.

2a] THE STORY OF HAGAR

Present location unknown.

A picture called by this title was shipped on 3 July 1651 to Field-Marshal Wrangel, the Swedish Governor-General of Pomerania. Along with other Dutch pictures, including three more Steens, it had been bought for thirty-six florins at The Hague by Wrangel's agent there, H. Appelboom. This information comes from a letter of 3 July 1651 from Appelboom to the Field-Marshal; the letter was to accompany the shipment of pictures. (There were, besides the Steens, works by G. ter Borch, J. Danckerts, J. van Duijnen, A. va Beyeren, H. de Meyer, and W. van Diest.) The letter was discovered in Sweden in 1904 by Olof Granberg (1) (2).

If this picture still exists, its whereabouts is unknown. Further, one cannot tell precisely what was the subject. "The story of Hagar" could refer to several episodes from the Old Testament. Bredius either knew or assumed that it was a dismissal of Hagar (4), but certainly not the picture in Dresden (Cat. 2); this opinion is correct. Others have assumed that the subject was Hagar and Ishmael in the wilderness, and have associated it with Cat. 2b (3). The latter position is also untenable on stylistic grounds.

The other three Steen pictures in the shipment were *The Well-Fed Family* (HdG 115a), its pendant *The Starved Family* (HdG 115b), and a *Winter Landscape* (HdG 881a). In 1927 Martin published a pair of pictures that might well be 115a and 115b—though they are 121 and 122 in Hofstede de Groot's catalogue (5). The *Winter Landscape* was rediscovered in 1928 by Wolfgang Stechow in the collection of Baron Rutger von Essen, a descendant of Wrangel, at Skokloster, Sweden (6). This painting, remarkably like those of Isaac van Ostade, and signed "J S," was exhibited in the large Steen show at The Hague during the winter of 1958/59 (7) (Fig. 22).

For a further discussion of the problem of *The Story of Hagar* see Cat. 2b.

Bibliography: (1) Granberg, *O-H*, XXV, 1907, p. 132; (2) Gransberg, *Inventaire Général*, 1911, I, p. 92; (3) Lilienfeld, *Monatshefte für Kunstwissenschaft*, IV, 1911, pp. 50–53; (4) Bredius, *Steen*, 1927, pp. 17, 27; (5) Martin, *ZfbK*, LXI, 1927/28, p. 333; (6) Stechow, *ZfbK*, LXII, 1928/29, pp. 173-74; (7) Cat., Jan Steen, The Hague, 1958/59, No. 1.

2b*] HAGAR AND ISHMAEL IN THE WILDERNESS*

Fig. 46

Canvas; 24 x ½ x 20 inches; signed in full at lower right.

Elizabeth M. Drey collection, New York.

Provenance: The Handex lists the picture as belonging at one time to the Dribel collection at The Hague, but offers no date. In the early part of this century it belonged to Dr. Karl Lilienfeld of Leipzig (1); and during 1912/13 it was at the Boymans Museum in Rotterdam, on loan from Dr. Lilienfeld (2). It was still in the Lilienfeld collection in 1927 (4). Between 1940 and 1946 it was exhibited several times in the United States. In 1951 Walter P. Chrysler of New York owned it, and in 1952 it went to the T. Gilbert Brouillette Gallery in New York. That same year it was in possession of E. William Cooper of Atcheson, Kansas. The Bob Jones University Collection of Religious Painting, Greenville, South Carolina, acquired it in 1954 (8). It was traded in 1960 to the Paul Drey Gallery of New York. The picture entered a European collection in the mid-1960's, but was subsequently acquired by the Paul Drey Gallery.

Exhibitions: Rotterdam, Boymans Museum, 1912/13; Leipzig, 1914; Grand Rapids Art Gallery, Grand Rapids, Michigan, 1940; Milwaukee Art Institute, Milwaukee, Wisconsin, 1943; Indiana University, Bloomington, Indiana, 1946.

The Biblical source for the subject is Genesis 19:15–17. The painting was not listed by Hofstede de Groot in his original catalogue. It is added in the Handex at The Hague as No. 2b. The Catalogue of the Bob Jones Collection of Religious Paintings (8) is in error in listing it as HdG 2a and in stating that it was in the collection of Field-Marshal Wrangel (see Cat. 2a). Trautscholdt also confused it with HdG 2a (6). And Kurt von Freise also felt the identification with HdG 2a was a possible one, believing the painting to be an early work (2).

If this picture were HdG 2a, it would have to be dated 1651 or earlier; but it could not possibly be from so early in Steen's career. The hazy evening landscape and soft foliage indicate a mature work of the mid-1660's. An idea of the kind of landscapes Steen painted in his early years can be derived from the *Winter Landscape* in the Rutger van Essen collection in Sweden (HdG 881a), which was certainly part of the Wrangel purchase (see Cat. 2a). Steen's early attachment to Haarlem landscape painting, apparent in the Van Essen picture, is documented by others of his early landscapes (9) (5) (Figs. 12–14 and 22).

Comparison with Steen's earliest dated picture, *The Death of Ananias* of 1651 (Cat. 66, Fig. 1) also demonstrates the later date of the present painting. There are connections, especially the tendency to foreshorten the heads; but the figures, the space, the composition of the *Ananias*, are tightly constricted compared to the openness of the *Hagar and Ishmael*. Further, the *Ananias* has little of the rhythm of narrative present in *Hagar and Ishmael*, and characteristic of all of Steen's mature works.

All the evidence, then, indicates that the present picture must be dissociated from HdG 2a and given a later place in Steen's career, perhaps in the mid-1660's. Both Bredius and E. Plietzsch share this opinion, maintaining that both this picture and the Dresden *Dismissal of Hagar* (Cat. 2) are too late to be associated with the picture sent to Wrangel (4) (10).

Bibliography: (1) Lilienfeld, *Monatshefte für Kunstwissenschaft*, IV, 1911, pp. 50–53; (2) Von Freise, *Cicerone*, IV, 1912, p. 662; (3) *Jaarverslag*, Boymans Museum, Rotterdam, 1912, p. 6; (4) Bredius, *Steen*, 1927, pp. 27–28; (5) Martin, *Burlington*, LXVII, 1935, pp. 211–12; (6) Trautscholdt, *T-B*, XXXI, 1937, p. 511; (7) *Art Quarterly*, XVII, 1954, p. 430; (8) Cat. Bob Jones Collection, 1954, pp. 114–15; (9) Martin, *Steen*, 1954, pp. 154, 29; (10) Bode, *Malerschulen*, ed. 1958, p. 156, n. 1.

3] THE DEPARTURE OF LABAN

Canvas; 46 1/2 x 71 inches.
Present location unknown.

Hofstede de Groot lists a picture of this title in the W. Wreesman sale in Amsterdam on 11 April 1816 (No. 174). It was sold for 500 florins to Roos. It may be identical with Cat. 4/652a, but substantiating proof is missing. Research has revealed no further information on the picture.

A painting of *Laban Searching for the Idols Hidden by Rachel* was in the W. C. Drossaart van Dusseldorp sale at Rotterdam in 1937. The size (37 x 48 inches), however, does not correspond; and though there are Steen-like elements in the picture, the attribution to Steen is not convincing.

4/652a] LABAN SEARCHING FOR THE IDOLS HIDDEN BY RACHEL*
Fig. 89

Canvas; 44 x 58 inches.
Stedelijk Museum "De Lakenhal," Leiden.

Provenance: Sale, J. van der Linden van Slingelandt, Dordrecht, 22 Aug. 1785, No. 401, with measurements 42 x 64 1/2 inches (HdG); the Turenne collection, Paris, ca. 1830/1852 (HdG); sale, Turenne, Paris, 17 May 1852, No. 89, bought by Nieuwenhuys (HdG); sale, London, 28 June 1879 (HdG); sale, C. J. Nieuwenhuys, London, 17 July 1886, No. 99 (HdG); collection, C. J. Lembruggen, Leiden (HdG); Lembruggen gave it to "De Lakenhal" in 1889.

Exhibitions: Leiden, "De Lakenhal," "L'exposition de tableaux, et de dessins de Rembrandt et d'autre maîtres de Leyde," 1906, No. 57; Leiden, "De Lakenhal," "Jan Steen Tentoonstelling," 1926, No. 15; Amsterdam, Rijksmuseum, "Bijbelse Kunst," 1939, No. 18; The Hague, Mauritshuis, "Jan Steen Tentoonstelling," 1958/59, No. 48.

The Biblical source for the subject is Genesis 31:32–35. Hofstede de Groot suggests that the picture Smith called "A Village Fair" (HdG 652a) and described as a preparation for market may be identical with this listing. The description given by Smith (1) accurately fits the present picture: "Towards the side are a man in Asiatic dress, with an assistant, busy over a large coffer"—and the dimensions, 44 x 65 inches, are so close, that the identity seems certain. Furthermore, Smith in 1833 gave the owner as Count de Turenne of Paris; that datum agrees with the history of the present painting. Trautscholdt, however, does not confirm the correspondence (8).

The picture has generally been reported signed. The signature is confirmed as late as 1958 in the catalogue of the Steen show at The Hague (12). Yet this confirmation seems to be in error, since neither my own observations nor those of J. N. van Wessem, director of "de Lakenhal" at Leiden, have discovered a signature. Records at the museum do not tell when the signature disappeared. When the painting was cleaned about 1953, its condition was described as "very good indeed."

According to the Turenne sale catalogue of 1852, the picture was dated 1660. But the date disappeared with later restoration (12). Bredius states that he saw the date 1661 on the painting before the cleaning (7), which must have occurred early in the century since Hofstede de Groot (1907) notes that the date was not visible. Both Bredius and Martin (11) accept the date—either 1660 or 1661—as correct. Their position is challenged in the catalogue to the Hague show of 1958/59, where it is said that the date most probably should have been read 1669 (12). The latter opinion is the more correct one, though the probability is that the picture was made some few years later, around 1671, at which time Steen opened up his backgrounds. To begin with, the reported date may have been false.

Jan Steen loved the shimmering still-life details, the richness and texture of silk, the light shining on bronze or silver. This is particularly true of his later works in which he fractured his surfaces with light. Indeed he has been accused of losing the subject in distracting details (10). The dullness of some of the objects in this picture suggests that he left it unfinished. The trunk on the right, the saddle, wagon, and horse on the other side, the basket in the center, the parasol, the foreground landscape to the left, and the little figures in the distance, share a sketchy opacity compared with the shimmering brilliance of the figures of Rachel and Laban and Jacob. One may compare the rich, foliated foreground beneath them with the barrenness of that on the left; compare the sleeping dog, so alive even in sleep, with the biological inertness of the horse. It is true that Steen often gave to his major figures a grandeur he denied the "extras," but this is not enough to account for the sketchiness of some areas of the picture.

Some of the animals, particularly the cows, with their backs making an awkward horizontal across the light sky, are disconcerting. The shepherd too seems awkward and out of scale. One is tempted to assign these to an inept hand attempting to make an incomplete work seem finished.

There is a strong possibility also that the distant landscape, some of the foliage, and especially the sky is the work of another hand. Steen did not silhouette his figures against the open sky. The horizon rarely lies so low; and if it does, as in some of his early outdoor scenes, like the picture called *Mooy Uyt* or *Rustic Feast* (HdG 621), the figures are always placed below the horizon line, and trees or houses are used on one side as a kind of backdrop for the action. *David Returning Victorious* (Cat. 13, Fig. 83) of 1671 shows the way Steen handled outdoor scenes similar to that in the present picture in his later years: all the activity is still placed below the horizon. Steen probably planned this picture of Laban and Rachel to be of roughly the same construction. The very best comparison is with *Moses Striking the Rock* (Cat. 9, Fig. 88), which Steen painted at about the same time, and which like *The Worship of the Golden Calf* (Cat. 7, Fig. 85), is superbly finished in all its details.

From all the evidence present, the conclusion is that the picture left unfinished by Steen was completed by a later hand and falsely signed and dated.

Bibliography: (1) Smith, *Catalogue Raisonné*, 1833, No. 171; (2) Moes, *Oud en Nieuw*, 1889, p. 67ff; (3) Martin and Overvoorde, *Stedelijk Museum Leiden*, 1902, p. 48; (4) Bredius, *Leidse Tentoonstelling in 1906*, pl. 14; (5) Martin and Moes, *Oude Schilder-Kunst*, 1912, Vol. II, No. 68; (6) Cat., Steen, Leiden, 1926, No. 15; (7) Bredius, *Steen*, 1927, pp. 30–31; (8) Trautscholdt, *T-B*, XXXI, 1937, p. 512; (9) Cat., "De Lakenhal," 1949, No. 404; (10) de Groot, *Beeld en Woord*, 1952, pp. 170–71; (11) Martin, *Steen*, 1954, p. 52; (12) Cat., Steen, The Hague, 1958/59, No. 48.

5] JOSEPH AND POTIPHAR'S WIFE

Panel; 26½ x 32½ inches.

The picture was in the de Robiano sale in Brussels on 1 May 1837, No. 616. According to Hofstede de Groot, the catalogue of that sale described it as a "caricature." Research has revealed no further information on this picture.

6] THE TRIAL OF THE INFANT MOSES*

Fig. 69

Panel; 31 x 31½ inches; signed in full on column at left.

Wetzlar collection, Amsterdam.

Provenance: Sale, Grenier, Middelburg, 18 Aug. 1712, No. 53 (HdG); sale, E. van Dishoek, The Hague, 9 June 1745, No. 20 (HdG); sale, J. Viet, Amsterdam, 12 Oct. 1774, No. 197 (Handex). It remained unknown until in 1953 a Dutch dealer discovered it in a French castle (1). Dealer, Heim Gerrac, Paris; dealer, Nijstad, The Hague; collection, Wetzlar.

Exhibitions: Delft, Antiekbeurs, 1953; The Hague, Mauritshuis, Jan Steen Tentoonstelling, 1958/59, No. 50.

The story of Moses told here is not found in the Bible. It is a synthesis of stories that came to embellish the history of Moses as found in Exodus. The catalogue of the 1958/59 exhibition at The Hague relates the popular story (for which it gives no source) of how the young Moses was forced to choose between the crown of Pharaoh and hot coals; guided by the invisible angel Gabriel, he chose the coals, thus saving his life. Also mentioned in the catalogue is the story from Josephus (*Antiquities of the Jews*, Book II, Chapter X) in which the young Moses is presented to Pharaoh as a possible successor. Taking the crown from his own head, Pharaoh placed it jokingly on the boy's, whereupon Moses threw off the crown and playfully trod upon it. The omen was easily read, and advisors witnessing the scene called for the death of Moses. Pharaoh's daughter intervened, God softened the heart of Pharaoh, and Moses' life was spared.

The two stories must have been combined by Steen. One explains the crown on the floor with a piece broken from it, and the other the brazier.

Another story from Talmudic literature fuses these episodes into one. At the table of Pharaoh, Moses, then three years old, audaciously removed the crown from Pharaoh's head and placed it upon his own. The omen was explicated, and the advisors called for the death of the child. One minister, however, who according to some sources was the angel Gabriel in disguise, proposed a test to see if the boy had sense enough to do such a deed deliberately. Shining gold or jewels were put on a plate together with a hot coal. The angel Gabriel guided the choice; young Moses put the hot coal into his mouth; it burned his tongue, causing him to stutter from then on, but saving his life. This burn accounts for the lines "but I am slow of speech and of a slow tongue" uttered by Moses to the Lord (Exodus 4:10). (For the sources of this legend and others, see *The Jewish Encyclopedia*, IX, p. 47ff.)

This story explains the bag of gold on the floor, and also that Moses points to his tongue. Steen must have known the story from a source uniting all three of these apocryphal tales and making the incident with the crown the reason for the test. That he united them himself is unlikely. Such stories are common even today among the Jews, and it may very well be that the painting was made, as Martin suggests, for a Jewish patron in Haarlem or Amsterdam (2).

The agitated old man in the background has been identified as Moses' older brother Aaron (4) (2). This is incorrect. According to Exodus 4:14–31, where the Lord gives Aaron as a mouthpiece, the brothers were near-contemporaries. If any figure could be identified as Aaron, it would have to be the boy kneeling beside the brazier—but this also seems unlikely.

Martin's date for the picture, about 1660 (2), is too early. A better date, around 1670, is given in the catalogue of the 1958/59 show at The Hague (4), and this agrees with Stechow's dating of the picture around 1668 (3), here accepted.

Bibliography: (1) Maandblad "Het Kind," IX. 1953, p. 287; (2) Martin, *Steen*, 1954, pp. 41–42, pl. 28; (3) Stechow, *Allen Memorial Art Mus. Bull.*, 1958, p. 97; (4) Cat., *Steen*, The Hague, 1958/59, No. 50.

7] THE WORSHIP OF THE GOLDEN CALF*

Fig. 85

Canvas; 70 x 61½ inches; signed in full on the gourd at right.
North Carolina Museum of Art, Raleigh, North Carolina.

Provenance: Sale, Amsterdam, 14 May 1749, No. 15 (Handex); sale, B. Beschey, Antwerp, 1 July 1776, No. 13, to Beschey (HdG); sale, J. F. Beschey, Antwerp, 21 Aug. 1786, No. 33 (HdG); collection, A. M. Vroeg, Mookesherde, around 1926/27 (5); unknown private collection, 1954 (6). It was acquired in 1954 by the Museum in Raleigh.

Exhibition: Leiden, "De Lakenhal," 1926, No. 69.

The Biblical source for the subject is Exodus 32:1–6. Steen was inspired here by Lucas van Leyden's painting of the same subject now in the Rijksmuseum in Amsterdam (Fig. 107). The compositional structure of the two pictures is the same. A strong foreground group surrounds a central couple and extends across the lower part of the canvas like a wall, while in a background clearing the Israelites dance around the Golden Calf raised upon a column. In both cases the man (perhaps a modified self-portrait in the Steen) and woman in the center are set off in a kind of inverted triangle of space (stronger in Steen) by the diagonal *coulisses* in either corner. The reversal of the man and the woman, and also of the background space, suggests that Steen may have known Lucas' picture through a print. However, no known print after the painting exists (see Hollstein, X, p. 240 ff.). The Lucas painting itself was owned by Jacob Wuytiers, perhaps of Amsterdam, before 1679 (7), and there is the possibility that Steen could have known it.

Steen's use of archaic costume elements, particularly the hat of the central woman and the leggings of her companion, seems also to be related to Lucas' picture. The drummer might have stepped out of a late sixteenth-century picture. The boy with the bird at the far left, with his plumed hat and abundant curls, also hints at the earlier century, and may find a counterpart in the half-hidden boy at the far left of Lucas' painting.

Once, Martin called this "a courageous early work" and dated it about 1648 (3). Criticised on this dating (4), he later dated it in the 1670's (6). The latter is surely a more accurate date. Stylistically the work is related to *The Sacrifice of Iphigenia* at the Rijksmuseum dated 1671 (Cat. 74, Fig. 82). Structurally they share the open center, with diagonal stage-wing sides giving the center the shape of an inverted triangle. In painting too they are close. At the beginning of the 1670's, Steen painted his figures with a sparkling clarity and brilliant color.

Bibliography: (1) Cat., *Steen*, Leiden, 1926, No. 69; (2) Bredius, *Steen*, 1927, p. 29; (3) Bredius, *ZfbK*, LXI, 1927/28, p. 330; (4) Stechow, *ZfbK*, LXII, 1928/29, p. 175; (5) Trautscholdt, *T-B*, XXXI, 1937, p. 511; (6) Martin, *Steen*, 1954, p. 57, pl. 65; (7) Cat., Rijksmuseum, Amsterdam, 1956, No. 1452–A2.

7a] THE WORSHIP OF THE GOLDEN CALF

According to Hofstede de Groot, the picture was in the Bryan sale, London, 1864. Research has yielded no further information. Perhaps 7a is identical with 7, since the known history does not conflict; but there is no substantiating proof of the identity.

8] MOSES STRIKING THE ROCK FOR WATER*

Fig. 27

Panel; 21½ x 17½ inches; signed in full at bottom center.
Städelsches Kunstinstitut, Frankfurt-am-Main.

Provenance: Sale, W. Lormier, The Hague, 1763 (HdG) (according to HdG, Lormier purchased the picture from the stock of van Th . . . for 110 florins, but this reference is obscure); sale, Jacobs, Brussels, 24 June 1774, No. 40 (Handex); sale, Hoofman, Haarlem, 1799 (Handex); dealer, George, Paris (HdG); collection, Georg Finger, Frankfurt a/M (HdG). It was sold in 1874 to the Städelsches Kunstinstitut.

The Biblical source for the subject is Genesis 17:1–7. Two of Jacob de Wet's pictures of the subject bear close resemblance to the present painting. One, now in the National Museum in Warsaw, has both the grotto and the rider of Steen (Fig. 31). Also, Moses is elevated above the crowd and is highlighted against the dark rock. The spotlighting quality is similar and the figures, small in their environment, distinctly recall those of Steen. Another picture, sold at Bad Kissingen on 24 Sept. 1955 (No. 137) as a de Wet, shows similar features. Bode suggested de Wet as one of Steen's early teachers in Haarlem (7); and van Gelder strongly supported this position (1). The landscape here has, as Gerson points out, some affinity with those in the mythological scenes of Cuylenburgh (5); and this may also establish an early Utrecht connection. Nevertheless, the close correspondence with the de Wet pictures emphasizes Haarlem and the Rembrandt influence.

Stechow felt that this picture, along with another *Moses Striking the Rock* (Cat. 9, Fig. 88) and *The Worship of the Golden Calf* (Cat. 7, Fig. 85), was a late work (3). The painting should rather be associated with *The Village Wedding* in the Boymans/van Beuningen Museum (HdG 445, Fig. 25) of 1653, and forms with *St. John the Baptist Preaching in the Wilderness* (Cat. 28, Fig. 29) and *The Adoration of the Shepherds* (Cat. 35, Fig. 28) a group of works of the early 1650's under the influence of Rembrandt (1).

Bibliography: (1) Van Gelder, J. G., *O-H*, XLIII, 1926, pp. 205–6; (2) Martin, *ZfbK*, LXI, 1927/28, p. 325ff; (3) Stechow, *ZfbK*, LXII, 1928/29, p. 175; (4) Martin, *Burlington*, LXVII, 1935, pp. 211–12; (5) Gerson, *Kunsthistorische Mededelinging*, III, 1948, p. 53; (6) de Groot, C. W., *Beeld en Woord*, 1952, p. 171; (7) Bode, *Malerschulen*, ed. 1958, p. 123.

9] MOSES STRIKING THE ROCK FOR WATER*

Fig. 88

Canvas; 38 x 40 inches.
Johnson collection, Museum of Art, Philadelphia.

Provenance: Sale, Seger Tierens, The Hague, 28 July 1743, No. 176 (HdG); sale, J. Tak, Soeterwoude, 5 Sept. 1781, No. 18 (HdG); sale, P. N. Quarles van Ufford, Amsterdam, 19 Oct. 1818, No. 50 (HdG); sale, Roothaan, Amsterdam, 29 March 1826, No. 103, bought by De Vries for Count de Robiano (HdG); sale, Robiano, Brussels, 1 May 1837, No. 615 (HdG); dealer, Nieuwenhuys; collection, Prince Demidoff, San Donato; sale, Demidoff, Paris, 18 April 1868 (HdG); sale, Hulst, Paris, 9 May 1892, No. 48 (Handex); collection, Baron Koenigswarter, Vienna (HdG); sale, Koenigswarter, Vienna, July 1893. John G. Johnson acquired the picture in that year. C. Sedelmeyer, the Paris dealer, published it in 1898 as having at one time been in his collection; but at the time of publication of his catalogue the painting belonged to Johnson (1).

The Biblical source for the subject is Genesis 17:1–7. In the catalogue of the Roothaan sale of 1826, the landscape was attributed to Jan Wils. The landscape is not at all in keeping with Wils' style. The explanation may involve a printing error. This picture was followed in the sale by Steen's *John the Baptist Preaching in the Wilderness* (Cat. 28), the landscape of which has been attributed to Wils with some reason.

The picture has until now been reported signed in the center foreground. Recent examination, however, reveals no trace of a signature. The picture was cleaned in 1942; but no record notes the disappearance of the signature at that time.

Almost twice as large as the picture in Frankfurt of the same subject (Cat. 8, Fig. 27), it shows the openness, more even light, and brilliant foreground colors of Steen's later style. The figure of the woman being helped to a drink at the right repeats the major figure in *The Worship of the Golden Calf* (Cat. 7, Fig. 85) and is also reminiscent of Rachel in *Laban Searching for the Idols* (Cat. 4, Fig. 89). All three pictures must have been made about the same time, around 1671. Both Martin and Stechow agree with this late dating (8) (5)—though at one time Martin thought it an early work.

Bibliography: (1) Sedelmeyer, *300 Paintings by Old Masters*, Paris, 1898, No. 194; (2) Valentiner, W. R., Cat. Johnson Collection, 1914, II, pp. 100–101; (3) Antal, *Art in America*, XIII, 1925, pp. 107–16; (4) Martin, *ZfbK*, LXI, 1927/28, p. 330; (5) Stechow, *ZfbK*, LXII, 1928/29, p. 175; (6) Tietze, Hans, *Masterpieces of European Painting in America*, 1939, No. 182; (7) Cat. Johnson Collection, Philadelphia, 1941, No. 509; (8) Martin, *Steen*, 1954, pp. 56–57, pl. 64.

10] SAMSON AND DELILAH*

Fig. 67

Canvas; 26½ x 32¼ inches; signed in full on right-hand corner of step and dated 1668.
Private collection, The Netherlands.

Provenance: Sale, G. Bruyn, Amsterdam, 16 March 1724, No. 7 (HdG); sale, Wynand Coole, Rotterdam, 6 Aug. 1782, No. 65 (HdG); sale, D. de Jongh, Rotterdam, 26 March 1810 (HdG); collection, N. Oosthuyzen, The Hague (HdG); collection, Huldschinsky, Berlin, 1898 (1); sale, Huldschinsky, Berlin, Cassirer-Helbing Galleries, 10-11 May 1928, No. 36; sale, L. van den Bergh, Mak v. Waay, Amsterdam, 5–6 Nov. 1935; dealer, Bachstitz, The Hague, 1938.

During World War II the picture was among those taken by the Germans. Returned to Holland after the war, it went back to Bachstitz and was probably sold when his collection was dissolved upon death in 1951. It then passed through the hands of several other dealers before it was acquired by its present owners.

Exhibitions: Berlin, Kaiser-Friedrich Museum, 1906, No. 32; Amsterdam, Rijksmuseum, "Bijbelse Kunst," 1939, No. 45a; United States (fourteen cities), "Paintings Looted from Holland," 1946/47, No. 44 (organized by the Dutch government).

The Biblical source for the subject is Judges 16:17–21. The picture corresponds in some details to Abraham Koninck's play *The Tragedy of Samson* of 1618, which has often been cited as a possible literary source (5), (8), (7), (10). One of the scenes in the play, where a barber is called to cut the hair of the sleeping Samson, is the same as that represented by Steen (7). The play and picture have a common source in the Biblical narrative where a barber is called to cut the hair of Samson. The motif was used by Rubens in his painting in the Höser collection, which predates the play (Fig. 111). Van Dyck used it again in a painting now at Dulwich College (Fig. 112), indicating an independent pictorial tradition.

One of the rare drawings attributed to Jan Steen has been connected to this picture. In 1937 it belonged to A. Welcker of Amsterdam, who wrote an article showing it to be a study for this painting; he believed the changes between drawing and painting were meant to make the Biblical narrative more convincing and direct (6). Heppner attributed those differences to the influence of theatrical performance (8). Neither argument is convincing. The drawing is singularly unrelated to the painting, and the attribution, which rests heavily upon the connection, is suspect. Van Regteren-Altena in his important article on Steen's drawings does not include the drawing in his discussion (9).

Its explicit style and its date make this painting crucial in the reconstruction of the chronology of Steen's historical pictures. From it a clear idea can be gained of his style in the late 1660's while he was living in Haarlem. The thrusting of the main group forward out of a monochrome background becomes typical of his construction around this time (11).

Bibliography: (1) Sedelmeyer, *300 Paintings by Old Masters*, Paris, 1898, No. 195; (2) Bode, *Sammlung Oscar Huldschinsky*, 1908, pp. 19–20, No. 28; (3) Bredius, *Steen*, 1927, p. 28, pl. 4; (4) Sales Cat., Huldschinsky, Cassirer-Helbing, Berlin, May 10–11, 1928, No. 36; (5) Van Gils, *O-H*, LII, 1935, pp. 130–33; (6) Welcker, *O-H*, LIV, 1937, p. 254; (7) Gudlaugsson, *Ikonographische Studien*, 1938, pp. 66–68; (8) Heppner, *J of W&CI*, III, 1939/40, *passim*; (9) Van Regteren-Altena, *O-H*, LX, 1943, pp. 97–117; (10) de Groot, W. C., *Beeld en Woord*, 1952, pp. 34ff.; (11) Stechow, *Allen Art Museum Bulletin*, XV, 1958, pp. 97ff.; (12) de Jonge, *Jan Steen* (Palet Series), n.d., p. 51.

10a] SAMSON AND DELILAH*

10a is identical with 12; see entry for 12/10a.

10b] SAMSON AND DELILAH

HdG10A*

30 x 36 inches.
Present location unknown.

Sale, G. Vogel, Rotterdam, 3 July 1755, No. 29 (Handex); sale, Rotterdam, 20 July 1768, No. 75 (Handex).

The picture is added in the Handex, where the following descriptive phrase is offered: "Samson dressed in white satin lies in the lap of Delilah, who cuts his hair." A picture on canvas following this description, and of the same dimensions, was in the possession of the London dealer Matthiesen in 1939. The pictures may be the same, but the Matthiesen picture raises some questions of attribution; particularly the landscape background is strange for what must otherwise be a late painting. It may be that the figures of Samson and Delilah are Steen's, and the background the work of another hand. The probability is that the picture should be removed from the catalogue of the authentic pictures. Verification from the original is necessary.

11] SAMSON MOCKED BY THE PHILISTINES*

Removed from the Catalogue; see Addendum 1.

12/10a] SAMSON MOCKED BY THE PHILISTINES*

Fig. 63

Canvas; 53 x 79 inches; signed in full in the lower right corner.
Wallraf-Richartz Museum, Cologne.

Provenance: Sale, J. van Hoek, Amsterdam, 1719 (HdG); sale, anonymous, 1825 (HdG); collection, J. Taylor, London, 1856 (HdG); sale, London, 1863 (HdG 10a); sale, C. J. Nieuwenhuys, London, 17 July 1886, No. 100 (HdG); sale, D. Sellar, Paris, 6 June 1889, No. 71 (HdG); sale, London, 17 March 1894, No. 124 (HdG). It was presented to the Wallraf-Richartz Museum in that same year by the "Kölner Kunstfreunde."

Exhibition: Leiden, "De Lakenhal," Jan Steen Tentoonstelling, 1926, No. 14.

The Biblical source for the subject is Judges 16:19–21. Like Cat. 10 this picture has also been connected with contemporary Biblical drama. Several details seem to support the contention. Heppner has pointed to the standard-bearer in the left background as an indication of the connection of this painting with the Rederijkers' guild (5). The drunken comical soldier in the right background has his source in "Capitano" from Commedia del' Arte, also known in Holland at that time. Capitano became the burlesque of the long traditional enemy, the Spanish soldier (6).

Over six feet in length, this is one of Steen's largest pictures. It displays magnificently his love of comically exaggerated gesture and expression. This penchant, as C. W. de Groot comments, connects Steen with the baroque aesthetics of the direct externalization of emotion (7).

The painting is related in style to the *Samson and Delilah* of 1668 (Cat. 10, Fig. 67) and must have been made about that year.

Bibliography: (1) Bredius, *Steen*, 1927, pp. 28–29, pl. 5; (2) Schmidt-Degener and Van Gelder, *Steen*, 1927, p. 17; (3) Van Gils, *O-H*, LII, 1935, pp. 130–33; (4) Gudlaugsson, *Ikonographische Studien*, 1938, p. 32; (5) Heppner, *J of W&CI*, III, 1939/40, p. 41; (6) Gudlaugsson, *De Komedianten*, 1945, p. 34; (7) de Groot, C. W., *Beeld en Woord*, 1952, pp. 169–70; (8) Martin, *Steen*, 1954, p. 70, pl. 80; (9) Cat., Wallraf-Richartz Museum, Cologne, 1959, No. 1024; (10) de Jonge, *Steen* (Palet Series), n.d., p. 51.

12a] SAMSON AND DELILAH

HdG12A*

Panel; 17 x 14 inches.

This entry is added in the Handex. Sale: G. J. Drummond *et al.*, London, 22 Dec. 1919, No. 108. A painting of the same subject measuring 17¼ x 14 inches on panel was in the Pearson sale, 6 Dec. 1912, Christies, London, No. 101. The pictures might be the same. The given dimensions do not coincide with those of any other listed painting of the same subject.

13] DAVID RETURNING VICTORIOUS

Fig. 83

Canvas; 43 x 63½ inches; fully signed on the bottom step at the left, and dated 1671.
Kronborg Castle, Elsinore, Denmark; property of the Royal Museum of Fine Arts, Copenhagen.

Provenance: Sale, J. Hoogenbergh, Amsterdam, 10 April 1743, No. 41 (HdG); sale, Amsterdam, 8 June 1763, No. 41 (HdG); sale, Amsterdam, 14 Aug. 1793, No. 115 (Handex); sale, Maria Theresia Wittebol and Labistraten, Antwerp, 19 June 1804, No. 163 (HdG). The painting was reported to have been in the collection, Werbrouck, Antwerp (HdG), but was not part of the sale on 12 Sept. 1859 (HdG). Purchased in 1809 from the West collection for the Danish Royal Collection at Copenhagen.

The narrative fuses elements from I Samuel: 17 and 18. David's victory over Goliath occurs in Chapter 17; from Chapter 18 comes his joyous welcome after a subsequent victory over the host of the Philistines and mention of Saul's daughter Michal. The inscription on the pedestal reads:

Soli Deo gloria
T heeft Godt behaeght
Dat Davit t heeft gwaeght
Als hij Goliat verslogh
En Saul in t hart wrogh
Victorieus hij treet voruyt
Hier verwelkomt van sijn bruyt.

Soli Deo gloria
It pleases God
That David dared
To slay Goliath
And hurt Saul to the heart
Victorious he steps forth
Here welcomed by his bride.

The source of this inscription, whether by Steen or another hand, is unknown (5).

The similarities of the subject matter to a play *David ende Goliat* written by Job van der Wael in 1619 for the Schiedam guild of Rederijkers led Van Gils to postulate a direct dependency (2). He used details such as the damp and smoky atmosphere and the red dress and hair of the woman playing the lute (a reference to "Het Rood Roosjen," the blazon of the Schiedam group) to support his contention, with which Heppner concurs (3). Neither the correspondence with the subject matter which occurs in earlier painting nor the details cited are enough, however, to establish convincingly a direct link between Steen's picture and the play.

This picture, as well as *The Sacrifice of Iphigenia* (Cat. 74, Fig. 82), also of 1671, indicates a shift in Steen's style in the early 1670's. The exaggerated drama with its deep full color abates in favor of a delicacy of line, rhythm, and lighter color.

The picture shows a jointing or fold about ten inches from the top and five inches from the bottom. Whether this indicates an addition or repair is not known to the author.

Bibliography: (1) Bredius, *Steen*, 1927, p. 31, pl. 6; (2) Van Gils, *O-H*, LII, 1935, pp. 130–33; (3) Heppner, *J of W&CI*, III, 1939/40, p. 40; (4) Cat., Royal Museum of Fine Arts, Copenhagen, 1951, No. 682; (5) W. C. de Groot, *Beeld en Woord*, 1952, p. 35; (6) Martin, *Steen*, 1954, pp. 56 and 71; (7) de Jonge, *Steen* (Palet Series), n.d., p. 55.

14] BATHSEBA RECEIVING DAVID'S LETTER

Fig. 70

Panel; 15 x 13 inches; signed in full at bottom left-hand corner.
Present location unknown.

Provenance: Sale, J. van Zaanen, The Hague, 16 Nov. 1767, No. 16 (HdG); collection, M. van Slingelandt, The Hague (HdG); collection, Griffier Fagel; sale, Fagel, London, Coxe, Burrel, & Foster, 22 May 1801 (HdG); collection, Marquis of Bute, London, 1884 (HdG). When it left the Bute collection is unknown. Dealer, Galerie Internationale, The Hague, 1938 (RKHD); collection, Nathan Katz; sale, Katz, Paris, Rheims, 7 Dec. 1950, No. 58.

Exhibition: London, Dowdeswell Gallery, "Jan Steen," 1909, No. 10.

The picture was sold as a pair with *Ascanius and Lucilla* (HdG) 70/408—see Add. 14, Fig. 110) as early as 1767. Their sizes are the same. They remained together through the nineteenth century. The Marquis of Bute owned them both (2); they were separated while in that collection. It is difficult to say whether the pictures were in fact painted as pendants. Though the subjects seem disparate, one coming from contemporary drama (see (5), where Bredero's play *Lucelle*, from which Steen took his subject, is described) and the other from the Old Testament, the love theme unites them, and their structure permits an interpretation as pendants—i.e., the table, the curtains, the figural arrangement.

One distressing observation if they are taken as pendants is the difference in quality. Judging from photographs, *Ascanius and Lucilla* is a magnificent Steen in every detail; *Bathseba* is weak in several areas, particularly in the painting of the old woman and the landscape. Perhaps it was this weakness that led van den Marck to declare it a copy (Handex).

The Biblical source for the subject is II Samuel 11:2–4. Through the arched window King David can be seen upon a terrace watching the scene. If not for this, the scene could be mistaken for one of the many love-letter scenes so popular in seventeenth-century Holland. The procuress is a familiar figure in Dutch painting. The letter begins "*Lieve minne—*," "sweet love—" (3).

Stylistically the painting should be placed in the late 1660's. It is close to *Samson and Delilah* of 1668 (Cat. 10, Fig. 67).

Bibliography: (1) W. Buchanan, *Memoirs of Painting*, 1824, Vol. I, p. 304, No. 45; (2) Richter, *Catalogue of the Collection of the Marquis of Bute,*

1884, No. 161; (3) Martin, *L'art flamand et hollandais*, XII, 1909, p. 156; (4) Schmidt-Degener and Van Gelder, *Steen*, 1927, pp. 17–18; (5) Gudlaugsson, *Ikonographische Studien*, 1938, pp. 72–73.

14a/814a] BATHSEBA WITH
HdG14A* DAVID'S LETTER*

Fig. 90
Canvas; 25¾ x 21 inches; signed in full at top left corner.
Wetzlar collection, Amsterdam.

Provenance: Sale, Paris, 22 March 1845, No. 37 (Handex); sale, Ulrich, Vienna, Wawra, 13 March 1911 (FRL); collection, W. Duschnitz, Vienna; on loan to the Frans Hals Museum (1920/26) from Duschnitz; collection, van Diemen, Berlin, 1927 (FRL). After that it belonged to C. Thierling, Berlin, and H. Stokvis of Brussels, 1939 (FRL) and to a number of dealers: Schaeffer, N.Y.; Douwes, Amsterdam; Brod, London (FRL). Wetzlar bought it from Brod in 1958.

Exhibitions: Leiden, "De Lakenhal," Jan Steen Tentoonstelling, 1926, No. 38; Amsterdam, Rijksmuseum, Bijbelse Kunst, 1939, No. 54a.

The Biblical source for the subject is II Samuel 11:2–4. Here, as in his other paintings of Bathseba (Cat. 14, 15, Figs. 70 and 34) Steen only hints at the Biblical subject. The inscription on the letter is not entirely legible: Scho . . . Bersc (*or* Berse). . . . Still, it is clear that it is addressed to Bathseba. In this case Steen has not included David in the garden—an omission which disguises the subject even more than usual.

Bredius, who praised Steen's handling of the satin dress, suggested that it might be a portrait of Steen's second wife, the widow Maria van Egmont, whom he married in 1673 (2). Though the date is quite possible for the picture, there is no evidence that this is a portrait and one might wonder why he would choose to depict a new wife in such a guise.

Bibliography: (1) Cat., Steen, Leiden, 1926, No. 38; (2) Bredius, *Steen*, 1927, p. 68, pl. 73; (3) Cat., Bijbelse Kunst, Amsterdam, 1939, No. 54a.

14b/348*]** BATHSEBA RECEIVING
Fig. 71 DAVID'S LETTER*

Canvas; 13 x 11½ inches; signed on the wall at the middle.
Virginia Museum of Fine Arts, Richmond, Va.

Provenance: Sale, de Beurmonville, Paris, 21 May 1883, No. 96 (HdG). The dealer S. Nystad of The Hague had the picture around 1960. It was purchased for the Virginia Museum of Fine Arts in 1964.

The Biblical source for the subject is II Samuel 11:2–4. Hofstede de Groot knew the picture only from the de Beurmonville sale and identified it as a genre subject—a *Love-Letter at the Toilet*. The Museum has it catalogued simply as "The Letter." Though the Biblical subject is not identified by the address of the letter as in Cat. 14a (Fig. 90) and 15 (Fig. 34) or by the presence of David as in Cat. 14 (Fig. 70), the iconographic type along with the generalized historical dress of Bathseba and the exterior towers establish the Biblical allusion and allow its inclusion in the catalogue. Along with Cat. 14 (Fig. 70) it should be placed around 1668.

Bibliography: European Art in the Virginia Museum of Fine Arts, 1966, No. 94, p. 59.

15] BATHSEBA RECEIVING
Fig. 34 DAVID'S LETTER*

Panel; 16½ x 13 inches; signed in full on the pediment above the door in the background.
Private collection, Sussex, England.

Provenance: Sale, J. Enschede, Haarlem, 30 May 1786, No. 16 (HdG); sale, P. Lyonet, Amsterdam, 11 April 1791, No. 232 (Handex); sale, B. de Bosch, Amsterdam, 3 Nov. 1840, No. 102 (HdG) (in that sale it was described as a canvas "by or after" Jan Steen); sale, Van Saceghem, Brussels, 2 June 1851, No. 60 (Handex); sale, Theodor Patureau, Paris, 20 April 1857, No. 34 (Handex); collection, Lord Powerscourt at Powerscourt (HdG); collection, Liechtenstein, Vienna, 1908 (HdG); collection, Murat, Paris, 1911; dealer, Knoedler & Company, New York City, 1926 (exhib. cat.); dealer, Colnaghi, London, 1935 (1); collection, E. Nicolas, Paris, 1939 (3). This collection was bought by E. Speelman the London dealer, and from there the work entered a private collection in Sussex.

Exhibitions: London, Burlington House, Winter Exhibition, Old Masters, 1878 (No. 123, as "Le billet-doux"); Paris, Murat Collection, 1911, No. 157; New York, Knoedler Galleries, Loan Exhibition of Dutch Masters of the Seventeenth Century, 1925, No. 21.

The Biblical source for the subject is II Samuel 11:2–4. Dressed in gold, red, and white satin, Bathseba here is elegant and vain. The inscription reads: *Alderschonte Barsabe—omdat*; Most beautiful Bathseba—because. In the garden behind can be seen David dressed in red. In this painting Steen has brought history and genre very close together. It is not surprising that it was exhibited at one time simply as "Le billet-doux." Were it not for the inscription on the note, the Biblical reference might be completely missed.

The motif may have its source in theatrical comedy. Gudlaugsson reproduces a fragment of a wall painting taken from the "Narrentreppe" which repeats the central motif of Steen's picture, save that the card has only a heart on it and no message (2). He points out, however, that the theme of the young woman and the old servant dame (sometimes as procuress) has a long history in Dutch painting, and it is more likely that in this case Steen drew his idea from that tradition.

The painting dates from about 1659/60, and must be compared to *The Music Lesson* in the National Gallery at London (HdG 409, Fig. 35), the date of which most certainly should be read as 1659 (4).

Bibliography: (1) Trautscholdt, E., "Steen," *T-B*, XXXI, 1937, p. 511; (2) Gudlaugsson, *De Komedianten*, 1945, p. 66, pl. 66; (3) Martin, *Steen*, 1954, p. 49; (4) Maclaren, *The Dutch School*, Cat. National Gallery, London, 1960, No. 856; (5) Kunoth-Leifels, *Bathseba im Bade*, 1962, pp. 73–74.

15a*] BATHSEBA

Canvas.

This picture is listed in the Handex. There is a single sales reference: J. H. G. van Dosterdijk *et al.*, Amsterdam, 8 Oct. 1800, No. 79; sold to Dirk Versteeg for 24 florins. It might be identical with 14a or 14b.

16] TAMAR AND AMNON*

Fig. 72

Panel; 25½ x 32 inches; signed in full at the lower left.
Wallraf-Richartz Museum, Cologne.

Provenance: Sale, J. Pompe van Meerdervoort-Soeterwoude, 19 May 1750, No. 25 (Handex); sale, J. H. van Heemskerck, The Hague, 29 March 1770 (HdG); sale, Etienne Le Roy, Brussels, 1848, No. 190 (HdG); sale, Matthieu Neven, Cologne, 17 March 1895 (described as a "Stratonice and Antiochus") (HdG); collection, Carstanjen, Berlin, 1908 (HdG). That collection was on long-term loan in the Wallraf-Richartz Museum from 1928 until 1936, when the entire collection was purchased by the Museum.

Exhibition: Dusseldorf, Art History, 1904, No. 383.

The Biblical story from II Samuel 13:1–17 is not frequently treated. Amnon, one of the sons of King David, desired Tamar, his virgin half-sister and sister of Absalom. By feigning sickness, he brought her to his chambers and took her by force, after which his desire turned to hate and he had her dismissed by a servant. Absalom avenged his sister's honor by killing Amnon (II Samuel 13:29).

The story was the subject of a play by J. C. Mayvogel, *De Verleiding van Thamar of Amnon's Verleidende Liefde*, written in 1642 for the rhetoricians' guild at Hoorn. The same piece was played in 1659 in Amsterdam (1) (3). Little evidence can be adduced to show Steen's actual dependence upon either play or performance, though the servant is dressed in a type of theatrical costume which has its source in the sixteenth century.

The picture can be placed at the very end of the 1660's. It is close in style to *Samson and Delilah* of 1668 (Cat. 10, Fig. 67) and *The Merry Company* of 1668 in the Rijksmuseum (HdG 88).

Bibliography: (1) Heppner, *J of W&CI*, III, 1939/40, p. 43; (2) Gudlaugsson, *Ikonographische Studien*, 1938, pp. 16–17; (3) de Groot, W. C., *Beeld en Woord*, 1952, p. 35; (4) Cat., Wallraf-Richartz Museum, Cologne, 1959, No. 2536.

16a] THE IDOLATRY OF SOLOMON

HdG16A*

Removed from the Catalogue. See Addendum 2.

17] ESTHER BEFORE AHASUERUS

Fig. 73

Panel; 42 x 33 inches; signed in full on the throne of Ahasuerus.
The Hermitage, Leningrad.

Provenance: Sale, P. van Dorp, Leiden, 16 Oct. 1760, No. 5 (HdG); sale, Hendrik Verschuuring, The Hague, 17 Sept. 1770, No. 162 (HdG). The later history of this picture before it entered the state collection is unknown to this researcher.

The Biblical source for this episode is Esther 8:1–3. In general the story of Esther's saving of the Jews from the treachery of Haman was very popular in Holland during the seventeenth century. Steen himself painted it numerous times (see the following entries) and it was the subject of at least two seventeenth-century Dutch plays: Nicolaes Fonteyn's *Esther, or The Picture of Obedience* of 1638, and Joannes Serwouter's *Hester, or The Deliverance of the Jews*, first published in 1659 with numerous later editions. The latter (in the 1659 edition) is introduced by an engraved frontispiece, perhaps by Pieter Quast (Fig. 114), which Heppner found similar to Steen's painting, and used as evidence of Steen's theatrical dependence (1). It would seem more probable, however, that Steen and Quast(?) shared a common iconographic tradition stemming from the Biblical narrative, which tells how Esther swooned before the king. A drawing by Engelbrechts in the Albertina and Lucas van Leyden's engraving of 1518 (Fig. 115) use the same motif, indicating that the tradition predates seventeenth-century plays and engravings. The Lucas engraving is much closer in feeling to the Steen than is the Quast(?).

Van Westrheene and Kuznetsov were both incorrect in associating the "scholar-figure" in the foreground with Haman (5). According to the Biblical narrative, Haman was already dead and Mordecai in a position of trust when Esther came to plead that the Jews be freed from Haman's evil laws (Esther 8:1–3). The old man is clearly Mordecai, and his benevolence is enough to so identify him. This figure, highly refined by Steen, probably has its source in the scholar-pieces of Rembrandt such as *St. Jerome in a Dark Study* etching (4).

Kuznetsov dates the picture 1669/70, which, judging from a photograph, seems correct (5). It is similar in style to other narrative paintings from the end of the 1660's—i.e., *Samson and Delilah* of 1668 (Fig. 67, Cat. 10) and *Antony and Cleopatra* of 1667 (Cat. 86, Fig. 56).

Bibliography: (1) Heppner, *J of W&CI*, III, 1939/40, pp. 41–42; (2) Gudlaugsson, *De Komedianten*, 1945, pp. 51–52; (3) de Groot, *Beeld en Woord*, 1952, p. 35; (4) Münz, *Etchings*, 1952, No. 247; (5) Kuznetsov, Ezhegodnik Akademiia nouk SSSR, Institut Istorii Iskusstv, 1957, pp. 406–7; (6) Cat., The Hermitage, Leningrad, 1958, No. 878; (7) Bulletin, Cleveland Museum of Art, LII, 1965, No. 4, p. 98.

18] THE WRATH OF AHASUERUS*

Fig. 59

Canvas; 50½ x 65½ inches; signed in full at the lower left-hand corner.
The Barber Institute of Fine Arts, Birmingham University, Birmingham, England.

Provenance: Sale, R. Pickfatt, Rotterdam, 12 April 1736, No. 44 (HdG); collection, Hankey, Beaulieu, Hastings (HdG). In 1899 it was in the possession of the Paris dealer C. Sedelmeyer (1), who sold it to the collector Rudolf Kann. Kann's collection was bought by Duveen in 1907, after which the picture passed to the dealers F. Kleinberger (1926) and K. Bachstitz (1929/39). It was purchased from Bachstitz for the Barber Institute in 1939 (13).

Exhibitions: Leiden, Jan Steen Tentoonstelling, "De Lakenhal," 1926, No. 48; London, Dutch Art, Royal Academy, 1929, No. 208; Amsterdam, Oude Kunst, 1929, No. 139; London, Bachstitz Gallery Exhibition, Knoedler House, 1938, No. 29; Sheffield, Dutch Exhibition, Graves Art Gallery, 1956, No. 49; The Hague, Jan Steen Tentoonstelling, Mauritshuis, 1958/59, No. 49.

Narratively this picture precedes 17. Its Biblical source is Esther 7:1–7. Haman is accused of treachery against the Jews. He shrinks from the wrath of the glaring Ahasuerus. Heppner feels that the picture may illustrate lines taken from Joannes Serwouter's play *Hester, or The Deliverance of the Jews* of 1659:

> —Shame on thee, Haman, now curse the hour of thy birth.
> —Where shall I hide myself? I dare not look upon the face of the King. (12)

As in other cases of theatrical parallels, there is an equally strong tradition in painting which seems to indicate a common source rather than a direct dependency (see Cat. 17). The picture in its theatrical orientalism is closely related to Rembrandt's early work, most strongly to the controversial painting of the same subject in the Museum at Raleigh, North Carolina (B. 631) (Fig. 117) and to *Belshazzar's Feast* in London (B. 497) (Fig. 58).

Steen has been severely criticized for this picture. Schmidt-Degener thought it beyond the scope of his power (7), and C. W. de Groot felt that he lost himself in details like the still-life falling from the table, and that the whole was like a children's Bible story (14). Steen is certainly at his most bombastic here, but the exaggeration is conscious. By it he achieves the sense of the ridiculous which is part of his historical vision.

The picture must have been made around 1668. It is stylistically close to *Samson and Delilah* of that year (Cat. 10, Fig. 67). It would seem that in his mature years he turned to Rembrandt's work of the 1630's for dramatic inspiration.

Bibliography: (1) Sedelmeyer, *100 Paintings*, 1899, No. 59; (2) Bode, *Die Gemälde-Galerie des Herrn Rudolf Kann*, 1900, p. xii, pl. 19; (3) Michel, G., *GdBA*, XXV, 1901, pp. 292–93; (4) Marquillier, *Les Arts*, II, 1903, pp. 24–25; (5) Bode, *Catalogue of the Rudolf Kann Collection*, 1907, I, p. 85, pl. 84; (6) Bredius, *Steen*, 1927, p. 29; (7) Schmidt-Degener and Van Gelder, *Steen*, 1927, pp. 17, 15, pl. xxi; (8) Cat., Exhibition of Dutch Art, London, 1929, pp. 129–30; (9) Hobson, *Country Life*, LXV, 1929, p. 244; (10) Martin, *Bulletin of the Bachstitz Gallery*, 1935, pp. 34–35; (11) Martin, *De Hollandsche Schilderkunst*, II, 1936, pp. 258–60; (12) Heppner, *J of W&CI*, III,

1939/40, p. 42; (13) Cat., Barber Institute, Birmingham, 1952, pp. 102–3; (14) de Groot, *Beeld en Woord*, 1952, p. 168; (15) Martin, *Steen*, 1954, pp. 55–56; (16) Cat., Steen, The Hague, 1958/59, No. 49; (17) de Jonge, *Steen* (Palet Series), n.d., pp. 51, 54.

19] THE WRATH OF AHASUERUS

Fig. 75

Canvas; 33 x 40 inches, signed on the column at the right.
Present location unknown.

Provenance: Sale (probable), Goldsmith, Paris, 27 Feb. 1869, No. 74 (HdG); collection, Prince Potocki, Paris, 1908 (HdG). In 1927 Bredius reported it as still being in that collection (1). Sale, Vienna, Dorotheum, 12 Sept. 1957. Sale, London, Christies, 16–17 July 1970, No. 177; sale, Amsterdam, Brandt, 14 Nov. 1972, No. 13.

The Biblical source of the subject is Esther 7:1–7. For a discussion of the subject and its sources, see Cat. 18.

According to certificates by Friedlaender and Bode, both of August 1912, the picture was in good condition and an authentic work. The certificates were reprinted in the sales catalogue of 1957 and in that of the Brandt sale of 1972. The original certificates have been lost (2). The existence of another, slightly smaller, version of the painting now in Cleveland (Cat 19a, Fig. 74) casts some doubt upon the authenticity of the present picture. The major compositional differences between the two are the position of Haman and presence (in the Cleveland picture) of the jester at the right.

Though the Cleveland picture is the stronger of the two, this variant, judging from a good photograph, is close enough in treatment particularly of the main figures to be identified as a repetition, possibly by Steen himself. Bredius, who knew both pictures, did declare the present one a repetition (1). Any final conclusion as to the authenticity of the picture, however, must await inspection of the original.

Bibliography: (1) Bredius, *Steen*, 1927, p. 29; (2) Sales Cat., Amsterdam, Brandt, 14 Nov. 1972, No. 13.

19a]** THE WRATH OF AHASUERUS*

Fig. 74

Canvas; 27 x 36 inches.
Museum of Art, Cleveland.

Provenance: The early history of this picture is unknown. It might be identical with the one in the Goldsmith sale, Paris, 27 Feb. 1869 mentioned under Cat. 19. It might also be identical with Nos. 20a, 20b, or 21, but no proof exists. Dealer, Douwes, Amsterdam, prior to 1926; collection, Dreesman, Amsterdam, 1926–1960; sale, Dreesman, Muller, Amsterdam, 22–25 March 1960; dealer, Douwes, Amsterdam, 1960.

Exhibitions: Leiden, Jan Steen Tentoonstelling, "De Lakenhal," 1926, No. 37; Amsterdam, Tentoonstelling, van oude kunst . . . van Handelaren, Rijksmuseum, 1929, No. 140; Amsterdam, Bijbelse Kunst, Rijksmuseum, 1939, No. 60f; Amsterdam, Jubileum Tentoonstelling Kunsthandel Gebr. Douwes, 1955, No. 59; Tel-Aviv, "Holland's Golden Age," Museum, 1959, No. 106.

The Biblical source for the subject is Esther 7:1–7. For a discussion of the subject and its sources see Cat. 18.

The catalogue of the Leiden exhibition of 1926 lists this picture as HdG 19 with a question mark (1). Trautscholdt made it a separate entry: 19a (4). The picture is probably the original of Cat. 19 which may be a repetition by Steen himself. (See Cat. entry and Fig. 75.) The major compositional differences are the position of Haman and the presence of the jester at the right in the present picture.

Bredius knew both pictures and rightly declared this version the better of the two (2). He also reported the picture signed, but no trace of a signature can be found (7).

The main figures around the table are light in tone—blues and pinks, purples—variegated and changing as in silk. From the foreground the colors deepen step by step so the main figures stand out against a deep red-brown monochrome. This kind of coloring is found in the late 1660's. The picture is most closely related to *Esther Before Ahasuerus* in the Hermitage (Cat. 17, Fig. 73) and must be of similar date, about 1668.

Bibliography: (1) Cat., Steen, Leiden, 1926, No. 37; (2) Bredius, *Steen*, 1927, p. 29, pl. 7; (3) Cat., Tentoonstelling van oude kunst, Amsterdam, 1929, No. 140; (4) Trautscholdt, "Steen," *T-B*, 1937, p. 511; (5) Cat., Bijbelse Kunst, Amsterdam, 1939, No. 60f; (6) Cat., Jubileum Tentoonstelling Kunsthandel Gebr. Douwes, Amsterdam, 1955, No. 59; (6) Sales Cat., Dreesman, Muller, Amsterdam, 22–25 March 1960; (7) Bulletin, Cleveland Museum of Art, LII, 1965, No. 4, pp. 94–100.

20] THE WRATH OF AHASUERUS

Fig. 76

Panel; 16½ x 19½ inches; signed with monogram J.S.
Private collection, England.

Provenance: Sale, Rotterdam, 14 May 1831, No. 175 (Handex); sale, Amsterdam, 6 May 1845, No. 126 (HdG); sale, Amsterdam, 23 Aug. 1850, No. 70 (HdG); sale, Rotterdam, 14 May 1851, No. 175 (HdG); collection, J. S. Bruyn, Rotterdam, 1856 (W 38); collection, J. M. Ulrich, Berlin, 1913 (Handex); collection, J. M. Hudig, Rotterdam, 1917 (Handex). The dealer Hageraats of The Hague bought it in an Amsterdam sale on 11 Dec. 1923, No. 508 (Handex). Collection, Carl Thürling, Amsterdam, about 1930 (Handex); collection, Plietzsch, Berlin, 1939 (Handex); dealer, Goudstikker, Amsterdam, about 1940. The picture was sold with a certificate of authenticity from Walther Bernt on 22 July 1967 in Munich (3). Subsequently it was in the collection of Mr. and Mrs. Eugene Ferkauf, New York. It was sold from that collection at Christies on 7 July 1972, No. 95, to the London dealer, Alan Jacobs, and from there passed to its present owner.

Exhibitions: Rotterdam, 1917 (Handex); London, Winter Exhibition of Fine XVIIth Century Dutch and Flemish Old Masters, A. Jacobs, 1972.

The Biblical source for the subject is Esther 7:1–7. For a discussion of the subject and its sources see Cat. 18.

In the general composition this picture recalls the previous listed work (Cat. 19a, Fig. 74). It is, however, less excited—which in this case may indicate an earlier, rather than later, date. Comparison of the two shows in Cat. 19a the table shifted to the left and a servant figure added to the foreground. The composition (again in comparison with 19a) seems weak. The table is awkwardly low and unconvincing in depth. Some of the same spatial confusion is found in the relationship between the two servant figures at the left. The elaborate still life in the right foreground, for all that it appears well painted, is troublesome as a solution to a corner problem and weakens the dramatic structure of the picture. Some of the difficulties in the picture may be accounted for by its small size. There is a great deal of Steen in this painting (the types are clearly his) but the tendency of the present writer is to consider it a close version of the subject rather than an original by Steen. Such a conclusion, however, must await examination of the original.

According to the Handex, a copy on canvas (32½ x 39 inches) was sold at a London dealer's in 1919 (see Cat. 21a).

Bibliography: (1) Trautscholdt, "Steen," *T-B*, 1937, p. 511; (2) Bulletin, Cleveland Museum of Art, LII, 1965, p. 98; (3) Sales Cat., London, Christies, 7 July 1972, No. 95.

20a] to 23] ESTHER AND AHASUERUS

Sale, Amsterdam, 17 Sept. 1727, No. 16 (HdG). There is no further information on this picture. The reference might belong to another listed picture of the subject.

20b] ESTHER AND AHASUERUS

Sale, Willem Six, Amsterdam, 12 May 1734, No. 125 (HdG). There is no further information on this picture. The reference might belong to another listed picture of the subject.

21] ESTHER, AHASUERUS, AND HAMAN

Sale, D. Reus, Amsterdam, 24 May 1752, No. 24 (HdG). There is no further information on this picture. The reference might belong to another listed picture of the subject.

21a*] ESTHER, AHASUERUS, AND HAMAN

Canvas; 32 x 39 inches.
Sale, J. Vliet, Amsterdam, 12 Oct. 1774, No. 198 (Handex). Added by the Handex, 21a is possibly the copy of 20 sold in London in 1919 (see Cat. 20), but there is no proof of that identity. The measurements suggest that it may possibly be identical also with 19.

21b*] ESTHER, AHASUERUS, AND HAMAN

Canvas; 30½ x 31 inches.
Dealer, O. Mündler (Handex); sale, Charles Sedelmeyer's, Vienna, 20 Dec. 1872, No. 150 (Handex). This number was added by the Handex. There is no further information on the picture. The reference might belong to another listed picture of the subject.

22] HAMAN AND MORDECAI

Sale, C. Wittert van Valkenburg, Rotterdam, 11 April 1731, No. 60 (HdG). There is no further information on this picture.

22a*] ESTHER, AHASUERUS, AND HAMAN

14½ x 12½ inches.
Sale, J. M. Cok, Amsterdam, 16 Dec. 1771, No. 173 (Handex). There is no other information available on this picture. The reference might belong to another listed picture of this subject.

22b*] ESTHER, AHASUERUS, AND HAMAN

Sale, S. van der Stel, Amsterdam, 25 Sept. 1781, No.

150 (Handex). There is no other information on this picture. The reference might belong to another listed picture of this subject.

23] **TOBIAS PRAYING**

Van Haeften sale, Leiden, 15 June 1764, No. 20 (HdG, Handex). Hofstede de Groot adds only that it is a small picture.

24] **TOBIAS HEALING HIS FATHER**

Canvas; 28½ x 32½ inches.
Destroyed.

The Biblical source for the subject is Tobit 11:15.

The picture was destroyed by fire at the Boymans Museum in 1864. The 1811 catalogue of the Boymans collection lists it as attributed to Gerard Dou (1)—an attribution tentatively supported by Bürger-Thoré when he saw it around 1860:

> Mais il n'a pas été heureux dans sa tentative à la Gerard Dou, avec son combat de lumières factices—Le tableau est assez grand, pres d'un metre en largeur; une douzaine de personages,—sans comter l'ange.

In the first catalogue of the Museum of 1849 the picture was given to Steen. Van Westrheene accepted this attribution, believing it to be an early work.

The following description is taken from Hofstede de Groot, which he in turn took with little change from van Westrheene:

> The young Tobias is completing the operation. He wears an Oriental costume, while the other personages wear the Dutch costumes of the time. His mother holds a candlestick in her left hand; with her right she grasps the hand of old Tobias to give him courage. Beside her stands the angel. Two old people and children look on. In the left background are three figures beside the fire. The scene is illumined by two lamps. The mingled sympathy and curiosity of the spectators are well suggested. The angel's figure is unusually large, for Jan Steen.

This last line is misleading. Van Westrheene says: "la figure de l'ange est empreinte de tant de dignité qu'on se sent presque étonné de rencontrer ce degré d'élévation sous le pinceau de l'artiste." He adds that the hesitation in the brushstroke and the confusing effect of the light indicate an early work. J. G. van Gelder accepted this conclusion, dating the picture 1644/46 and using it with others in an attempt to establish an early style influenced by Rembrandt (6). Van Gelder also points out that both Rembrandt and Dou (4) painted the subject in a similar way. In particular the Rembrandt, which originally was larger and had five more figures, shows Anna holding tightly the hands of the suffering Tobias (B. 502). Though that picture has been lost, Steen's dependency upon it is a strong possibility.

Bibliography: (1) Cat., Boymans Collection, 1811, No. 29; (2) Cat., Boymans, Rotterdam, 1849, No. 256; (3) Bürger-Thoré, *Musée de la Hollande*, II, 1860, p. 267; (4) Hofstede de Groot, "Dou," *Catalogue Raisonné*, 1908, I, No. 2; (5) Haverkorn van Rijsewijk, *Het Museum-Boymans te Rotterdam*, 1909, pp. 82–83; (6) Van Gelder, *O-H*, XLIII, 1926, p. 208; (7) Bredius, *Steen*, 1927, p. 34; (8) Van Harderwijk, *Kunstkronijk*, XI, 1950, pp. 79–80.

25/487] **THE MARRIAGE OF TOBIAS AND SARAH***
Fig. 86

Canvas; 41 x 50 inches; signed on base of table at the lower right.
M. H. de Young Memorial Museum, San Francisco.

Provenance: Sale, Westerhof, Amsterdam, 16 May 1781, No. 53 (HdG); collection, Hoofman, The Hague and Haarlem, 1781–1842 (Sm Supp No. 73); after the death of Mme. Hoofman sometime before 1856 (the date of Van Westrheene's catalogue) it was sold by Quarles van Ufford to the dealer M. Nieuwenhuys (W 214 bis); collection, Duc de Morny, Paris, 1863; sale, de Morny, Paris, 31 May 1865, No. 78 (2); collection, Princess Murat. It remained in the Murat family until 1961, when it was sold as part of their collection at Palais Galliéra—at which time the de Young Society bought this picture as a gift for the Museum.

Numbers 25 and 487 (*The Marriage Contract*) are identical. It is also related to 457, likewise called *The Marriage Contract* (Cat. 25a/457, Fig. 66). Both represent the marriage between Tobias and Sarah (3). The story comes from the Book of Tobit, 7:11–15.

Sarah, the cousin of the young Tobias, had taken seven husbands and each had perished on the wedding night before they had lain with her. Raphael, Tobias' guardian angel, whom we see behind the couple, taught him how to exorcise the jealous devil who loved Sarah, making it flee "into the uppermost parts of Egypt" and to bondage. Tobias gets Sarah, and half the family's wealth as dowry, and fulfills a prophecy of his own marriage.

The story of Tobias was popular in the seventeenth century, possibly because of its moralistic overtones. Mention of it is found in Jacob Cats' *Trou-Ringh* of 1637 (3) (6). It was also the subject of a play by Elizabeth Hartloop, *Tobias*, published in 1688 (4).

This is Steen's most complicated treatment of the

subject (see Cat. 25a/457, Fig. 66, and 25b, Fig. 77). It abounds with symbols and emblems of love and marriage. Steen has also included three self-images: as the bridegroom, the notary, and the old celebrant at the left. Such inclusions may indicate that he made the picture to celebrate his second marriage in 1673.

A date of 1673 would accord well with his work of the period. See *The Sacrifice of Iphigenia* of 1671 (Cat. 74, Fig. 82).

Bibliography: (1) Lagrante, *GdBA*, XIV, 1863, p. 300; (2) Cat., le Duc de Morny, 1865, p. 49, No. 78; (3) Fink, *ZfbK*, LX, 1926/27, pp. 230–33; (4) Heppner, *J of W&CI*, III, 1939/40, p. 42; (5) Fink, *Atlantis*, XXI, 1949, pp. 181–82; (6) de Groot, *Beeld en Woord*, 1952, p. 30; (7) Cat., Steen, The Hague, 1958/59, No. 44.

25a/457*]** THE MARRIAGE OF TOBIAS AND SARAH*
Fig. 66

Canvas; 52½ x 68½ inches; signed in full at the bottom left hand corner.
Staatliches Herzog Anton-Ulrich Museum, Brunswick, W. Germany.

Provenance: Arnold Houbraken owned the picture and described it in his life of Steen of 1721 (1). He reported that the picture had been sold to the Duke of Brunswick-Wolfenbüttel, in whose collection it was by 1710 (13). That collection formed the core of the present collection in Brunswick. The painting was one of many carried off by Napoleon, and later returned.

Exhibitions: Paris, 1808, as "Van Stren;" Schaffhausen, Rembrandt und seine Zeit, 1949, No. 162; The Hague, Jan Steen Tentoonstelling, Mauritshuis, 1958/59, No. 44.

Like Cat. 25/487 (Fig. 86), this painting has been generally known as *The Marriage Contract.* Hofstede de Groot lists it only as that. August Fink first recognized the true subject of the picture (5), thereby explaining many of the previously puzzling details. The Biblical source for the subject is Tobit 7:11–15. For a discussion of the subject matter and its sources, see Cat. 25/487.

The picture has been reported as dated by several sources (13) (8) (16). This is incorrect however; there is no date on the picture and none is reported as having disappeared (7). A date of around 1667/68 can be given the picture. Stylistically, the jutting forward of the main group against a monochrome background is characteristic of Steen's work of the late 1660's (15). This dating has been challenged because of the association with another painting by Steen, *The Prayer of Tobias and Sarah* (Cat. 25c, Fig. 65).

The two paintings are most certainly related, not only in subject, but also in figural types and dress. Steen took his composition for *The Prayer of Tobias and Sarah,* the particular emotional quality of the scene, and the physical types of Tobias and Sarah from Nicholas Knüpfer's painting of the same subject now in the Centraal Museum in Utrecht (Fig. 6). Steen's work has been cut, removing the angel which originally appeared on the right paralleling Knüpfer's (see Cat. 25c). The Knüpfer is signed and dated 1654. The fact that all three paintings are related [Friederich Schlie in his study of Knüpfer noted the similarity between the figures in the present picture and those in Knüpfer's painting in Utrecht; he did not know of Steen's *Prayer of Tobias and Sarah* (4)] led Kurt Simon to assume an earlier date for both pictures, perhaps 1660 (10). On stylistic grounds this is too early. The paintings should be moved not six years away from their source, but thirteen or fourteen, to 1667/68, which would make better sense stylistically.

The Marriage of Tobias and Sarah was one of Steen's most popular works; besides the three possible originals (Cat. 25/487, 25a/457, 25b), there are at least six variants and copies. A full-size copy (47 x 72 inches) was sold at Parke-Bernet on 18 April 1956. It was presented as a gift to the Rose Art Museum at Brandeis University in Waltham, Massachusetts, in 1957. Previously it was in the collection of M. Helsleuter.

There was a copy in the Sierstoroff collection at Brunswick. In the catalogue of 1817 compiled by Caspar Heinrich Sierstoroff himself, the painting was considered original, though a version of the painting in the Royal collection. He also mentions a third "original," which was a little overworked (2).

Smith (No. 155) reported a copy (32 x 34 inches) in the collection of Count Brühl which was engraved in the eighteenth century by Charles Bagnoy. His entry under No. 73 of the Supplement to his Catalogue gives the impression that the engraving was after the picture in the Hoofman collection now in San Francisco (Cat. 25/487). This is incorrect. Hofstede de Groot repeats this error resulting from the vagueness of Smith's pronouns.

Van Westrheene (No. 167) mentioned seeing an analogous picture in the home of the Brugmans at Leiden. He could not decide whether it was a copy or a poor original damaged by retouching.

Hofstede de Groot (457) reported a copy (47 x 38½ inches) in the Hoogendijk collection at The Hague with the following history: Rupprecht exhibition, 1889, No. 21; collection, Count Festetics; sale, Hoch,

Munich, 1892, No. 197; sale, Lanfranconi, Cologne, 1895; dealer, Kleinberger, Paris. This might well be the same as a picture of similar dimensions (38 x 48 inches) in the W. A. Freund sale of 1906, No. 141.

Another copy, according to Hofstede de Groot (457), was at the Palazzo Tosio in Brescia.

A small copy (20 x 26 inches) on wood was in the Sandor sale, at Kende's in Vienna on 10 May 1918.

Some of these copies may be identical, but without descriptions or accurate measurements it remains impossible to bring them together.

Bibliography: (1) Houbraken, *De Groote Schouburgh*, III, 1721, p. 16; (2) Cat., Sierstoroff collection, 1817, No. 101, p. 255; (3) Mündler, *ZfbK*, III, 1868, p. 190; (4) Schlie, *Über Nickolaus Knüpfer*, 1896, p. 16; (5) Fink, *ZfbK*, LX, 1926/27, pp. 230–33; (6) Bredius, *Steen*, 1927, p. 23; (7) Cat., Herzog Anton-Ulrich Museum, Brunswick, 1932, No. 313; (8) Trautscholdt, "Steen," *T-B*, 1937, p. 510; (9) Heppner, *J of W&CI*, III, 1939/40, p. 42; (10) Simon, *Pantheon*, XXV, 1940, p. 162; (11) Fink, *Atlantis*, XXI. 1949, pp. 181–82; (12) de Groot, *Beeld en Woord*, 1952, pp. 30–31; (13) Martin, *Steen*, 1954, pp. 10, 51, pl. 50; (14) Cat., Steen, The Hague, 1958/59, No. 44; (15) Stechow, *Allen Memorial Art Museum Bulletin*, XV, 1958, p. 97; (16) de Jonge, *Steen* (Palet Series), n.d., p. 44; (17) *Duits Quarterly*, VII, Spring 1965, pp. 4–9.

25b] THE MARRIAGE OF TOBIAS AND SARAH

HdG25B*

Fig. 77

Canvas; 31½ x 40½ inches; signed in full on the base of the column at left.

Present location unknown.

Provenance: Probably the one in the Piérard collection which was sold in Paris on 20–21 March 1860, No. 28 (HdG 457); collection, Levesque, Paris; Drouot, 27-28 March 1914, No. 13; collection, Czempin, Berlin; dealer, Haberstock, Berlin; collection, Buchenau, Niendorf near Lübeck, 1930's (1). It passed as inheritance to the grandson of Buchenau at Barcelona (2). Collection, Girardet, Kettwig, Germany, 1959/63. In 1965 it was in the possession of the London dealer Duits, who acquired it from Girardet.

Exhibition: Bremen, Kunsthalle, 1931.

The Biblical source for the subject is Tobit 7:11–15. For a discussion of the subject see Cat. 25/487.

The painting is a close variant of the one in Brunswick (Cat. 25a/457, Fig. 66). Its existence was noted by Walther Bernt in the Handex. The main figures are closely followed, the only variation being the dress of Tobias and Sarah.

The interior, also very similar, has been garlanded with flowers and leaves with a large wreath above the heads of Tobias and Sarah. A curtain has been drawn across the kitchen at the back. The table carpet has been changed and a white rose placed on the empty chair in the foreground.

It would seem that this picture should be labeled a copy, since the authenticity of the Brunswick picture (Cat 25a/457) cannot be doubted. However, the quality of the painting, as judged by a photograph, forces its inclusion in the catalogue. It has recent (1958) certificates of authenticity from Plietzsch and Bernt. Both maintain that it is an earlier version, by Steen, of the Brunswick picture. It is here maintained, however, that it is a repetition or, better, a variant of that picture, perhaps by Steen himself, and that chronologically it falls between it and the one now in San Francisco (Cat. 25/487), here dated ca. 1673 (Fig. 86). The flower wreath and the strewn floor appear in the later version, and the cloth with which Tobias has wrapped himself drapes the table to the right in the San Francisco picture. Thus the present picture contains elements from both the other two, giving the idea that while it relied on one, it inspired the other. This seems to be borne out also in the greater openness of the present picture and in the lightness of the figures of Tobias and Sarah. In the Brunswick picture they are earthbound and a little cloddish. In the San Francisco version they have an almost elegant lightness. The present picture again seems the mean between the two.

Bibliography: (1) Trautscholdt, "Steen," *T-B*, 1937, p. 512 (under No. 457); (2) Cat., Steen, The Hague, 1958/59, No. 44; (3) *Duits Quarterly*, VII, Spring 1965, pp. 4–9.

25c] THE PRAYER OF TOBIAS AND SARAH*

HdG25a/b

Fig. 65

Canvas; 32½ x 26¼ inches.

Centraal Museum, Utrecht, on loan from the Dutch Government (Dienst voor 's Rijks Verspreide Kunstvoorwerken, The Hague).

Provenance: According to Trautscholdt, this picture is probably the same as both 25a and 25b in Hofstede de Groot's catalogue (6). That would mean that it was delivered by Barent van Lin to the notary Dispontijn in payment for a debt at The Hague, 18 April 1676 (HdG 25a) and that it was sold in Amsterdam on 6 March 1708, No. 4 (HdG 25b). However, since there is no conclusive evidence of the identity, these references can be given only tentatively. Collection, Count Contini, Rome; collection, Roerich, New York; sale, Roerich, New York, American Art Association, 27-28 March 1930, No. 144 (4); dealer, Goudstikker, Amsterdam, 1930/31 (5); dealer, P. de Boer, Amsterdam, 1940. After the war it became the property of the Dutch government and in 1948 was placed on loan at the Centraal Museum in Utrecht.

Exhibitions: Amsterdam/Rotterdam, Nouvelles acquisitions de la collection Goudstikker, 1930/31, No. 70; Amsterdam, Winter Tentoonstelling, P. de Boer, 1940, No. 13; Amsterdam, Rijksmuseum, Bijbelse Kunst, 1939, No. 68h.

The Biblical source for the subject is Tobit 8:3. Narratively the event immediately follows the marriage of Tobias and Sarah shown in Cat. 25/487, 25a/457, 25c. For a discussion of the subject see Cat. 25/487.

The 1952 catalogue of paintings in the Centraal Museum says "omsteeks of kort na 1654" (11). This date is deduced by the picture's close association with Knüpfer's work of the same subject also at Utrecht (Fig. 6). Steen borrowed his composition and his figural types from the Knüpfer (1) (9) (11) (see Cat. 25a/457). The use of fluttering cupid-angels, so rare an inclusion in his paintings, also reveals his indebtedness to Knüpfer.

The painting is also related to *The Marriage of Tobias and Sarah* in Brunswick painted around 1667/68 (Cat. 25a/457, Fig. 66). Given the closeness of the two works, their dates must be similar, despite the 1654 date of the Knüpfer. The possibility exists that Steen either owned or knew the Knüpfer and used it at the end of the 1660's. For another case of Steen's reliance on Knüpfer at this time see Cat. 59.

Steen's *Prayer of Tobias and Sarah,* in its original form, included the angel Raphael at the right exorcising the devil by burning the heart and liver of the fish, as told in the Biblical story, and seen in Knüpfer's picture (Fig. 6). In 1927 Hofstede de Groot postulated the presence of the angel to the right (1). A subsequent cleaning revealed the cut wings and part of a sword, thus proving Hofstede de Groot's hypothesis. At the same time he raised the question whether the so-called *"St. Michael and the Slain Dragon"* (Cat. 25d/69, Fig. 78), in the Bredius Museum, might not actually be the angel Raphael sacrificing the "fish," and thus the missing half of this picture. More recently Van Thiel of the Rijksmuseum has put forth the same hypothesis, suggesting that the painting had been cut on both sides as well as having a section taken out in the middle (12).

Though the subjects of the two fragments match (see Cat. 25d/69 for identification of the angel) and their dimensions make the joining possible, the hypothesis is unconvincing. The photographic reconstruction (12) shows the angel as being much too large to be considered part of the original bedroom scene. Besides the difference in size, the composition of such a reconstruction, so tight on the right and open on the left, would be decidedly awkward.

Bibliography: (1) Hofstede de Groot, *Art in America,* XVI, 1927/28, p. 251; (2) Hennus, *Maandblad voor Beeldende Kunst,* VII, 1930, p. 284; (3) Bredius, *Steen,* 1927, p. 14; (4) Sales Cat., Roerich, American Art Association, New York, 27–28 March 1930, No. 44; (5) Cat., Nouvelles Acquisitions, Goudstikker, Amsterdam, 1930/31 (No. 39), No. 70; (6) Trautscholdt, "Steen," *T-B,* 1937, p. 510; (7) Cat., Bijbelse Kunst, Amsterdam, 1939, No. 68h; (8) Heppner, *J of W&CI,* III, 1939/40, p. 42; (9) Simon, *Pantheon,* XXV, 1940, p. 262; (10) Cat., Museum Bredius, The Hague, 1945, p. 44; (11) Cat., Centraal Museum, Utrecht, 1952, Nos. 1321, 170; (12) *Duits Quarterly,* IX, 1965, pp. 6–10; (13) de Jonge, *Steen* (Palet Series), n.d., p. 9.

25d/69] THE ANGEL RAPHAEL
Fig. 78 CASTING OUT THE DEVIL

Canvas; 26½ x 22 inches; signed in full on the altar. Museum Bredius, The Hague.

Provenance: Dealer, Kleinberger, Paris (HdG). Collection, A. Bredius, The Hague (HdG).

Hofstede de Groot titled this picture "St. Michael and the Slain Dragon." The correct subject is the one given above. The angel Raphael binds the devil that had jealously guarded Tobias' new wife, Sarah (Tobit 8:3). In all probability it is a fragment of a picture showing the prayer of Tobias and Sarah. However, it is not to be associated with the Steen painting of that subject now at Utrecht (see Cat. 25c, Fig. 65). For a discussion of the subject matter see Cat. 25/487.

J. B. F. van Gils thought the subject to be *Daniel and the Dragon,* a story coming from the Apocryphal Book of *Bel and the Dragon,* connected with the Book of Daniel (4). There Daniel causes the Dragon-god of the Babylonians to eat chunks of pitch, fat, and hair seethed together—and the Dragon "burst in sunder," disproving his power as a god (Bel and the Dragon: 23–27). Van Gils believed it quite obvious that it was Daniel unbinding the choked dragon rather than Raphael binding the cast-out dragon. It is, however, impossible to tell if he is being bound or unbound. Alfrink correctly asserts that the traveling bag and stick are enough to associate the scene with Tobias (3). Also the figure is winged and one cannot accept Van Gils' idea that this winging of Daniel was Steen's "dichterlijke vrijheid." Van Gils had the last word in this small argument, maintaining that it was still Daniel, not Raphael, and adding that one cannot see the devil departing in Steen's picture as one does in Knupfer's of the whole subject at Utrecht (5). Be that as it may, the traveling case and hiking stick are so traditionally associated with the Tobias story that they denote the subject with certainty.

Bibliography: (1) Hofstede de Groot, *Art in America*, XVI, 1927/28, p. 251; (2) Heppner, *J of W&CI*, III, 1939/40, p. 42; (3) Alfrink, *O-H*, LIX, 1942, pp. 127–28; (4) Van Gils, *O-H*, LIX, 1942, p. 62; (5) Van Gils, *O-H*, LIX, 1942, pp. 184–85; (6) Cat., Museum Bredius, The Hague, 1945, p. 31; (7) *Duits Quarterly*, IX, 1965, pp. 6–10.

26] THE BEHEADING OF HOLOFERNES

Panel; signed in full.

Sale, Amsterdam, 10 Dec. 1822 (HdG). Research has revealed no further information on this picture. The following description is quoted by Hofstede de Groot:

> The spectator looks into a tent, whose canvas walls are turned back on the left. Judith, in the right foreground, holds the severed head of Holofernes in her right hand. Her old servant stands near her, somewhat further in, and holds out a sack. The corpse of the general lies on the bed. In the center is a table with a candlestick, cups, and other things.

27/27a] THE BIRTH OF ST. JOHN THE BAPTIST

Panel; 26½ x 35 inches.

Provenance: Sale, Willem Six, Amsterdam, 12 May 1734, No. 45 (HdG 27); collection, G. Braamcamp, Amsterdam, 1766; sale, G. Braamcamp, Amsterdam, 31 July 1771, No. 215 (HdG). Last known owner P. Fouquet.

Clara Bille in her study of Braamcamp's collection noted that Van Diemen, who bought a picture of this subject from Six in 1734, was a buyer for Braamcamp (2). Even though the latter's collection was started a few years later (about 1736/43), it seems evident that HdG 27 and HdG 27a are identical. The picture was in the Braamcamp collection in 1766, the date of de Bastide's catalogue.

The description from the sales catalogue of 1771 (Braamcamp) follows:

> The subject of his piece is the birth of St. John, a composition of 13 figures. Contrary to his habit, the artist has treated the subject very modestly. The brush-stroke is broad like Metsu's; it is executed in the manner of Dou; everything is in bright light and of a charming character. The finest piece of this master known in this country.

> Het onderwerp van dit stuk is de Geboorte van Johannes, zynde eene Ordonnantie van dertien Beelden. Dit Stuk is, tegen deezes Schilders gewoonte, zeer zedig behandeld. De Penceelstreek van dit stuk is breed als van G. Metzu, en uitgevoerd in de manier van G. Dova, alles is helder gedaagd en van eene bevallige gedaante, zynde dit stuk het fraaiste dat hier te lands van deezen Meester bekend is.

The description, especially the mention of Dou, creates the impression that this is one of Steen's early works; other works of his, such as the destroyed *Tobias Healing His Father* (Cat. 24), have also been associated with Dou. This is not strange, considering Steen's early Leiden connections.

Bibliography: (1) de Bastide, *Le temple des arts ou le cabinet de Monsier Braamcamp*, Amsterdam, 1766; (2) Bille, *De Tempel der Kunst*, Amsterdam, 1961, Vol. I, p. 120.

28] ST. JOHN PREACHING IN THE WILDERNESS*

Fig. 29

Canvas; 44 x 46 inches; signed in full at right foreground.

Nivaagaard collection, Nivaa, Denmark.

Provenance: Sale, Roothaan, Amsterdam, 29 March 1826, No. 105 (HdG) (the catalogue of that sale attributed the landscape to Jan Wils); sale, Comte F. de Robiano, Brussels, 1 May 1837, No. 614 (HdG) (in the catalogue the landscape was attributed to Jan Hackaert); collection, Malle, Brussels, 1840; collection, M. Govelo (HdG); sale, Emmerson, London, 1856; sale, Nieuwenhuys, Paris, 28 April 1881 (Handex). In the 1881 catalogue the landscape was again attributed to Hackaert and the *Moses Striking the Rock* (Cat. 9), which was also in the Robiano sale of 1837, is mentioned as a pendant. Sale, Paris, 27 Jan. 1882 (Handex); sale, Degenser, Paris, 13 May 1898, No. 39 (Handex); sale, G. T. Kortenhoef *et al.*, Amsterdam, 29 Nov. 1898, No. 34 (Handex); dealer, Kleinberger, Paris, 1898 (HdG); dealer, Goldhart, Amsterdam, 1901 (HdG). In 1902 it was bought for the Hage collection at Nivaa.

Hofstede de Groot erred in giving this as Westrheene No. 206. The identity is between HdG 30 and Westrheene 206. Van Westrheene was incorrect in associating 206 with Smith No. 102 and in listing it in the Roothaan sale (Amsterdam, 1926). See Cat. 30.

Exhibition: The Hague, Jan Steen Tentoonstelling, Mauritshuis, 1958/59, No. 2.

Simon, seeking strong connections with Utrecht, felt that the horse and rider at the right were similar to those in Knüpfer's *Search After Happiness* of 1651 at Schwerin (2) (Fig. 11). While this motif does seem borrowed, the direct connection with Knüpfer remains tenuous.

As stated in the provenance, the landscape has been attributed at one time to Jan Hackaert and at another to Jan Wils, both Italianate landscapists. Bredius supports the attribution of the landscape to Wils (1). And Martin (5) unwillingly admits that the background rocks may be his work. Hackaert seems rightly to have been dropped from consideration; but Jan Both has been added as a possible influence, though not as actual painter of the landscape (2) (3).

The date of this picture is established by its stylistic affinity with *The Village Wedding* of 1653 (HdG 455, Fig. 25). In figural style and general structure the picture is related to the work of Jacob de Wet, who influenced Steen during the early 1650's.

Bibliography: (1) Bredius, *Steen*, 1927, p. 37; (2) Simon, *Pantheon*, XXV, 1940, p. 162; (3) Gerson, *Kunsthistorische Mededelinging*, III, 1948, p. 52; (4) Cat., Malerisamlingen på Nivaagaard, Nivaa, 1949, No. 53; (5) Martin, *Steen,* 1954, p. 35; (6) Cat., Steen, The Hague, 1958/59, No. 2.

29] JOHN THE BAPTIST PREACHING IN THE WILDERNESS

69 x 91 inches

Sale, J. de Roore, The Hague, 4 Sept. 1747, No. 124 (HdG). "A large landscape with numerous figures, horses and wagons" (HdG).

Bredius comments on the picture, saying that it was lost and mentioning its very large size (1); if the picture is by Steen, this probably indicates a late date, though the subject does not seem to fit with a late date.

Bibliography: (1) Bredius, *Steen*, 1927, p. 37.

30] JOHN THE BAPTIST PREACHING IN THE WILDERNESS

Panel; 30½ x 30½ inches.

Sale, Reyersburgen van Couwerwen, Leiden, 31 July 1765, No. 56 (HdG); sale, Hendrik Verschuuring, The Hague, 17 Sept. 1770, No. 164 (HdG). This is Van Westrheene No. 206. He believed it to be the same as Smith No. 102. That is incorrect and Smith 102 should be associated with Cat. 28. Research has revealed no further information on this picture.

30a***] HEAD OF ST. JOHN THE BAPTIST

Fig. 44

Panel; 13¼ x 10¼ inches.

Private collection, London.

Exhibition: London, Dutch Pictures 1450–1750, Royal Academy, 1952/53, No. 144.

Attributed to Steen in the catalogue of the Exhibition of Dutch Pictures at the Royal Academy in 1952. The attribution is a good one, and finds support in other of his works. The type can be seen repeated in the head of the kneeling peasant in *The Adoration of the Shepherds* at the Rijksmuseum (Cat. 37/31, Fig. 37). The present picture probably dates from around 1659. It might also be compared to the disappearing head of Christ from *Christ at Emmaus* (Cat. 65, Fig. 45).

Bibliography: (1) Cat., Dutch Pictures, London, 1952/53, No. 144.

31] THE NATIVITY

HdG 31 is identical with HdG 31a and HdG 37; see entry under 37.

31a] THE NATIVITY

HdG 31a is identical with HdG 31 and HdG 37; see entry under 37.

32] THE ADORATION OF THE SHEPHERDS

Fig. 3

Canvas; 28 x 37 inches; signed in full on the manger. Museum, Aix-en-Provence.

Provenance: The picture was in the Museum at Aix-en-Provence as early as 1867. The catalogue of that year (No. 300) attributed it to Gerard Honthorst (1). The catalogue of 1901 (No. 362) gives it as a Jan Steen (2).

The Biblical source for the subject is Luke 2:16–20.

A pen and wash drawing of *The Adoration of the Shepherds* (Fig. 20) formerly in the Frits Lugt collection is close in form to the picture. Though Lugt attributed the drawing to Isaac Ostade, Van Regteren Altena attributed it to Steen, while commenting on the closeness to Ostade (4). The drawing here accepted as Steen cannot be taken, however, as a direct study for the painting; it is merely related in concept.

Cat. 38 (Fig. 4) is a smaller version of the picture with some variations. Both are among Steen's earliest Biblical paintings and date from around 1651, the year of the first dated picture, *The Death of Ananias* (Cat. 66, Fig. 1).

Bibliography: (1) Cat. du Musée d'Aix, Aix-en-Provence, 1867, No. 300; (2) Cat. du Musée d'Aix, Aix-en-Provence, 1901, No. 263; (3) Bredius, *Steen*, 1927, p. 35; (4) Van Regteren Altena, *O-H*, LX, 1943, p. 104.

33/36] THE ADORATION OF THE SHEPHERDS*
Fig. 36

Panel; 12½ x 16½ inches.
Museum Bredius, The Hague.

Provenance: In 1872, the year of a large Dutch exhibition at Amsterdam, the picture belonged to M. Y. Gruyter of Amsterdam (1). Sale, M. Y. Gruyter, Amsterdam, 24 Oct. 1882, No. 108 (HdG 36); collection, Schmetz, Aachen (HdG); collection, Bredius, The Hague, 1907 (HdG).

Exhibition: Amsterdam, Dutch paintings, 1872.

Number 33 is identical with 36. This is proven not only by the size, but also by the description of the Gruyter picture given by Henri Harvard in his review of the exhibition at Amsterdam in 1872:

. . . les bergers n'ont point été guidés vers le Dieu naissant par une étoile, comme le dit l'Ecriture, mais bien par une énorme lanterne, ce qui est infiniment plus pratique, quoique moins orthodoxe. . . . Rien qu'a voir toutes ces laìdes figures et à entendre les sons épouvantables de l'énorme cornemuse. . . . Il y a bien une vingtaine de personnages dans ce petit tableau . . . (1)

The Biblical source for the subject is Luke 2:16–20.

Hofstede de Groot mentions that the composition is influenced by Rembrandt. He probably had in mind Rembrandt's two paintings of the subject of 1646, one in London, the other in Munich (B.574, 575). Steen however adds a note of rough humor to the scene which is foreign to Rembrandt.

The picture was probably made at the end of the 1650's or early 1660's and is related in form to the larger work in the Rijksmuseum (Cat. 37/31, Fig. 37).

Bibliography: (1) Harvard, *GdBA*, VI, 1872, p. 378; (2) Bredius, *Steen*, 1927, p. 35; (3) de Groot, *Beeld en Woord*, 1952, pp. 33–34.

34] THE ADORATION OF THE SHEPHERDS
Fig. 126

Removed from the Catalogue; see Addendum 3.

35] THE ADORATION OF THE SHEPHERDS
Fig. 28

Canvas; 50½ x 40½ inches; signed in full on rock at lower left.
Bishop's Residence, Leitmeritz, Czechoslovakia.

Provenance: Unknown except that in 1892 it was in the Cathedral at Leitmeritz (1).

The Biblical source for the subject is Luke 2:16–20.

The band of frolicking cherubs is a strange inclusion for Steen. As seen in the other adoration scenes discussed (Cat. 32, 33/36, 37/31, Figs. 3, 36, 37), he generally leaves out any exterior manifestation of the event.

Like the *Adoration* in the Bredius Museum (Cat. 33/36, Fig. 36), this work is strongly influenced by Rembrandt. J. G. van Gelder included it as part of an early Rembrandtesque group of pictures which he assigned to the years 1644/46 (Cat. 8, 28, Figs. 27, 29) (2).

This dating now seems too early, and the picture along with the others mentioned should be dated around 1653 in association with *The Village Wedding* of that year (HdG 455, Fig. 25).

Bibliography: (1) Hofstede de Groot, *Nederlandsche Spectator*, 10 Feb. 1892, pp. 104–5; (2) Van Gelder, *O-H*, XLIII, 1926, p. 206.

36] THE ADORATION OF THE SHEPHERDS*

HdG 36 is identical with HdG 33; see that entry.

37/31/31a] THE ADORATION OF THE SHEPHERDS*
Fig. 37

Canvas; 21 x 25½ inches; signed in full at lower left.
Rijksmuseum, Amsterdam.

Provenance: Sale, Honas Witsen, Amsterdam, 31 March 1717, No. 131 (HdG); sale, Amsterdam, 17 Sept. 1727, No. 15 (HdG 31a); collection, Lord of Tabley, 1827 (Sm); collection, Franks, London, 1842 (Sm, HdG); dealer, Sabin, London, 1933; dealer, Hoogendijk, Amsterdam, 1934 (1); collection, A. A. van Sandick, Rotterdam, 1937/47. It was purchased for the Museum from Sandick in 1947 (5).

Exhibitions: London, British Gallery, 1835; London, Twenty-Five Dutch and Flemish Masters, Sabin (dealer), about 1933/34, No. 20; Rotterdam, Meesterwerken uit vier eeuwen, Museum Boymans, 1938, No. 141; Amsterdam, Bijbelse Kunst, Rijksmuseum, 1939, No. 78c; Zurich, Holländer des 17. Jahrhunderts, 1953, No. 143; Rome, 1954, No. 146; Milan, 1954, No. 149; Antwerp, De Madonna in de Kunst, 1954, No. 95; Utrecht, 1954/55, No. 95; Sheffield, Dutch Masterpieces, 1956, No. 50; The Hague, Jan Steen Tentoonstelling, Mauritshuis, 1958/59, No. 10.

The picture is identical with Nos. 31 and 31a.

The Biblical source for the subject is Luke 2:16–20.

Smith says that the picture is painted in imitation of the "Italian school." Van Westrheene repeats this idea, and Hofstede de Groot says: "The picture shows traces of Italian influence." More recently Van Guldener tried to connect this with Italy via Wttewael and Steen's Utrecht background (3) (7). If such overtones of Italian influence are present in the picture, they are indeed obscure.

De Jonge is in error in calling the picture an early work (7), and so also is the Catalogue of the 1958/59 exhibition at The Hague, which offers a date of "[plus or minus] 1670." It should rather be placed about 1659/60 and related in style to *The Music Lesson* of 1659 in the National Gallery, London (HdG 409, Fig. 35).

A close replica of the picture is in the State Collection of Art at Wawel Castle, Cracow; see Addendum 3.

Bibliography: (1) Cat., Twenty-Five Paintings by Dutch and Flemish XVIIth Century Masters, London, Sabin, about 1933/34, No. 20; (2) Bremmer, *Die Constghesellen,* I, 1946, p. 163; (3) Van Guldener, *Phoenix,* III, 1948, pp. 18–21; (4) de Groot, *Beeld en Woord,* pp. 33–34; (5) Cat., Rijksmuseum, Amsterdam, 1956, No. 2250-A4; (6) Cat., Steen, The Hague, 1958/59, No. 10; (7) de Jonge, *Steen* (Palet Series), n.d., p. 14; (8) Leeuwen, *De Kroniek van de Vriendenkring van het Rembrandthuis,* XX, 1966, pp. 57–64.

38] THE ADORATION OF THE SHEPHERDS

Fig. 4

Panel; 7 x 8 inches; signed in full on the manger. Present location unknown.

Provenance: Sale, T. Hellincx, Leiden, 6 April 1778, No. 21 (Handex); collection, Duke of Arenberg, Brussels. The picture had been sold by the time of the publication of Hofstede de Groot's catalogue (1907). An undated note in the Handex says that after the First World War it was probably in Nordkirchen in Westphalia. Dealer, Nystad, The Hague, 1957. Last reported in a private collection in Italy.

Exhibition: Delft, Oude Kunst en Antiekbeurs, Prinsenhof, 1957.

The identity of the present picture with the one from the Arenberg collection is made on the basis of a lithograph done by P. Simonau and Co. and included in the Arenberg catalogue of 1829.

The Biblical source for the subject is Luke 2:16–20.

This little painting relates directly to the one at Aix-en-Provence (Cat. 32, Fig. 3); and though much rougher in its handling, probably dates from around the same time—the early 1650's—a dating supported by Bredius (3). It is also close in conception to the painting in the Bredius Museum (Cat. 33/36, Fig. 36).

Bibliography: (1) Cat., Arenberg collection, 1829, No. 75; (2) Bürger-Thoré, Galerie d'Arenberg à Bruxelles, 1859, No. 59; (3) Bredius, *Steen,* 1927, p. 36.

38a***] NATIVITY

9½ x 12 inches.

Sale, New York, American Art Association, 21 Jan. 1914, No. 9. Purchased by H. D. Estabrook. Research has revealed no further information on this picture.

39] REST ON THE FLIGHT TO EGYPT*

Fig. 79

Canvas; 75 x 54½ inches.
Museum, Dunkirk.

Provenance: Sale, C. Wittert van Valkenburg, Rotterdam, 11 April 1731, No. 59 (HdG). It may also have been No. 27 in the Brun sale at Paris on 30 Nov. 1841, at which time the measurements were given either as 62½ or 74½ x 56½ inches (HdG). Collection, Van Ruth, Antwerp (HdG); collection, Coffyn, Antwerp. It entered the Dunkirk Museum by 1891 from the Coffyn bequest (1).

Exhibition: Paris, Le Siècle de Rembrandt, Petit Palais, Jan. and Feb. 1971.

Hofstede de Groot calls the picture "apparently genuine." Later repainting and patching, especially in the landscape, may account in part for his doubt. Furthermore, the religious content in itself is strange for Steen. He has shown the scene taken from Matthew 2:14 in a Catholic manner with angels, diffused haloes for mother and child, and religiously ecstatic expressions. He added also the adoring infant St. John. Though Steen was himself a Catholic, in no other known religious painting is such an image found. The large size of the picture may indicate that it was made as a commissioned altarpiece for a Catholic chapel.

The landscape is unconvincing as Steen, as is the awkwardly flattened figure of Joseph. The catalogue of the Van Valkenburg sale (1731) attributed the landscape to I. Lievens; and it reminded Hofstede de Groot of Eeckhout.

For all the problems with the picture, the figure of Mary leaves no doubt that it is a mature work made either in the late 1660's or the early 1670's. She is almost a replica of Rachel from *Laban Searching for the Idols* (Cat. 4, Fig. 89), a picture which stylistically must be placed in the early 1670's.

Under No. 40a, Hofstede de Groot gives a description of a painting called *Flight into Egypt* which exactly describes the present picture. However, the measurements differ. It is possible that it is a copy of the present picture, but since No. 40a is unknown, no definite conclusion can be drawn. Possibly the measurements given by Hofstede de Groot for 40a are incorrect and its history properly belongs to the present picture.

Bibliography: (1) Cat., Museum, Dunkirk, 1891, No. 314; (2) Martin, G. "Seventeenth-century Dutch Painting at the Petit Palais," *Apollo*, XCIII, 1971, pp. 118–19.

39a] FLIGHT INTO EGYPT

HdG39A**

Removed from the Catalogue; see Addendum 4.

40] FLIGHT INTO EGYPT

Sale, Amsterdam, 4 June 1729, No. 43 (HdG). There is no further information on this picture. The reference may belong to another listed picture of this subject.

40a] FLIGHT INTO EGYPT

Canvas; 25½ x 22 inches.

Sale, G. Groeninx van Zoelen *et al.*, Rotterdam, 25 June 1800, No. 10 (HdG).

The Biblical source of the picture is Matthew 2:14. Steen, as the description shows, has added St. John:

The Virgin sits in a landscape with the Child, who gives grass to a lamb. Beside Him is John. Joseph, leading an ass, salutes the Virgin. To the right Elizabeth brings vegetables, with Zachariah behind her. In the sky is a radiant company of angels.

This description exactly corresponds to Cat. 39 in the Dunkirk Museum (Fig. 79). Only the measurements differ. It may be a copy of that painting, or the measurements given by Hofstede de Groot may be incorrect; but since it is untraceable no definite statement to that effect is possible.

40b] FLIGHT INTO EGYPT

HdG 40A*

Canvas; 39 x 34 inches.

Sale, Leiden, 26 Aug. 1788, No. 135 (Handex). Added by the Handex as 40A. There is no further information on this picture and the reference might belong to another listed picture of this subject.

41] FLIGHT INTO EGYPT

Canvas; 21½ x 18 inches.

Sale, Pieter Oets, Amsterdam, 31 Jan. 1791, No. 5 (HdG).

The description given by Hofstede de Groot leaves the impression that it might be a simple outdoor genre scene such as Steen did, particularly in his early years—e.g., *Gypsies in a Landscape* (HdG 223, Fig. 14).

In the foreground of a landscape sits a woman with a child at her breast; near her is a youth asleep. Beside her stands a servant saddling an ass. Among the trees are a peasant hut and other buildings; a woman draws water. The whole is rendered with spirit in a lively and vigorous manner.

If the title of the picture as given is correct, the reference might belong to another listed picture of the subject.

42] MASSACRE OF THE INNOCENTS

Present location unknown.

The picture was part of the H. A. J. Munro collection; however, it was not in the sale on 1 June 1878 in London.

The Biblical source for the subject is Matthew 2:16.

Waagen saw the picture in the Munro collection and was repelled by it. "A picture which in its revolting coarseness shows the utter incapacity of the artist to comprehend the only legitimate mode of conceiving the subject" (1).

There is no further information on the picture.

Bibliography: (1) Waagen, *Treasures of Art in Great Britain*, II, 1854, p. 138.

43] THE HOLY FAMILY

Removed from the Catalogue; see Addendum 5.

44] THE CHILD JESUS IN THE TEMPLE*

Fig. 39

Canvas; 33 x 40 inches; signed with monogram at the lower left.

Kunstmuseum, Basel.

Provenance: Sale, M. Stategaart, Alkmaar, 27 July 1802, No. 1 (HdG); sale, 1803 (HdG); collection, Marquis Maridon (Marialva, according to Sm), 1823 (Sm, HdG); collection, Smith, London (HdG); collection, J. Fisher, London, 1833 (HdG); sale, J. Fisher, London, 1858 (Handex); collection, Countess Wilmar Festetits, Budapest (Handex); sale, H. Theodore Hoech, Munich, 19 Sept. 1892, No. 198 (HdG). In 1908 the painting was owned by Hans van der Mühel in Basel, from whose collection it entered the Museum.

Exhibition: Delft, Bijbelsekunst, 1952, No. 160.

The moment shown is when Mary and Joseph, after searching for the young Jesus, find him disputing in the temple (Luke 2:46–48).

Smith says, "The painter evidently intended in this picture to imitate the richness of colour and effect of Rembrandt." In no other work, not even *Lot and His Daughters* (Cat. 1, Fig. 48), taken in part from a Rembrandt/van Vliet etching, was Steen so imitative of Rembrandt's manner. The rabbinical mood and quality of the scene has its source in Rembrandt, and can be seen in Eeckhout's work of the same subject in the Hamburg Künsthalle. Even within this dependence, the central group—Mary, Joseph, and the young Christ—stand out as typically Steen within a Rembrandtesque environment.

A note in the Handex says the authenticity of the monogram is questionable. That seems correct, since Steen used the monogram only with rare exception in his early years.

The Virgin resembles Steen's treatment of her in *The Adoration of the Shepherds* in the Rijksmuseum (Cat. 37/31, Fig. 37). A similar date of around 1659/60 is assigned to both.

Bibliography: (1) Bredius, *Steen*, 1927, pp. 31–32, pl. 10; (2) Cat., "Offentliche Kunstsammlung," Basel, 1946, No. 906, p. 83; (3) de Groot, *Beeld en Woord*, 1952, p. 179; (4) Martin, *Steen*, 1954, p. 61, pl. 26.

45/50a] THE MARRIAGE AT CANA

Fig. 2

Panel; 11 x 14½ inches; signed on the right.

Present location unknown.

Provenance: Collection, Baumgärten, Leipzig, 1863 (HdG, 50a) (3); collection, Rudolf Mosse, Berlin, 1907 (HdG); sale, Mosse, Berlin, 29 May 1934, No. 113 (1). It was purchased at that sale by Berlin dealer Haberstock. Efforts to trace the later history of the picture have been unsuccessful.

Exhibition: Berlin, Schäffer Gallery, 1929, No. 87.

According to Stechow, on the basis of a communication with Trautscholdt, this picture is identical with HdG 50a (3), which is described in the original catalogue as "with many figures, one of whom is the painter himself."

The Biblical source for the subject is John 2:1–10.

Hofstede de Groot saw this picture and described it in considerable detail:

On the left is the full-length figure of Christ, surrounded by four persons. A servant standing in front of Him pours wine out of a jug. Three metal pans are placed near. To the left of a marble-topped table sits a young woman, drinking from a goblet. At the back of the table a carpet hangs on the wall; before this are five persons. Two men on the right are conversing; the younger of them holds a shallow cup. In the right background are two figures, and a boy playing a flute at the foot of a staircase, which leads to a gallery in the center of the picture. A maid-servant with a plate of cakes comes down the stairs. There are in all twenty-five or thirty figures. It is an excellent work, beautiful as a composition, delicate and harmonious in color, and well preserved; it resembles in style the picture of a wedding in the Six collection (455).

Though the painting conforms mostly to the description, there are certain differences. Twenty-five or thirty figures are not to be found. The woman with the tray appears to be going *up* the stairs and the servant who pours the wine kneels rather than stands. These are minor differences; and on the basis of the provenance (this is the picture from the Mosse sale) and size, the identity is certain (1). Stechow suggests that the inaccuracies of Hofstede de Groot's description may rest with a confusion with another picture of the subject, possibly Catalogue 50b (Fig. 30) (3).

On study of the picture, even in a photograph, one must wonder at Hofstede de Groot's praise of it. It is a rough and awkward picture, flatly composed and unclear in details. Bredius, who knew the picture from the Mosse collection, felt that it was uneven and perhaps not entirely finished by Steen (1). Compositionally it differs from all the other treatments of the subject by Steen (see Cat. 46–50b, Figs. 62, 95, 30) and is most certainly his earliest.

Hofstede de Groot associated it with *The Village Wedding* of 1653 in the Boymans/van Beuningen Museum (HdG 455, Fig. 25), but that dating, early though it may be, is too late; and the picture should be assigned to 1651, or even a few years earlier. It is one of Steen's earliest religious paintings. The dating here is opposed to Stechow's belief that the picture must date from the late sixties or "even later" (3). That late dating is unacceptable because, as Stechow himself points out, the picture shows none of the developed motifs which Steen used again and again in later versions of the subject and which were clearly set by the 1650's (see Cat. 50b, Fig. 30). Stechow believes the picture to be a "quick sketch" rather than an "independent composition" (3).

Bibliography: (1) Bredius, *Steen*, 1927, p. 33; (2) Trautscholdt, "Steen," *T-B*, 1937, p. 511; (3) Stechow, W., *Nederlands Kunsthistorisch Jaarboek*, XXIII, 1972, p. 77, 82, note 12.

46] THE MARRIAGE AT CANA

Fig. 96

Canvas; approximately 45½ x 54½ inches.

Present location unknown.

Provenance: Sale, A. van Lennek, Amsterdam, 24 July 1792, No. 5 (HdG); sale, Paillet, Paris, 1814

(HdG); sale, van Leyden, Warmond, 31 July 1816 (HdG); sale, Duchess de Berry, Paris, 1816 (HdG); sale, P. Perrier, Paris, 1843 (HdG); collection, Duke of Arenberg, Brussels, 1859 (1).

There were several sales of Arenberg pictures (15 Nov. 1[illegible]; 22–24 Nov. 1926; 17–18 March 1939); however, the *Marriage at Cana* was in none of these.

Exhibition: Brussels, 1855.

The Biblical source for the subject is John 2:1–10.

The painting was praised by those who knew it; "[It] was painted in the best period of the master and is distinguished for the clearness and beauty of the colouring" (Smith, No. 98); "tableau frappant de vérité et de naïveté. Il témoigne du savoir faire de l'artiste" (W. No. 192). Bürger-Thoré in his catalogue of the Arenberg pictures called it "une des plus vastes et des plus importantes compositions de Jan Steen" (1).

Hofstede de Groot's description gives a good idea of the picture:

> In a large hall, which has a green curtain hanging from the ceiling, numerous persons sit at a table which stands on a daïs. Among them is Christ, who gives an order to the servants. On the steps leading to the daïs a man and a woman converse about the miracle; near them a young man praises the wine to an old woman. Among other groups in the foreground is a man who fills another man's glass. There are musicians in a gallery beneath which is another table. In all there are about sixty figures. Various incidents are introduced to give movement and effect to the piece, such as a child rolling along an empty cask, a mother caressing her infant, and a merry-andrew; these, together with numerous accessories, tend to the perfecting of the composition.

Hofstede de Groot adds that it should be compared to 601, called *Rustic Feast in a Large Tavern* and dated 1674 (Fig. 93). If correct, this correspondence means the picture was one of Steen's latest works of this subject. The picture is unique among Steen's representations of the subject in that the hall, half hidden by a large painted dust cover, is very much larger and the figures correspondingly smaller than in any of the other versions. The picture is also distinguished from other representations by the table to the left which is placed perpendicular to the picture plane (4). Hofstede de Groot's association of the picture with the *Rustic Feast* of 1674 is correct. Stechow concurs with the late date, saying that it can hardly be dated before 1670 (4).

Bibliography: (1) Bürger-Thoré, *Galerie d'Arenberg à Bruxelles*, 1859, No. 58; (2) Bredius, *Steen*, 1927, pp. 33–34; (3) de Groot, *Beeld en Woord*, 1952, pp. 81–82; (4) Stechow, W. *Nederlands Kunsthistorisch Jaarboek*, XXIII, 1972, p. 78.

47] THE MARRIAGE AT CANA

Fig. 97

Panel; 22½ x 19 inches; signed in full on the steps at lower right.

Staatliche Kunstsammlungen, Dresden.

Provenance: Sale, W. Fabricius, Haarlem, 19 Aug. 1749, No. 13 (HdG). It was in the Royal collection at Dresden (No. 1725) as early as 1905, when it appeared in the catalogue (2).

Hofstede de Groot gives this as Sm 100. The reference is incorrect; Sm 100 is Cat. 48/49. See that entry.

As reported by Stechow, Frau Dr. A. Mayer-Meintschel corroborated the fact that the figure of Christ shows unfortunate retouching which may date from the eighteenth century (6).

The Biblical source for the subject is John 2:1–10.

Of all Steen's treatments of the subject this is the most concentrated. He shows only a few figures, rather than giving the entire hall with all the secondary activities of the wedding feast, as he does, for instance, in the picture in the Beit collection (Cat. 48/49, Fig. 62).

The dating of the picture is extremely difficult without personal inspection. Tentatively it is placed late in his career, around 1676, and might best be associated with *The Marriage at Cana* of that year in the Norton Simon collection (Cat. 50, Fig. 95). The looseness of the painting, particularly in the background, supports such an association. Stechow, however, suggests a somewhat earlier date, 1667/68, and associates the picture with the *Antony and Cleopatra* in Göttingen (see Cat. 86, Fig. 56) (6).

Bibliography: (1) Bredius, *Steen*, 1927, p. 33; (2) Cat., Staatlichen Gemälde-Galerie, Dresden, 1930, No. 1725; (3) Furst, *Apollo*, XXX, 1939, pp. 217–18; (4) Heppner, *J of W&CI*, III, 1939/40, p. 43; (5) Rudloff-Hille, *Die Dresdner Gemäldegalerie*, 1960, p. 109; (6) Stechow, W., *Nederlands Kunsthistorisch Jaarboek*, XXIII, 1972, p. 77.

48/49] THE MARRIAGE AT CANA

Fig. 62

Panel; 25 x 32½ inches; signed with a monogram, IHS, on the vat at left.

Sir Alfred Beit collection, Blessington, Ireland.

Provenance: Sale, A. van Hoek, Amsterdam, 7 April 1806 (HdG); sale, Bicker and Wijckersloot, Amsterdam, 19 July 1809, No. 51 (HdG); sale, Delahante, London, 1814 (HdG); sale, London, 1815 (HdG); sale, Constantin, Paris, 1829 (HdG); dealer, Nieuwenhuys, London (HdG); sale, Nieuwenhuys, London, 1833 (HdG); sale, Lord Northwick, Cheltenham, 1838 (HdG); sale, Perier, Paris, 1848 (HdG 49); collection, J. Walter, Bearwood (HdG); collection, Lansdowne, Bowood. Alfred Beit acquired it from the Lansdowne collection. It appears in the 1904 catalogue of the Beit collection.

Exhibitions: London, The British Institute, 1837, No. 174; Manchester, Art Treasures, 1857, No. 946; London, The British Institute, 1862, No. 69; London, Winter Exhibition, Royal Academy, 1882, No. 55; London, Burlington Fine Arts Club, 1900, No. 44; London, Jan Steen, Dowdeswell Galleries, 1909, No. 5; Leiden, Jan Steen, 1926, No. 23; London, Dutch Art, 1450–1900, Royal Academy, 1929, No. 206; Nottingham, British Council, 1945, No. 56; Capetown, 17th Century Dutch Paintings, National Art Museum, 1952, No. 58; Dublin, Paintings from Irish Collections, Municipal Gallery of Modern Art, 1957, No. 157; The Hague, Jan Steen, Mauritshuis, 1958/59, No. 51.

According to an unsigned note in the Handex, 48 and 49 are identical. This seems reasonable since their measurements as given by Hofstede de Groot are just about the same (i.e., 25 x 32½ inches and 32 x 25 inches).

As with the other pictures of this subject, the Biblical source is John 2:1–10. In Steen's interpretation the festivities are as important as the miracle itself, and drinking is particularly emphasized. Schmidt-Degener pointed out that Steen, in signing the picture IHS on the wine-barrel rolled along by a little boy, may have been making an ironic and humorous pun on *In Hoc Signo (vinces)* (8), thus setting off the drinking theme even more strongly. The possibility exists that this picture and the others of the subject were made to hang in taverns. This would account in part for Steen's interpretation of the subject, and accords well with his own life as a brewer and tavern owner. Stechow declares that the IHS should be taken as a reference to the monogram of Christ (IHS = Jesus) and the double meaning taken as a reference to the miracle of the Eucharist in which wine is turned into the blood of Christ (19). The meaning of the picture, if such an interpretation is accepted, would be more directly doctrinal than has generally been recognized.

As can be seen from the list of exhibitions, this is one of Steen's most widely known religious paintings. Always praised for the quality of its painting, and rightly connected with the "Feinmalerei" of Leiden (8) (17), it has been at the same time criticized for its religious conception. Smith says of the picture:

The total incapacity of Jan Steen to render the necessary dignity of character and expression to his figures, so indispensable to an historical subject, is no less evident in this picture than in every other example of a similar kind; in all other respects the talents and genius of the artist are strikingly evinced. (Smith, 100.)

Waagen says: "The subject is degraded to a level of his [Steen's] sphere of art, but the picture is rich and careful" (1).

This particular type of criticism is not limited to the nineteenth century but is current in this century as well. H. E. van Gelder, talking of the painting, says: "In general it does not seem advisable to look for a deep significance in the work of Steen, whose realism is almost too child-like" (8). He adds, however, that in Steen's very realism may lie a deeper meaning as regards our experience with divine presence and miracle (6). F. J. B. Watson, describing the pictures in the Beit collection, comments that the picture is extraordinary, and impressive, but that the religious theme is "perhaps treated too curiously in the Dutch genre style to appeal greatly to the modern taste" (18). Stechow, however, has sought to find a deeper symbolic and perhaps even doctrinal significance in Steen's mixture of the sacred and the profane (19).

C. W. de Groot maintained that Steen based his composition upon Raphael's *School of Athens*, which he may have known through a print or drawing (16). There is good reason for accepting this idea. The structure of the space with steps and arches in the background, while not directly imitative of the fresco in the Vatican, is certainly reminiscent of it. So also is the group of figures in the left foreground. One cannot help wondering if Steen did not particularly enjoy using one of the great paragons of history painting for his own somewhat indecorous presentation. He replaced Diogenes with a drunken peasant.

Martin, in his monograph of 1954, dates the picture in the early 1660's (17), which is a correction of his earlier estimate that it was a work of the early 1650's (9). J. G. van Gelder and Stechow contradict both of Martin's estimates, and place the work at the end of the 1660's (6) (10), the date accepted here.

Bibliography: (1) Waagen, *Treasures of Art in Great Britain*, IV (supplement), 1857, p. 296; (2) Bode, *Kunstsammlungen des Herrn Alfred Beit*, 1904, p. 58; (3) Martin, *L'art flamand et hollandais*, XII, 1909, p. 155; (4) Bode, *Catalogue of the Collection of Mr. Otto Beit*, 1913, pp. 14–15, No. 57; (5) Cat., Steen, Leiden, 1926, No. 23; (6) Van Gelder, *O-H*, XLIII, 1926, p. 210; (7) Bredius, *Steen*, 1927, p. 32; (8)

Schmidt-Degener and Van Gelder, *Steen*, 1927, pp. 11–12, 34, pl. VII, VIII; (9) Martin, *ZfbK*, LXI, 1927/28, p. 332; (10) Stechow, *ZfbK*, LXII, 1928/29, p. 175; (11) Fischel, *Burlington*, LXVI, 1935, p. 65; (12) Heppner, *J of W&CI*, III, 1939/40, p. 44; (13) Gudlaugsson, *De Komedianten*, 1945, p. 6; (14) Bax, *Skilders wat Vertel*, 1951, pp. 216ff; (15) Bax, *Hollandse en Vlaamse Schilderkunst in Zuid-Afrika*, 1952, pp. 113–15; (16) de Groot, *Beeld en Woord*, 1952, pp. 81, 153, 181–82; (17) Martin, *Steen*, 1954, p. 40; (18) Watson, *Connoisseur*, XLV, 1961, p. 158; (19) Stechow, W., *Nederlands Kunsthistorisch Jaarboek*, XXIII, 1972, pp. 78–79.

50] THE MARRIAGE AT CANA*

Fig. 95

Canvas; 31 x 40 inches; signed in full below the table at the lower right, dated 1676.
The Norton Simon collection, Los Angeles.

Provenance: Sale, Edward O . . . , Paris, 1877 (FRL); sale, Prince Demidoff, San Donato, 15 March 1880, No. 1126 (HdG); collection, Febvre (HdG); sale, Febre (Febvre), Paris, 1882 (FRL); sale, Laurent Richard, Paris, 28–29 May 1886, No. 45 (FRL); sale, Charcot, Paris, 1900 (FRL); collection, Sedelmeyer, Paris (HdG); sale, Sedelmeyer, Paris, 25–28 May 1907, No. 176 (HdG); dealer, Katz, Dieren, 1933 (7); dealer, Goudstikker, Amsterdam, 1939 (6). In 1955/56 it belonged to the Amsterdam dealer P. de Boer, who sold it to the Kleiweg de Zwaan collection in Neerlangbroek (The Netherlands). The picture passed from that collection to that of Norton Simon.

Exhibitions: Amsterdam, Tercentenaire de Rembrandt, Müller Gallery, 1906, No. 115; Amsterdam, Gedenck-Clank, Municipal Museum, 1938, No. 102; Amsterdam, Bijbelse Kunst, Rijksmuseum, 1939, No. 121b; Amsterdam, Kersttentoonstelling, P. de Boer, 1955; Dordrecht, Mens en Muziek, Museum, 1957; Bordeaux, La Découverte de la Lumière, Galerie des Beaux Arts, 1959; Utrecht, Het Wonder-Miracula Christi, Artsbisshoppelijk Museum (Centraal Museum), 1962.

It is noted in the Handex and reported elsewhere that the picture is a pendant to the *Expulsion from the Temple* dated 1675 (Cat. 62, Fig. 94) (3). Though the pictures are of the same size and general format, no definite evidence connects the two. The subjects, both from the life of Christ, are possible as pendants, though as Stechow points out, they have no cogent iconographical relationship (12). Space and composition do not work collaterally between them. The connection should be rejected.

The Biblical source for the subject is John 2:1–10. For a discussion of Steen's use of the theme see Cat. 48/49.

Oscar Fischel believed there to be a direct link between the setting of the picture and Jacob van Campen's design for the stage at the Amsterdam Schouwburg (5). Several things make his contention questionable. The theater, built in 1637, was replaced by a new one in 1665 complete with a new facade and more modern stage that did not have an architectural facade structure. Though Steen may have recalled the older stage, which did not have a continuous colonnade but partial ones, it would have been impossible for him to have seen a performance of the *Marriage at Cana* on the stage. Gudlaugsson, in commenting upon Fischel's idea, cited a decree issued by the Synod of Dordrecht of 1617 which forbade the showing of episodes from the life of Christ upon the stage (9). Though it is not known how long the decree was in effect, none of the plays of the time known to the author deal with the life of Christ. According to Heppner, pageant versions of the marriage at Cana were performed by Rederijker groups as entertainments at wedding celebrations (8). Stechow, however, rejects that contention as seeming to be without foundation (12).

Gudlaugsson erred in thinking that Fischel was talking about the picture in the Beit collection (Cat. 48/49, Fig. 62).

The picture is Steen's latest treatment of the theme, which he repeated throughout his life. It shows the expansive space and the predominantly light colors he used in his late years. It also shows Steen's constant re-use of motifs. The landlord, the central couple, the boy rolling the keg, the scattered Orientals, and the hazy figure of Christ are found in the Beit picture of a few years earlier (Cat. 48/49, Fig. 62) and in the still earlier version formerly in the Hudig collection (Cat. 50b, Fig. 30).

Bibliography: (1) de Saint-Groux, André, "La collection Ch. Sedelmeyer," *Les Arts*, VI, 1907, p. 20; (2) Sales Cat., Sedelmeyer Sale, Paris, 25–28 May 1907, No. 176; (3) Van Gelder, *O-H*, XLIII, 1926, p. 210; (4) Bredius, *Steen*, 1927, p. 34; (5) Fischel, *Burlington*, LXVI, 1935, p. 65; (6) Cat., *Bijbelse Kunst*, Amsterdam, 1939, No. 121b; (7) Trautscholdt, "Steen," *T-B*, 1937, p. 511; (8) Heppner, *J of W&CI*, III, 1939/40, p. 44; (9) Gudlaugsson, *De Komedianten*, 1945, p. 6; (10) Cat., La Découverte de la Lumière, Bordeaux, 1959; (11) de Jonge, *Steen* (Palet

Series), n.d., p. 56; (12) Stechow, W., *Nederlands Kunsthistorisch Jaarboek*, XXIII, 1972, pp. 74, 81.

50a] THE MARRIAGE AT CANA

HdG 50a is identical with HdG 45; see entry under 45.

50b] THE MARRIAGE AT CANA

HdG 50A**

Fig. 30

Panel; 29½ x 36 inches; signed in full on the terrace and dated 1653 (?).

Destroyed.

Provenance: Sale, Sir William A. Clavering, 18 March 1921, London, Christie's No. 111 (Handex); dealer, Krantz and de Bruyn, Amsterdam, 1922 (Handex); sale, Bringenberg, Amsterdam, 25 June 1925, No. 241 (Handex); collection, J. M. Hudig, Rotterdam, 1926 (2); dealer, London, 1930. The painting was destroyed during World War II (8).

Exhibition: Leiden, Jan Steen Tentoonstelling, "De Lakenhal," 1926, No. 79.

The Biblical source for the subject is John 2:1–10. For a discussion of Steen's use of the theme see Cat. 48/49.

This painting was added to Hofstede de Groot's catalogue by Trautscholdt (6).

The painting, first publicly seen in 1926 at Leiden, became immediately the center of a controversy. Its authenticity has never been doubted. The controversy developed over the half-obliterated date. The catalogue of the 1926 show reported the date as 1655 (2). In the following issue of *Oud-Holland*, J. G. van Gelder claimed that in a strong light it was clearly visible as 1646 and used the picture to establish an early style under the tutelage of a Rembrandt disciple, probably in Haarlem. He offers Jacob de Wet as a possible teacher (3).

Van Gelder's position was challenged by Bredius in the following issue of *Oud-Holland* (1); he felt that the partially obliterated date should better be read 165?. Further, he adds, this is too mature a work to be that of a beginner; and he mentions the well established fact that Steen began his career as a painter of small landscapes. There is general concurrence that Bredius was correct in these assertions (6) (5). According to Stechow, Van Gelder subsequently abandoned the 1646 reading in favor of 1656, a position with which Stechow concurs (8). In his study of Steen a year later, Bredius, without explanation, gave the date as 1663 (4), too late to be accepted.

Van Gelder may have been incorrect in seeking a date in the 1640's, but he was correct in establishing an early Rembrandtesque style under the tutelage of de Wet. (See Cat. 8, 28.) Several of the motifs and the use of chiaroscuro document that influence. A better date for it would be around 1653, the year of the *Village Wedding* (HdG 455, Fig. 25), which reveals a similar dependency.

Bibliography: (1) Bredius, *O-H*, XLIII, 1926, pp. 267–68; (2) Cat., Steen, Leiden, 1926, No. 79; (3) Van Gelder, J. G., *O-H*, XLIII, 1926, p. 206; (4) Bredius, *Steen*, 1927, p. 34; (5) Martin, *ZfbK*, LXI, 1927/28, p. 326; (6) Trautscholdt, "Steen," *T-B*, 1937, p. 510; (7) Martin, *Steen*, 1954, p. 78; (8) Stechow, W., *Nederlands Kunsthistorisch Jaarboek*, XXIII, 1972, pp. 74, 82 note 7.

51] CHRIST IN THE HOUSE OF MARY AND MARTHA

Fig. 40

Panel; 30 x 28 inches; signed in full on edge of fountain.

Donald Maxwell Macdonald, on show at Pollok House, Glasgow.

Provenance: Sale, G. Kamermans, Rotterdam, 3 Oct. 1825, No. 4 (HdG). The picture entered the Stirling-Maxwell collection prior to 1907 (HdG). From there it passed to its present owner.

Exhibition: London, Jan Steen Exhibition, Dowdeswell Galleries, 1909, No. 1.

The Biblical source for the subject is Luke 10:38–42.

Of this picture Hofstede de Groot wrote: "It is a very good picture with many well painted accessories." Despite this overall acceptance, the picture presents certain difficulties, which Martin brought to light on the occasion of its exhibition in London in 1909. In general, he did not find the painting very exciting; and what troubled him most was the still life in the foreground. He found the technique so foreign to Steen that he hesitated to declare it his work. Further, he suggests that the whole might be a work by Steen's son, Cornelis (born 1656), retouched and corrected by the master (2).

Martin's assertion that Steen's son painted the picture lacks evidence; however, he is correct in questioning the still life, which most probably is a later addition. It appears as if someone, dissatisfied with the vacant foreground, filled it in with a still life acceptable to the subject. In so doing, however, space and scale have been distorted.

Waagen, who saw and described the picture, thought it an admirable work (but in neglected condition) and close in style to *The Marriage at Cana* then in the Arenberg collection (Cat. 46, Fig. 96) (1). In both pictures the scene is separated from the view by a large curtain pulled aside to reveal the action. The Arenberg picture, however, is almost certainly too late to be here directly associated.

A note in the Handex calls it "probably an early work" and thus perhaps explains its weakness. C. W. de Groot repeats this possibility (3), which the present writer finds difficult to accept. In use of light and in composition the painting is close to *The Child Jesus in the Temple* (Cat. 44, Fig. 39) and should probably be dated around the same time, 1659/60.

Bibliography: (1) Waagen, *Treasures of Art in Great Britain*, 1859, IV (supplement), p. 452; (2) Martin, *L'art flamand et hollandais*, XII, 1909, p. 56; (3) de Groot, *Beeld en Woord*, 1952, pp. 176–77.

51a] CHRIST IN THE HOUSE
HdG 51A** OF MARY AND MARTHA

Removed from the Catalogue; see Addendum 6.

52/440] THE PRODIGAL SON
(THE GARDEN PARTY)

Removed from the Catalogue; see Addendum 13.

53] THE PRODIGAL SON

Removed from the Catalogue; see Addendum 7.

54] THE PRODIGAL AMONG THE HARLOTS

Subject redesignated as *Antiochus and Stratonice*. See Cat. 84b/54.

54a*] THE PRODIGAL SON

No information on this painting is available. It was added by the Handex without comment. It may be a reference to another listed picture of the subject.

54b*]** THE PRODIGAL SON

Removed from the Catalogue; see Addendum 8.

55] THE RETURN OF THE PRODIGAL SON
Fig. 80

Canvas; 48 x 38 inches; signed in full in the lower left corner.

Countess Brita Wachmeister, Kulla Gunnarstorp (Sweden).

Provenance: Collection, Finspong (HdG); collection, Van Plafen (HdG); collection, Count Carl de Geer, Kulla Gunnarstorp (5); collection, Wachtmeister, Kulla Gunnarstorp (1).

Exhibition: Lund, Gamla Holländare, University, 1953, No. 49.

The picture was restored and relined about 1950.

The Biblical source for the subject is Luke 15:18–24.

This is Steen's only known interpretation of the scene. It is, judging from a photograph, not a very inspired painting. In particular, the organization is common for the subject and the depiction of the emotions not very convincing.

The figural type of the Prodigal is familar from a number of Biblical and historical paintings from the late 1660's—e.g., *The Marriage of Tobias and Sarah* (Cat. 25a/457, Fig. 66), *Tamar and Amnon* (Cat. 16, Fig. 72), *The Banquet of Antony and Cleopatra* (Cat. 86a/b, Fig. 60). Along with those paintings it should be dated around 1668/69.

A close copy of this painting was sold at the Herrenberger sale at Lepke's in Berlin on 1 Dec. 1908, No. 87. This copy is possibly identical with Cat. 56 (2) here given as Addendum 9.

Bibliography: (1) Granberg, Cat., Wachmeister Collection, 1886, No. 50; (2) Bredius, *Steen*, 1927, p. 36, pl. 11; (3) Trautscholdt, "Steen," *T-B*, 1937, p. 511; (4) de Groot, *Beeld en Woord*, 1952, p. 21; (5) Cat., Gamla Holländare I, Skänska Hem, Lund, 1953, No. 49.

56] THE RETURN OF THE PRODIGAL SON

Removed from the Catalogue; see Addendum 9.

57/61?] THE UNJUST STEWARD

58½ x 78 inches.

Sale, Pook and Theodorus van Pee, The Hague, 23 May 1747, No. 12 (HdG).

Hofstede de Groot quotes the following descriptive phrase, "with many figures. Good in composition and execution." He adds that it is probably identical with 61. No further information is available on the picture. The identity between it and 61 is tentative.

58] THE PARABLE OF THE RICH MAN
Fig. 103 AND LAZARUS*

Canvas on panel; 32 x 26 inches; signed in full on balustrade in front.

Private collection, New York.

Provenance: Collection (dealer) Hoogendijk, Amsterdam, 1899 (HdG); in 1907 Hoogendijk lent the picture to the Rijksmuseum, where it was exhibited until 1912 (1); sale, Hoogendijk, Amsterdam, Muller, 14 May 1912, No. 76 (2); dealer, Goudstikker, Amsterdam, 1920 (3); collection, Preyer, The Hague, 1930's (FRL); collection, Willinck, Winterswijk, 1930's; dealer, Katz, Dieren, 1935; collection, A. Bronkhorst, The Hague, 1937 (4); dealer, Schaeffer, New York, 1938 (FRL); dealer, Goudstikker, Amsterdam, 1940 (Handex); collection, Wetzlar, Amsterdam; dealer, Borghouts, Utrecht; sale, Paris, Charpentier, 6 June 1958; dealer, Weitzner, London, 1959. Weitzner lent the picture to the Bob Jones University Museum, Greenville, South Carolina. It was purchased by the present owner from Weitzner.

Exhibitions: Rotterdam, 1899, No. 14; The Hague, Collection Goudstikker, "Pulchri Studio," 1920, No. 108; The Hague, Kunstzaal Kleykamp, 1934; Nijmegen, Huize Belvoir, 1936, No. 63; Dieren, Summer Exhibition, D. Katz, 1937, No. 94; Deventer, 1948, No. 36; The Hague, 1956, No. 21; Greenville, South Carolina, Bob Jones University Museum, 1959.

The Biblical source for the subject is Luke 16:19–21.

This is Steen's only religious picture which contains a moralizing inscription. *In weelde ziet toe* (in wealth take care) is chiseled in a free script in the stone of the low balustrade at the foreplane of the painting. The saying implies that in wealth it is necessary to beware of moral depravity, and the story of Lazarus is used to show one aspect of such depravity: the lack of charity. Steen consciously compares the begging of the poodle with the begging of the desperate Lazarus. He used the same proverb in his *Dissolute Living* in Vienna (HdG 102), where the same idea of moral weakening is expressed through the proverb. In both cases, however, he delights in displaying the lovely ruins of indulgence, and moralization cannot be taken as his primary concern (5).

Hofstede de Groot found the picture " . . . spirited in color, but, as a composition, lacking in harmony." It was not, he felt, among Steen's best works. The judgment is a fair one, especially when the painting is compared to Steen's outstanding treatment of the subject in another picture now with Lehmann in Cologne (Cat. 59, Fig. 57).

The painting was probably made in the late 1670's, and can be associated in style with the so-called "Prodigal Son" or *Garden Party* (see Add. 13, Fig. 98) dated 1677. He achieves in both a wispy elegance which characterizes his later works.

Bibliography: (1) Cat., Rijksmuseum, Amsterdam, 1911, No. 2250c; (2) Sales Cat., Hoogendijk, Amsterdam, 14 May 1912, No. 76; (3) Cat., Collection Goudstikker, The Hague, 1920, No. 108; (4) Trautscholdt, "Steen," *T-B*, 1937, p. 511; (5) de Groot, *Beeld en Woord*, 1952, pp. 63–64.

59] THE PARABLE OF THE RICH MAN AND LAZARUS*

Fig. 57

Canvas on panel; 32½ x 27½ inches, signed in full at the lower left and dated 1667.
Fritz Lehmann, Cologne.

Provenance: Sale, Thomas Schwendke, The Hague, 6 Oct. 1767, No. 30 (HdG); sale, Hendrik Verschuuring, The Hague, 17 Sept. 1770, No. 173 (HdG); sale, Bicker and Wijkersloot, Amsterdam, 19 July 1809 (No. 50) (HdG); dealer, Woodburn, London, 1833 (HdG); the order of its subsequent owners is hard to establish; however, we know it belonged to Dr. Walter Cohen in Dusseldorf (probably 1939); Goudstikker, the Amsterdam dealer; and Frits Lugt, Utrecht. After the war, it was in the collection of Joseph Hanstein in Cologne (?), and it passed through the auction house Lempertz at Cologne to Fritz Lehmann.

The Biblical source for the picture is Luke 16:19-21.

This is one of Steen's best religious pictures. Its date of 1667 makes it an historically important picture as well—for, though coming fairly late in his career, the picture shows a connection with Nicholas Knüpfer. Indeed, this painting, with its platforms and its striking diagonal light, is the closest Steen gets to Knüpfer.

In 1927, Martin attempted to show that a painting of *Lazarus on the Steps*, signed Metsu, at Strasbourg (Fig. 61), was really by Steen, and that he had taken the central motif and general setting from Knüpfer's painting of the same subject at the museum in Liege, there mistakenly given to J. B. Weenix (Fig. 7) (1). Though the pictures are connected, Martin's attribution of the Strasbourg picture to Steen is dubious, and has not found general acceptance. Martin does not mention it in his monograph of 1954. The picture in Strasbourg, though generally given to Metsu (2) (3), may be a second version by Knüpfer himself. Kuznetsov, however, does not list it in his catalogue of Knüpfer's works (8).

Steen clearly knew the Strasbourg picture and based his own work upon it. He repeats with some variation the servant girl going up the stairs, the figures around Lazarus, and (though in changed perspective) the architectural setting. The date of the picture makes it clear that Steen's connection with Knüpfer cannot be limited to his early years, as often held (6) (7) (4). This picture, along with *The Prayer of Tobias and Sarah* (Cat. 25c, Fig. 65), also made around 1667/68 and showing even more direct dependence on Knüpfer, offers the only documentary evidence of Steen's reliance on the older master.

In both the present picture and the one in Strasbourg, the scene around Lazarus has been altered. In the latter the servant was originally urinating on Lazarus. In the Steen, the little boy, as part of an unpleasant joke, was urinating into a stein, apparently to be offered to Lazarus. Both motifs have been painted out.

Bibliography: (1) Martin, *ZfbK*, LXI, 1927/28, p. 329; (2) Plietzsch, *Pantheon*, XVII, 1936, p. 6; (3) Trautscholdt, "Steen," *T-B*, 1937, p. 512; (4) Simon, *Pantheon*, XXVI, 1940, p. 162; (5) Gudlaugsson, *De Komedianten*, 1945, pp. 52–53; (6) de Groot, *Beeld en Woord*, 1952, p. 176; (7) Martin, *Steen*, 1954, pp. 27–28; (8) Kuznetsov, *Trudy Gosudarstvennogo ermitazha*, VIII, No. 3, n.d., pp. 212–13.

60] CHRIST BLESSING THE LITTLE CHILDREN*
Fig. 5

Panel; 15 x 17 inches; signed in full (?).
Private collection, Amsterdam.

Provenance: Sale, J. B. van den Bergh, Amsterdam, 15 July 1833 (No. 230) (HdG); its subsequent history until 1951 cannot be reconstructed. In that year it belonged to the Amsterdam dealer P. de Boer, from whom it was acquired by its present owner.

Exhibition: Amsterdam, P. de Boer, Old Masters, July/Aug. 1951, No. 43.

The Biblical source for this subject is Mark 10:13–16.

This is one of Steen's early pictures, and it must be dated in the first years of the 1650's. It is associated in style with *The Death of Ananias* (Cat., 66, Fig. 1), dated 1651. The probability is that the painting falls between the *Ananias* and *The Village Wedding* (HdG 455, Fig. 25) at the Boymans/van Beuningen Museum, of 1653.

It is outstanding in the tenderness of the blessing that Christ offers the children, and in the warmth of the diffused evening light, which Steen may here have painted for the first time.

Bibliography: Cat., *Old Masters*, P. de Boer, Amsterdam, 1951, No. 43.

61] THE STEWARD PAYING THE MEN THEIR WAGES
(The Workers in the Vineyard)

Sale, David Ietswaart, Amsterdam, 22 April 1749, No. 87 (HdG); sale, Amsterdam, 4 June 1766, appendix, No. 10 (HdG).

According to Hofstede de Groot, the picture is "probably" identical with Cat. 57; see that entry.

62] THE EXPULSION FROM THE TEMPLE*
Fig. 94

Canvas; 32 x 43½ inches; signed in full and dated 1675 on the paper in the foreground.
Stedelijk Museum "De Lakenhal," Leiden; on loan from the Dutch Government (Dienst voor 's Rijks Verspreide Kunstvoorwerpen, The Hague).

Provenance: Sale, Lord Harrington, London, 1781 (HdG); sale, Duchess de Berry, Paris, 4 April 1837 (in Lemaître catalogue, but not in Berry catalogue—see below) (HdG); sale, Mafait of Lille, Paris, 19 Dec. 1864, No. 43 (HdG); sale, Lemaître, Paris, 5 March 1870, No. 74 (HdG); sale, G. Rothan, Paris, Galerie Georges Petit, 29 May 1890 (HdG); collection, Yerkes, N.Y. (Handex); sale, Yerkes, N.Y., American Art Association, 5–8 April 1910, No. 139 (Handex); dealer, Katz, Dieren, 1939; collection, S. J. van Oss, The Hague (Handex); after the war it became the property of the Dutch government, and is presently on loan to "De Lakenhal," Leiden.

Exhibitions: Paris, Old Masters Exhibition, Palais Bourbon, 1874; Leiden, Jan Steen, "De Lakenhal," 1926 (No. 54); The Hague, Oude Kunst uit Haagsbezit, Gemeente Museum, 1936/37 (No. 187); Amsterdam, Bijbelse Kunst, Rijksmuseum, 1939 (No. 98a); The Hague, Herwonnen Kunstbezit, Mauritshuis, 1946 (No. 61).

The Biblical source for the subject is John 2:13–16. In his treatment of the theme Steen shows familiarity with Rembrandt's etching of 1635. The interior architectural structure seems related and they share the motif of the man grasping the money in his arms. Steen has included several rabbinical types among his peasants to give the whole an air of authenticity.

The similarity of style, date, and size between this picture and *The Marriage at Cana* of 1676, in the Norton Simon collection (Cat. 50, Fig. 95), has led to the suggestion that they were made as pendants (2). Though the scale and general mood of the pictures might allow such a contention, the space does not work collaterally in both pictures, and the subjects, though both from the life of Christ, are not iconographically connected. The idea that they are pendants must be rejected.

Along with *The Marriage at Cana* the picture can be taken as an indication of the less elegant side of Steen's late style. In this respect it contrasts markedly with the *Garden Party* of 1677 (see Add. 13, Fig. 98), which reveals his late proclivities for greater elegance.

Bibliography: (1) Cat., Steen, Leiden, 1926, No. 54; (2) Van Gelder, J. G., *O-H*, XLIII, 1926, p. 210; (3) Bredius, *Steen*, 1927, p. 34; (4) Martin, *ZfbK*, LXI, 1927/28, p. 327; (5) Cat., Bijbelse Kunst, Amsterdam, 1939, No. 98a; (6) Martin, *Steen*, 1954, p. 71; (7) de Jonge, *Steen* (Palet Series), n.d., p. 56.

63] THE LAST SUPPER

26 x 25 inches.

Sale, G. van Lill, Dordrecht, 18 June 1743, No. 10 (HdG).

Hofstede de Groot gives the following descriptive phrase: "A masterpiece of the artist's." There is no further information on the painting.

64] THE BETRAYAL OF CHRIST

Removed from the Catalogue; see Addendum 10.

65] CHRIST AT EMMAUS*

Fig. 45

Canvas; 53½ x 41½ inches; signed in full in the lower left-hand corner.

Rijksmuseum, Amsterdam.

Provenance: Sale, Macalester Loup, The Hague, 20 Aug. 1806, No. 4 (HdG); sale, A. van der Werff van Zuidland, Dordrecht, 31 July 1811, No. 99 (HdG); sale, J. Hulswit, Amsterdam, 28 Oct. 1882 (HdG); sale, Earl of Clancarty, London, 17 March 1892, No. 83 (HdG); dealer, Colnaghi, London, 1893 (HdG); collection, G. de Clercq, Amsterdam, 1894 (HdG); in 1900 it was bought for the Rijksmuseum by the Rembrandt Society.

Exhibitions: Utrecht, Old Masters, 1894, No. 431; Amsterdam, Bijbelse Kunst, Rijksmuseum, 1939, No. 116a.

The Biblical source is Luke 24:28–32. Steen chose a moment rarely represented. He shows Christ's disappearance after his recognition. Its representation of religious mystery sets this picture apart within Steen's oeuvre. He rarely touched upon such phenomena. It is the mystery in the picture that led H. E. van Gelder to find in it, of all Steen's paintings, a "truly religious atmosphere" (2). Schmidt-Degener, on the other hand, found it a grand failure precisely because it lacked miracle (2). Van Gelder and Hofstede de Groot describe the pilgrims as lost in prayer as Christ vanishes. Such a description misses the point. Steen's pilgrims are in a profound hallucinatory sleep, and the remarkable stillness of the servants creates a world of dream-trance.

C. W. de Groot suggests correctly that Steen was dependent upon Rembrandt in his treatment of the subject (3). A drawing in the Fitzwilliam Museum attributed to Rembrandt shows the same seldom represented moment of Christ's disappearance. Rembrandt's interpretation, however, is one of startlement and excitation on the part of the disciples, rather than Steen's essential quiet.

The probable date of the picture is 1659/60. It is close in style to *Grace Before Meat* dated 1660 in the Simon Morrison collection (HdG No. 375). In both, one finds the forms are composed of large planes; and the colors are fairly uniform. This is generally characteristic of Steen's paintings of this time (5). The two paintings share also a certain sober piety.

Bibliography: (1) Bredius, *Steen*, 1927, p. 37, pl. 13; (2) Schmidt-Degener and Van Gelder, *Steen*, 1927, pp. 16, 54; (3) de Groot, *Beeld en Woord*, 1952, pp. 172, 179; (4) Cat., Rijksmuseum, Amsterdam, 1956, No. 2250; (5) Martin, *Steen*, 1954, p. 39.

65a] CHRIST AT EMMAUS

The moment shown is the same as in the previous picture and is found in Luke 24:31.

According to Jacob Campo Weyerman's biography of Steen, a picture of this subject was in the house of Jakob le Beuf at Leiden. He praised the picture highly, saying "Sometimes, rarely but excellently, he painted histories in a wonderful way. Look at, among others, a painting to be seen at the house of Heere Jakob le Beuf at Leyden, which contains the vanishing Christ and the astonished disciples at Emmaus. Truly one can, and must say that he made that artful piece with the exertion of all the powers of his soul. . . . " (1).

This description does not allow the identification of this picture with Cat. 65 (Fig. 45). The pilgrims in that painting in the Rijksmuseum cannot really be described as astonished. For this reason, this work is kept as a separate entry, though it may actually be identical with 65.

Bibliography: (1) Weyerman, *De Levens-Beschrijving*, II, 1729, p. 364.

65b] THE DISCIPLES AT EMMAUS

Canvas.

Sale, Van Berneveld, Van den Haute, *et al.*, Antwerp, 26 Feb. 1844, No. 15 (HdG). There is no further information on this picture. The reference might belong to either HdG 65 or HdG 65a.

66] THE DEATH OF ANANIAS
Fig. 1

Panel; 18 x 14½ inches; signed in full at the bottom right-hand corner and dated 1651.
Present location unknown.

Provenance: Sale, Halfwassenaar, The Hague, 31 March 1770 (HdG); sale, Amsterdam, 6 Aug. 1810, No. 94 (HdG); sale, H. Crosse, Amsterdam, 18 Sept. 1811, No. 1701 (HdG); sale, J. Hulswit, Amsterdam, 28 Oct. 1822, No. 112 (HdG); collection, D. J. van Eewijck van der Bildt of Haarlem (HdG); sale, Roos, Amsterdam, 31 Oct. 1871, No. 285 (HdG); collection, Besier, Utrecht, 1872; dealer, Herbrand, Paris, 1943 (Handex); collection, H. A. J. Stenger, The Hague, 1951 (Handex). Its most recent owner was Dr. Boas of Amsterdam, but its present location is unknown to this writer.

Exhibitions: Amsterdam, 1872; Paris, Palais Bourbon, 1874 (as Terborch).

The subject, representing an episode from the life of St. Peter found in Acts 5:1–6, is one of the few Catholic subjects in Steen's work, and indicates his Catholic background, which for the most part is not revealed in his painting.

The Death of Ananias is Steen's earliest dated picture (3) (2). (Hofstede de Groot lists a *Preparation for Blood Letting* of 1650, No. 150a, but says it is probably a copy; the work is untraceable.) The picture is not Steen's earliest work, but very likely represents the beginning of his efforts in historical painting. Only *The Seven Acts of Mercy* (Cat. 67, Fig. 15) may precede it in date, but in many ways that painting, though it has a religious theme, is really a village street scene. Despite the awkwardness of some parts of the painting, Henri Harvard in his review of the Amsterdam exhibition of 1872 said of *The Death of Ananias,* " . . . ce petit panneau est un vrai tableau d'histoire" (1), a compliment rarely paid Steen's historical paintings in the 19th century.

Martin felt that Steen's debt to the Raphael cartoon of the subject in London was apparent (3). Outside of the correspondence of subject, that connection is dubious. One can more easily find touches of Rembrandt in the picture—the Jew, the Oriental, and particularly the head of Peter, who resembles some of Rembrandt's early studies of Orientals.

Bibliography: (1) Harvard, *GdBA*, VI, 1872, p. 378; (2) Trautscholdt, "Steen," *T-B*, 1937, p. 512; (3) Martin, *Steen*, 1954, pp. 24, 31.

67] THE SEVEN ACTS OF MERCY
Fig. 15

Canvas; 18½ x 22½ inches; monogrammed at the lower left.
Private collection, Holland.

Provenance: Prior to 1899 sold as a Droochsloot (HdG). Sale, Brunswig, Cologne, 1899 (listed as a school piece) (HdG); sale, Van der Meulen, Amsterdam, 3 April 1900, No. 83 (HdG). Since 1937 it has been at its present location.

Probably Steen's earliest picture with a religious theme. It predates *The Death of Ananias* of 1651 (Cat. 66, Fig. 1) by several years and reveals Steen's early Utrecht connections, particularly those with the elder Droochsloot, whose village paintings, such as the one in the Boymans/van Beuningen Museum (Fig. 17), Steen's work resembles (3). As both Gerson and Martin have shown, Steen began his career neither as a genre painter nor as a historical painter, but as a landscapist (2) (3). It is not at all surprising that the picture was at one time sold as a Droochsloot.

The givers of mercy all appear to be monks, perhaps indicating Steen's own Catholic background, which for the most part does not reveal itself in the later religious paintings.

Bibliography: (1) Trautscholdt, "Steen," *T-B*, 1937, p. 511; (2) Martin, *Burlington*, LXVII, 1935, pp. 211–12; (3) Gerson, *Kunsthistorische Mededelinging*, III, 1948, pp. 50 ff; (4) Martin, *Steen*, 1954, p. 27.

68] THE CONCERT OF ST. CECILIA

43½ x 33 inches.

Sale, Amsterdam, 18 May 1756, No. 3 (HdG); sale, the widow Philip van Dijk, The Hague, 26 Nov. 1763, No. 6 (HdG).

There is no further information on this picture. Hofstede de Groot gives the following descriptive phrase: "with numerous figures, very carefully executed."

69] ST. MICHAEL AND THE SLAIN DRAGON*

Subject redesignated as *The Angel Raphael Casting Out the Devil.* See Cat. 25d/69.

HISTORICAL AND MYTHOLOGICAL WORKS

69a] LAUGHING BACCHUS, HOLDING UP A BUNCH OF GRAPES

Canvas.
Sale, Amsterdam, 15 Aug. 1825, No. 243 (HdG). Research has revealed no further information on the picture.

69b/520?] THESEUS AND ACHELOÜS

Fig. 52

Panel; 14½ x 18½ inches; signed in full on the edge of the table.
Present location unknown.

Provenance: Sale, J. K. van der Meir, Antwerp, 23 June 1755, No. 3 (HdG 520); dealer, Muller, Amsterdam, before 1908 (HdG); collection, Max Rosefeld, Stuttgart, 1908 (HdG); collection, Philips, The Hague, 1937 (2); collection, Hoos, or Haas, San Raphael, Calif. (RKHD). The picture was sold as "The Grotto of Neptune" at Christies, 7 July 1972 (No. 96) as the property of Mr. and Mrs. Eugene Ferkauf of New York (5). Purchased by De Wilt.

Exhibition: The Hague, "Oude Kunst uit Haagsch Bezit," Gemeente Museum, 1936/7 (as "Het Gastmaal van Naptunus").

Van Gils correctly identified the subject of this painting, earlier known as *The Grotto of Neptune* (3). Hofstede de Groot declared it possibly identical with *The Feast of the Gods* (HdG 520). The story, which has its source in Ovid's *Metamorphoses* (Book VIII), tells how Theseus on his return from the Calydonian boar-hunt was entertained by the river god Acheloüs until the river receded from flood stage. Van Gils reproduced along with the Steen a print by Martin Bouché from Durijer's 1677 translation of the *Metamorphoses* showing a similar scene identified as the given subject. This translation of Ovid is certainly too late for Steen to have used, but there were at least twelve Dutch translations made since 1552. It is impossible to tell with which Steen might have been familiar (4).

The painting shows similarities to *Christ in the House of Mary and Martha* (Cat. 51, Fig. 40), such as the distribution around the table and the alternation of light and dark areas. That picture probably was made about 1659/60. If the same date is accepted for this picture, it would be identifiable as Steen's earliest classical motif. However, since the author has not examined the painting, this suggestion is offered as a tentative one. The attribution to Steen is not at all certain. Some of the painting seems far too flat and opaque to be convincing.

Bibliography: (1) Cat., Oude Kunst, The Hague, 1936/37; (2) Trautscholdt, "Steen," *T-B*, 1937, p. 511; (3) Van Gils, *O-H*, LVII, 1940, pp. 145ff; (4) de Groot, *Beeld en Woord*, 1952, pp. 68, 71.

69c] CUPID REPOSING

Canvas.
Sale, Amsterdam, 15 Aug. 1825, No. 244. Research has revealed no further information on this picture.

70/408] ASCANIUS AND LUCILLA (LUCELLE)

Removed from the Catalogue; see Addendum 14.

71] VERTUMNUS AND POMONA

Canvas; 31 x 25 inches.
Sale, J. A. van Dam, Dordrecht, 1 June 1829, No. 120 (HdG). "Half-lengths, powerfully rendered; according to the catalogue, one of the artist's best works" (HdG). Research has revealed no further information on the picture.

72] CERES SEEKING FOR PROSERPINE

Canvas; approximately 27 x 22½ inches.
Sale, Donner, de Béez, Antwerp, 27 May 1777, No. 115 (HdG); sale, F. A. E. Bruijnincx, Antwerp, 1 Aug. 1791, No. 81 (HdG).

Hofstede de Groot quotes a description, probably taken from one of the sales catalogues: "Ceres drinks with avidity the wine mingled with honey that an old woman of Eleusis offers her. To the left a boy mocks her and is by way of punishment transformed into a lizard. Ceres' torch diffuses soft light over the scene. It is one of the artist's best works."

Research has revealed no further information on the picture.

72b]** APOLLO AND DAPHNE

Removed from the Catalogue; see Addendum 11.

73] ERYSICHTHON SELLING HIS DAUGHTER*

Fig. 51

Canvas; 26½ x 24½ inches; signed in full on the tree trunk at the right.
Rijksmuseum, Amsterdam.

Provenance: Sale, C. Baron Droste, The Hague, 21 July 1734, No. 39 (HdG); sale, van Zvieten, The Hague, 12 April 1741, No. 207 (HdG); dealer, Fischhof, Paris (HdG); collection, Hoogendijk, The Hague. In 1912 the picture was presented by the Hoogendijk heirs to the Rijksmuseum.

The story, seldom represented, is taken from Ovid's *Metamorphoses* (Book VIII). Erysichthon the woodsman cut down a grove of trees sacred to Ceres, for which act he was punished with eternal and raging hunger. Here he sells his daughter, Hypermnestra, to a stranger for the food that lies on the ground.

Schmidt-Degener felt that Steen turned to a direct literal translation of the story in order to ridicule humanistic learning (1). There is much to make this contention creditable. Steen has placed the herrings given as part of the price immediately below Hypermnestra, who with bared breast bewails her fate. Her emaciated father receives some coins to close the bargain.

C. W. de Groot's dating of about 1670 is unacceptable (3), it being clearly too late; by that time Steen had opened up his landscapes (see *David Returning Victorious* of 1671, Cat. 13, Fig. 83). The painting was probably made around 1667 and might be compared to *The Rich Man and Lazarus* of that year (Cat. 59, Fig. 57) or *The Trick-Track Players* also of that year in The Hermitage (HdG 719, Fig. 53). In all three, Steen seems interested in the creation of broken accents within an enclosed space.

Bibliography: (1) Schmidt-Degener and Van Gelder, *Steen*, 1927, p. 10; (2) Trautscholdt, "Steen," *T-B*, p. 512; (3) de Groot, *Beeld en Woord*, 1952, pp. 69–70; (4) Cat., Rijksmuseum, Amsterdam, 1960, No. 2250–A1.

74] THE SACRIFICE OF IPHIGENIA*

Fig. 82

Canvas; 64 x 59 inches; fully signed at lower left, and dated 1671.

Rijksmuseum, Amsterdam; on loan from the Dutch Government (Dienst voor 's Rijks Verspreide Kunstvoorwerpen, The Hague).

Provenance: Sale, Fouquet, London, 10–11 Feb. 1773, No. 58 (Sales Cat.); collection, Lady Cremorne, 1842 (HdG, Sm); probable collection, Rawdon (HdG); collection, A. Preyer, Versailles (3); sale, A. Preyer, Muller, Amsterdam, 8 Nov. 1927 (10); dealer, Goudstikker, Amsterdam. After the Second World War it became the property of the Dutch government (Dienst voor's Rijks verspreide Kunstvoorwerpen). Since 1948 it has been on loan to the Rijksmuseum.

Exhibitions: London, The British Gallery, 1835; Leiden, Jan Steen Tentoonstelling, "De Lakenhal," 1926, No. 60.

Steen could have known the subject from Ovid's *Metamorphoses* (Book XII). However, of all of Steen's paintings, it shows the greatest dependency upon stage construction, especially in the architectural wings in the middle ground (7), and Van Gils attempted to show a direct connection between the painting and Samuel Coster's play *Iphigenia* (5). The last performance of the play was in 1630 (8), and though Steen may have come to know it later on, it is hardly possible for him to have seen it. A better possible connection would be Vondel's 1666 translation of Euripides' *Iphigenia in Tauris* (8). While that play does not center around the theme of the sacrifice, it recalls that event as an important part of its exposition.

Joshua Reynolds in 1786 described and commented upon the picture in his Eighth Discourse before the Royal Academy. He used it as an example of inappropriate mixing of "higher" and "lower" classes art, and of misdirected ambition. He found Steen "perfectly ridiculous" in this attempt at history painting (1). Waagen, who described the picture in 1854, felt similarly that "No subject can be well imagined more foreign to the talent and mode of thought of the painter" (2). These opinions are characteristic of the adverse critical opinion which Steen's history paintings often incited during the eighteenth and nineteenth centuries.

The Sacrifice of Iphigenia is dated 1671 and helps establish Steen's style in the early 1670's. Along with *David Returning Victorious* of the same year (Cat. 13, Fig. 83), it shows the greater lightness of color, and the openness of structure and grouping of these years, especially when compared to the work of the late 1660's—i.e., *Samson and Delilah* of 1668 (Cat. 10, Fig. 67).

Bibliography: (1) Reynolds, *Discourses*, VIII, 1786, p. 236; (2) Waagen, *Treasures of Art in Great Britain*, 1854, II, p. 250; (3) Cat., Steen, Leiden, 1926, No. 60; (4) Bredius, *Steen*, 1927, p. 39; (5) Van Gils, *Op de Hoogte*, XXXIV, 1937, pp. 92–93; (6) Heppner, *J of W&CI*, III, 1939/40, p. 36; (7) Gudlaugsson, *De Komedianten*, 1945, p. 66, n. 53; (8) de Groot, *Beeld en Woord*, 1952, p. 69, n. 8; (9) Martin, *Steen*, 1954, pp. 56 and 71, pl. 62; (10) Cat., Rijksmuseum, Amsterdam, 1960, No. 2250–A5; (11) de Jonge, *Steen* (Palet Series), n.d., p. 55.

75] THE STORY OF MITHRAS

Presently unknown, the painting was mentioned by

Houbraken. He criticized Steen for the anachronism of introducing pickled herring in a classical subject. He identifies the subject as the Fable of Mithras from Naso (*"de Fabel van Mitra, uit Naso"*) (1) (2).

Bibliography: (1) Houbraken, *De Groote Schouburgh*, II, 1719, pp. 245–46 (Swillen's ed., 1944, p. 193); (2) Hofstede de Groot, *Arnold Houbraken und Seine Groote Schouburgh*, 1893, I, p. 168.

76] THE RAPE OF THE SABINE WOMEN

Fig. 50

Canvas; 27½ x 36½ inches; signed in full, lower right. John and Mabel Ringling Museum of Art, Sarasota, Florida.

Provenance: Sale, H. A. Bauer, Amsterdam, 11 Sept. 1820, No. 122 (HdG); collection, W. Gruyter, Amsterdam, 1833/1882 (2) (3); sale, W. Gruyter, Amsterdam, 24 Oct. 1882, No. 107 (HdG); sale, F. H. Wente, Paris, 22 Feb. 1893 (HdG); sale, Schönlank, Cologne, 28 April 1896, No. 172 (as "Benjaminites Carrying Off Shiloh's Daughters") (HdG); dealer, F. Kleinberger, Paris (HdG); collection, W. Dahl, Düsseldorf; collection, A. Preyer, Vienna, 1901 (HdG); collection, W. A. Clark, New York (1); sale, Clark, Anderson Galleries, New York, 1928 (3). (The picture was not part of the larger Clark sale 11–12 Jan. 1926 in New York.)

Exhibition: Amsterdam, 1867, No. 186.

There is no consensus about the identification of the subject. Smith believed it a *Rape of the Sabines* and said of it: " . . . the writer leaves it to the connoisseur's imagination to conceive the singular effect of Roman heroes and Sabine women being represented by Dutch *boers* and *boerins*, while under the influence of the drunken god" (No. 197). Actually, though Steen did not make a heroic picture in the traditional sense, he did costume his figures in other than contemporary dress, thus creating something of a historical milieu. The story of the rape of the Sabines is told by Livy, *History*, I:9. The picture was, however, sold in 1896 as *The Benjaminites Carrying Off Shiloh's Daughters* (Judges 21:21–24). Though the Roman subject is here accepted, it is impossible correctly to identify it. The possibility that the subject is the Biblical one is strengthened by the fact that the episode, an obscure one biblically, appears in Jacob Cats' *Trou-Ringh* of 1637 (II, p. 32), with which Steen was most certainly familiar. (See Cat. 25/487, 25a/457, 85, and 86a/b.)

The probable date of the picture would be the mid-1660's; it is close in style to *Hagar and Ishmael in the Wilderness* (Cat. 2b, Fig. 46) and *Rustic Love* (HdG 819, Fig. 47) in "de Lakenhal" at Leiden, a copy of which (HdG 796) bears the date 1659.

Bibliography: (1) Bredius, *Steen*, 1927, p. 40, pl. 15; (2) *Art News Annual*, Part II (Nov. 1949), p. 25; (3) Cat., John and Mabel Ringling Museum, Sarasota, 1949, No. 269.

[NOTE: HdG 77–81 have been omitted from this catalogue. They are all representations of *The Satyr and the Peasant*. Though the story includes a mythological creature, it is essentially legend rather than myth, and Steen treats it as folk-genre.]

82] DIOGENES

Canvas; 42½ x 37½ inches.
Sale, C. van Wolffen, Leiden, 31 Aug. 1741, No. 3 (HdG); sale, J. P. Wierman, Amsterdam, 18 Aug. 1762, No. 44 (HdG).

Hofstede de Groot gives the following description: "He goes with a lantern in daylight round the marketplace at Athens seeking a man; the boys mock at him. There are numerous figures. Among them is a quack who gives performances on his stage; below is a drunken woman on a barrow, with a woman and children near her. It is a very spirited and amusing composition."

Research has revealed no further information on this picture.

83] THE GENEROSITY OF SCIPIO*

Fig. 84

Canvas; 34½ x 58½ inches; signed in full at lower left on the step.
Present location unknown.

Provenance: Sale, J. C. Pruyssenaar, Amsterdam, 27 Feb. 1804, No. 98 (HdG); sale, B. Ocke, Leiden, 12 April 1817, No. 127 (HdG); collection, Z. Zschille, Dresden (HdG); dealer, Triepel, Grünberg, 1878 (HdG); collection, Weber, Hamburg, 1892 (purchased from Triepel in 1878) (HdG); sale, Weber, Lepke, Berlin, 20–22 Feb. 1912, No. 292 (4); collection, C. J. K. van Aalst, Huis-te-Hoevelaken, Holland; collection, N. J. van Aalst; sale, N. J. van Aalst, Christies, London, 1 April 1960, No. 47; the dealer, Leger, bought it at that sale. Collection C.H. Nordmark; sale, Nordmark Sotheby's, London, 25 Nov. 1970 (No. 108). Leger bought it again at the sale (13).

Exhibition: London, Antique dealers' fair and exhibition, 1960, Leger.

The story is found in both Livy (XXVI, 50) and Polybius (X, 17, 19). A later and perhaps more important source for the popularity of the story during the Renaissance and later is Petrarch's *Africa* (IV, 375–388), in which Scipio is presented as an example of classical virtue.

A small version of this picture (8½ x 12½ inches), possibly an original sketch (8), is in the Michaelis Gallery, Cape Town, South Africa (Fig. 124). It is signed on the lower left. It has been in the gallery since 1913 (3), before which it was in the Arthur Kay sale at Christies, 11–12 May 1911 (No. 129). Trautscholdt mistook this small panel for HdG 83 and reported it in Cape Town (5); and Heppner believed that there were two sketches, one in the Arthur Kay collection, the other in Cape Town (7). If the panel in Cape Town is indeed a preliminary sketch of the painting, it would be the only one in existence and would supply evidence as to Steen's manner of work. The two paintings are just different enough in detail to make the hypothesis of a sketch a strong possibility, but an examination of the original would be necessary before any such conclusion could be reached. If it is a sketch, one of the most interesting things is to see how Steen went from a very rough conception to a highly finished one, while incorporating all the major details. This would seem to parallel his manner of drawing (see Van Regteren-Altena on Steen drawings, *O-H*, LX, 1943, pp. 97 ff).

The openness of the painting, its light tones and clear air, and the elegance of the gestures of the main figures, indicate that the painting was made in the early 1670's. It is related in style to *The Sacrifice of Iphigenia* of 1671 (Cat. 74, Fig. 82) and *David Returning Victorious* of the same year (Cat. 13, Fig. 83).

Bibliography: (1) Von Pflugk-Hartung, *Repertorium für Kunstwissenschaft*, VIII, 1885, p. 85; (2) Cat., Weber collection, 1892, No. 245; (3) Wood, *The Max Michaelis Gift to the Union of South Africa—Flemish and Dutch Paintings*, Michaelis Gallery, Cape Town; London, 1913, No. 54; (4) Sales Cat., Weber, Berlin, 20–22 Feb. 1912, No. 292; (5) Bredius, *Steen*, 1927, p. 39; (6) Trautscholdt, "Steen," *T-B*, 1937, p. 512; (7) Valentiner, "Van Aalst Collection," 1939, p. 286, plate lxix; (8) Heppner, *J of W&CI*, III, 1939/40, p. 39; (9) Bax, *Hollandse en Vlaamse Schilderkunst in Zuid-Afrika*, 1952, pp. 115–16, pl. 66; (10) Martin, *Steen*, 1954, p. 33; (11) *Connoisseur*, CXLVI, 1960, p. 61 (Antique Dealers' Fair and Exhibition Number); (12) *Connoisseur*, CXLVII, 1961, p. 135. (13) Sales Cat., Sotheby's, London, 25 Nov. 1970, No 108.

84] MANIUS CURIUS DENTATUS AND
Fig. 100 THE SAMNITE AMBASSADORS*

Panel; 26 x 31 inches; signed in full on the stone in center.
Present location unknown.

Provenance: Sale, Amsterdam, 29 April 1817, No. 96, as "Marcus Curius" (HdG); sale, London, 1833 (HdG); collection, Matthew Anderson, Desmond Cottage, near Manchester, 1857 (HdG) (1); dealer, Branner Gallery, Paris, 1921 (Witt); collection, A. L. Nicholson, London, 1922 (2); collection, Ehrhardt, Berlin, 1927 (Witt); collection, A. Heppner, Amsterdam, 1936 (cat. Exhib. Rijksmuseum); sale, Barratt, Christies, 14 July 1950 (Witt); dealer, E. Speelman, London (Witt); dealer, St. Lucas, The Hague (RKHD); dealer, de Bos en Hamel, The Hague (RKHD); collection, H. Schellekes, The Hague (RKHD); sale, Sotheby, London, 27 March 1963, No. 52.

Exhibition: Amsterdam, Oude Kunst uit het Bezit van den Internationalen Handel, Rijksmuseum, 1936, No. 154.

This picture has often been called, and is listed by Hofstede de Groot as, *Roman Envoys Inviting Cincinnatus to Take Command of the Army*. That story, which has its source in Livy's *History of Rome* (III:26), might well be accepted as the proper subject, were it not for the presence of the turnips. In his life of Cato, Plutarch tells how the general Curius Dentatus was found boiling turnips in the chimney corner of his rural home. He refused the gift of gold the Samnites offered in return for his help. He sent them away saying that he who was content with such a supper had no need of gold. Thus did stoic virtue triumph.

Heppner, who owned the picture in 1936, also believed it to represent the story of Manius Curius and that it made a pair in didactic theme with *The Generosity of Scipio* (Cat. 83, Fig. 84) (6). He mentions that Flink made a painting of Manius Curius for the Royal Palace in Amsterdam for which Vondel described the virtue of the Roman:

> In the care of her burgomaster Rome may sleep secure, for Marcus [sic] Curius, rejecting the offered gold with scorn, contents himself with a meal of turnips. Thus is a state built on moderation and virtue . . .

Steen has been particularly humorous in his treatment of the subject. As Schmidt-Degener has pointed out, "The whole scene seems to rock with laughter at the silly wisdom of the old Romans" (3). There is, he adds, the moralizing inscription on the standard, *Natura paucis contenta*, but every nook is filled with turnips, onions and pumpkins. With humor also Steen has used the traditional form of the adoration of the Magi for the picture. The envoys bearing gifts, including a chalice, approach Dentatus. In the background is their entourage, including camels, horses, and servants, as so often seen in pictures of the three kings. Steen has included himself, corpulent and wide-eyed, as one of the richly clad emissaries. A smaller version of the subject (Cat. 84a, Fig. 101) has a very similar structure.

The painting is very sketchy, and some areas seem unfinished—e.g., the ground area at the left on which the servant kneels is unresolved. The probability is that the painting was made in the late 1670's, when Steen's style was at its loosest. Because of the question of finish, the dating must remain tentative.

Bibliography: (1) Waagen, *Treasures of Art in Great Britain*, 1857, IV (Supplement), p. 483; (2) Bredius, *Steen*, 1927, p. 39; (3) Schmidt-Degener and Van Gelder, *Steen*, 1927, p. 11; (4) Cat., Oude Kunst uit het Bezit van den Internationalen Handel, Amsterdam, 1936, No. 154; (5) Trautscholdt, "Steen," *T-B*, 1937, p. 512; (6) Heppner, *J of W&CI*, III, 1939/40, p. 37.

84a*]** MANIUS CURIUS DENTATUS AND THE SAMNITE AMBASSADORS
Fig. 101

Panel; 14½ x 19½ inches; signed on top of the standard.
Present location unknown.

Provenance: Collection, F. A. Drey, London, 1940; dealer, H. van den Ploeg, Amsterdam, 1954 (as Marcus Dentatus Curius); collection, Wetzlar, Amsterdam, 1958; (Witt); sale, Wetzlar, Lempertz, Cologne, 11–14 June 1958, No. 129 (called Curius Dentatus); collection, Xenopaulo, Luzern (RKHD).

Exhibition: Delft, Kunst en Antiekbeurs, "Het Prinsehof," 1954.

This painting is a smaller variant of Catalogue No. 84 (Fig. 100). Though there are many differences in detail, the dependency is obvious. The boy in front of 84 and Steen's self-portrait have been eliminated. The position of the dog has changed from left to center, and the view shifted somewhat to the right. If it were not for the fact that the photograph reveals convincing Steen touches (e.g., the children), one might be tempted to declare this a copy or school piece. Study of the original might eliminate troublesome questions.

84b/54] ANTIOCHUS AND STRATONICE*
Fig. 81

Panel; 19 x 23½ inches; signed in full to the left.
Wetzlar collection, Amsterdam.

Provenance: Collection, H. A. J. Munro, London, 1842 (HdG, Sm) (the picture was not in the sale of that collection in London on 1 June 1878); dealer, Duits, London, 1925; dealer, Douwes, Amsterdam, 1926 (2); dealer, Malmedé, Cologne, 1949 (RKHD); dealer, Julius Bühler, Munich, 1956; sale, Rheims and Lauren, Paris, 3 Dec. 1959 (RKHD).

Exhibition: Leiden, Jan Steen Tentoonstelling, "De Lakenhal," 1926, No. 36.

The subject of this picture has been erroneously called "The Prodigal Son among the Harlots" and "The Dispute Between Jacob and Laban." H. Schneider correctly identified the subject as Antiochus and Stratonice (1). The story comes from Plutarch or the even earlier *Facta et Dicta Memorabilia* of Maximus (3). There it is told how Antiochus, the son of Seleucus, pined for his father's young bride Stratonice. Upon discovery of the cause of the youth's illness, the father ceded the woman to the prince. Stechow traces the long literary and pictorial tradition of this theme; it was, he notes, very popular in seventeenth-century drama and later in opera (3). Steen could possibly have known Quinault's drama of 1660 which, according to Heppner, was probably performed in Holland (4).

The picture was painted at the end of the 1660's. Exaggeration of gesture and expression, the vaulting forward of the center group, and the general richness of the setting recall the work of the period; see *Samson and Delilah* of 1668 (Cat. 10, Fig. 67).

Bibliography: (1) Cat., Steen, Leiden, 1926, No. 36; (2) Trautscholdt, "Steen," *T-B*, p. 511; (3) Stechow, *Art Bulletin*, XXVII, 1945, pp. 221–28; (4) Heppner, *J of W&CI*, III, 1939/40, p. 37.

85] THE BANQUET OF ANTONY AND CLEOPATRA
Fig. 87

Canvas; 42½ x 32½ inches; signed in full at lower left.
S. Nystad, The Hague.

Provenance: Sale, Klerk de Reus, The Hague (HdG); sale, J. Witsen, Amsterdam, 16 Aug. 1790, No. 60 (HdG); sale (probably), Lady Thomond, Christies, London, 18 May 1821, No. 54 (HdG 86; note: Hofstede de Groot lists this under No. 86, but that is incorrect since that picture had been in Göttingen since 1805—see Cat. 86). The catalogue of the Thomond sale calls the picture of cabinet size, which means it cannot be No. 86a/b, which is over six feet in length. This means that it is either this picture or 86c, with the likelihood that it is the present one because it was purchased at the sale by G. W. Taylor. It was subsequently in the Josiah Taylor collection. Sale (probable), Josiah Taylor, London, 1828 (HdG); sale, Martial du Blaisel, 1877; collection, Rothschild,

Frankfurt a/M, 1908 (HdG); dealer, Katz, Dieren (FRL); dealer, Schaeffer, New York, 1938 (FRL). It was in a private collection in the United States and then passed to its present owners.

Exhibitions: Poughkeepsie (New York), April 1938, Vassar College; Springfield (Mass.), July 1938, Museum; Providence (Rhode Island), "Dutch Painting in XVII C.," Rhode Island School of Design Museum, Dec. 1938, No. 53; Delft, Antique Dealers' Fair, Oct.–Nov. 1975.

Steen could have known the story of Antony and Cleopatra's banquet from several sources. The original tale appears in Pliny's *Natural History* (X:58), a Dutch translation of which was published in 1662. A play by Willem van Nieuwelandt, *Aegyptica ofte Aegyptische, tragoedie van M. Anthonius en Cleopatra* of about 1606 may have been known to Steen. Another *Cleopatra*, translated from French by Dieverina van Kouwenhoven, appeared in Amsterdam in 1669, and may have been played earlier (3) (4). Jacob Cats described the scene in full detail and richness in the *Huwelijk van Antonius en Cleopatra* in the *Trou-Ringh* of 1637.

Pliny tells how Cleopatra wagered with Antony that she could give a banquet costing ten million sesterces. The wager taken, she dissolved one of her great pearl earrings in vinegar and drank it down. About to do the same with the second, she was stopped by Lucius Plancus, who declared the wager over and Cleopatra the winner. (The second pearl, after Cleopatra's defeat, was split in half and made into earrings for the statue of Venus in the Pantheon at Rome.) The story was presented in many variations. Steen shows Antony begging Cleopatra to halt the great waste.

In the English version Hofstede de Groot's description includes: "To the left is a fish." This is clearly an unfortunate mistranslation. The German reads *Links ein Naar*. The correct reading tallies with the picture: "To the left is a fool."

The subject was a popular one with Steen. He painted it four times (Cat. 85–86c), once in large scale (Cat. 86a/b, Fig. 60). The theme allowed him the rich display of stuffs and emotions of which he became so fond towards the end of the 1660's. This particular version of the subject, however, should be dated in the mid-1670's. It shows some of the artificial elegance, especially in the background figures, which became part of Steen's vocabulary in his last years. It may be compared to *The Garden Party* of 1677 (HdG 52/440; see Add. 13, Fig. 98), and to *The Marriage at Cana* of 1676 (Cat. 50, Fig. 95). In the latter Steen uses a very similar background arcade.

For all that the picture can be placed within Steen's chronology, still, judging from a photograph, there are elements in it that raise questions as to its authenticity. The main figures of Cleopatra, Antony and the kneeling servant boy seem good enough. A number of the subsidiary figures, however, display a crudity of type which is not common in late Steen. This is particularly true of the man at the table to the right who picks his teeth and the old man with a cloth over his shoulder behind Cleopatra. These seem to be vulgarized Steen types. The painting of the servant women to the left is just unconvincing as authentic. Indeed, the whole architectural background seems askew. And though Steen often used foreground still-lifes, the bowl of fruit at the left appears mundane in invention and mechanical in incorporation. As comparison see Steen's brilliant use of still-life elements in *The Generosity of Scipio* (Cat. 83, Fig. 84).

Without examination of the original no final conclusions on the authenticity of this picture can be arrived at. Possible tentative conclusions are that it is either an original composition with unfortunate inclusions by later hands or a pastiche of Steen elements done by an imitator.

Bibliography: (1) Schmidt-Degener and Van Gelder, *Steen*, 1927, p. 9; (2) Bredius, *Steen*, 1927, p. 36; (3) Heppner, *J of W&CI*, III, 1939/40, p. 36; (4) de Groot, *Beeld en Woord*, 1952, pp. 32–33, note 34.

86] **THE BANQUET OF ANTONY AND CLEOPATRA***
Fig. 56

Panel; 17½ x 14½ inches; signed in full in the center foreground and dated 1667.
University Museum, Göttingen.

Provenance: Sale (probably), Amsterdam, 16 May 1696, No. 83 (HdG); sale, Amsterdam, 17 Sept. 1727, No. 21 (HdG); sale, Anthony Sijdervelt, Amsterdam, 23 April 1766, No. 35 (HdG); collection, Zschorn (possibly Hanover), 1789 (3). The picture was in the collection at Göttingen as early as 1805, when it was reported there by Fiorillo (1). In 1818 Fiorillo reported the picture as being in a small collection in Hanover (2). This however may be a reference to an earlier collection, possibly Zschorn.

Exhibition: Leiden, Jan Steen Tentoonstelling, "De Lakenhal," 1926, No. 169.

For a discussion of the subject matter and sources, see Cat. 85. The picture was either originally polygonal (twelve-sided) or cut down to that shape at some time. It was subsequently filled out or restored to a rectangle. A four-inch strip of wood was also added to the top.

Dated 1667, the painting is Steen's earliest use of the subject. The three other versions (Cat. 85, 86a/b, 86c) all date later. A comparison with 86a/b (Fig. 60), probably of about 1669 (5), shows how Steen expanded his concept of the subject in later years. This earlier painting is still somewhat tight. It is an intimate scene rather than a lavish banquet with onlookers and commentators. Antony is more like middle-aged Ahasuerus (Cat. 18, Fig. 59) than the ardent young lover of the later paintings.

Bibliography: (1) Fiorillo, *Beschreibung der Gemählde*, 1805, p. 23, No. 2; (2) Fiorillo, *Geschichte der Zeichnungen Künste*, III, 1818, p. 201; (3) Cat., Sammlung der Universität, Göttingen, 1926; (4) Cat., *Steen*, Leiden, 1926, No. 169; (5) Bredius, *Steen*, 1927, p. 38; (6) de Groot, *Beeld en Woord*, 1952, pp. 31–32; (7) Martin, *Steen*, 1954, p. 71; (8) de Jonge, *Steen* (Palet Series), n.d., p. 53.

86a/b] BANQUET OF ANTONY AND CLEOPATRA*

Fig. 60

Canvas; 44½ x 75 inches; monogrammed in the foreground "JS."

Rolzaal, Binnenhof, The Hague (on loan from Dienst voor 's Rijks Verspreide Kunstvoorwerpen).

Provenance: Collection, Reynolds, before 1798 (HdG 86); sale, Reynolds, London, 9 May 1798, No. 32 (2); in that sale the picture was bought by H. Phillips (an earlier Reynolds sale listed by Hofstede de Groot [No. 86], 11 March 1795, No. 53, also contained an *Antony and Cleopatra*, but there is no way of telling if it was the same picture); collection, Harry Phillips, London (HdG 86); sale, Hickman, London, 17 May 1856, No. 94 (HdG 86a); sale, Ribbesdale, London, 1867 (HdG 86b); collection, Sedelmeyer Galleries, Paris, 1908–1914 (1); collection, Ant. W. H. Mensing, Aerdenhout, Holland; sale, Mensing, Müller, Amsterdam, 15 Nov. 1938, No. 99 (6); dealer, N. Beets & Fontein, Amsterdam; collection, Henry Deterding. After the Second World War it became the property of the Dutch government.

Exhibitions: Madrid, "Dutch Exhibition," 1921; Copenhagen, 1922, No. 122; London, "Exhibition of Dutch Art," 1929, No. 210.

HdG Nos. 86a and 86b are identical.

For a discussion of the subject matter and sources see Cat. 85. This is Steen's largest painting of the subject, and in general his most ambitious historical painting. De Jonge called it "de volle glorie van zijn kunst" (10). Over six feet in length, it contains seventeen figures grouped around the dramatic episode in the center. Schmidt-Degener commented on this picture thus:

> Into the gorgeous setting of curtains, and carpets, blazing chandeliers, plates and dishes of precious metal, he introduced the regal orgies of Cleopatra. Stage riches:but stage riches plus life. Antony is a debauchee, Cleopatra in her sky blue robes a dissolute wench. With the vanity of an actor Steen delighted to show how well his own reveller's face fits into such company. What would have remained of the scene had it been treated in the rational manner of a Lebrun? Steen's genial lightness of touch infused the heaviness of his subject matter. He spiced his story with that fresh vulgarity which makes him so attractive. The pleasures we derive from his game, subtle at once and trivial, certainly do not spring from our nobler instincts. But then, suddenly, we are affected by his unique play on colour; he produces a harmony which transforms the whole impression: an unfamiliar combination which exactly fits the event—transparent silvery blue struggling with orange-browns and faded vermillions. (4)

The picture should be dated around 1669 (3)—that is, about two years later than the one in Göttingen (Cat. 86, Fig. 56). Structurally it is similar to *Samson and Delilah* of 1668 (Cat. 10, Fig. 67) and to the *Twelfth Night Feast* in Cassel of 1668 (Fig. 68) (HdG 494), but seems in its openness (the center group is recessed rather than vaulted forward) to anticipate the works of the early 1670's, particularly *David Returning Victorious* of 1671 (Cat. 13, Fig. 83).

Bibliography: (1) Sedelmeyer, *100 Masterpieces*, 1914, No. 55; (2) Graves, *Art Sales*, 1921, III, p. 175; (3) Bredius, *Steen*, 1927, pp. 38–39, pl. xiv; (4) Schmidt-Degener and Van Gelder, *Steen*, 1927, pp. 8–9; (5) Cat., Dutch Art, London, 1929, No. 210; (6) Sales Cat., Mensing, Müller, Amsterdam, 15 Nov. 1938, No. 99; (7) Heppner, *J of W&CI*, III, 1939/40, p. 36; (8) de Groot, *Beeld en Woord*, 1952, pp. 31–32; (9) Martin, *Steen*, 1954, p. 71; (10) de Jonge, *Steen* (Palet Series), n.d., p. 53.

86c***] BANQUET OF ANTONY AND CLEOPATRA*

Fig. 102

Canvas; 41½ x 35½ inches; signed in full at lower left.
Private collection, The Netherlands.

Provenance: No history of this picture can be definitely determined. It is possible that it was the cabinet piece in the Lady Thomond sale at Christies, 19 May 1821, but there is no definite proof (see Cat. 85). It was at one time in the Roëll collection in The Netherlands and has since been acquired for another collection.

For a discussion of the subject matter and sources see Cat. 85.

The picture is probably Steen's latest version of the subject. The silky brightness of the colors, and the sketchiness of the paint, indicate a date late in the 1670's. See *The Garden Party* of 1677 (HdG 52/440, Add. 13; Fig. 98).

87] THE STORY OF ARENT PIETER GHIJSEN

Removed from the Catalogue; see Addendum 15.

ADDENDUM TO THE CATALOGUE

The Addendum contains works which have been removed from Hofstede de Groot's Catalogue and from the additions to it. It is divided into two sections:

1. Biblical and historical paintings erroneously attributed to Steen.
2. Authentic or reportedly authentic paintings erroneously included in Hofstede de Groot's section on Biblical and historical subjects.

Biblical and Historical Paintings Erroneously Attributed to Steen

1/HdG 11] SAMSON MOCKED BY THE PHILISTINES
Fig. 125

Canvas; 26½ x 33 inhes; signed in full in the left foreground.
Musée Royal des Beaux-Arts, Antwerp.

Provenance: Sale, E. Hooft, Amsterdam, 31 Aug. 1766, No. 37 (HdG); collection, Spruyt, Ghent (HdG); collection, Baut de Rasmon (HdG). The Rasmon collection was bequeathed to the Museum in 1859 (4).

According to the catalogue of the Musée Royal, the picture is probably a copy by Jacobus Ignatius de Roore (Antwerp 1686—The Hague 1747), and the signature a false one (4).

The whole is based upon Steen's painting of the same subject in Cologne (Cat. 12/10a, Fig. 63). It is, however, not a literal copy; the artist has added and rearranged figures, and in part changed the composition. Perspective and scale are distorted, making all the figures dwarf-like and awkward. Since the copy reverses the original, there is the possibility that it was made from a print, though no print of the Cologne picture is known.

In a second version, close in size (27 x 34 inches) and structure to the present copy, a few details have been changed. The second was sold in Berlin at Lepke's, 7 March 1899, and again there in the Weustenberg sale on 27 Oct. 1908 (No. 68). It was sold at Christie's on 27 Nov. 1911 (No. 122). Its present whereabouts is unknown.

Bibliography: (1) Leclercq, *GdBA*, IX, 1861, pp. 47–48; (2) Burger, *GdBA*, XII, 1862, p. 161; (3) Bredius, *Steen*, 1927, p. 29; (4) Catalogue Descriptif, Musée Royal des Beaux-Arts, Anvers, 1958, No. 338.

2/HdG 16A*] THE IDOLATRY OF SOLOMON

Canvas; 19 x 22 inches.

"The king, surrounded by his wives, kneels in worship on a cushion before a statue of Venus. At left is the high priest by an offering stand. In the background is a courtyard. The picture is rich in figures and thoroughly worked." This is a translation of the description found in the Handex. It is probably taken from the sales catalogue—B. Zacharias *et al.*, Berlin, 1 May 1900, No. 65—which is the only reference to this picture.

The description given above roughly follows that of Knüpfer's painting in the Herzog Anton-Ulrich Museum at Brunswick (1). The size also roughly corresponds, the Knüpfer being 19 x 25 inches, but painted on a panel. Martin assumed that the picture in Brunswick was a Steen, but that was an error in information since the attribution to Knüpfer cannot be doubted (2).

There seems to have been a confusion here, and the Handex reference most probably belongs to the Knüpfer and not to an unknown painting by Steen. It is therefore withdrawn from the catalogue.

Bibliography: (1) Cat., Gemäldesammlung im Herzog Anton-Ulrich Museum, Brunswick, 1932, No. 193; (2) Martin, *Steen*, 1954, p. 28, n. 40.

3/HdG 34] THE ADORATION OF THE SHEPHERDS
Fig. 126

Canvas; 21 x 24½ inches; signed at lower right.
State Collection of Art, Wawel Castle, Cracow, Poland.

Provenance: Sale, J. F. Motte, Amsterdam, 20 Aug. 1794, No. 111 (Handex); sale, Rotterdam, 7 Aug. 1798, No. 62 (Handex); sale, Rotterdam, 25 April 1817, No. 82 (HdG); sale, Britten Flee, London, 25 March 1901, No. 40 (HdG); dealer, Schwartz, Vienna, 1902. It was perhaps through Schwartz that Leon Pininsky of Lemberg, Poland acquired the work, which he later donated to the National Collection.

Exhibitions: Leiden, Rembrandt Memorial Exhibition, 1906, No. 67; Lemberg (Lwow), 1908, No. 17.

This is an important replica of the painting now in the Rijksmuseum in Amsterdam (Cat. 37/31, Fig. 37). It has been considered original (4) (7), and has been in at least one important exhibition (2). A comparison with the original, however, reveals overall differences which identify the painting as a copy. In the present picture, a greater linear emphasis gives to the figures and drapery, particularly that of the virgin, a hardness not found in the original. In general the middle tones have been ignored; therefore the subtle gradations so much a part of Steen's work are lost.

Bibliography: (1) Czarnik, B. Wystawa Rembrandtowska w Lejdzie wr. 1906, 1908, p. 33; (2) Die Leidener Ausstellung von 1906, Leipzig-Haarlem 1907, No. 13; (3) Treter, M., Album Wystawy mistrzów dawnych, 1911, p. 17; (4) Bredius, *Steen*, 1927, p. 35, pl. 9; (5) *Album of Reproductions from Wawel Castle*, 1935, p. 29; (6) Trautscholdt, "Steen," *T-B*, 1937, p. 511; (7) Bialostoski and Wolicki, *Europäische Malerei in polnischen Sammlungen*, 1957, No. 310, p. 544; (8) Cat., Steen, The Hague, 1958/59, No. 10.

4/HdG 39A]** FLIGHT INTO EGYPT

Panel; 24½ x 23 inches; traces of a signature.
Present location unknown.

Provenance: Collection, Sir Samuel Wilson, London (Handex); dealer, Ehrich Gallery, New York, 1919 (FRL); dealer, Art Collectors Association, London, 1921 (FRL); collection, A. L. Nicholson, London, 1927 (Witt); collection, E. Bolton, London, 1927 (Witt); dealer, Goudstikker, Amsterdam, 1930/37 (1); sale, Gold, Berlin, 3 Dec. 1940, No. 174. After the war the picture became the property of the Dutch government, Dienst voor 's Rijks Verspreide Kunstvoorwerpen, The Hague. From 1948 to 1949 it was on loan to the Dordrecht Museum, after which it was publicly sold.

The painting was added to Hofstede de Groot's catalogue by Trautscholdt (2); however, it is an unimaginative picture and only distantly related to Steen. The figures are like flattened cutouts in a space artificially cleared for them. Joseph is a Steen type, but does not move with any of the assuredness that Steen always gave his figures.

In 1949 L. J. Bol, the director of the Dordrecht Museum, returned the picture to the Dutch government as unauthentic. It was sold at Mullers in Amsterdam on 3 July 1951 (No. 659). It was subsequently sold in Brussels on 3 June 1958 (No. 169). Its present location is unknown.

Bibliography: (1) Cat., *Nouvelles Acquisitions Goudstikker*, 1930/31, No. 74; (2) Trautscholdt, "Steen," *T-B*, 1937, p. 511.

5/HdG 43] THE HOLY FAMILY

Fig. 127

Canvas; 32½ x 36½ inches.
Present location unknown.

Provenance: Dealer, Yates, London, 1836 (HdG); collection, Pauwels (Allard), Brussels, 1907 (HdG). The collection of Mme. G. Pauwels was sold at auction on 21–22 Nov. 1927 at Gallerie Georges Giroux, Brussels; however, the present work was not among those up for sale.

Hofstede de Groot knew the picture and gives the following description:

> The Virgin, in a purplish-grey dress, sits in a room holding the Child in her lap. The youthful John, who has a cross in his hand and a lamb at his side, is playing with the child. In this part of the picture the figures are mostly undraped. Behind the children stands Elizabeth. On the left Joseph sits in a pensive attitude at a table and plots out a diagram with compasses. Through a doorway on the right is seen an adjacent room, in which several winged angels are busy. The picture has lost its freshness through over-cleaning; it must have been very fine. Several accessories are well preserved, such as a dress, a stone pan, and other things.

This description essentially agrees with that given by Bredius (1).

In 1935 the London dealer Leger had a picture of the Holy Family attributed to Jan Steen which corresponded to the description of the central group: Madonna, Child, and St. John with St. Elizabeth behind. The picture has been cut to the left, eliminating Joseph, though part of his table with a carpenter's square and papers was still visible. It would seem also that the picture has been cut to the right; hence the angels beyond the doorway are missing. Also, St. John and the lamb has been painted out. The aim of all this mutilation seems to have been to turn a religious picture into a genre piece.

The Leger picture, however, cannot be convincingly attributed to Jan Steen. Though there is something in common, the figures are too elongated and their features too sharp. The painting is opaque, and the spatial relationships do not work clearly, either between the Virgin and St. Elizabeth, or between the heads of the two children. Furthermore, Steen never elongated his figures in this way.

It is assumed that the fragment is a part of the picture from the Allard collection, and it is therefore removed from the Catalogue as unauthentic. It might be that it is a copy of the center of that picture, but the painting out of St. John substantiates the idea of general mutilation of the whole.

The fragment may well have been painted by the same artist responsible for the doubtful *Bathseba After the Bath* also attributed to Steen (see Add. 12, Fig. 132). The two paintings have the same hard contours and elongated figures. Possibly they identify the work of a late follower.

Bibliography: (1) Bredius, *Steen*, 1927, p. 36.

6/HdG 51a]** CHRIST IN THE HOUSE OF MARY AND MARTHA

Fig. 128

Canvas; 34½ x 41 inches.
Present location unknown.

Provenance: Collection, Count Kospoth, Briesse, Germany (not attributed to Steen). During the 1930's the painting was in a private collection at Twente, Holland, during which time it was cleaned, restored, and attributed to Steen. Dealer, Katz, Dieren, 1937 (2). It was acquired for the Weebers-Ten Bos collection, Nijmegen, from Katz; its present location is unknown.

Exhibition: Amsterdam, Bijbelse Kunst, Rijksmuseum, 1939, No. 96b.

The picture was added to Hofstede de Groot's catalogue by Trautscholdt (2), and was discussed by M. D. Henkel as a possible connection between Steen and Vermeer (1). There is little basis for such connection in this picture. While the figures, with the exception of Christ, are distantly reminiscent of Steen's types, they are too distortedly drawn and composed to be accepted as his. The picture is therefore removed from the Catalogue as a poor attribution.

Bibliography: (1) Henkel, *Kunstwanderer*, XIV, 1931/32, pp. 265–66; (2) Trautscholdt, "Steen," *T-B*, 1937, p. 511; (3) Cat., Bijbelse Kunst, Amsterdam, 1939, No. 96b.

7/HdG 53] THE PRODIGAL SON

Fig. 129

Panel; 23½ x 29½ inches; signed in full at lower left.
Present location unknown.

Provenance: Collection, Van Loon, Amsterdam (HdG); according to Hofstede de Groot it was "presumably" in one of the Rothschild collections either in Paris or in London, about 1907. Collection, Reginald Tilson Lee, Surrey, 1920 (Witt); sale, W. H. Durham *et al.*, London, Christie's, 31 May 1926, No. 63 (FRL) (measurements given as 31 x 38 inches); dealer, The Hague, 1942 (RKHD); dealer, W. Paech, Amsterdam, 1943 (RKH); sale, Jüngeling, Amsterdam, 1–2 March 1944, No. 32. In 1946 the picture was at the Munich collecting-point for recovered works of art, No. 1046/1. It was sent from Munich to Paris in that year with presumed owner listed only as Rothschild; it is not known to whom this refers.

Like *Christ in the House of Mary and Martha* (Cat. 51, Fig. 40) a curtain has been pulled aside and draped over its rod to reveal the scene. Showing a group seated around a table in the courtyard of an inn, the picture may possibly contain a reference to the Prodigal among the harlots (Luke 15:13). Even so, it must be withdrawn from the Catalogue for its attribution to Steen is doubtful. Though some of the figures are Steen-like, especially the seated women at the table, the whole is a patchwork of types indicating a pastiche by a copyist or follower. It may be that the picture is a heavily reworked original, but if so it has lost so much of Steen's ability to compose groups as to be no longer acceptable.

8/54b*]** THE PRODIGAL SON

Fig. 130

19 x 25½ inches; signed on the footstool.
Present location unknown.

Provenance: Bredius mentions a picture of the Prodigal from the Svenonius collection in Stockholm, which was not listed by Hofstede de Groot (1). The picture was sold at Paul Brandt's in Amsterdam on 22 May 1973 (No. 15). The catalogue of the sale gives the following provenance: L. Venou, Paris; Marcell von Nemes, Hungary (in Dusseldorf, 1912); Galerie F. Kleinberger, Paris; Berger Svenonius, Stockholm (2). The picture was sold from the Svenonius collection at Werthheim, Berlin, 30 Apr. 1930, No. 75.

Exhibitions: Stockholm, Lund University Museum of Art, 1927/1928, No. 54; Stockholm, Academy of Art, 1929, No. 63.

According to Bredius, the picture shows two separate episodes from the story. At the right the Prodigal is seen with his back against the table, foot on a foot-warmer. With his left hand he holds up a wine glass and with his right he pays a beautiful woman who stands behind him. At the left, before an open window, stands a young man who blows on a large trumpet. Through the window, in the distance, is seen the Prodigal by a farmhouse eating with the pigs (1). Though reportedly authenticated by a certificate from Hofstede de Groot, the attribution is a poor one, and the picture should be rejected as a Steen.

Bibliography: (1) Bredius, *Steen*, 1927, p. 36; (2) Sales Cat., Brandt, Amsterdam, 22 May 1973, No. 15.

9/HdG 56] THE RETURN OF THE PRODIGAL SON

Canvas; 41 x 33½ inches; signed at the left-hand corner.
Present location unknown.

Provenance: Sale, Berlin, 18 May 1897, No. 103 (HdG); sale (possible), A. von Herrenberger, Berlin, Lepke, No. 87 (1).

The Biblical source for the subject is Luke 15:18–24.

Hofstede de Groot gives a one-line description: "He is received by his father at the Threshold." Trautscholdt suggested that the painting sold in Berlin in 1908 might be identical with HdG 56. He added, correctly, that it was a copy (1). It is a repetition, close in size, of the painting in the Wachmeister collection (Cat. 55, Fig. 80); it is therefore withdrawn from the Catalogue.

One thing makes its identification as a copy problematical. Hofstede de Groot apparently knew both pictures, but did not declare one a version of the other. It may be that there is an error here, and that Hofstede de Groot was not really familiar with the painting from the 1897 sale, which he included as No. 56.

Bibliography: (1) Trautscholdt, "Steen," *T-B*, 1937, p. 511.

10/HdG 64] THE BETRAYAL OF CHRIST
Fig. 131

Canvas; 61 x 49½ inches.
National Gallery, Prague.

Provenance: Dealer, Otto Mayer, Barcelona, 1902 (HdG); collection, Joseph V. Novák, Prague, 1907 (HdG). The National Gallery purchased the picture from the Novák collection in 1950.

According to Hofstede de Groot, the picture was "probably by Steen" and made under the influence of the early *Betrayal of Christ* by Van Dyck in the Prado. It is difficult to understand how this picture ever was accepted as even a probable Steen. It is very close to Jordaens.

Whether by Jordaens himself or by a follower, the picture owes its conception to the Van Dyck in the Prado. The thrusting diagonal of heads rising from left to right culminating in the confrontation of Judas and Christ reveals the dependency. Compared with the Van Dyck, the Prague picture, also a night scene, is less dramatically unified and the figures less heroic. Peter and Malchus in the center foreground break the diagonal concentration of the composition, and are in reversed position. This may indicate that the artist was familiar with either a smaller, much more freely painted, and probably earlier version now in Minneapolis or the preparatory drawing for that painting in Hamburg (1). In both cases Peter and Malchus are reversed, but in neither are they separated so awkwardly from the main compositional movement.

The National Gallery lists it as the work of a "Dutch 17th century artist" (Inv. 0/2955—Do 2140).

Bibliography: (1) Stechow, *Bulletin,* Minneapolis Institute of Arts, XLIX, 1960, pp. 6–13.

11/HdG 72b]** APOLLO AND DAPHNE

Canvas; 24 x 28½ inches.
Present location unknown.

Provenance: Collection, N. N. (1); dealer, Goudstikker, Amsterdam, 1927/28 (Witt).

Exhibition: Leiden, Jan Steen Tentoonstelling, "De Lakenhal," 1926, No. 71.

The picture first appeared publicly as a Steen in the 1926 show in Leiden. Martin in his article following the show reproduced it and declared it to be a "most interesting late work in French taste" (2). Trautscholdt included it in his supplement to Hofstede de Groot's catalogue (3).

The painting has little resemblance to Steen, and particularly not to his late style with graceful elegance and fine textures. Furthermore Steen throughout his life conscientiously avoided painting the nude, and for this reason alone such a picture is out of place in Steen's work. Martin does not mention it in his 1954 monograph, and one would suspect that he dropped it as an authentic Steen.

Bibliography: (1) Cat., Steen, Leiden, 1926, No. 71; (2) Martin, *ZfbK*, LXI, 1927/28, p. 326; (3) Trautscholdt, "Steen," *T-B*, 1937, p. 512; (4) de Groot, *Beeld en Woord*, 1952, p. 70.

12/HdG 347/224] BATHSEBA AFTER THE BATH
Fig. 132

Panel; 22½ x 18 inches; signed in full on the archway to the left.
Museum der Bildenden Künste, Leipzig.

Provenance: Sale, C. M. Bronkhuyze van Leede and Oudewaard, Leiden, 13 Oct. 1863, No. 55 (HdG); sale, Reede van Oudtshoorn, Amsterdam, 14 April 1874, No. 43 (HdG); dealer, Ver Meer Gallery, London, 1925; dealer, Katz, Dieren, 1928; collection, E. Kummerlee, Germany (?). In 1953 the picture became state property.

HdG Nos. 347 and 224 (*The Fortune Teller*) refer

to the same picture now in Leipzig, the subject of which is *Bathseba After the Bath*. Though David is not visible in the background, Bathseba receiving a pedicure and approached by an old woman follows a traditional form for the subject. Bathseba holds David's letter in her right hand.

The picture in Leipzig follows Hofstede de Groot's description exactly, except the sides have been reversed. This may have resulted from a description given from the figure's point of view; such reversals occur elsewhere in Hofstede de Groot's catalogue. The size is the same as reported by Hofstede de Groot, but the picture is on a panel rather than on canvas.

Though the identity of the Leipzig picture and Nos. 347 and 224 is established, the painting is withdrawn from the Catalogue because its attribution to Steen is doubtful. Most probably it is the work of a follower who painted in a more traditional historical manner using Steen's types. The same painter may have been responsible for *The Holy Family*, also falsely attributed to Steen (Add. 5). In that picture there is a similar figural elongation and spatial uncertainty.

Authentic or Reportedly Authentic Paintings Erroneously Included in Hofstede de Groot's Section on Biblical and Historical Subjects

13/HdG 52/440 THE GARDEN PARTY (THE PRODIGAL SON)
Fig. 98

Canvas; 26 x 34½ inches; signed in full above the doorway; dated 1677.
Private collection, United States.

Provenance: Sale, Amsterdam, 12 Sept. 1708, No. 47 (HdG); sale, N. Tjark *et al.*, Amsterdam, 10 Dec. 1762, No. 28 (HdG); sale, J. v.d. Linden, Dordrecht, 1785, No. 398 (HdG 440); sale, Amsterdam, 5 Dec. 1796, No. 104 (HdG 440); sale, Emmerson, London, 1832 (HdG); collection, Lord Northwick, Cheltenham, 1833 (HdG); sale, Northwick, London, 1838 (HdG); sale, Meffre, Paris, 25 Feb. 1845, No. 86 (HdG 440); sale, Héris, Brussels, 19 June 1846, No. 69 (HdG 440); sale, D. v.d. Schrieck, Louvain, 1861, No. 104 (HdG 440); sale, Fürstenberg *et al.*, Cologne, 1877 (9); dealer, A. Gottschewski, Hamburg, 1920 (Handex); collection, de Burlett, Berlin, 1921 (Handex); dealer, Haberstock, Berlin, 1924 (Handex); collection, Semmel, Berlin, late 1920's (Handex); dealer, Duits, Amsterdam (9); dealer, Rozelaar, Amsterdam (9). When it came to the United States is unknown, but in 1954 Martin made reference to it as in a private American collection (8).

Exhibitions: Leiden, Jan Steen Tentoonstelling, 1926, "De Lakenhal," No. 72 (as "The Prodigal Son"); Brussels, Cinq Siècles d'Art, 1935, No. 783; The Hague, Jan Steen Tentoonstelling, 1958/59, No. 58 (as *The Garden Party*).

Hofstede de Groot's Nos. 52 and 440 are identical, and there has been a confusion as to subject. No. 440 is called *The Garden Party*. That is the more accurate title (9), since there is little to identify the scene of upper-class entertainment with the story of the Prodigal. The subject here, if it needs explication, should better be called a "Garden of Love" or "Fêtes Galantes," for it anticipates the French eighteenth century scenes of garden delights (4). The cushion in the foreground bears the arms of the family Paedts, the governing family in Leiden in 1677, and the house at the far end of the garden resembles theirs on the Rapenburg (1).

The picture, dated 1677, helps establish the style of Steen's last years. It is withdrawn from the present Catalogue only because of subject redesignation.

Bibliography: (1) Bijleveld, *O-H*, XLIII, 1926, pp. 132 ff; (2) Cat., Steen, Leiden, 1926, No. 72; (3) Bredius, *Steen*, 1927, p. 54; (4) Schmidt-Degener and Van Gelder, *Steen*, 1927, pl. XL; (5) Martin, *ZfbK*, LXI, 1927/28, p. 326; (6) Trautscholdt, "Steen," *T-B*, 1937, p. 511; (7) Gudlaugsson, *De Komedianten*, 1945, p. 46; (8) Martin, *Steen*, 1954, p. 57; (9) Cat., Steen, The Hague, 1958/59, No. 58; (10) de Jonge, *Steen* (Palet Series), n.d., pp. 56–57.

14/HdG 70/408] ASCANIUS AND LUCILLA (LUCELLE)
Fig. 110

Panel; 15½ x 12½ inches; signed in full on the paper held in the woman's hand.
Private collection.

Provenance: Sale, Fabricius, Haarlem, 19 Aug. 1749, No. 26 (HdG); sale, J. van Zaanen, The Hague, 16 Nov. 1767, No. 17 (HdG); collection, M. van Slingelandt, The Hague (HdG); collection, Griffier Fagel; sale, Fagel, London, 22 May 1801 (HdG 14). It was reported in the Bute collection in 1854 (1).

Exhibition: London, Dutch Painters 1450–1750, Royal Academy, 1952/53, No. 40A.

In 1767 the picture was sold as pendant to *Bathseba Receiving David's Letter* (Cat. 14, Fig. 70). They were together in the sale, and remained together in the Bute collection (2) until separated by the sale of the *Bathseba*. For a discussion of the pictures as possible pendants, see Catalogue 14.

The identity between Nos. 70 and 408 (*The Lute Player*) was first noted by Trautscholdt (4).

The picture is withdrawn from this Catalogue because its subject cannot be considered historical. Gudlaugsson has shown that the scene is one from Bredero's *Lucelle*, a non-historic comedy (5) (7).

Bibliography: (1) Waagen, *Treasures of Art in Great Britain*, III, 1854, p. 477; (2) Richter, *Catalogue of the Collections of the Marquis of Bute*, 1884, No. 162; (3) Van Gils, *O-H*, LII, 1935, pp. 130–33; (4) Trautscholdt, "Steen," *T-B*, 1937, p. 511; (5) Gudlaugsson, *Ikonographische Studien*, 1938, pp. 72–73; (6) Heppner, *JofW&CI*, III, 1939/40, p. 47; (7) Gudlaugsson, *Nederlandsche Kunsthistorisch Jaarboek*, I, 1947, pp. 178, pl. 4; (8) Martin, *Steen*, 1954, p. 71.

15/HdG 87] THE STORY OF PIETER GHIJSEN

38 x 29½ inches.

Sale, Pieter de Klok, Amsterdam, 22 April 1744, No. 176 (HdG).

Hofstede de Groot notes only that the picture was called "artistic in execution." The subject of this unknown work is a theme from Dutch history. It cannot be classified as "historical" in the strict sense of the word, for it does not refer to classical antiquity. The picture has therefore been withdrawn from this catalogue.

PLATES

Fig. 1. *The Death of Ananias,* 1651 (Cat. 66).
Present location unknown.

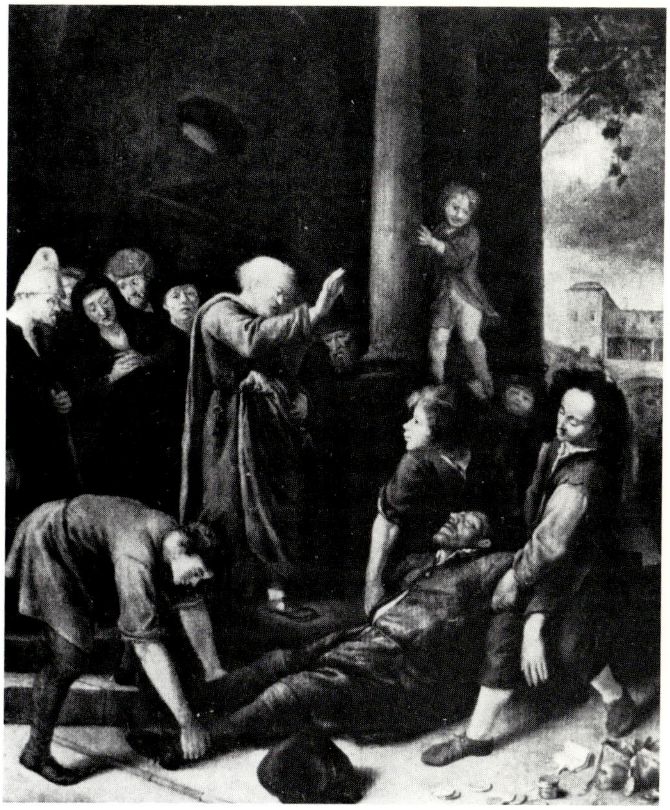

Fig. 2. *The Marriage at Cana* (Cat. 45/50a).
Present location unknown.

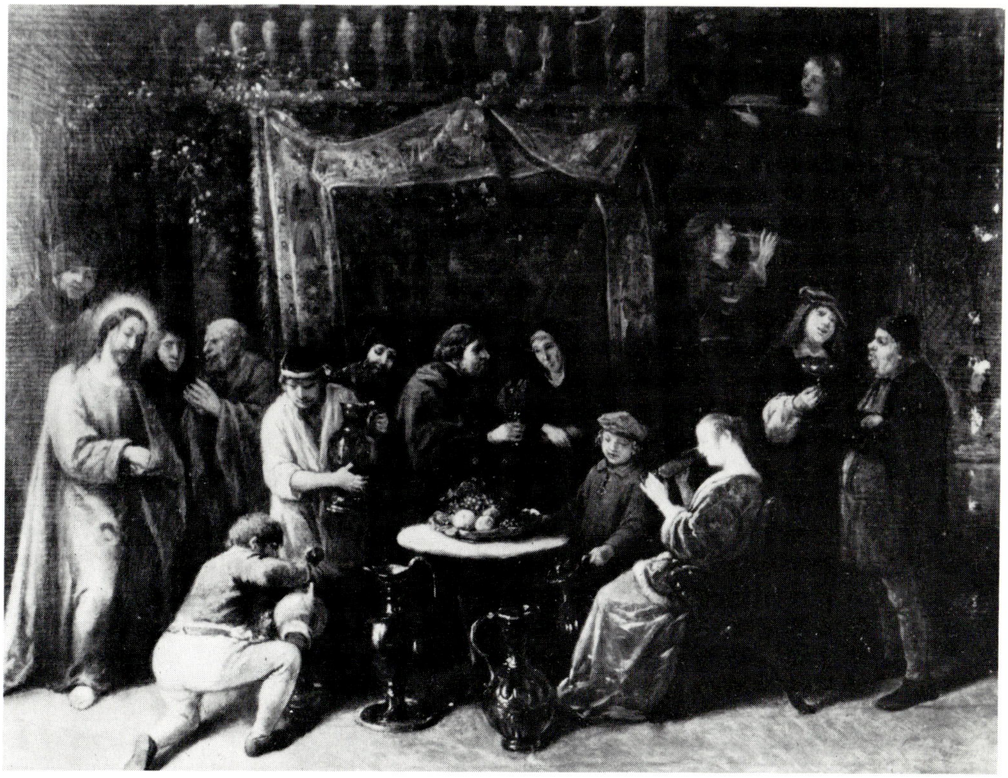

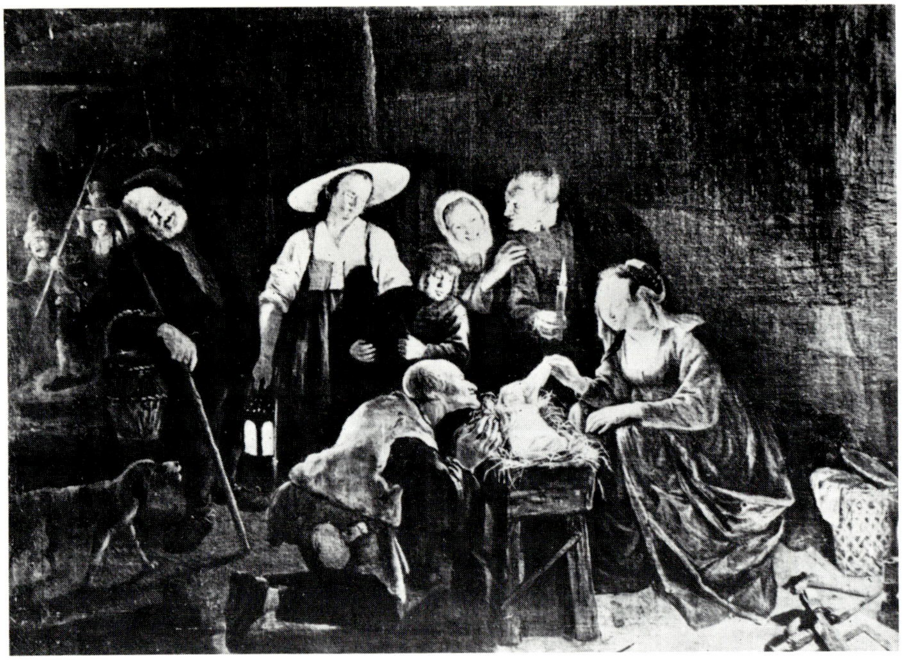

Fig. 3. *The Adoration of the Shepherds* (Cat. 32). Museum, Aix-en-Provence.

Fig. 4. *The Adoration of the Shepherds* (Ca 38). Present location unknown.

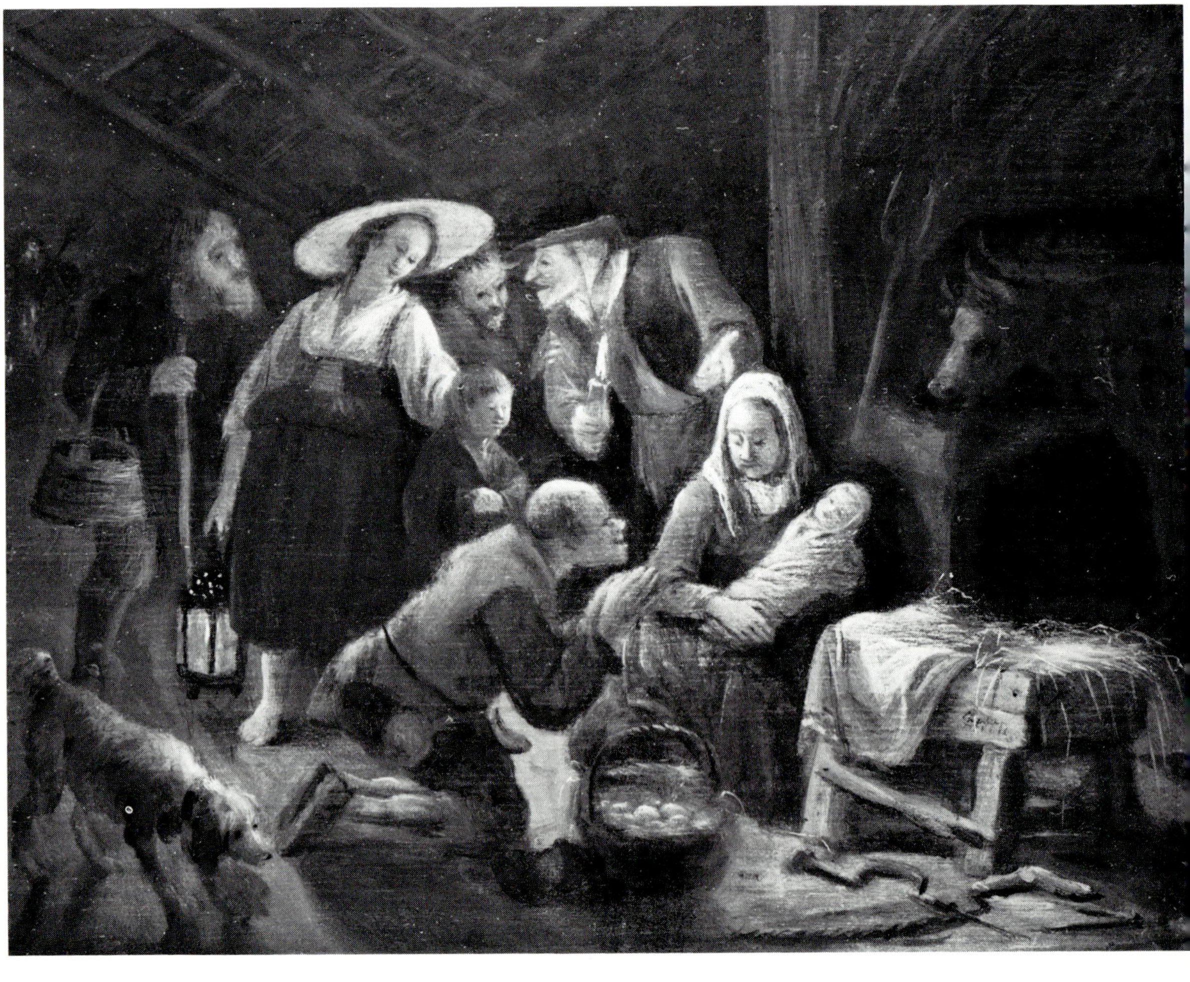

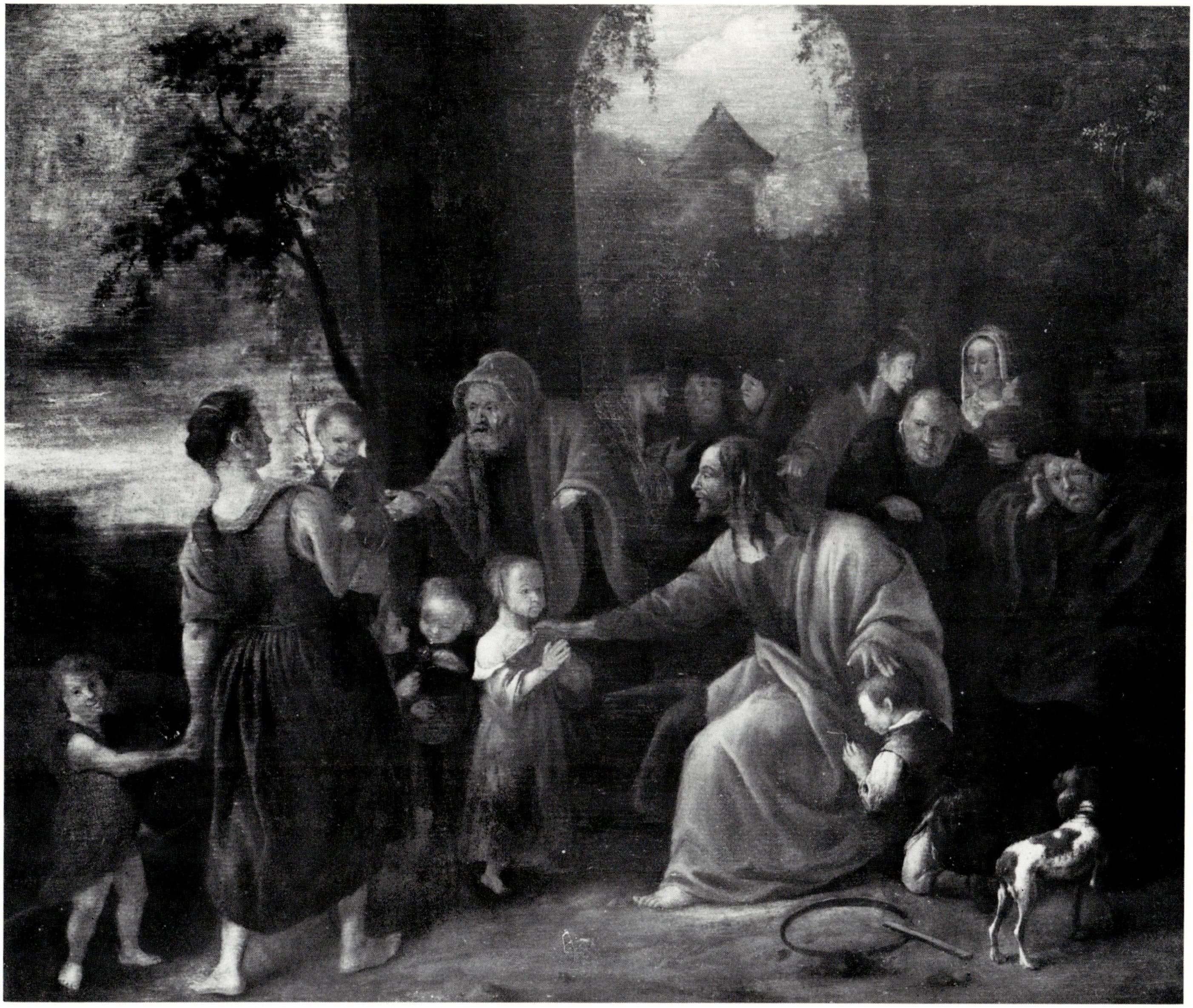

Fig. 5. *Christ Blessing the Little Children* (Cat. 60). Private collection, Amsterdam.

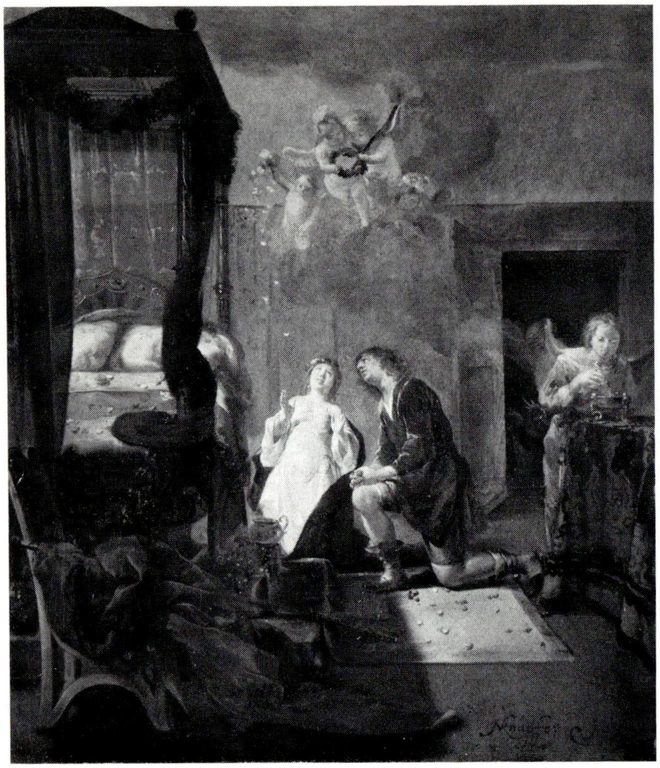

Fig. 6. Knüpfer, *The Prayer of Tobias and Sarah,* 1654. Centraal Museum, Utrecht.

Fig. 7. Knüpfer, *The Rich Man and Lazarus.* Musée des Beaux-Arts, Liege.

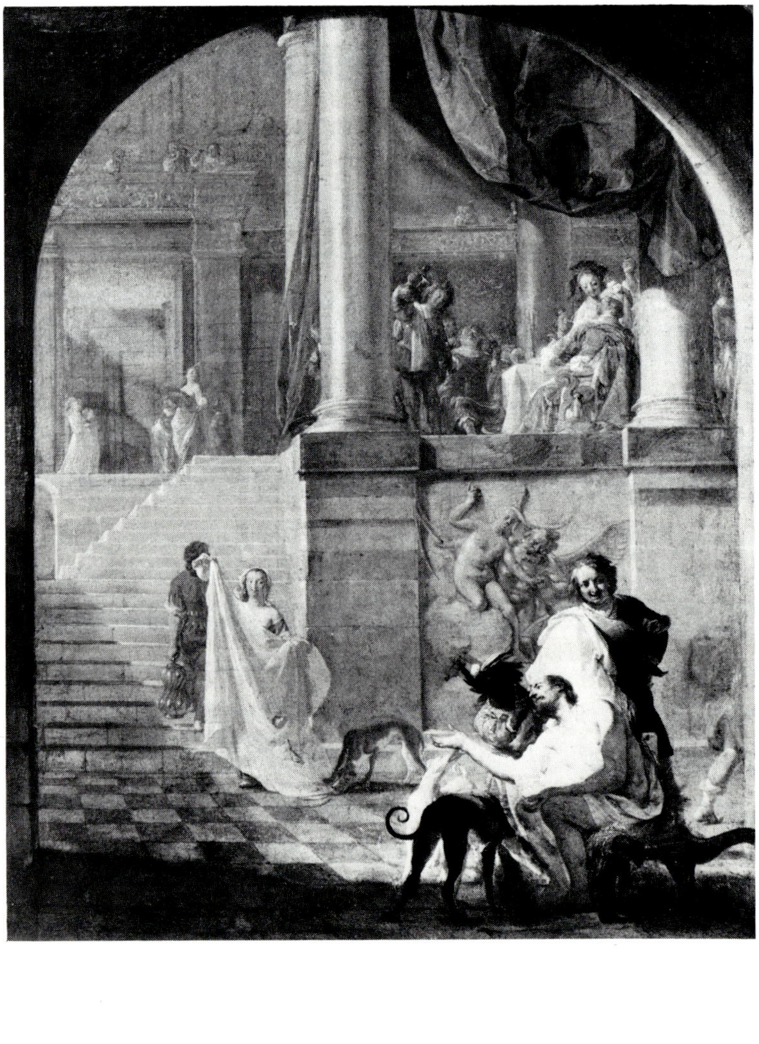

Fig. 8. Knüpfer, *Joseph Interpreting Dreams.*
Staatliches Museum, Schwerin.

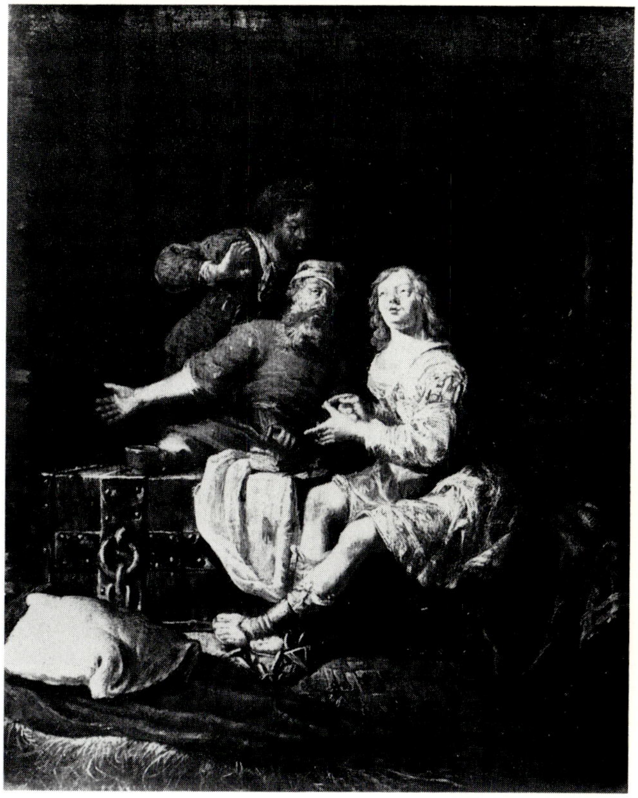

Fig. 9. Knüpfer, *The Seven Acts of Mercy.*
Staatliche Kunstsammlungen, Kassel.

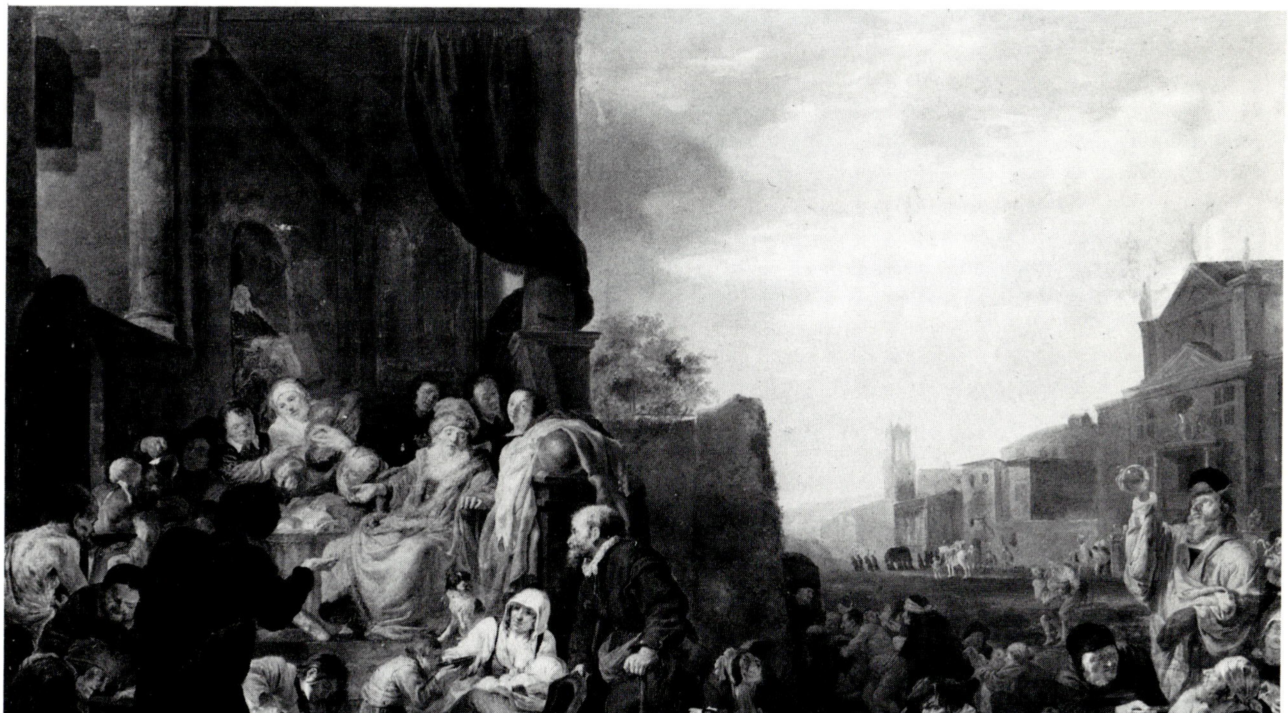

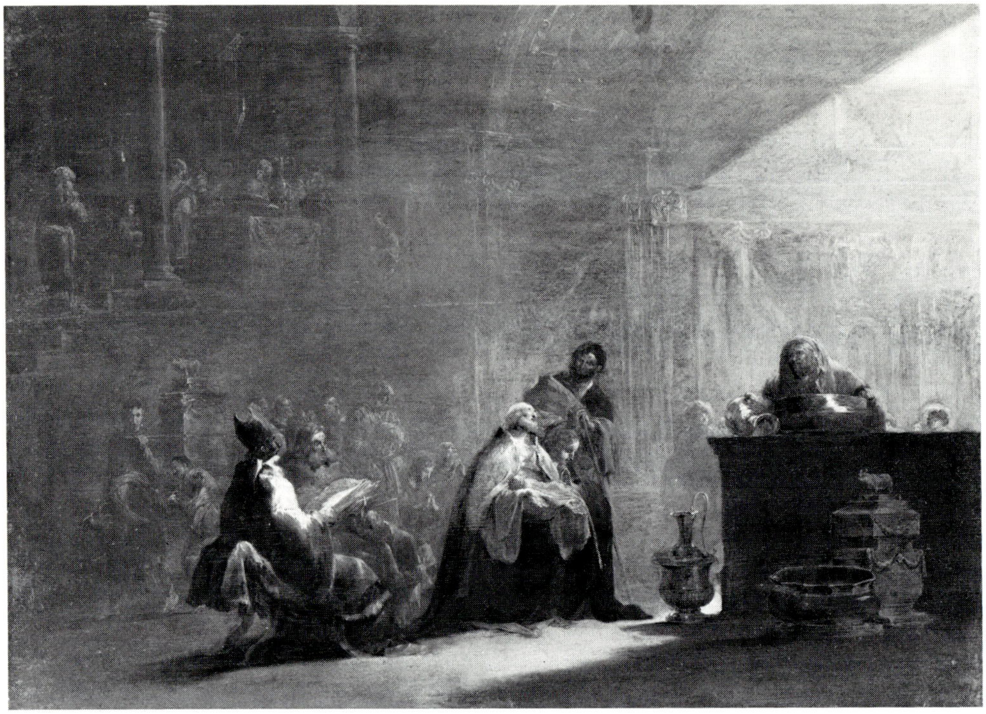

Fig. 10. Bramer, *The Presentation in the Temple.* Courtesy, John G. Johnson Collection, Museum of Art, Philadelphia.

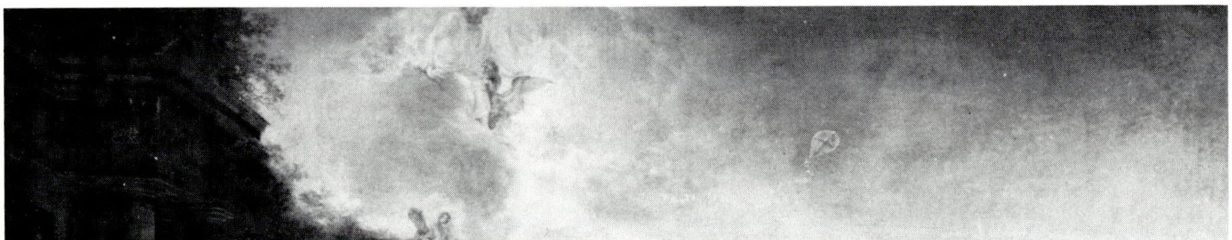

Fig. 11. Knüpfer, *The Search After Happiness,* 1651. Staatliches Museum, Schwerin.

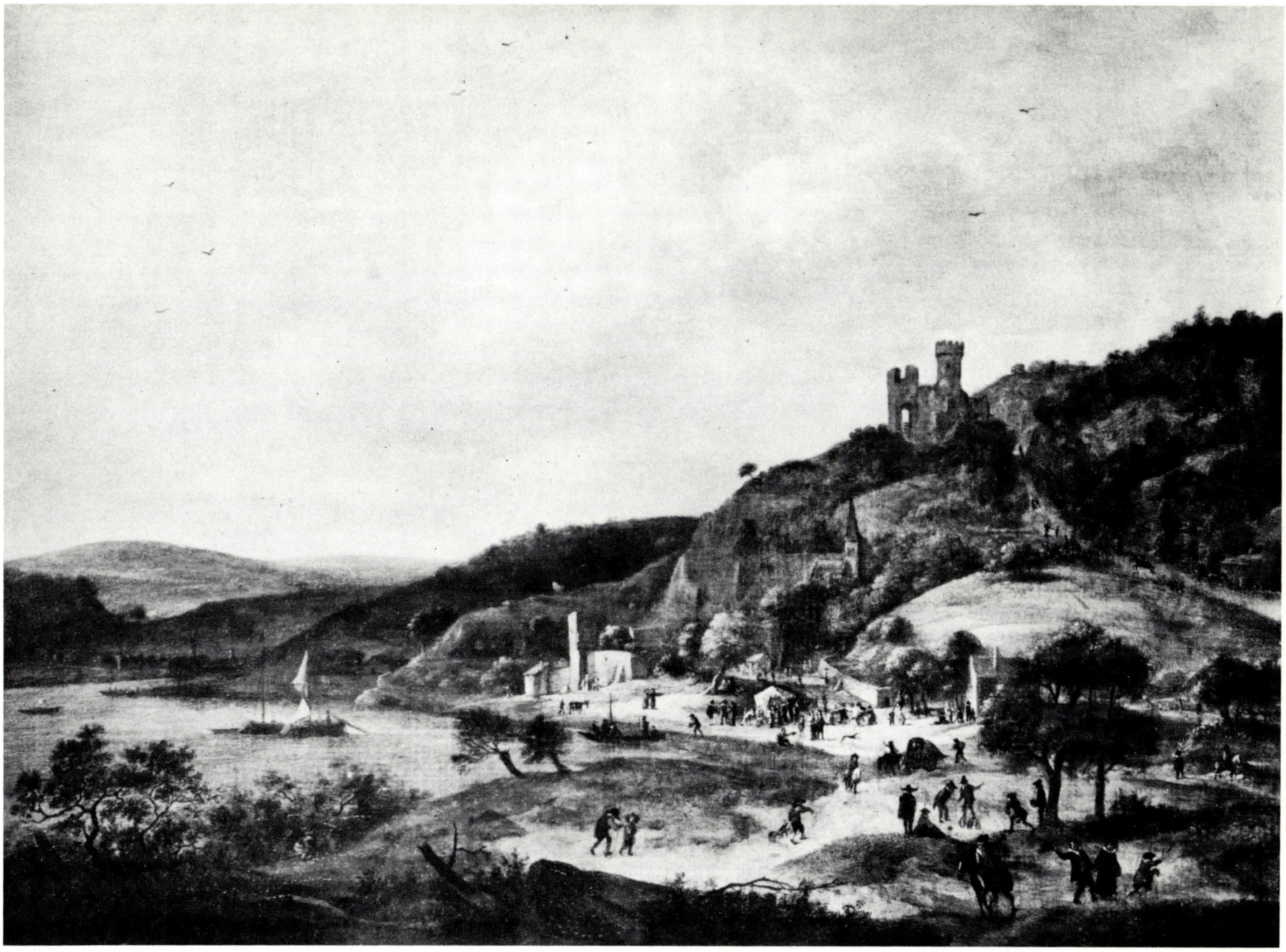

Fig. 12. *The Ruin on the Hill.* Formerly Baron van der Feltz, Brummen.

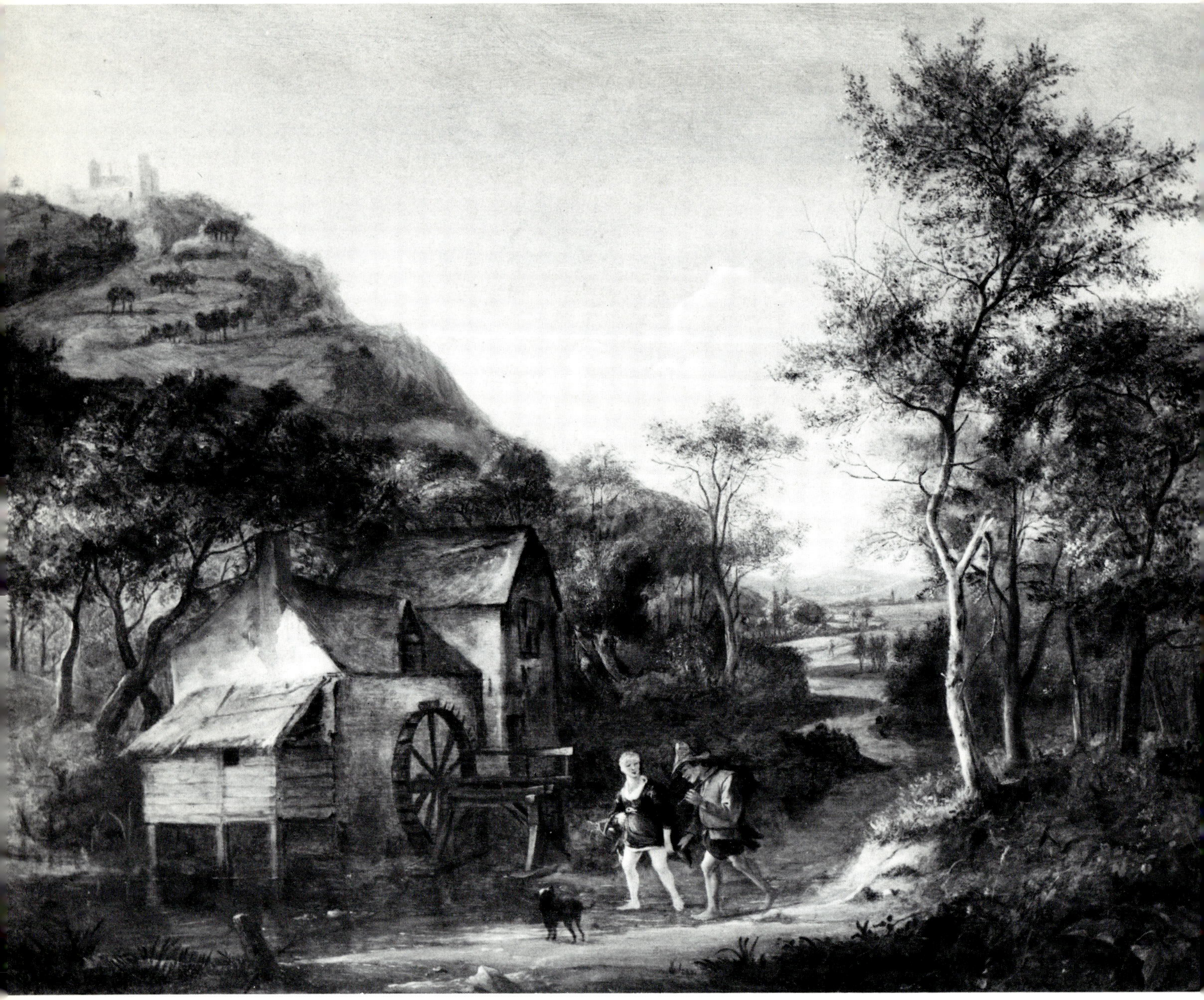

Fig. 13. *Wooded Landscape.* Formerly Nystad, The Hague.

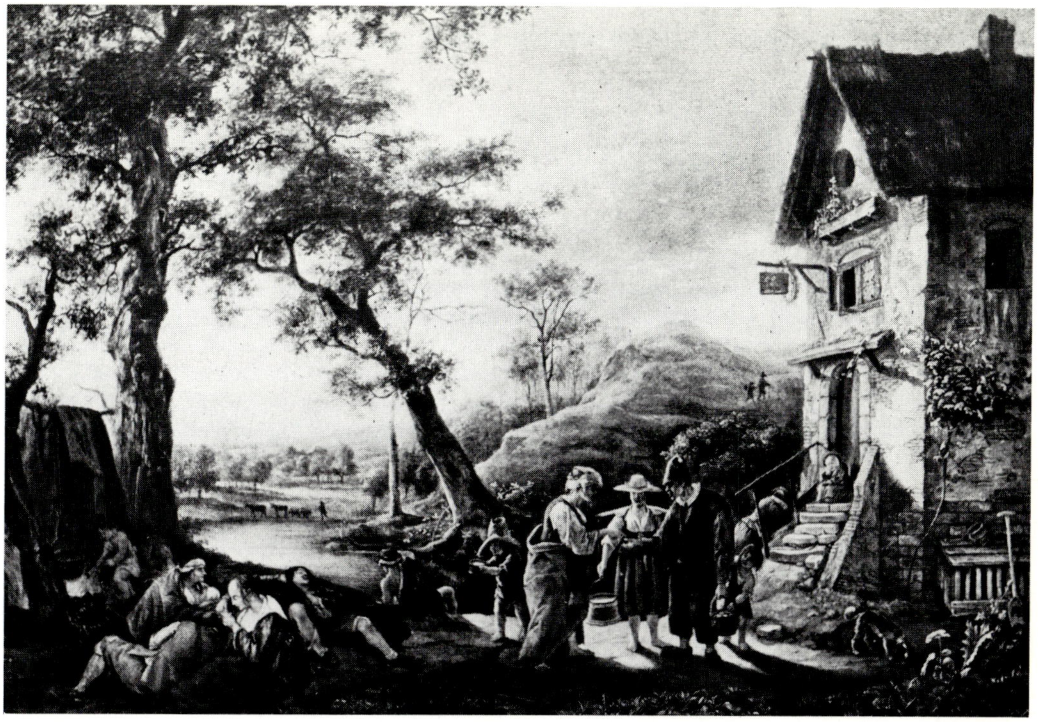

Fig. 14. *Gypsies in a Landscape* (HdG 223). Formerly Agnew, London.

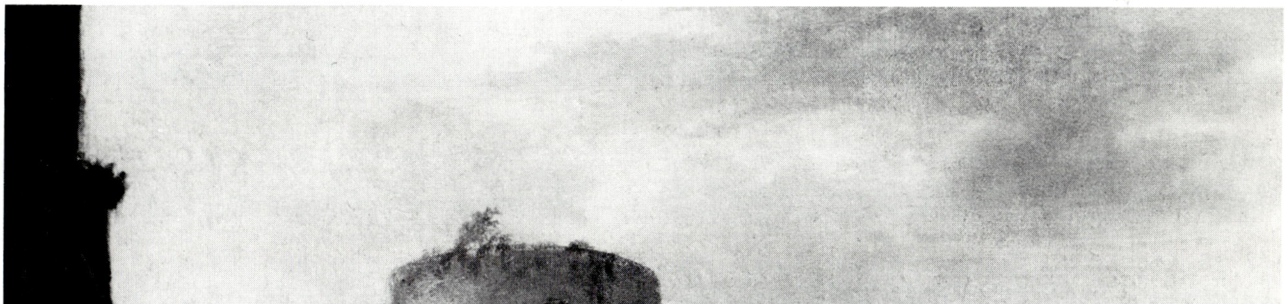

Fig. 15. *The Seven Acts of Mercy* (Cat. 67). Private collection, The Netherlands.

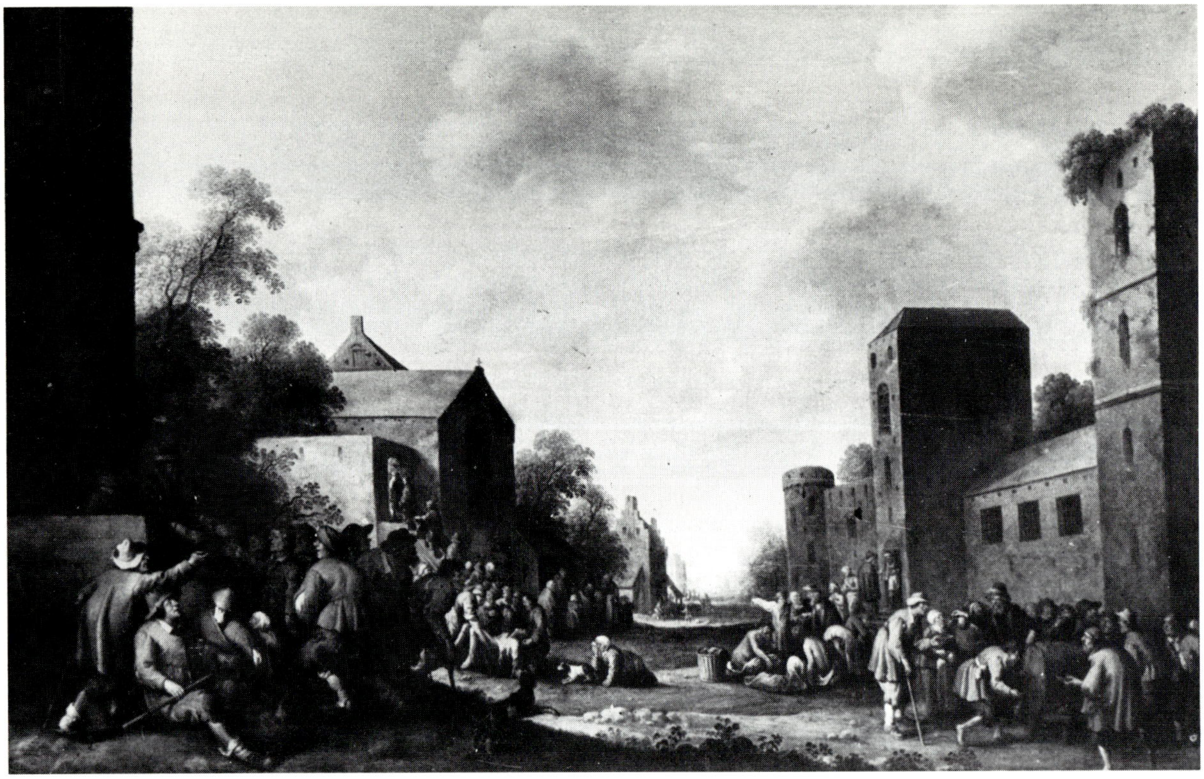

Fig. 16. Droochsloot, *The Seven Acts of Mercy*. Location unknown.

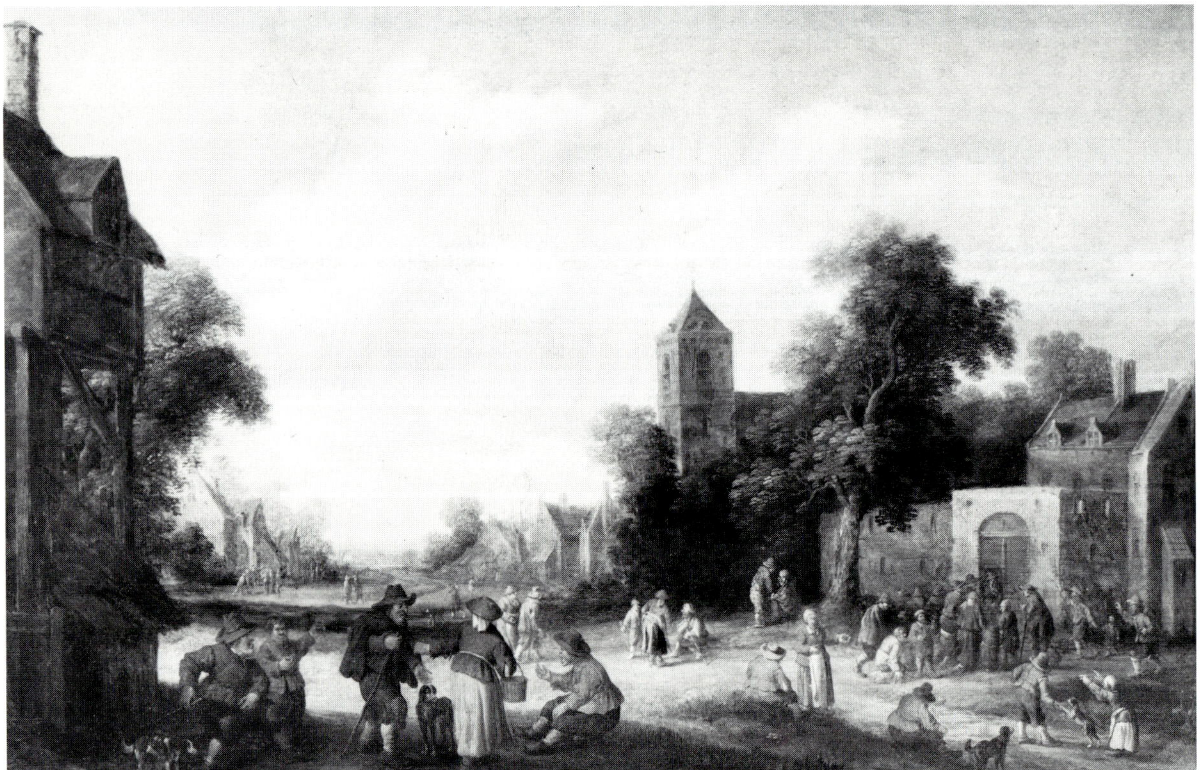

Fig. 17. Droochsloot, *Street Scene*. Boymans/van Beuningen Museum, Rotterdam.

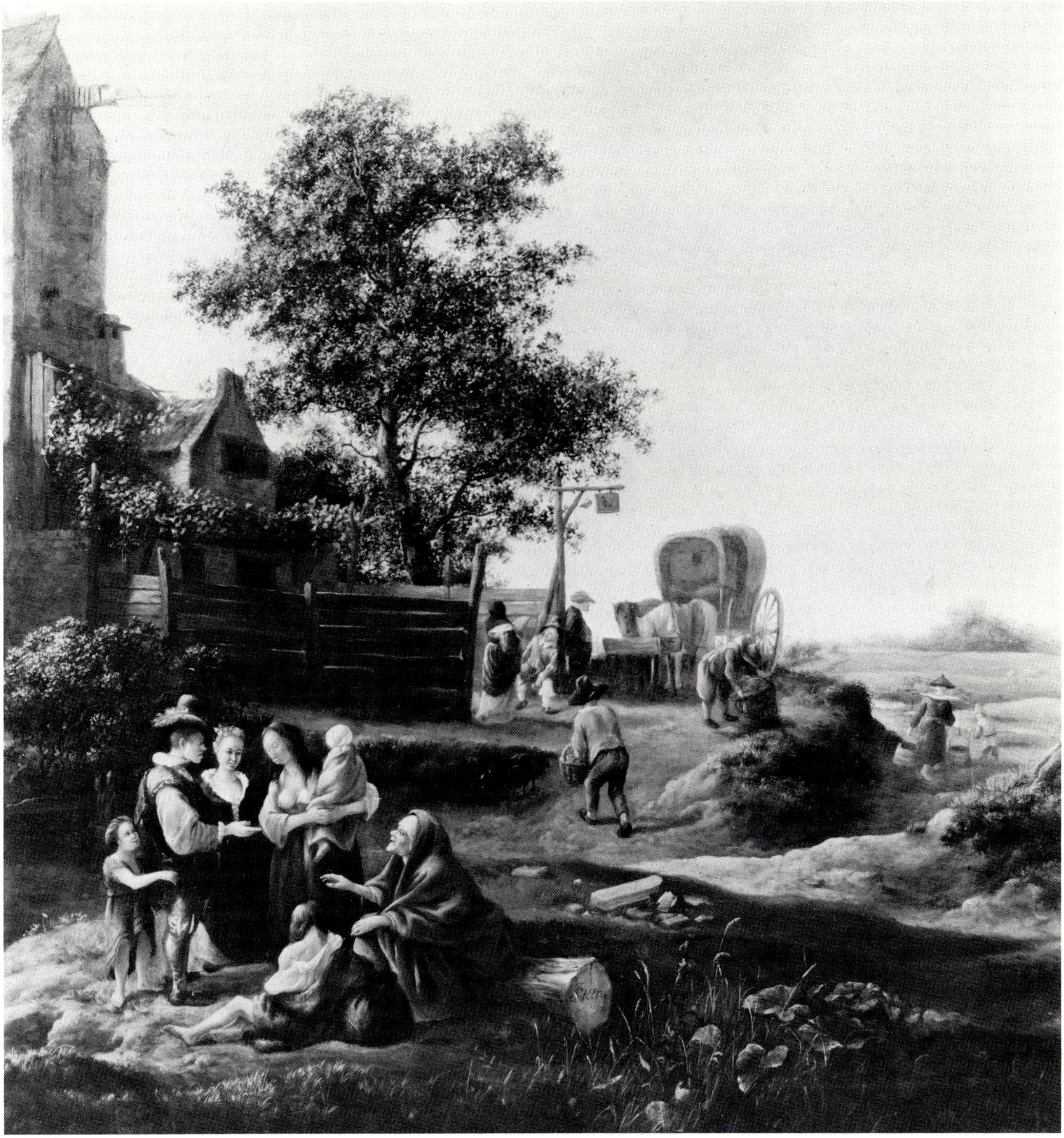

Fig. 18. *Landscape with Figures*. Museum of Art, Philadelphia.

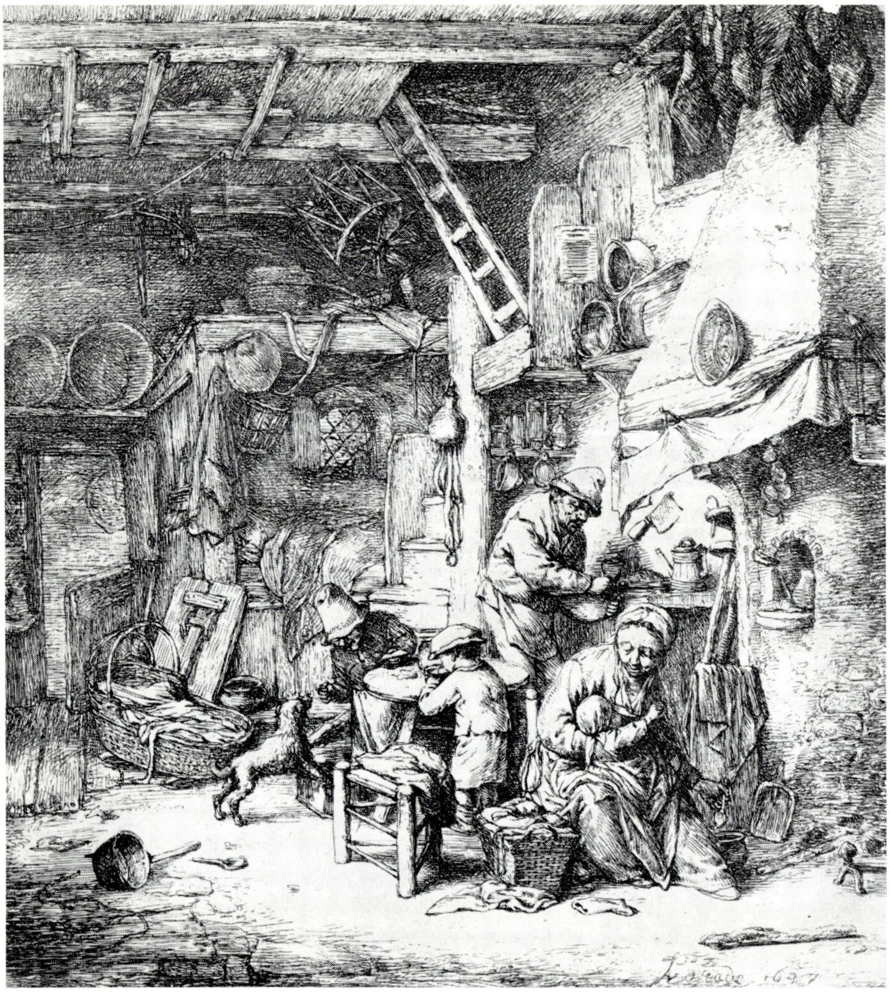

Fig. 19. Adriaen Ostade, *Family Scene,* etching, 1647. The Metropolitan Museum of Art, New York, Rogers Fund, 1917.

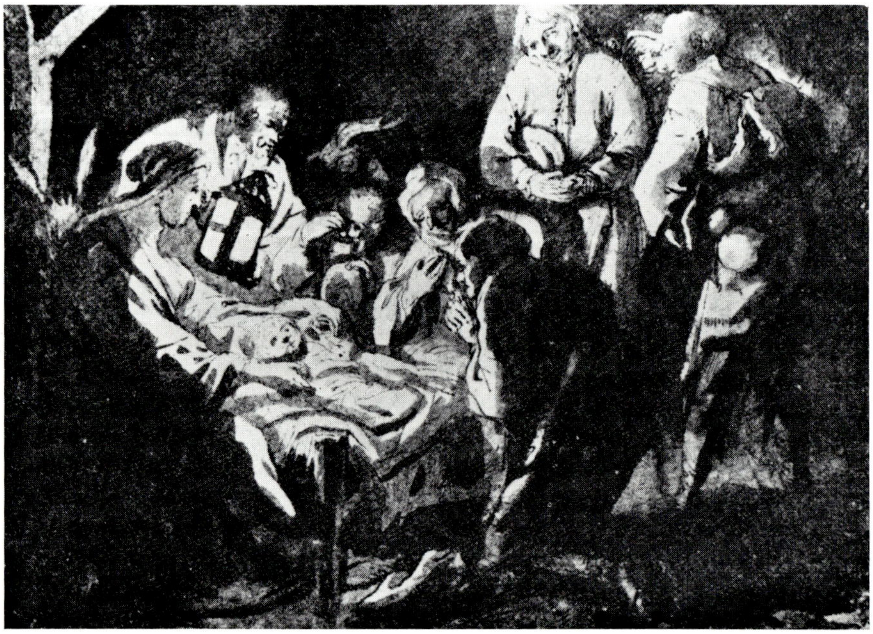

Fig. 20. *The Adoration of the Shepherds,* drawing. Formerly Frits Lugt, The Hague.

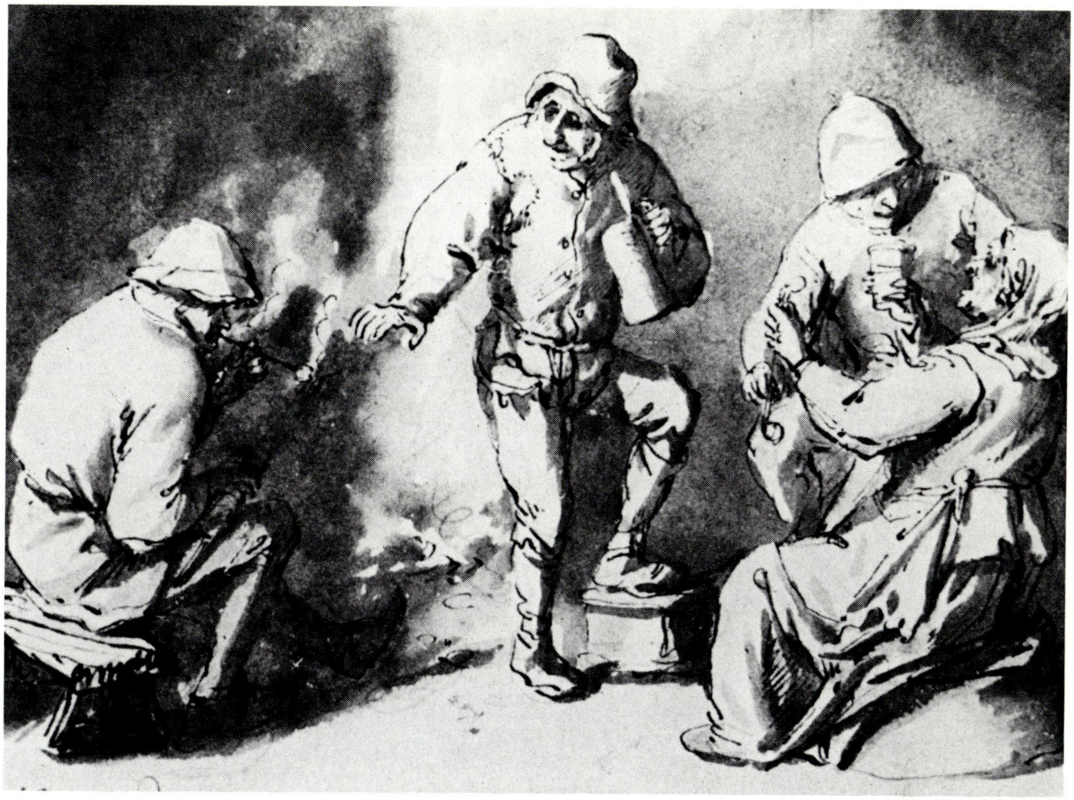

Fig. 21. Isaac Ostade, *Peasants Drinking,* drawing. British Museum, London.

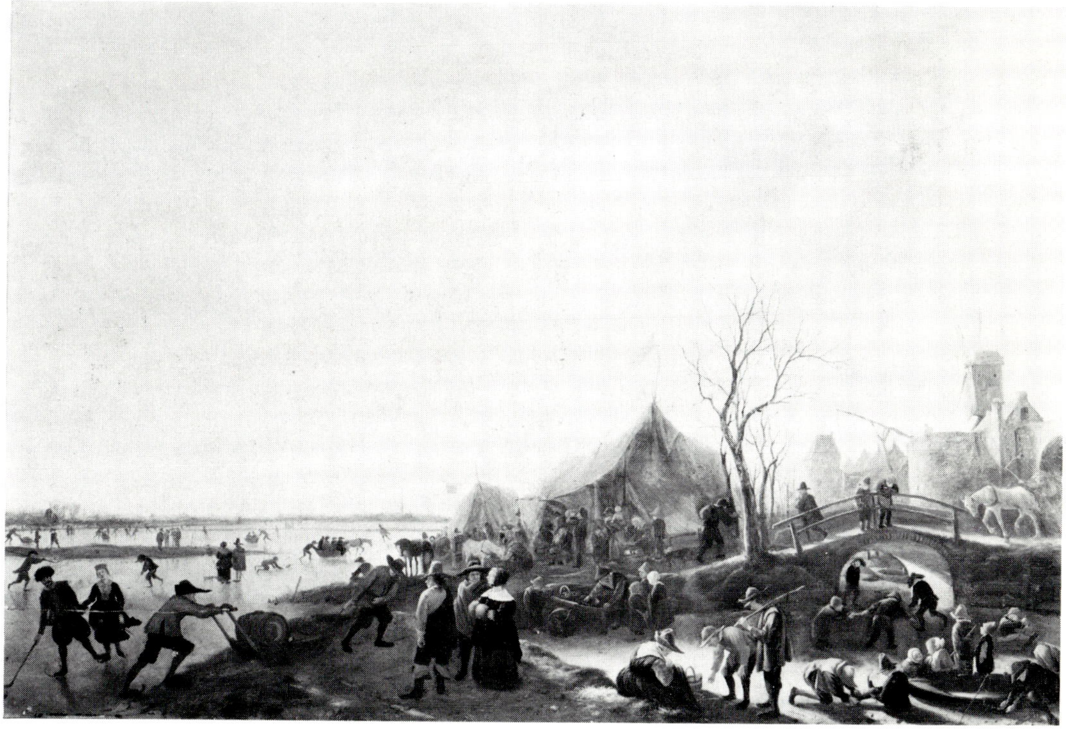

Fig. 22. *Winterlandscape* (HdG 881a). Skokloster Castle Collection, Skokloster, Sweden.

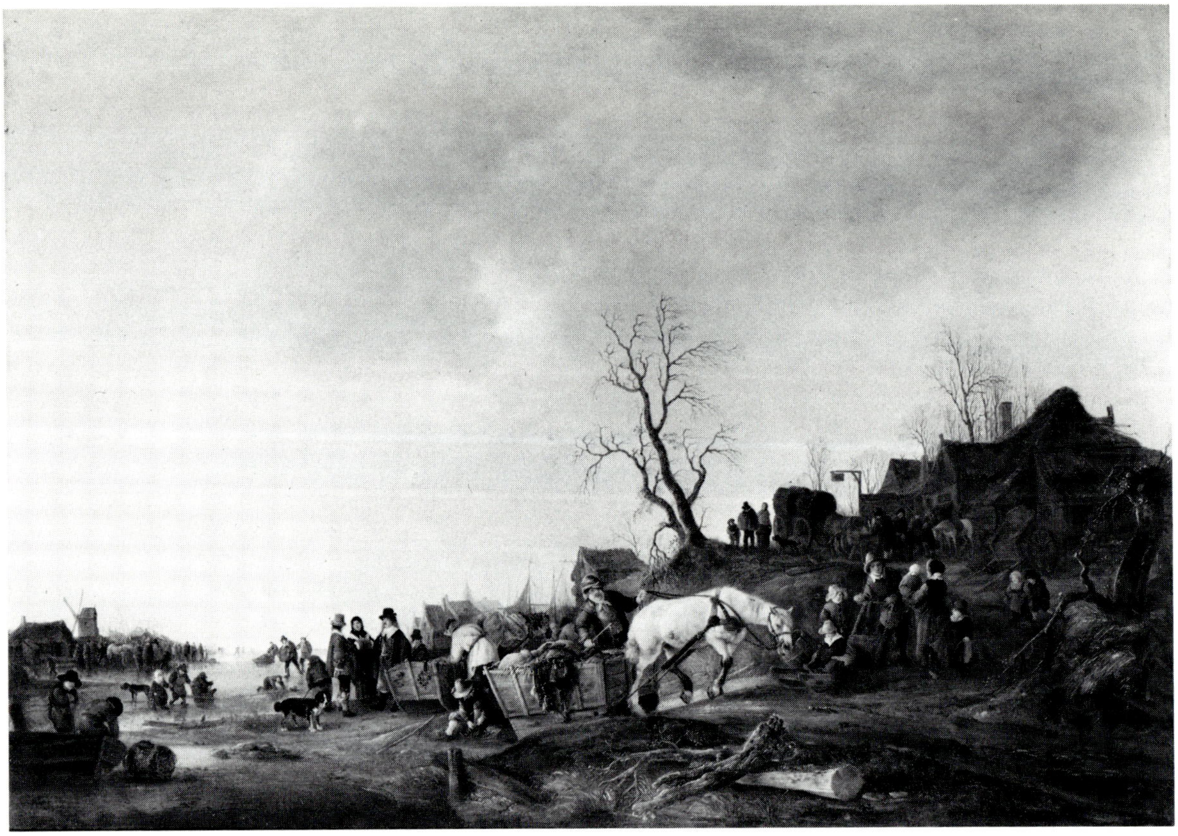

Fig. 23. Isaac Ostade, *Winterlandscape*. Alte Pinakothek, Munich.

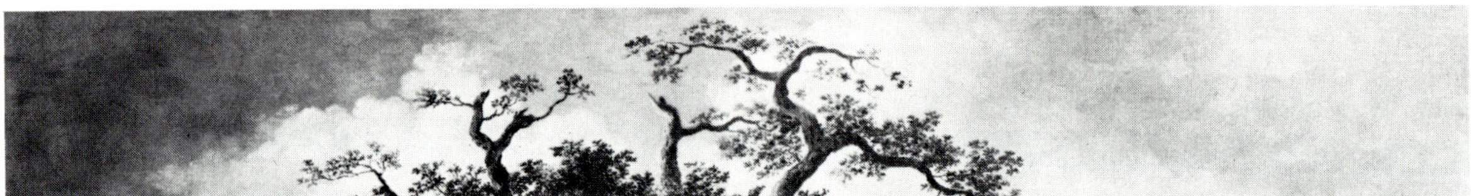

Fig. 24. Isaac Ostade, *Before an Inn*. Kunsthistorisches Museum, Vienna.

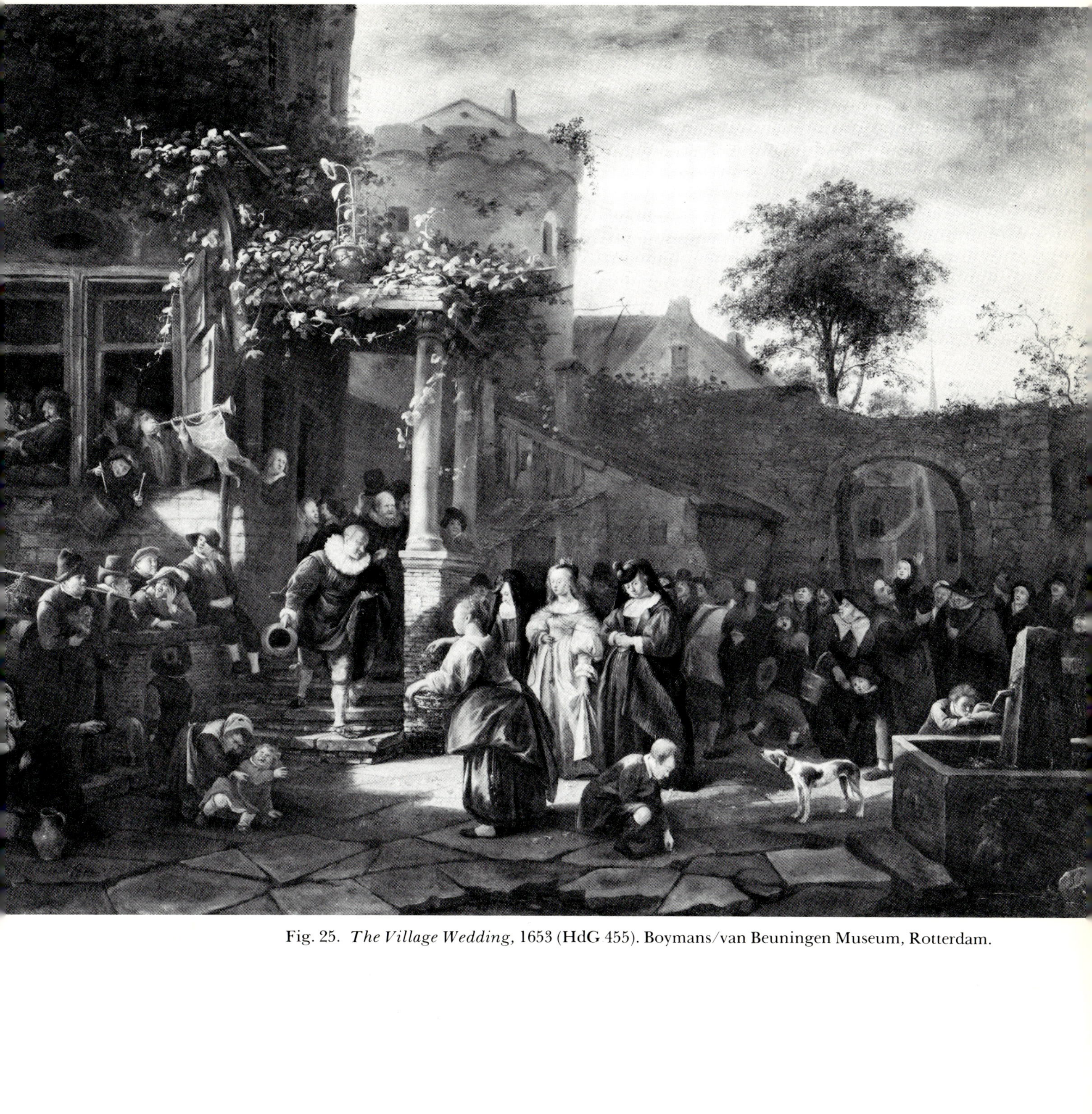

Fig. 25. *The Village Wedding,* 1653 (HdG 455). Boymans/van Beuningen Museum, Rotterdam.

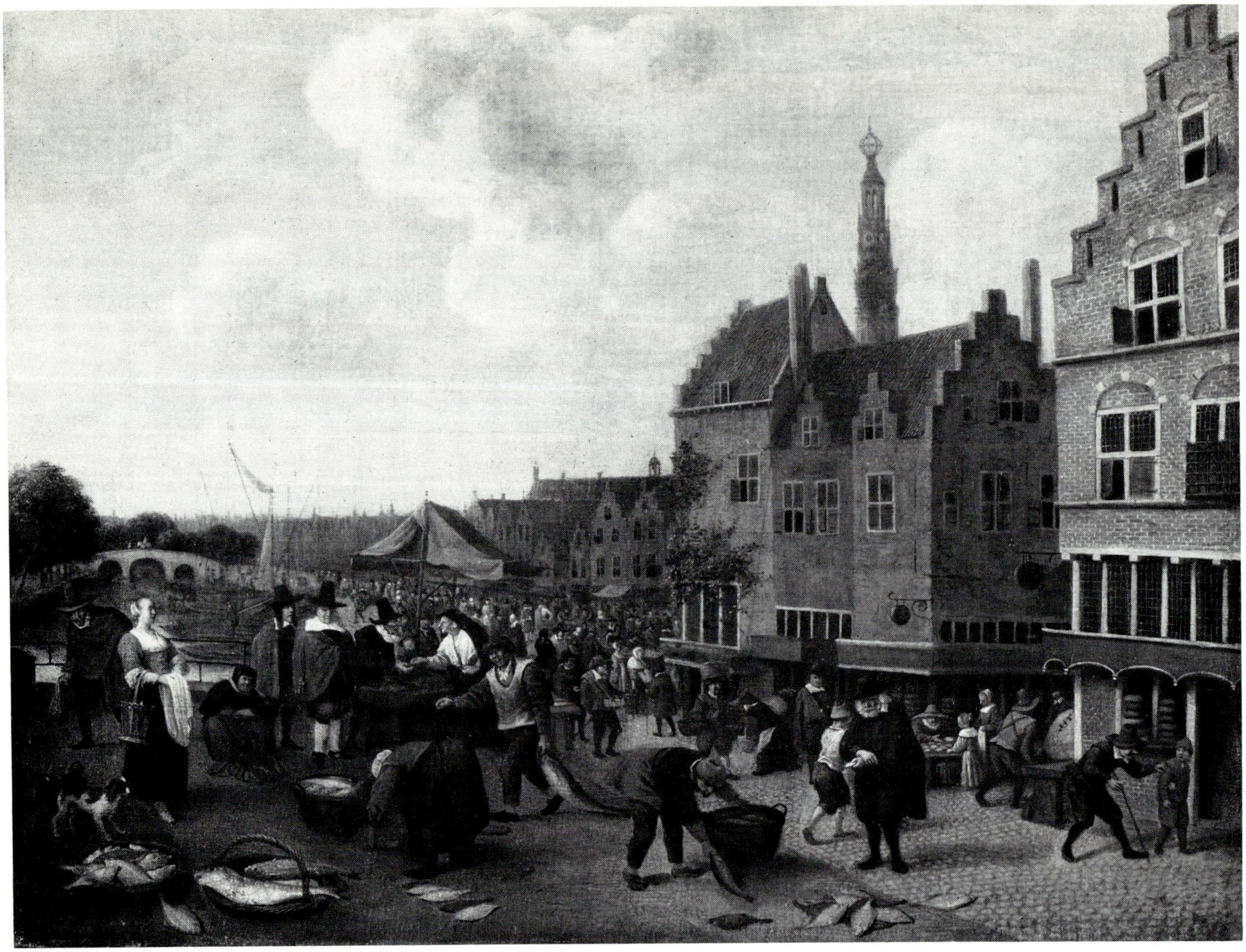

Fig. 26. *The Fishmarket at Leiden* (HdG 212). Städelsches Kunstinstitut, Frankfurt-am-Main.

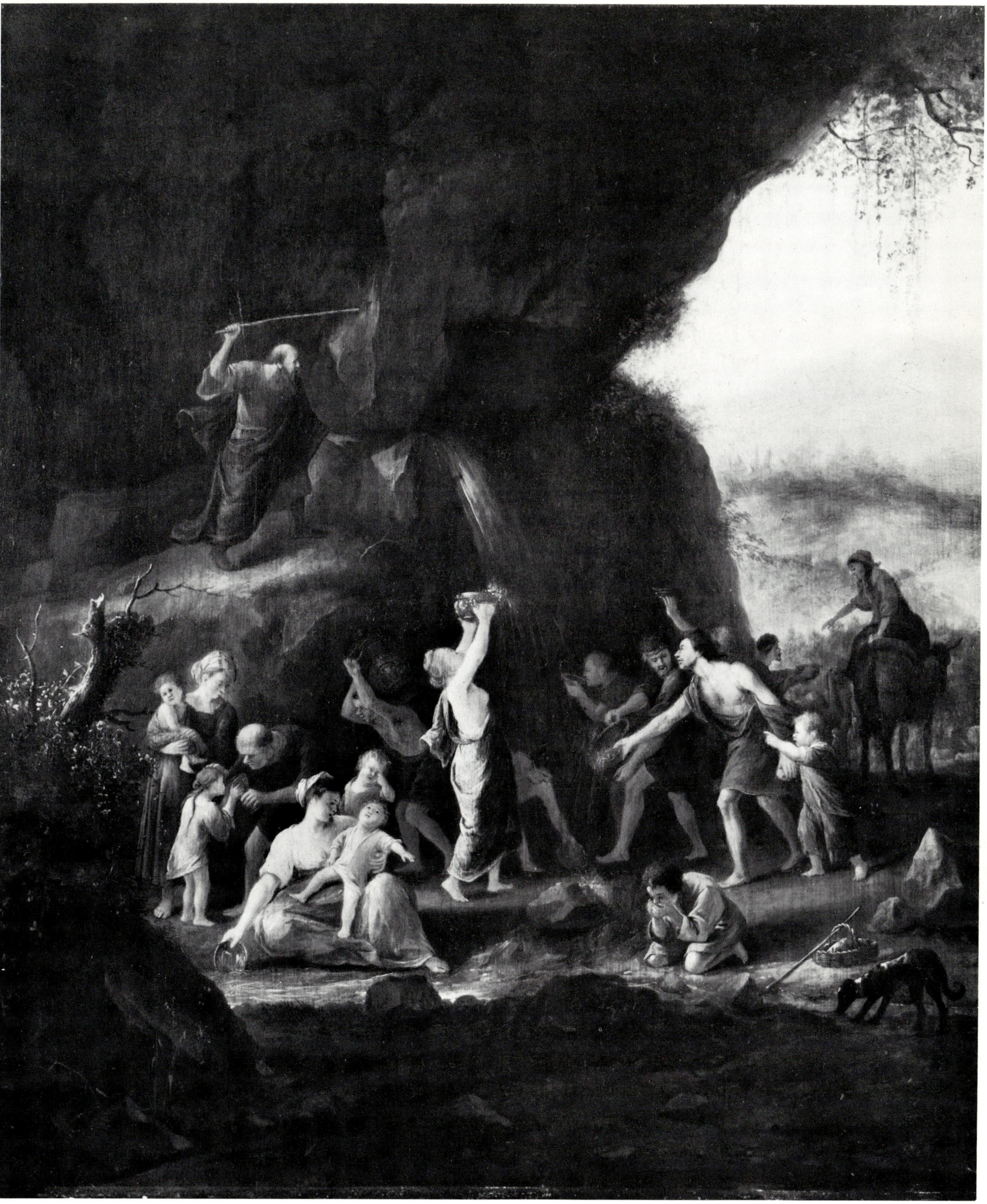

Fig. 27. *Moses Striking the Rock for Water* (Cat. 8). Städelsches Kunstinstitut, Frankfurt-am-Main.

Fig. 28. *The Adoration of the Shepherds* (Cat. 35). Bishop's Residence, Leitmeritz, Czechoslovakia.

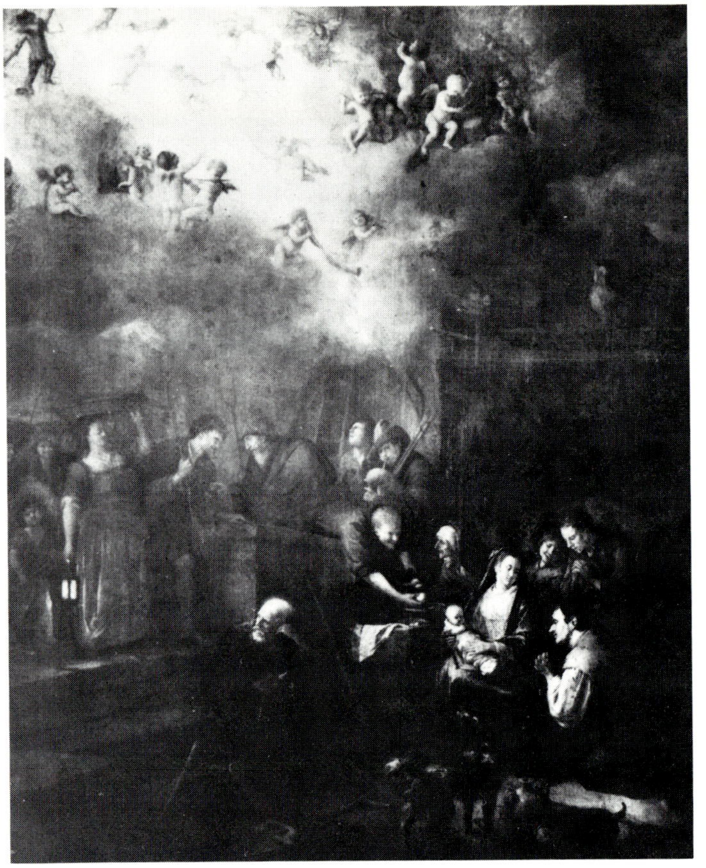

Fig. 29. *St. John Preaching in the Wilderness* (Cat. 28). Nivaagaard collection, Nivaa, Denmark.

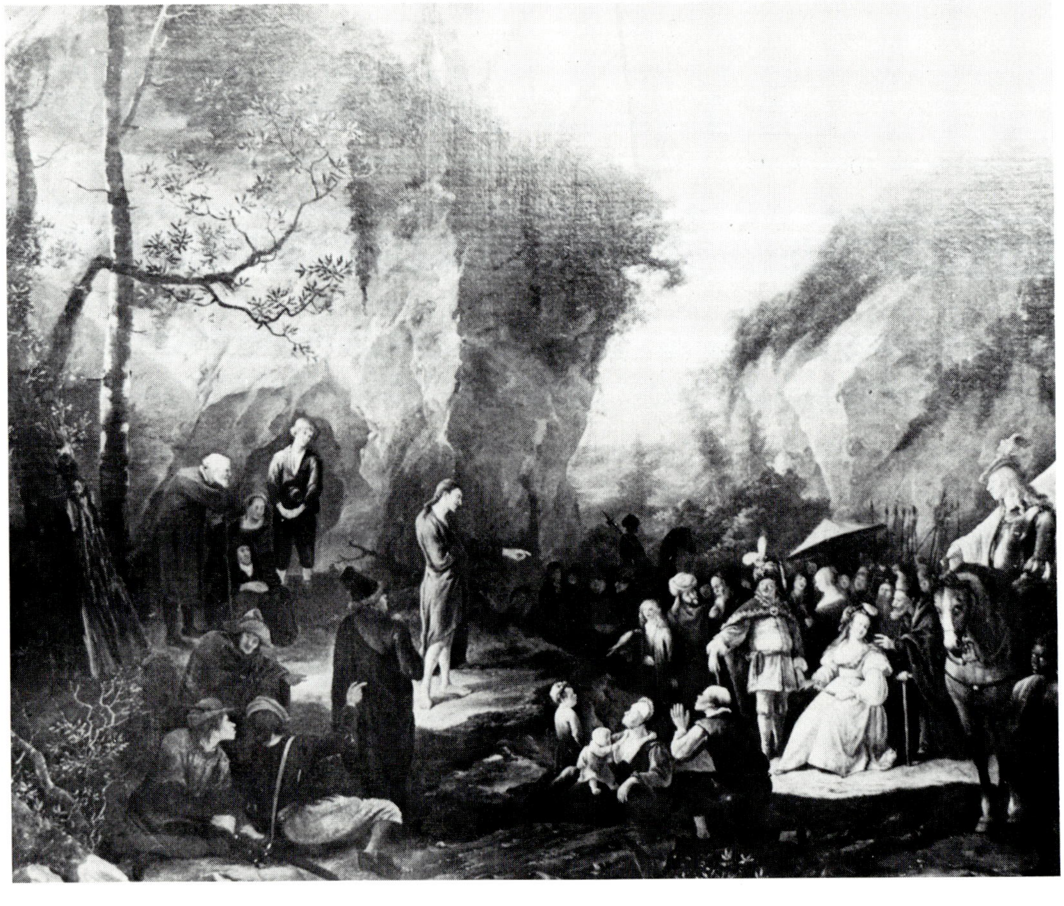

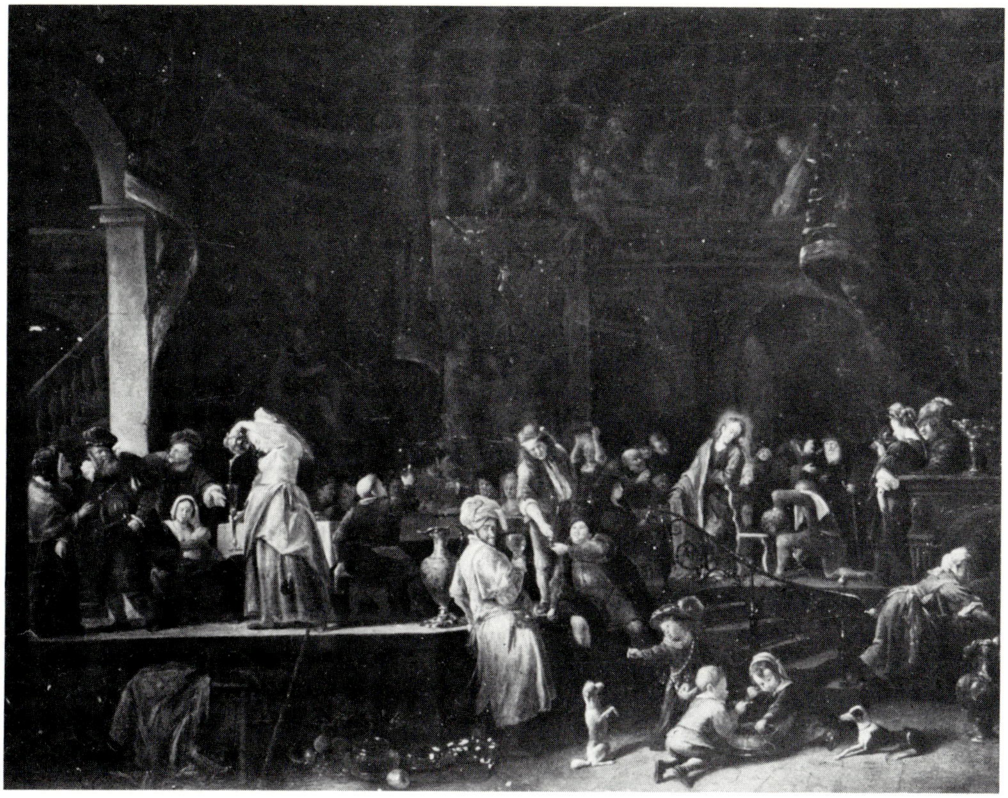

Fig. 30. *The Marriage at Cana* (Cat. 50b). Destroyed.

Fig. 31. De Wet, *Moses Striking the Rock for Water*. National Museum, Warsaw.

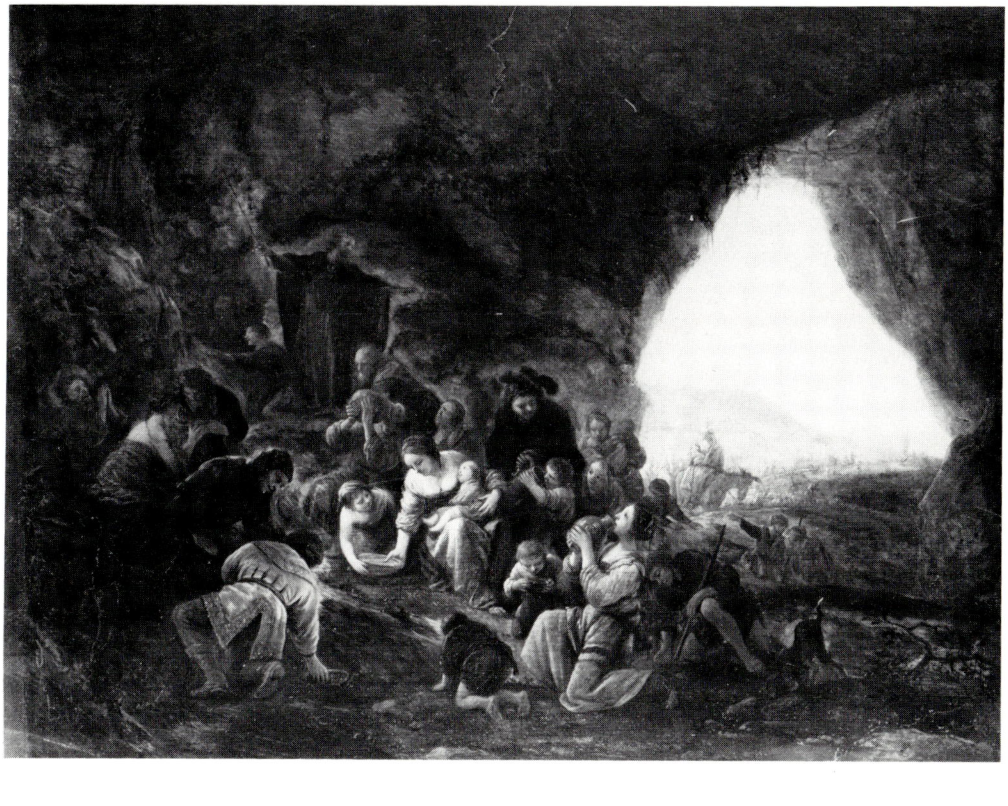

Fig. 32. *The Poultry Yard,* 1660 (HdG 330). Mauritshuis, The Hague.

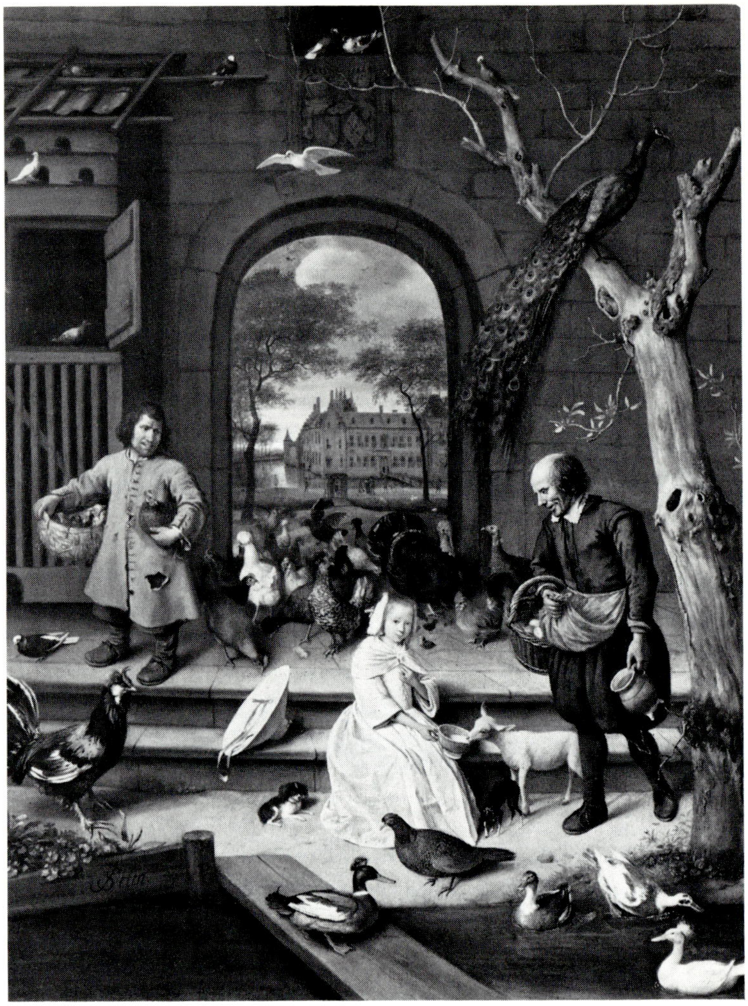

Fig. 33. *The Morning Toilet,* 1663 (HdG 340). Buckingham Palace, London.

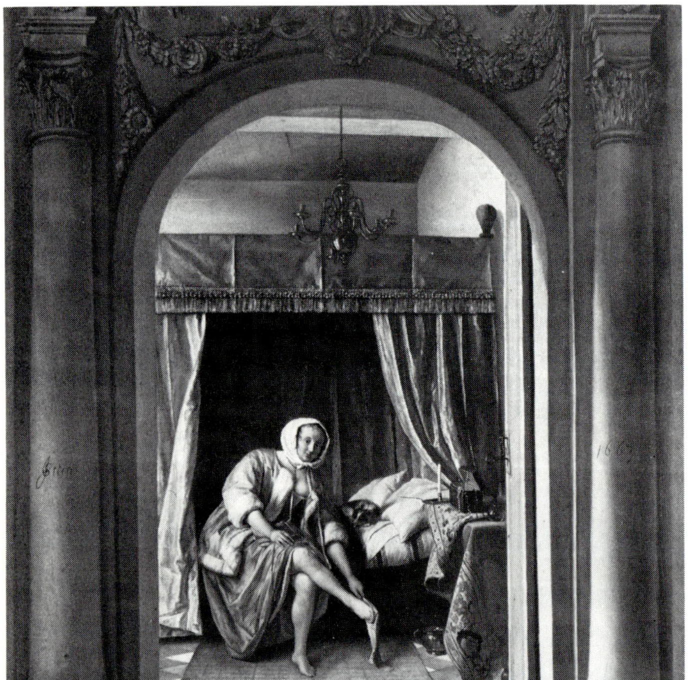

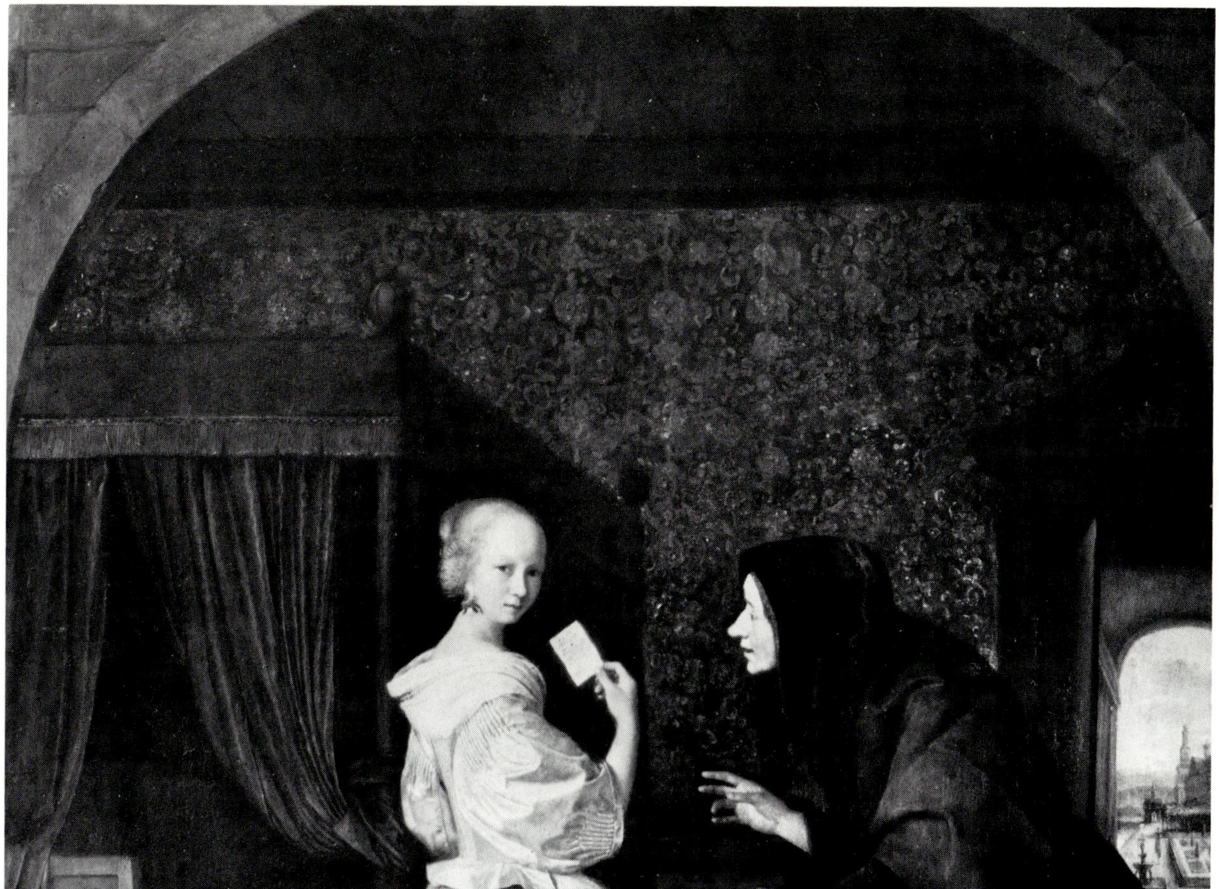

Fig. 34. *Bathseba Receiving David's Letter* (Cat. 15). Private collection, Sussex, England.

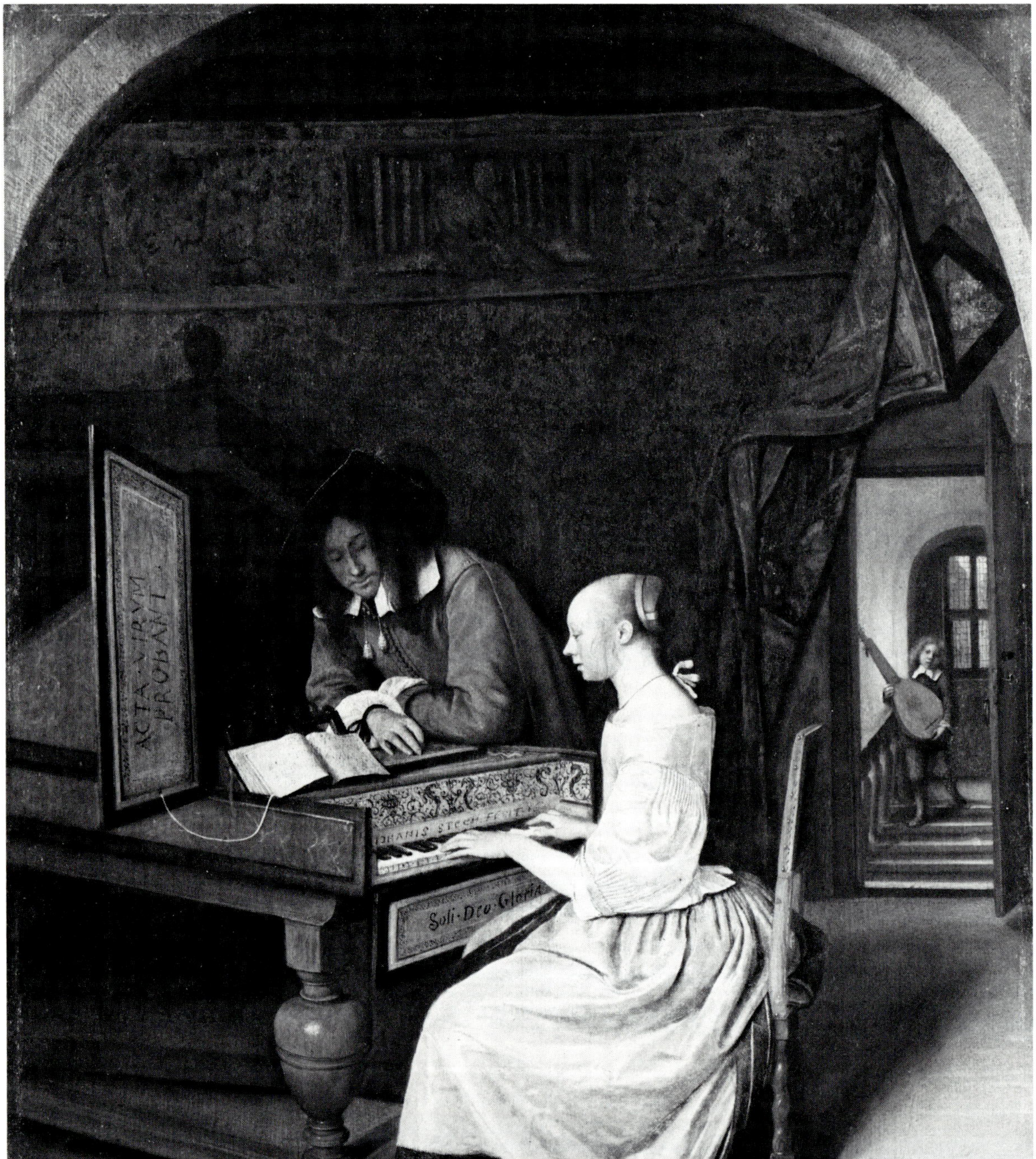

Fig. 35. *The Music Lesson,* 1669 (HdG 409). Reproduced by courtesy of the Trustees, The National Gallery, London.

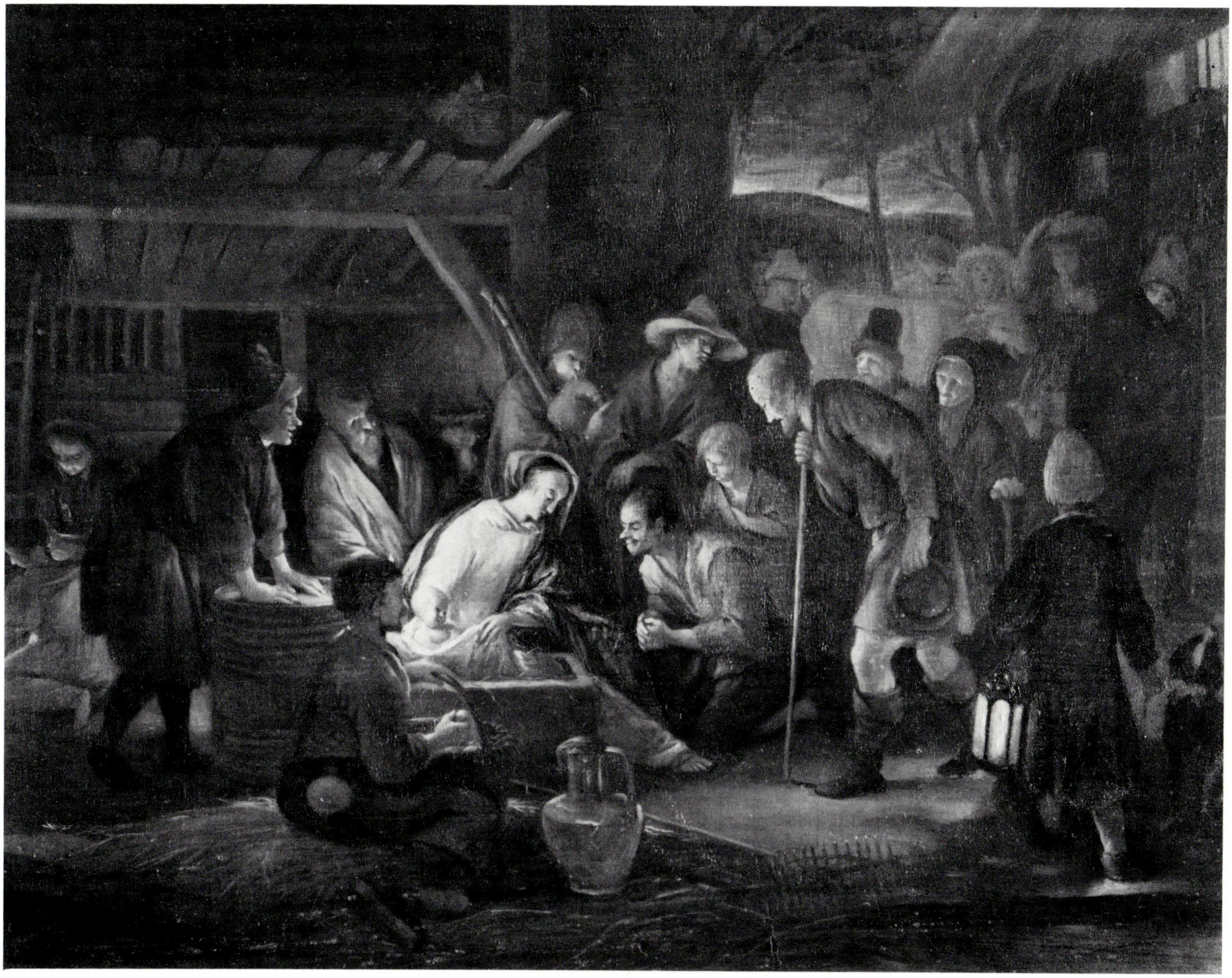

Fig. 36. *The Adoration of the Shepherds* (Cat. 33/36). Museum Bredius, The Hague.

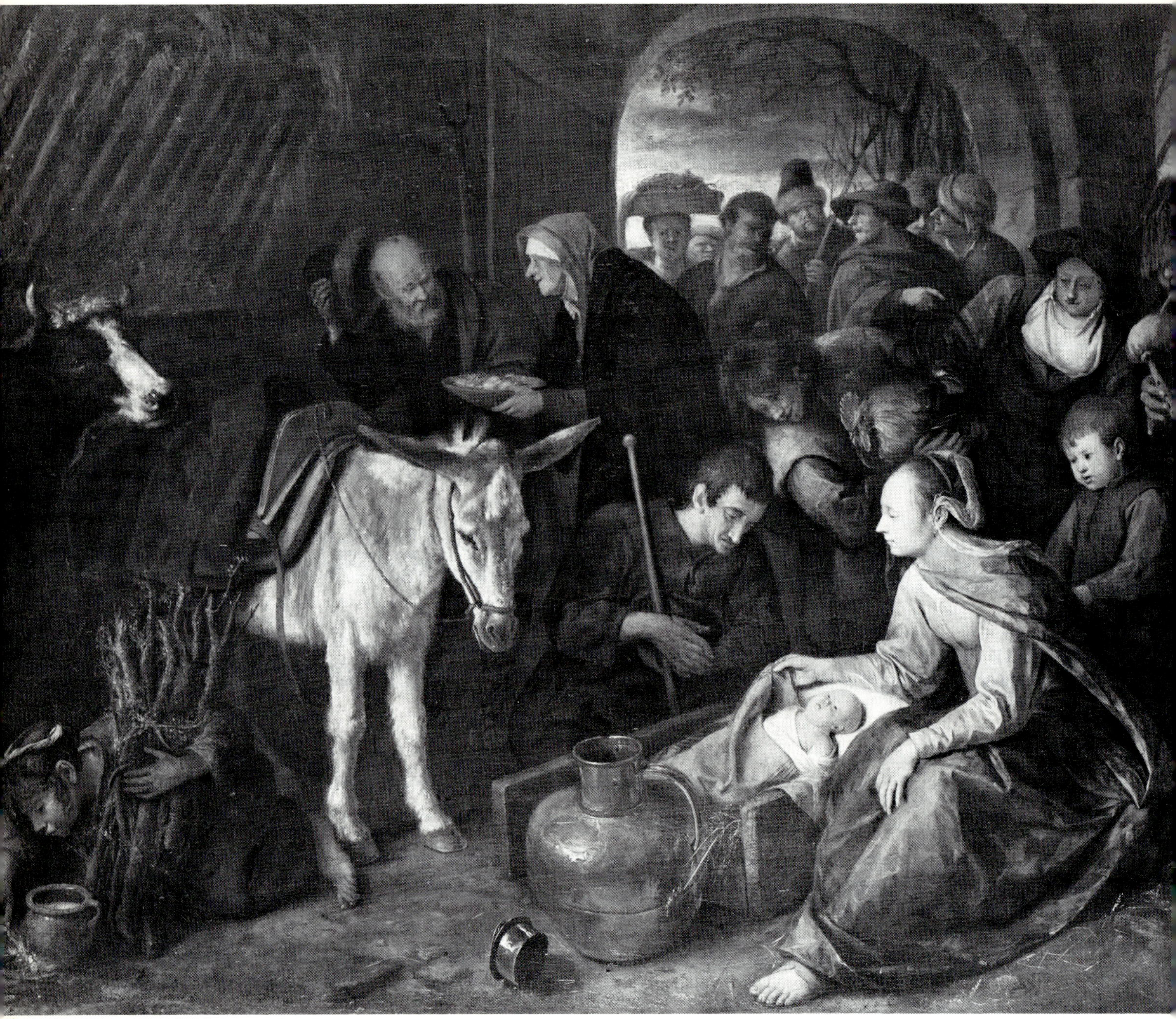

Fig. 37. *The Adoration of the Shepherds* (Cat. 37/31/31a). Rijksmuseum, Amsterdam.

Fig. 38. *Twelfth Night Feast,* 1662 (HdG 509c). Courtesy, Museum of Fine Arts, Boston.

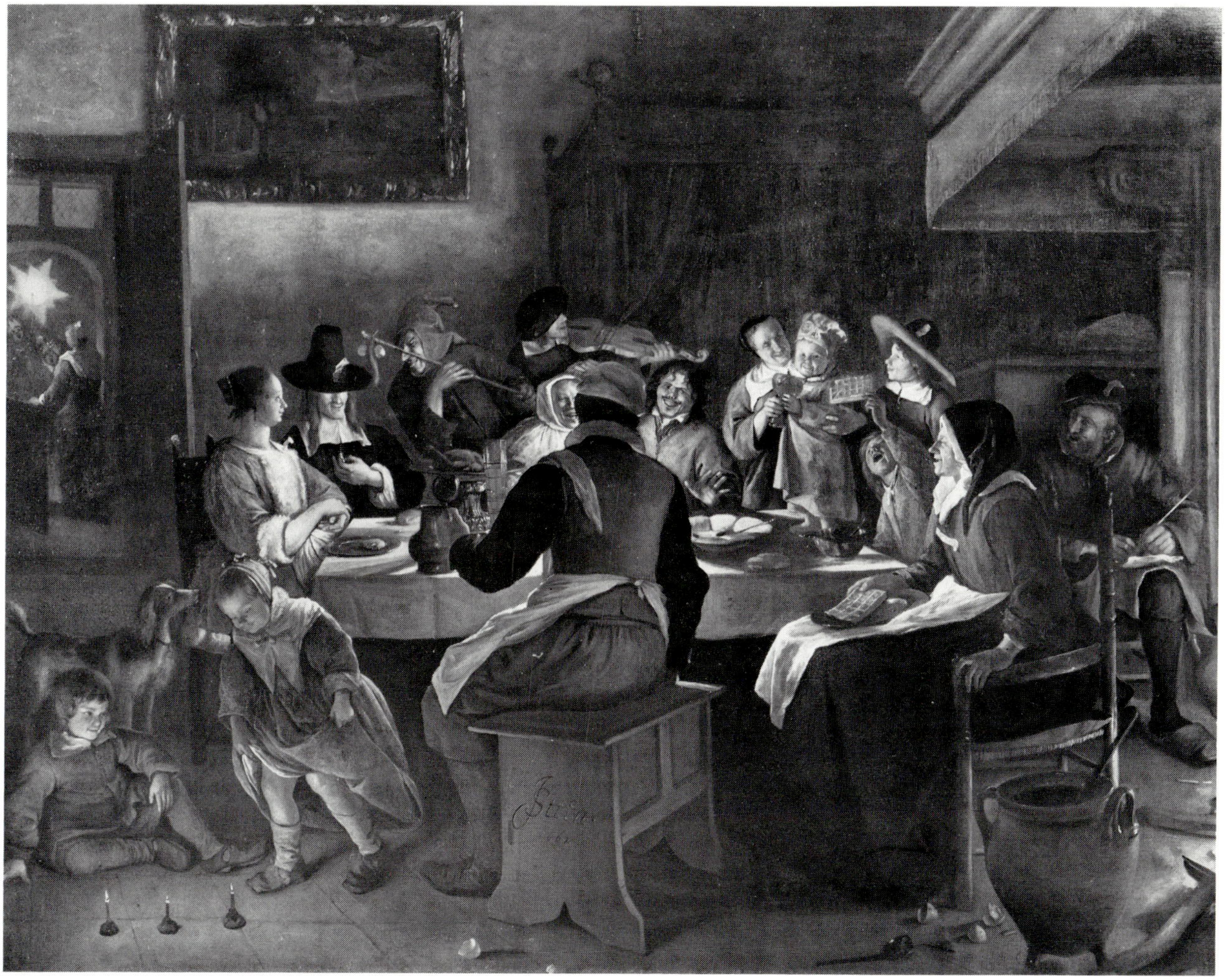

Fig. 39. *The Child Jesus in the Temple* (Cat. 44). Kunstmuseum, Basel.

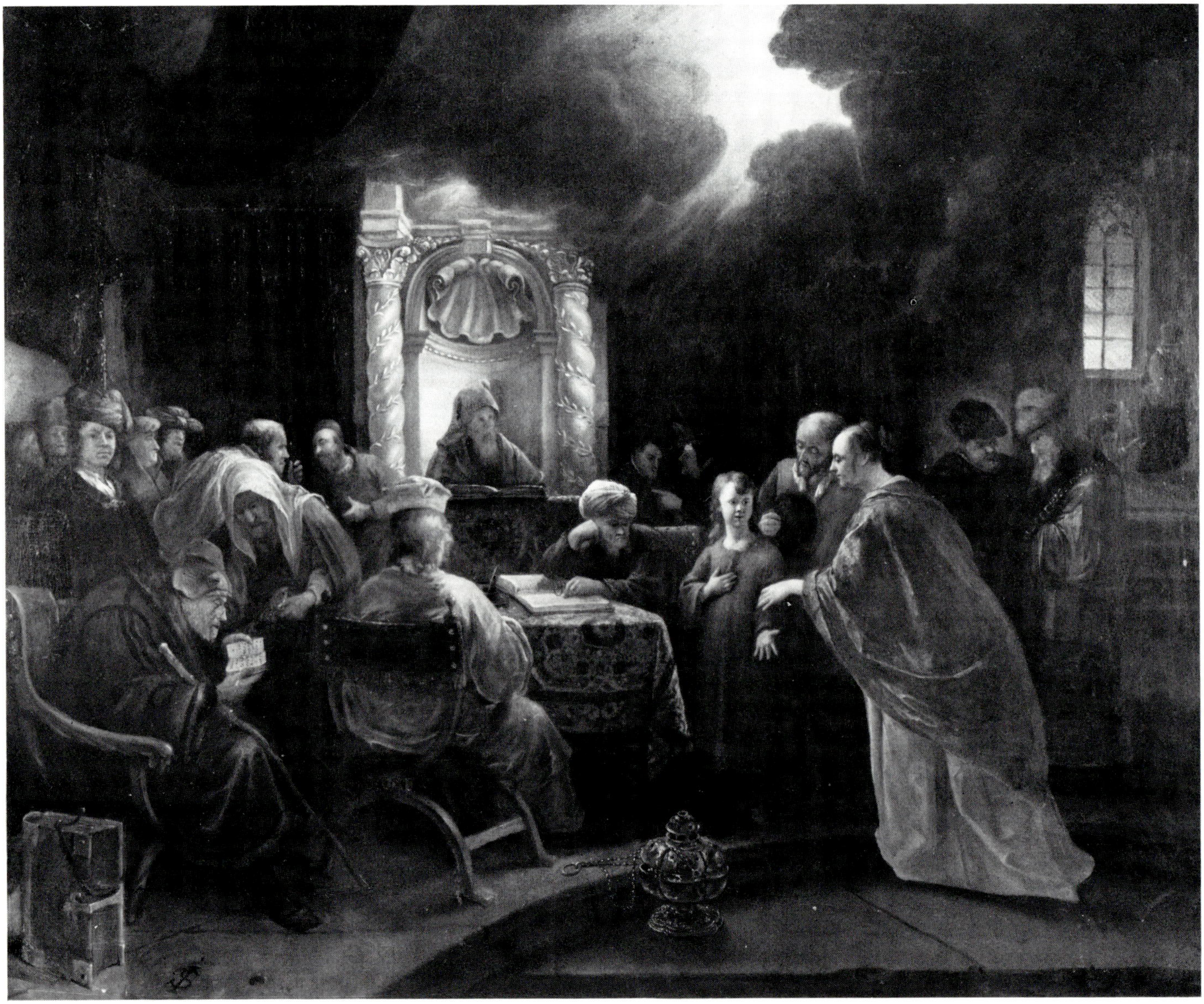

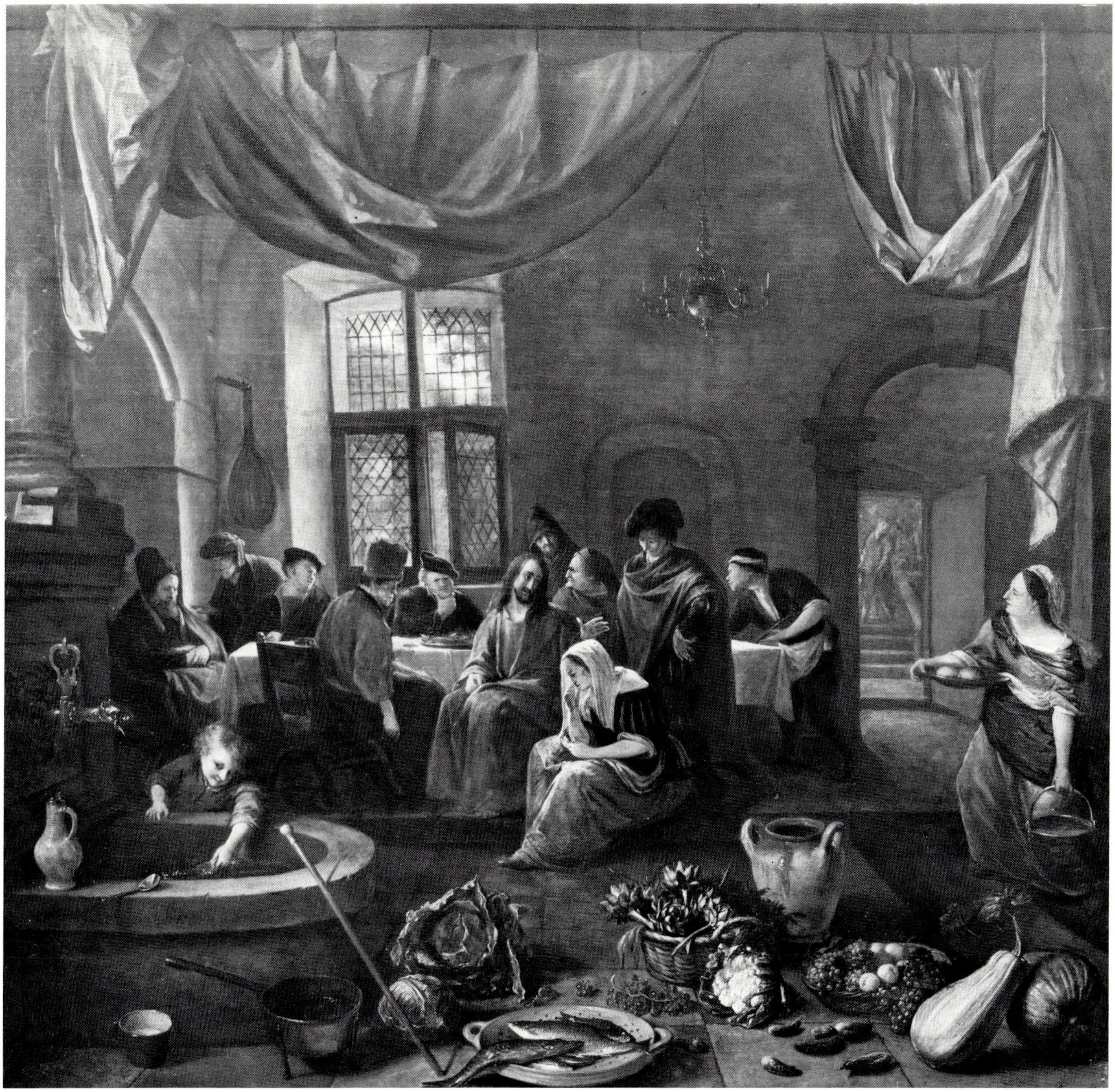

Fig. 40. *Christ in the House of Mary and Martha* (Cat. 51). Property of Donald Maxwell Macdonald, on show at Pollok House, Glasgow.

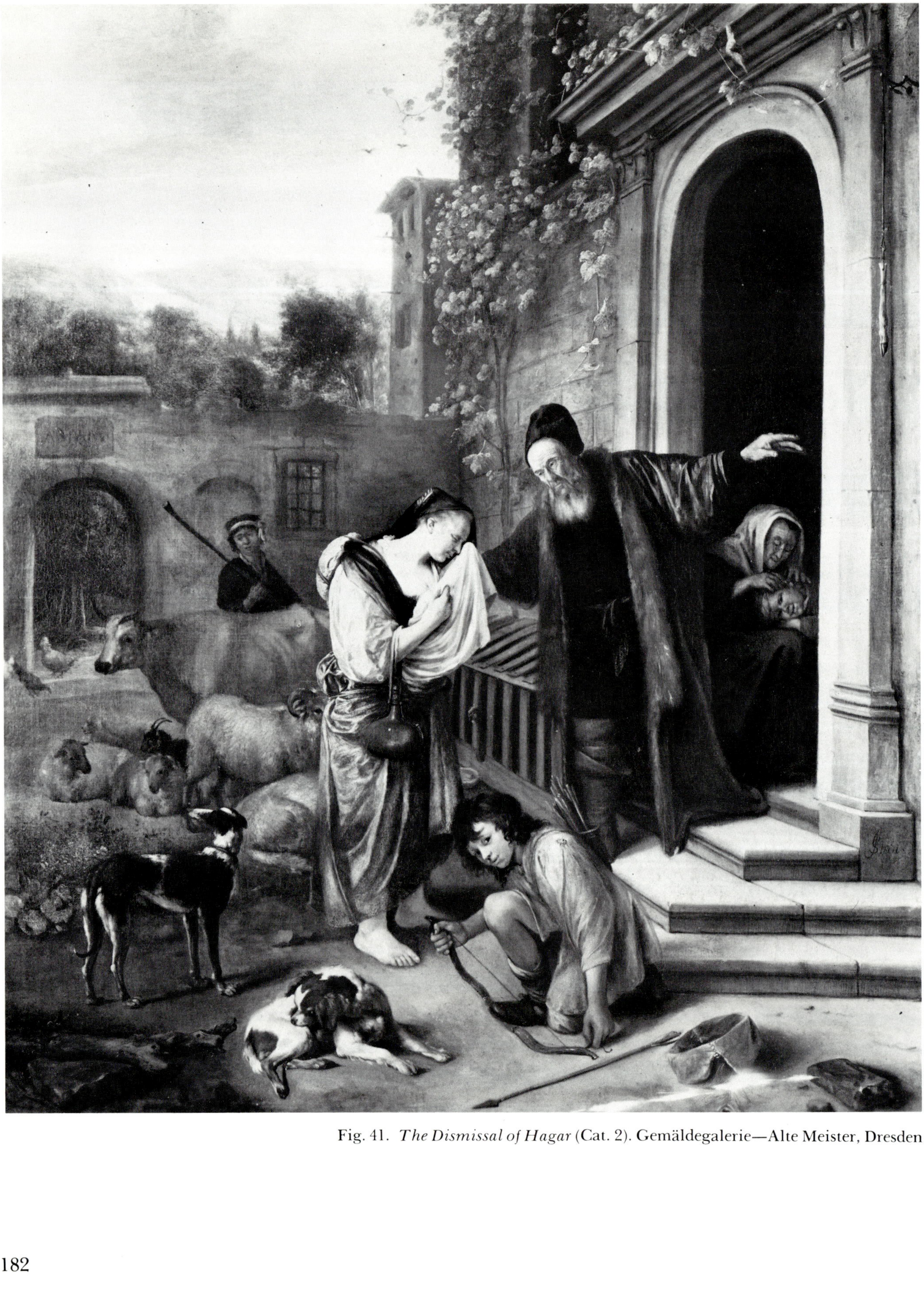

Fig. 41. *The Dismissal of Hagar* (Cat. 2). Gemäldegalerie—Alte Meister, Dresden.

Fig. 42. Rembrandt, *The Dismissal of Hagar,* etching, 1637. Courtesy, Museum of Fine Arts, Boston.

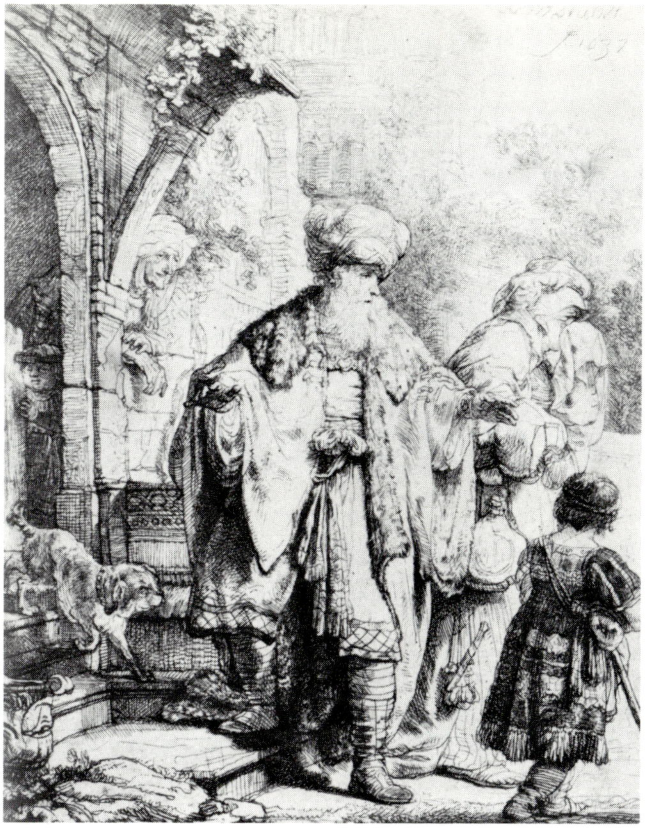

Fig. 43. Rembrandt, *Weeping Woman,* oil sketch. Gift of Mr. and Mrs. Henry Ford II, courtesy of The Detroit Institute of Arts.

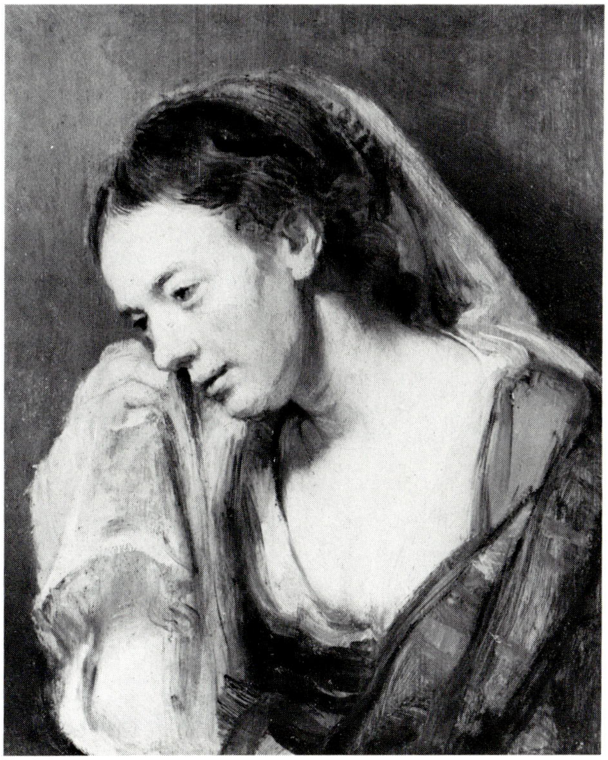

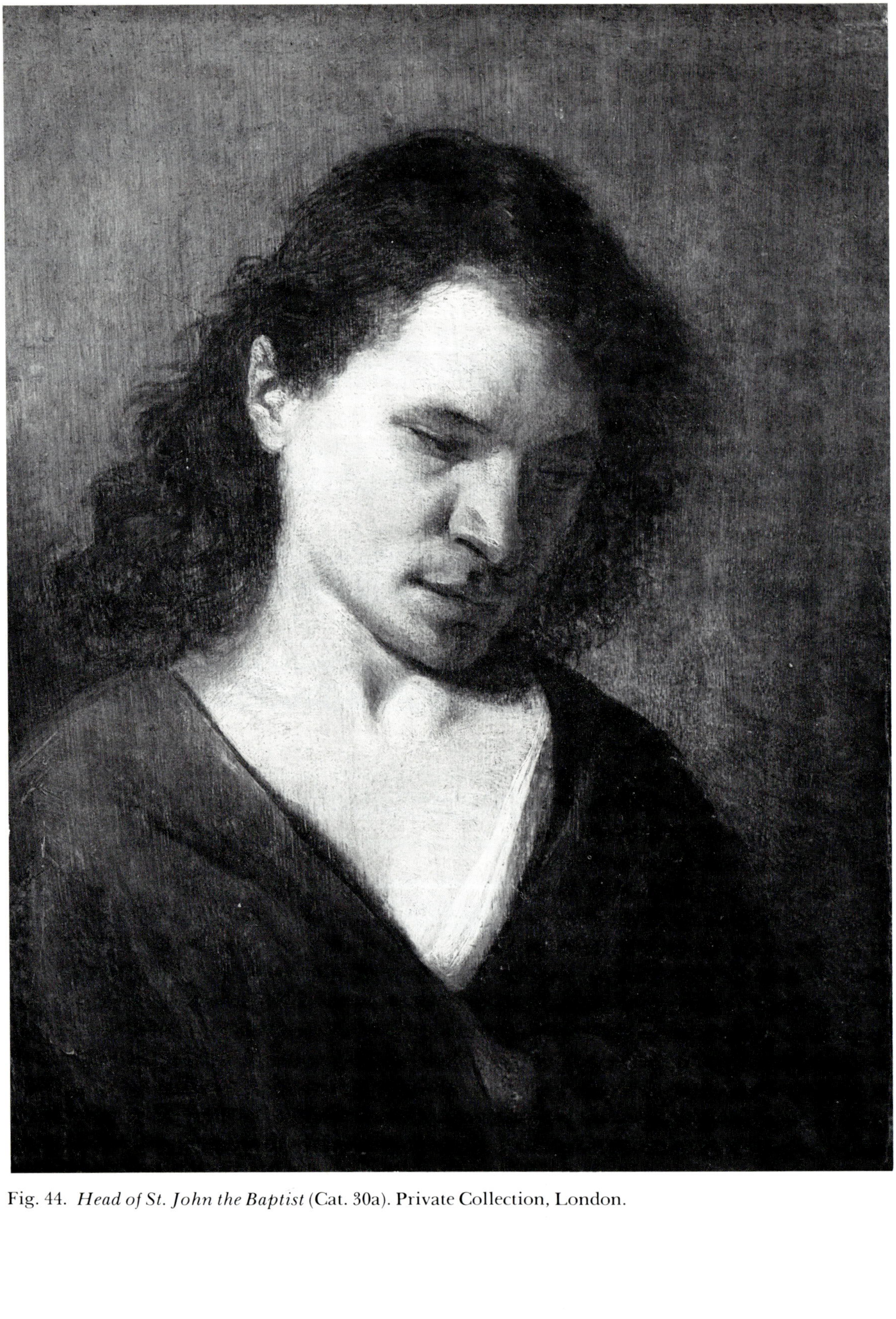

Fig. 44. *Head of St. John the Baptist* (Cat. 30a). Private Collection, London.

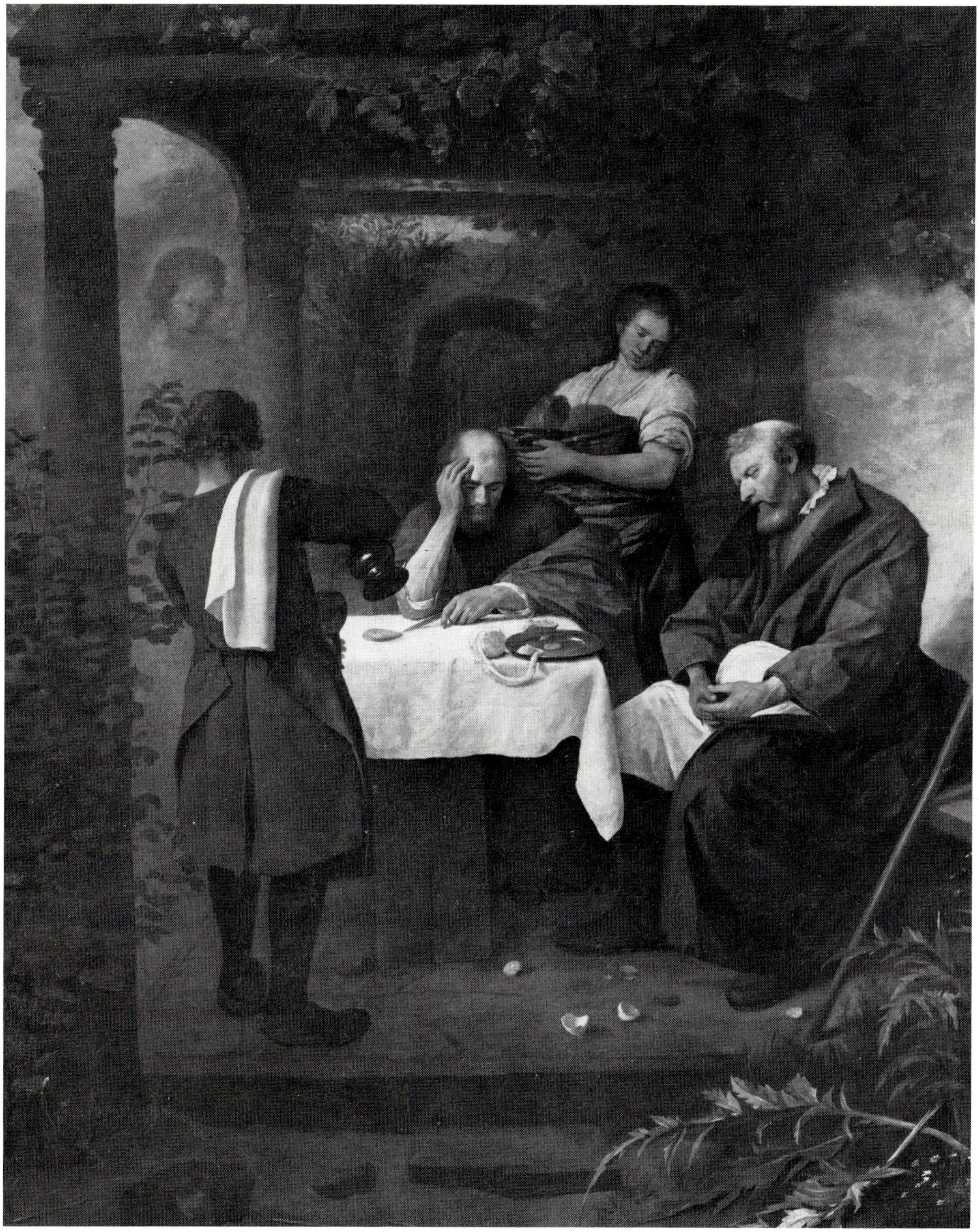

Fig. 45. *Christ at Emmaus* (Cat. 65). Rijksmuseum, Amsterdam.

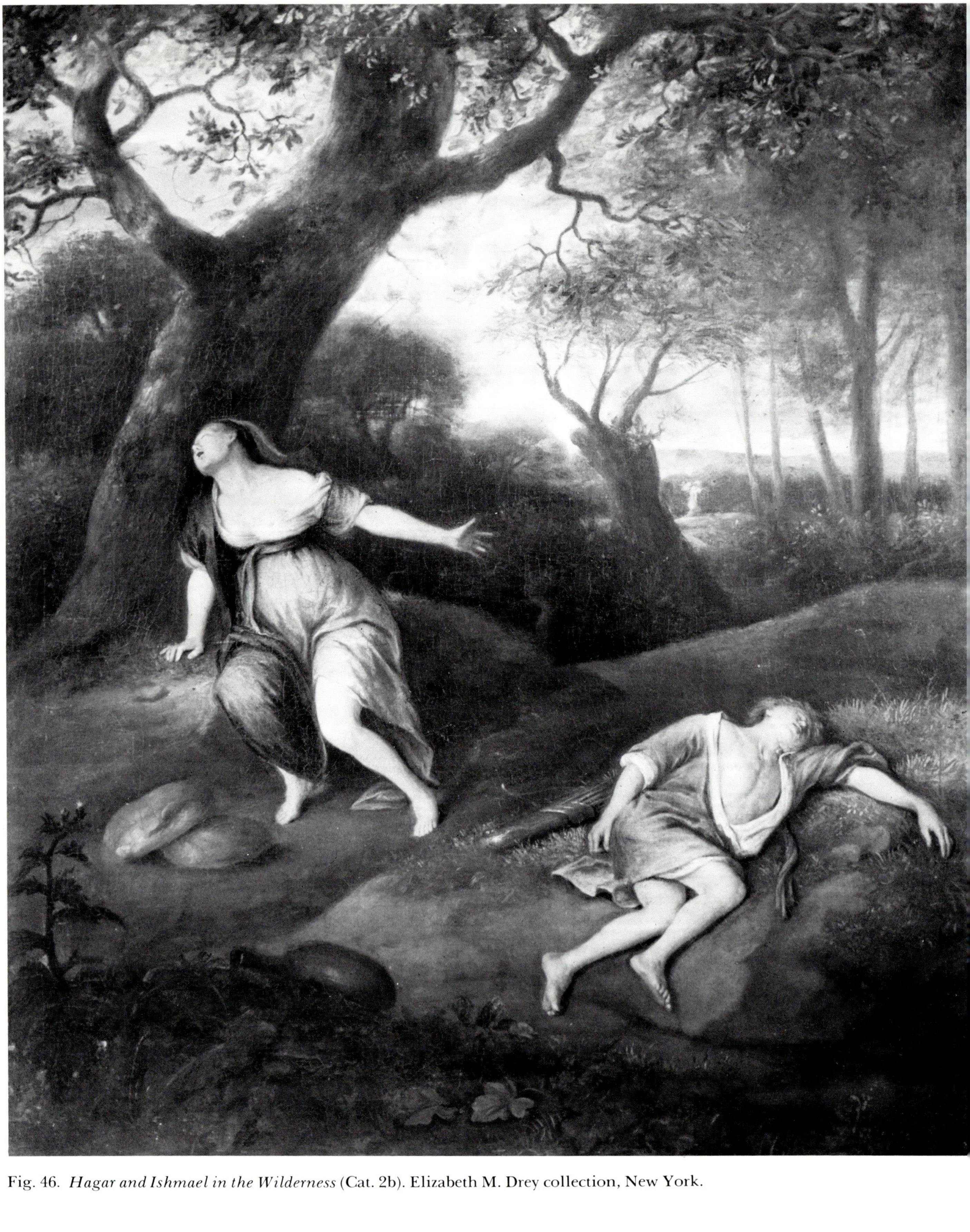

Fig. 46. *Hagar and Ishmael in the Wilderness* (Cat. 2b). Elizabeth M. Drey collection, New York.

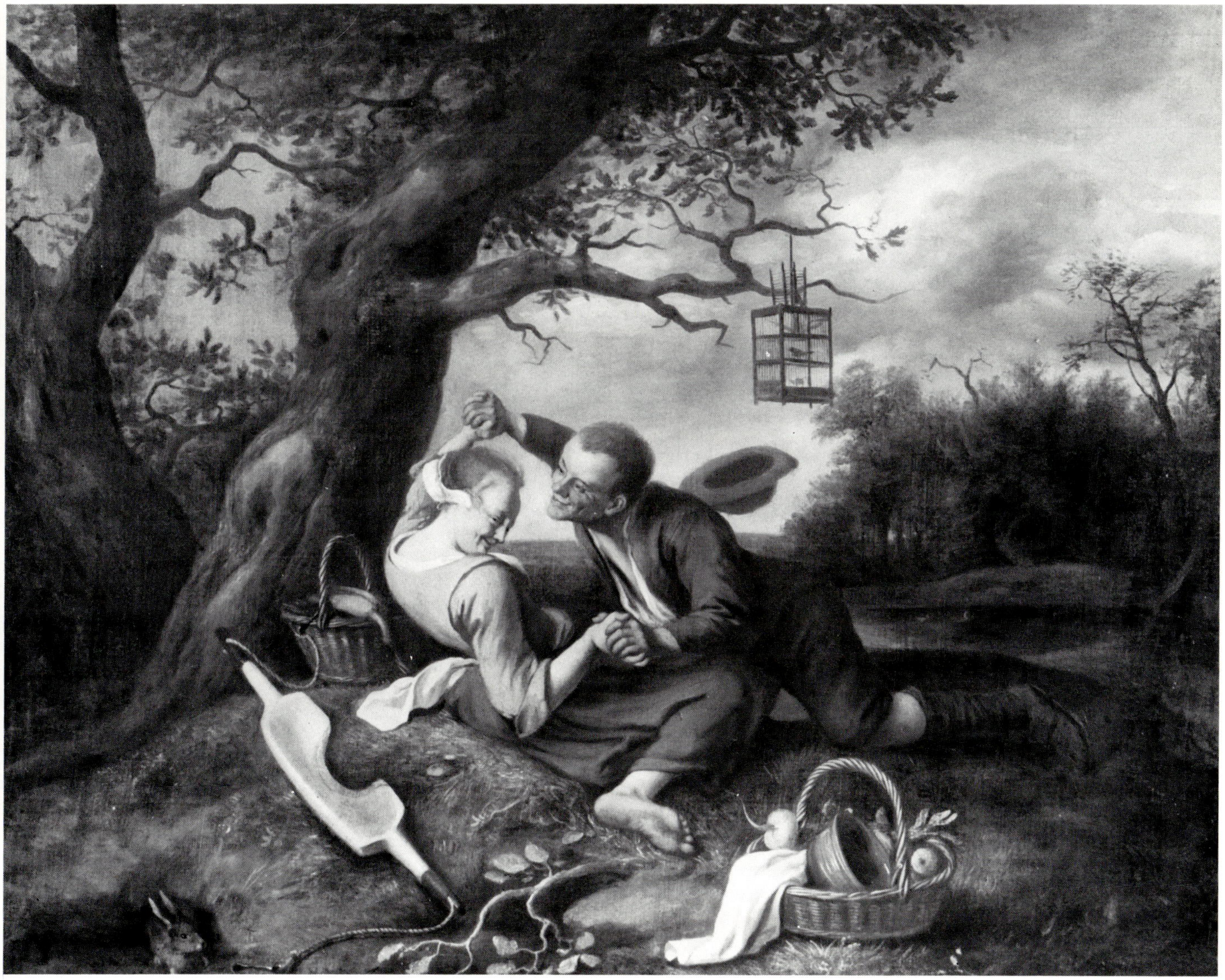

Fig. 47. *Rustic Love* (HdG 819). De Lakenhal, Leiden.

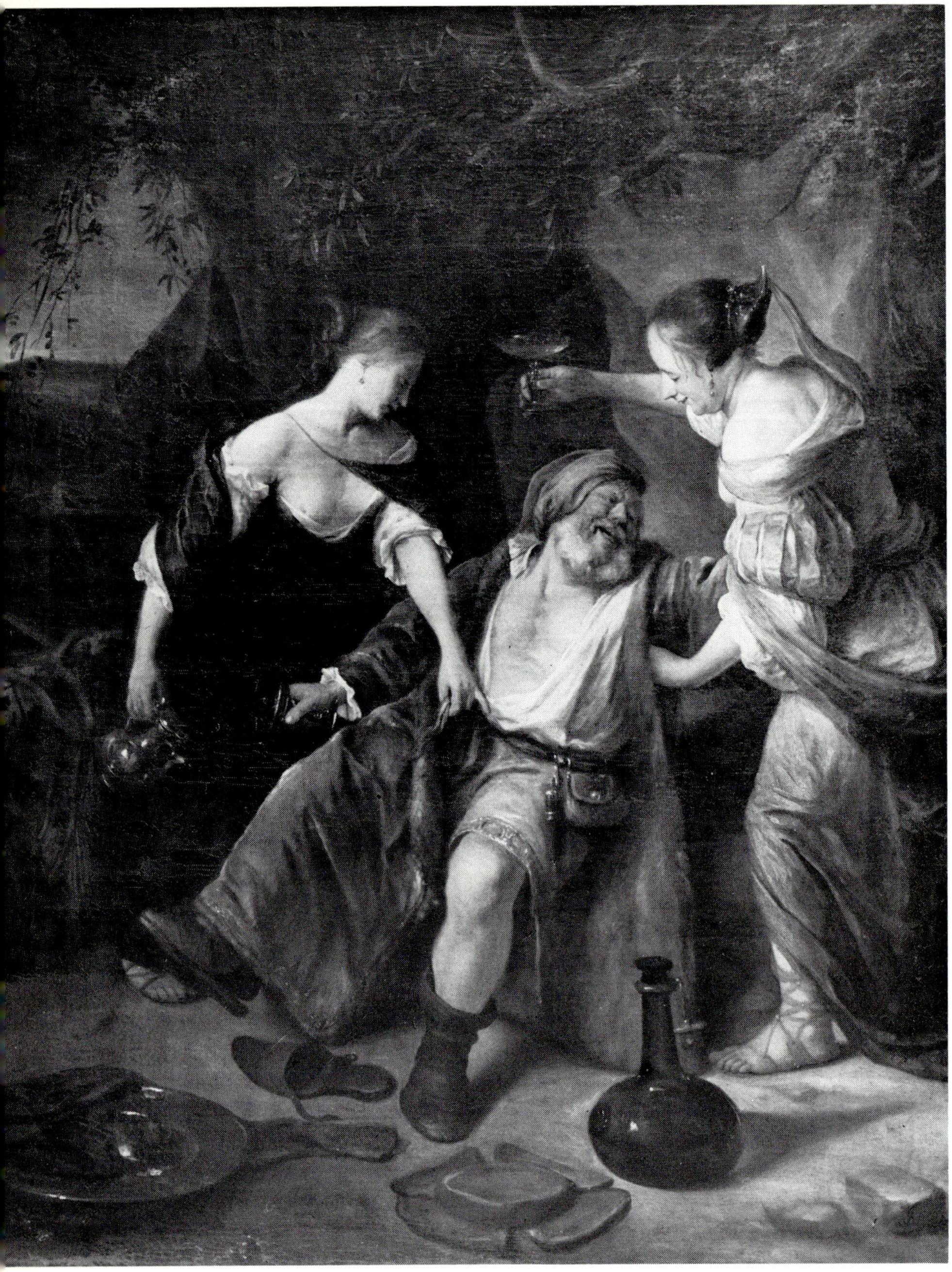

Fig. 48. *Lot and His Daughters* (Cat. 1). Wessenbergische Gemäldegalerie, Constance, West Germany.

Fig. 49. Van Vliet, *Lot and His Daughters*, etching, 1631.

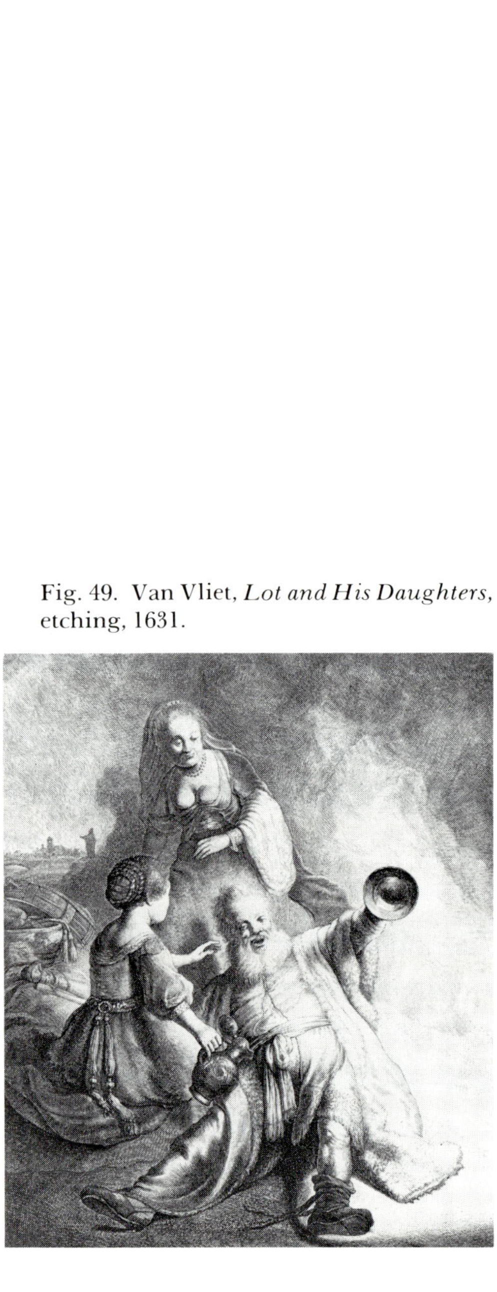

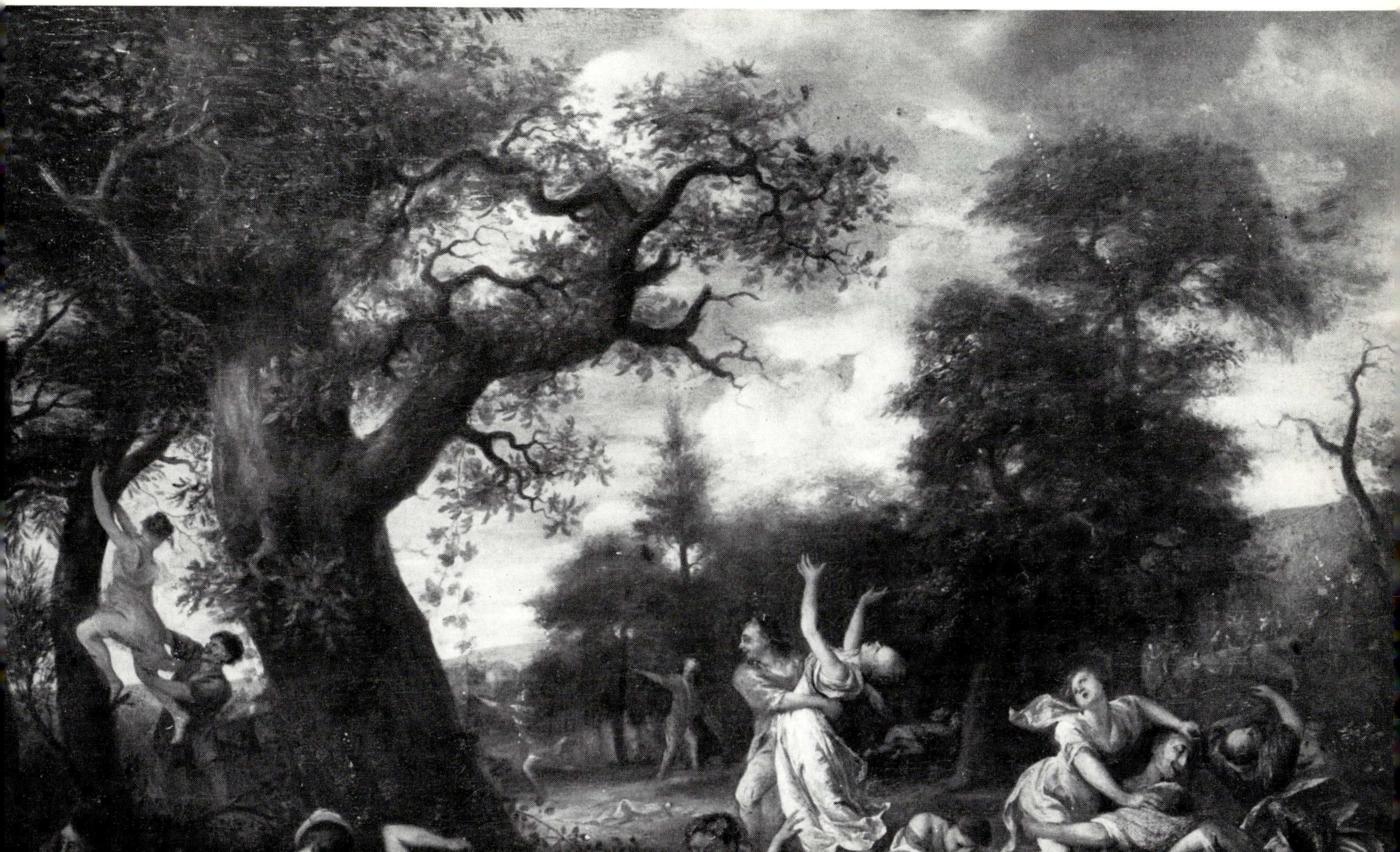

Fig. 50. *The Rape of the Sabine Women* (Cat. 76). John and Mabel Ringling Museum of Art, Sarasota, Florida.

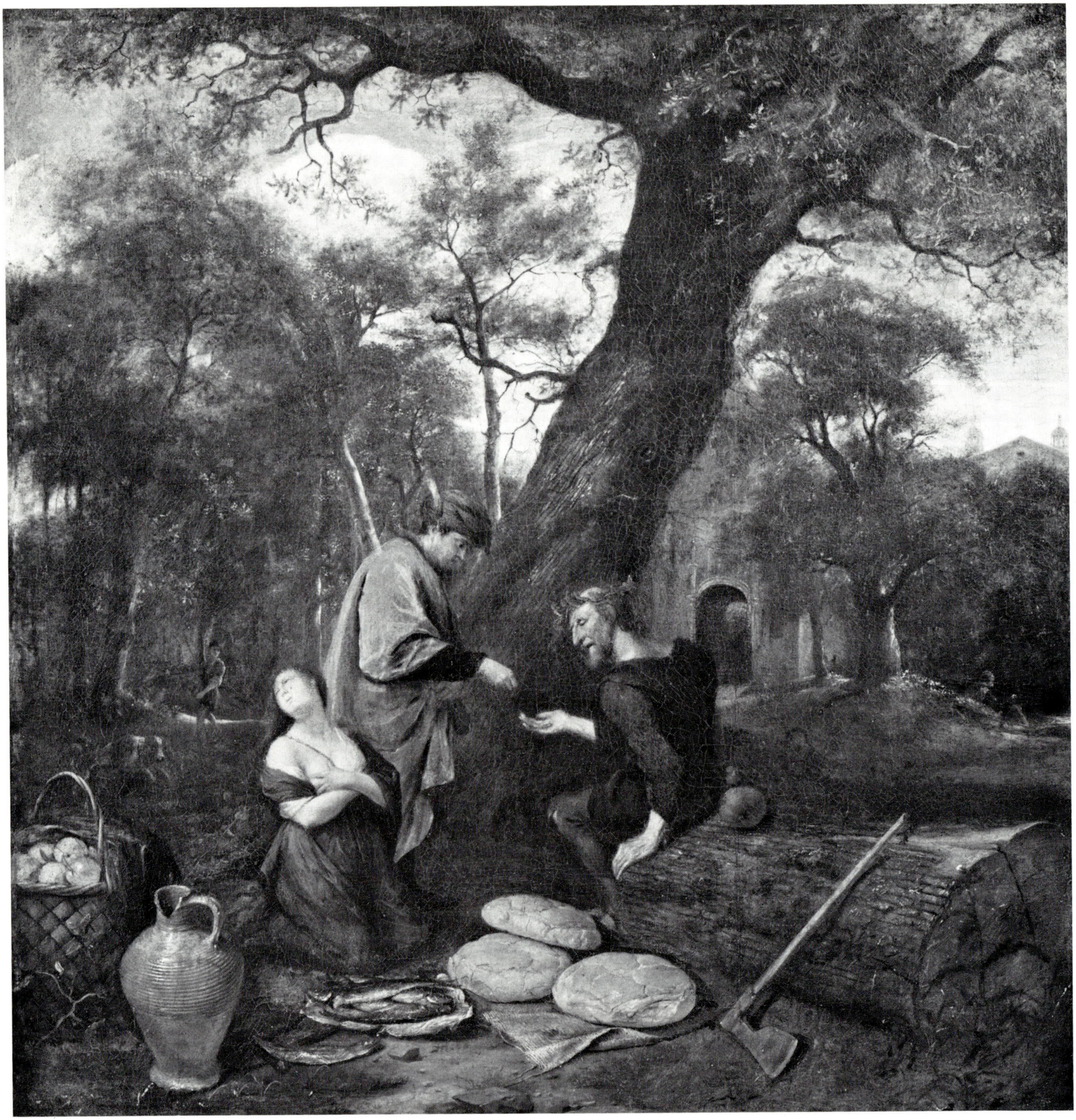

Fig. 51. *Erysichthon Selling His Daughter* (Cat. 73). Rijksmuseum, Amsterdam.

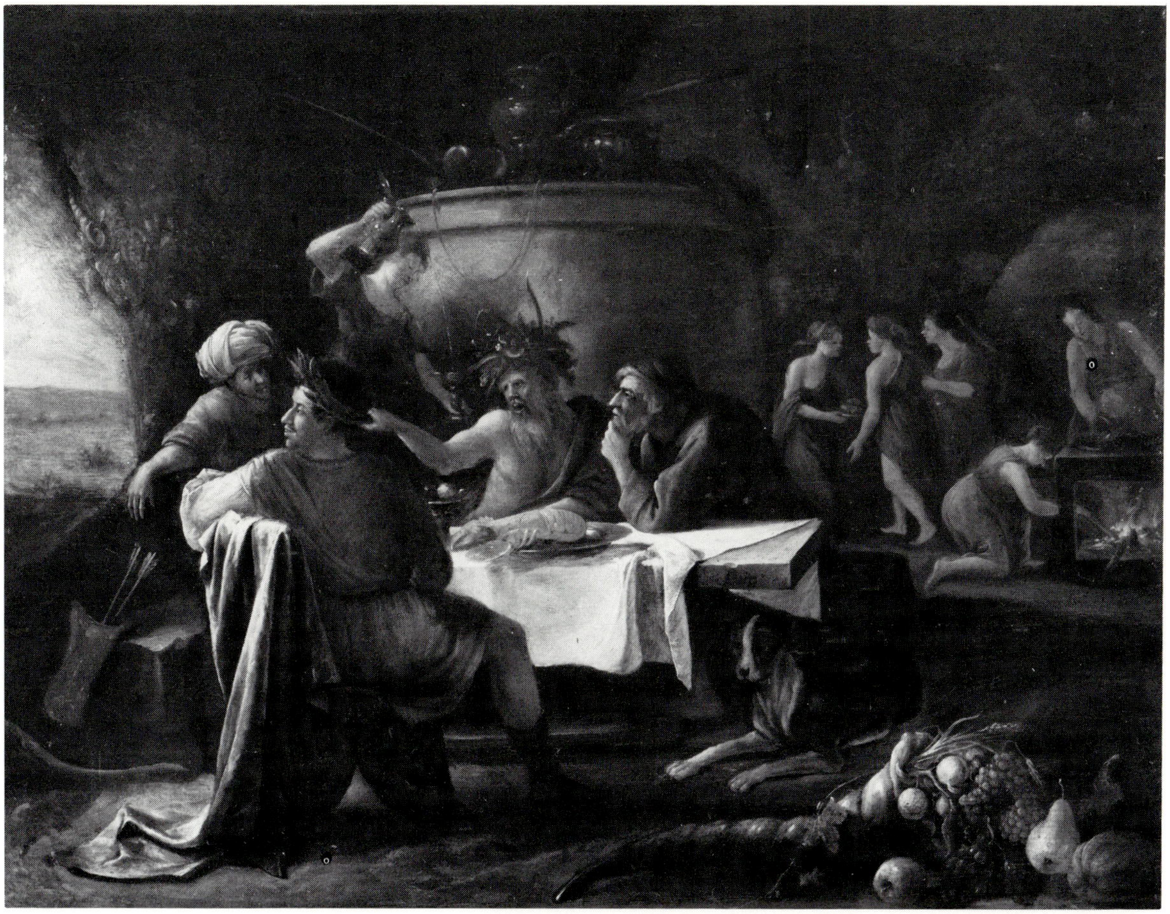

Fig. 52. *Theseus and Acheloüs* (Cat. 69b/520?). Present location unknown.

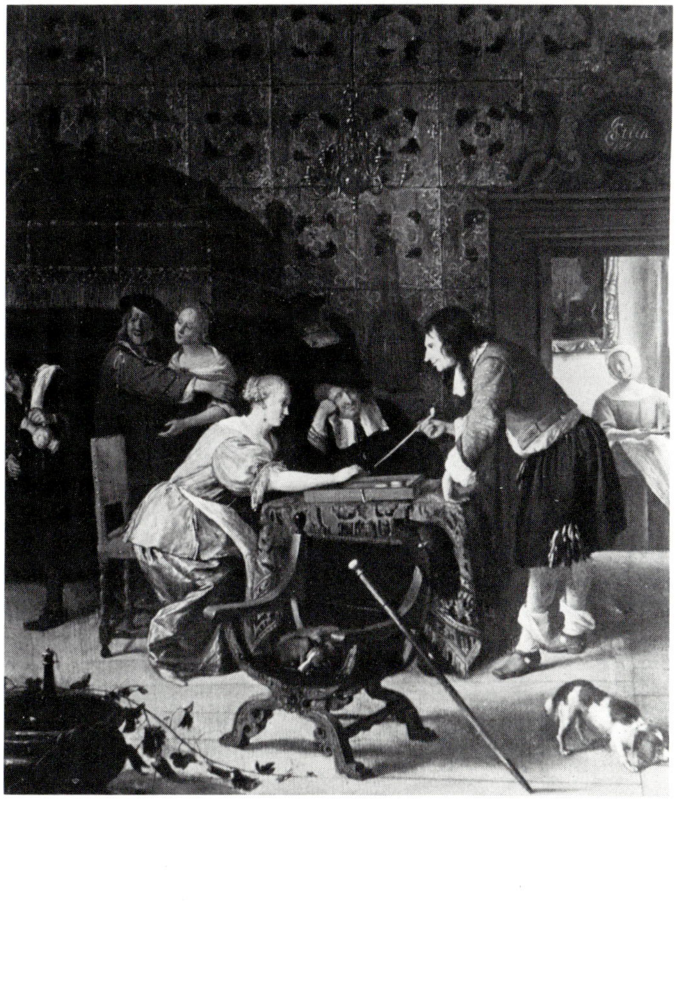

Fig. 53. *Trick-Track Players,* 1667 (HdG 719). Hermitage, Leningrad.

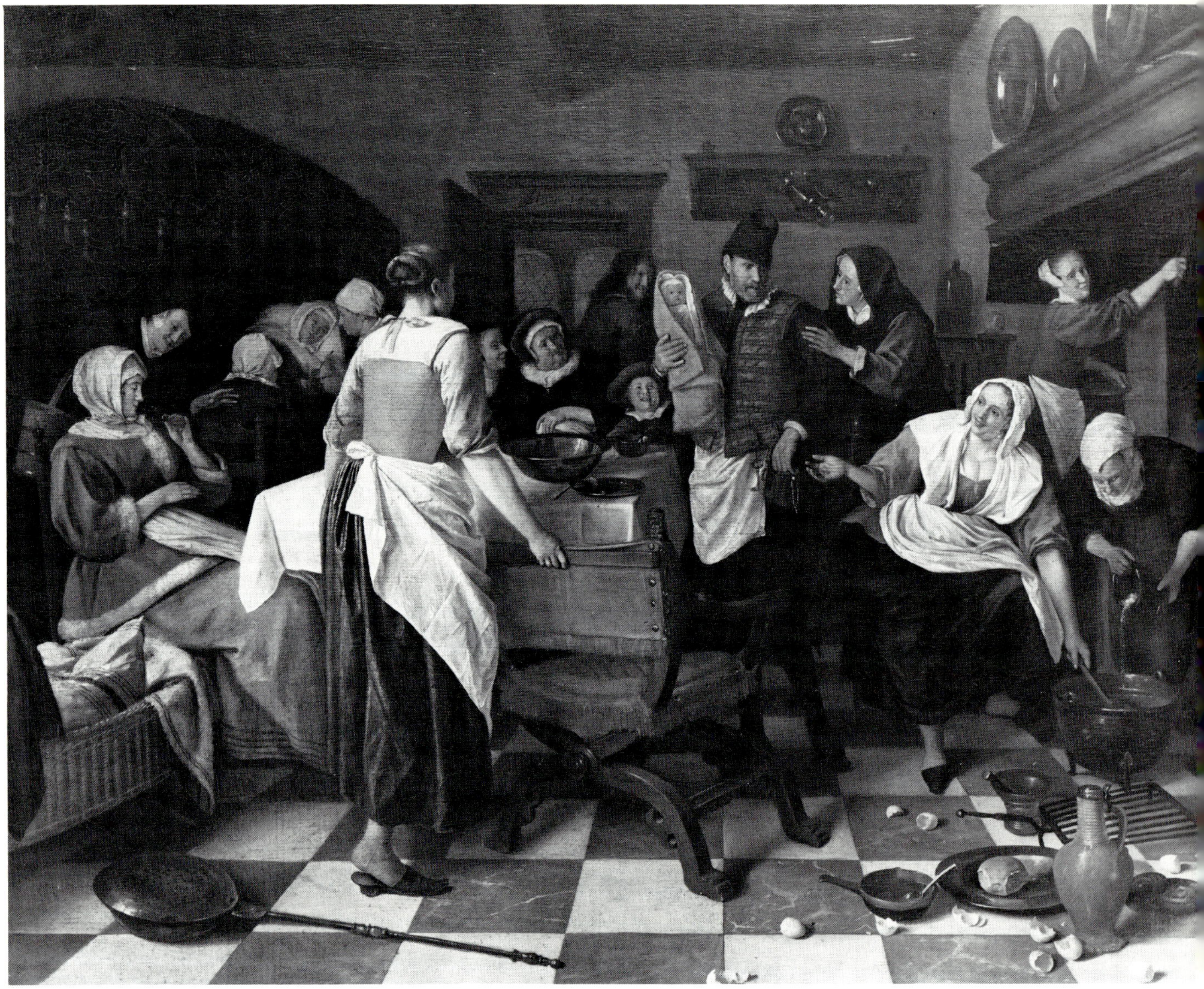

Fig. 54. *The Birth Feast,* 1664 (HdG 448). Wallace Collection, London.

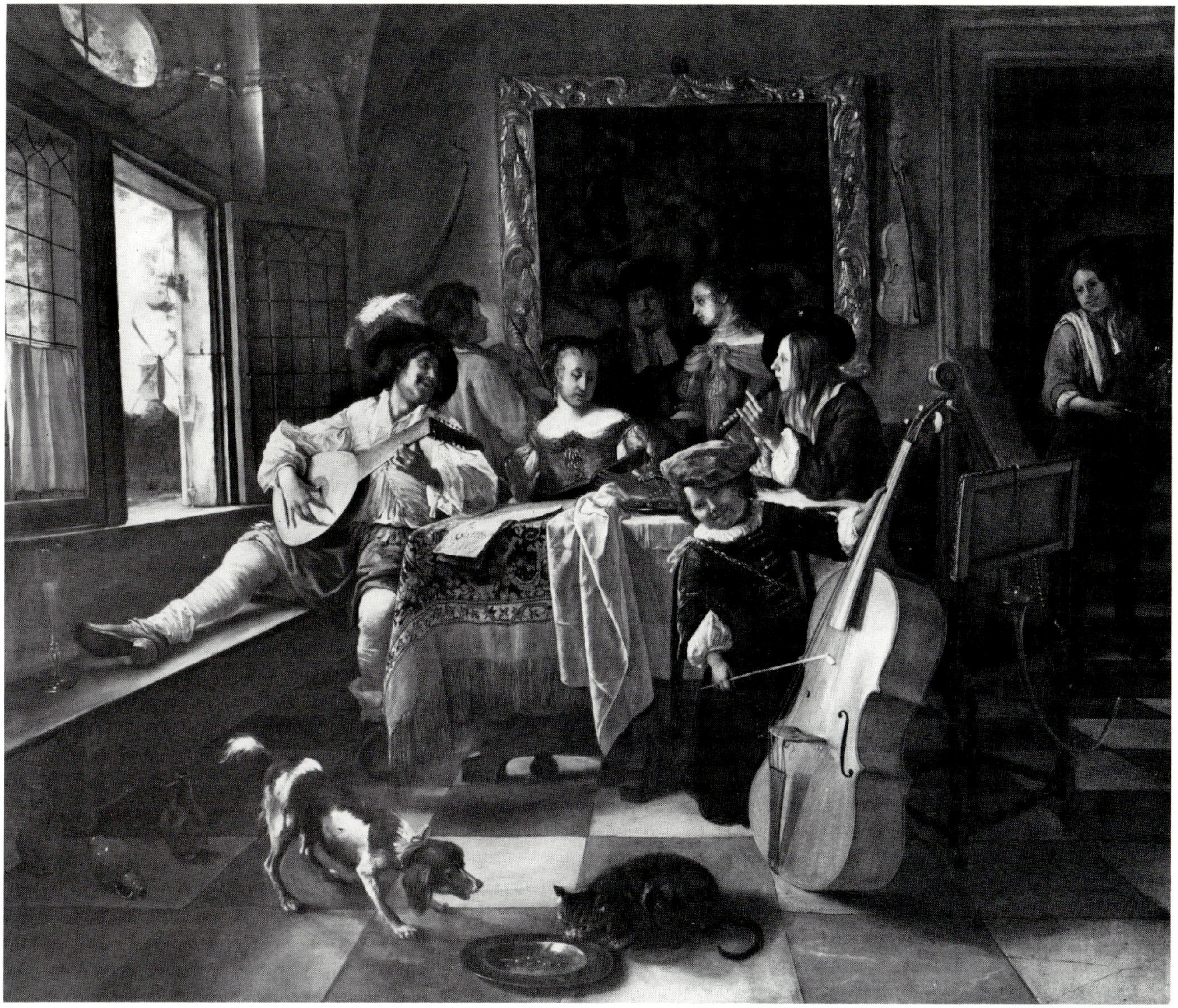

Fig. 55. *The Music Group,* 1666 (HdG 442). Courtesy of The Art Institute of Chicago.

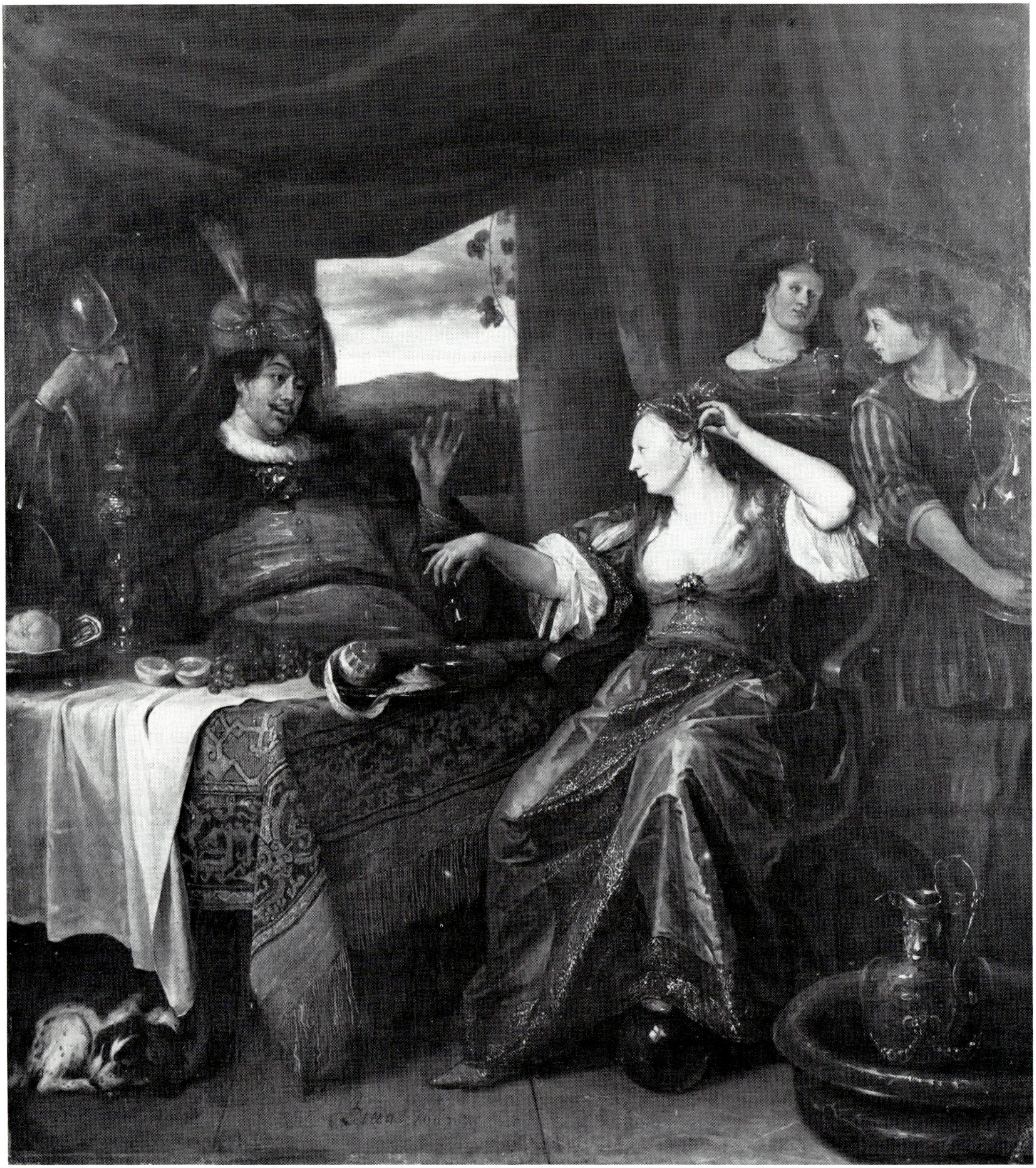

Fig. 56. *The Banquet of Antony and Cleopatra,* 1667 (Cat. 86). University Museum, Göttingen.

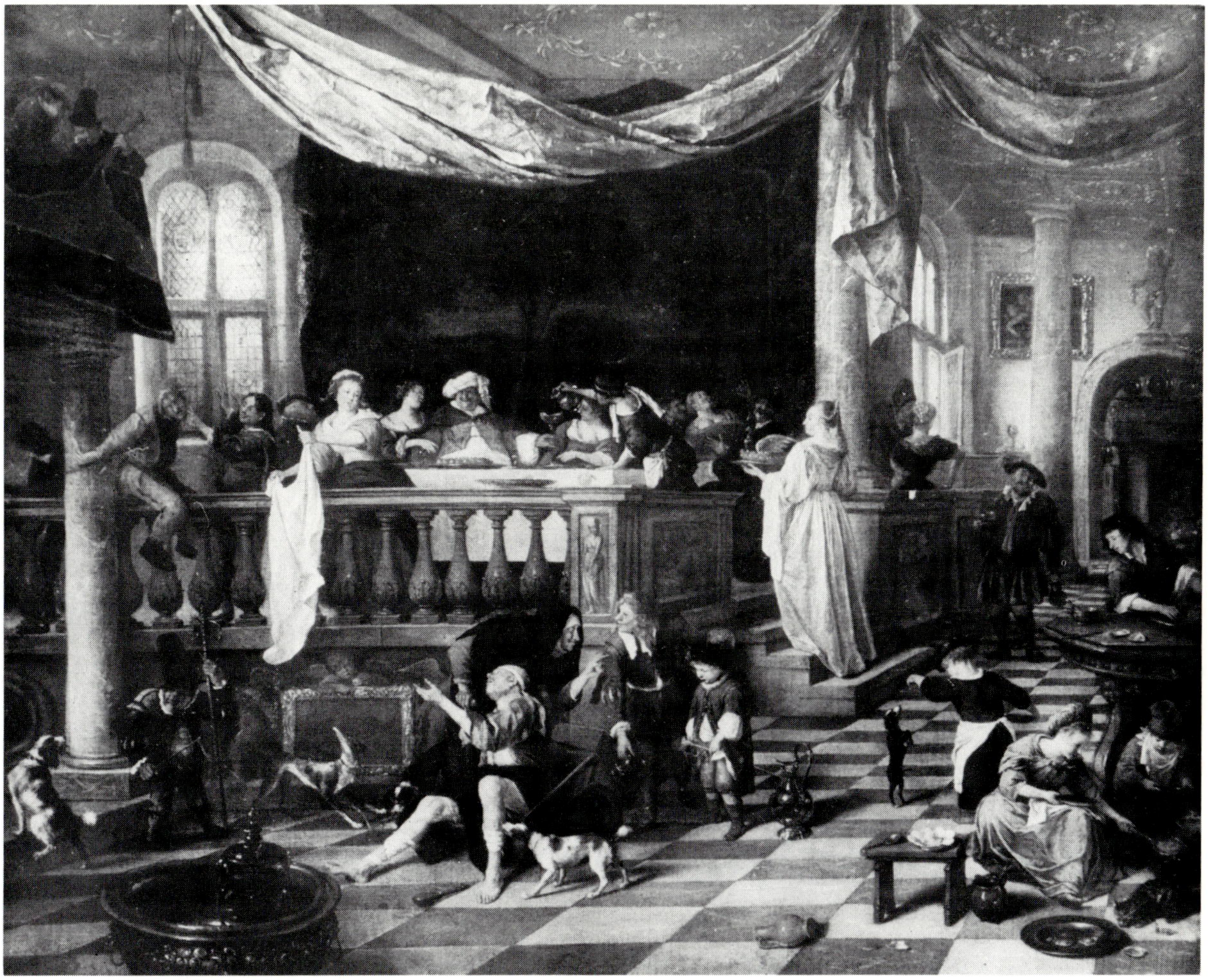

Fig. 57. *The Parable of the Rich Man and Lazarus,* 1667 (Cat. 59). Fritz Lehmann, Cologne.

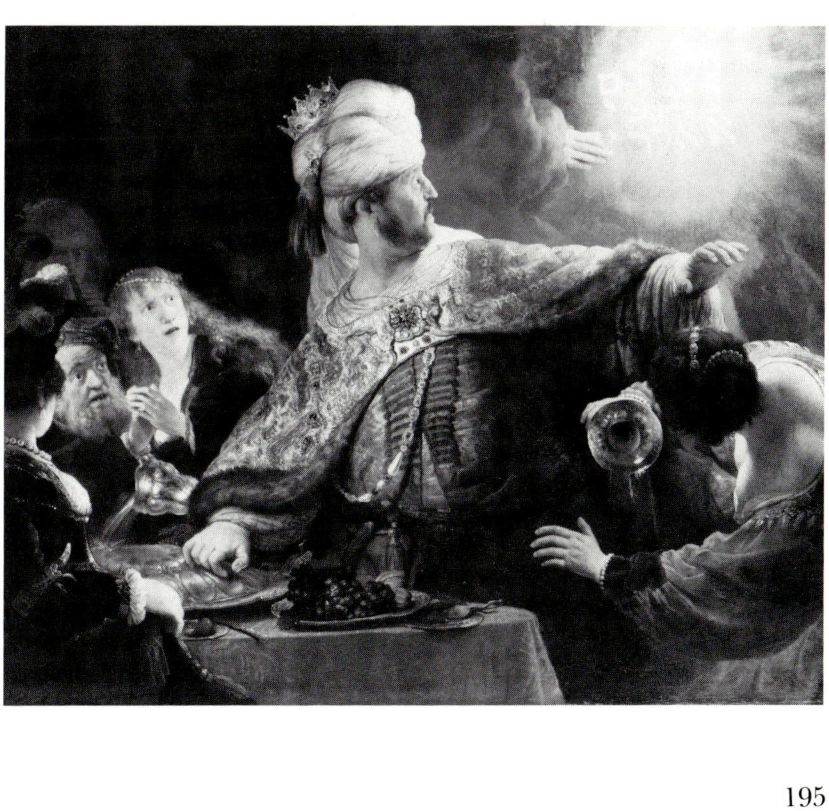

Fig. 58. Rembrandt, *Belshazzar's Feast.* National Gallery, London.

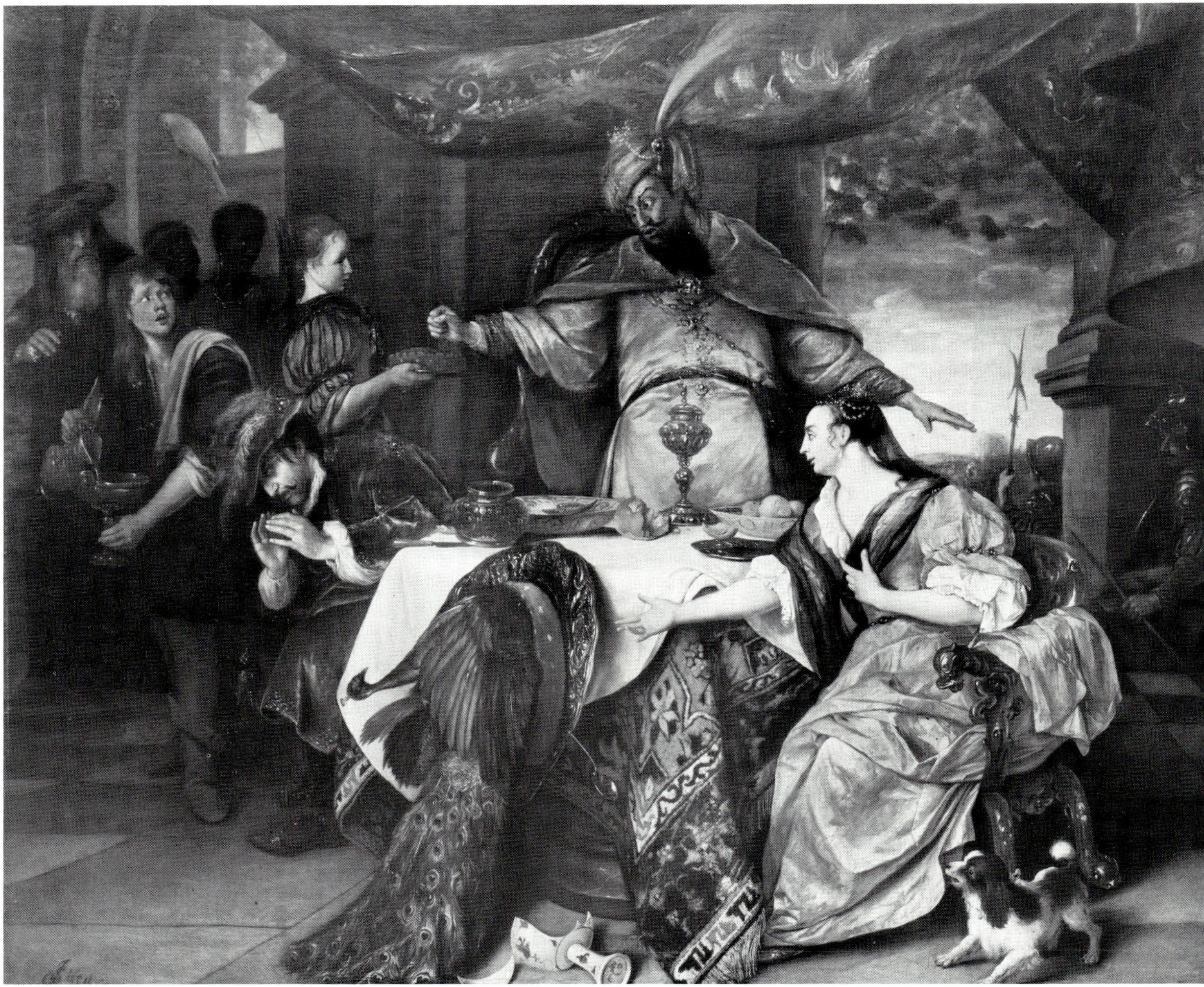

Fig. 59. *The Wrath of Ahasuerus* (Cat. 18). The Barber Institute of Fine Arts, University of Birmingham, Birmingham, England.

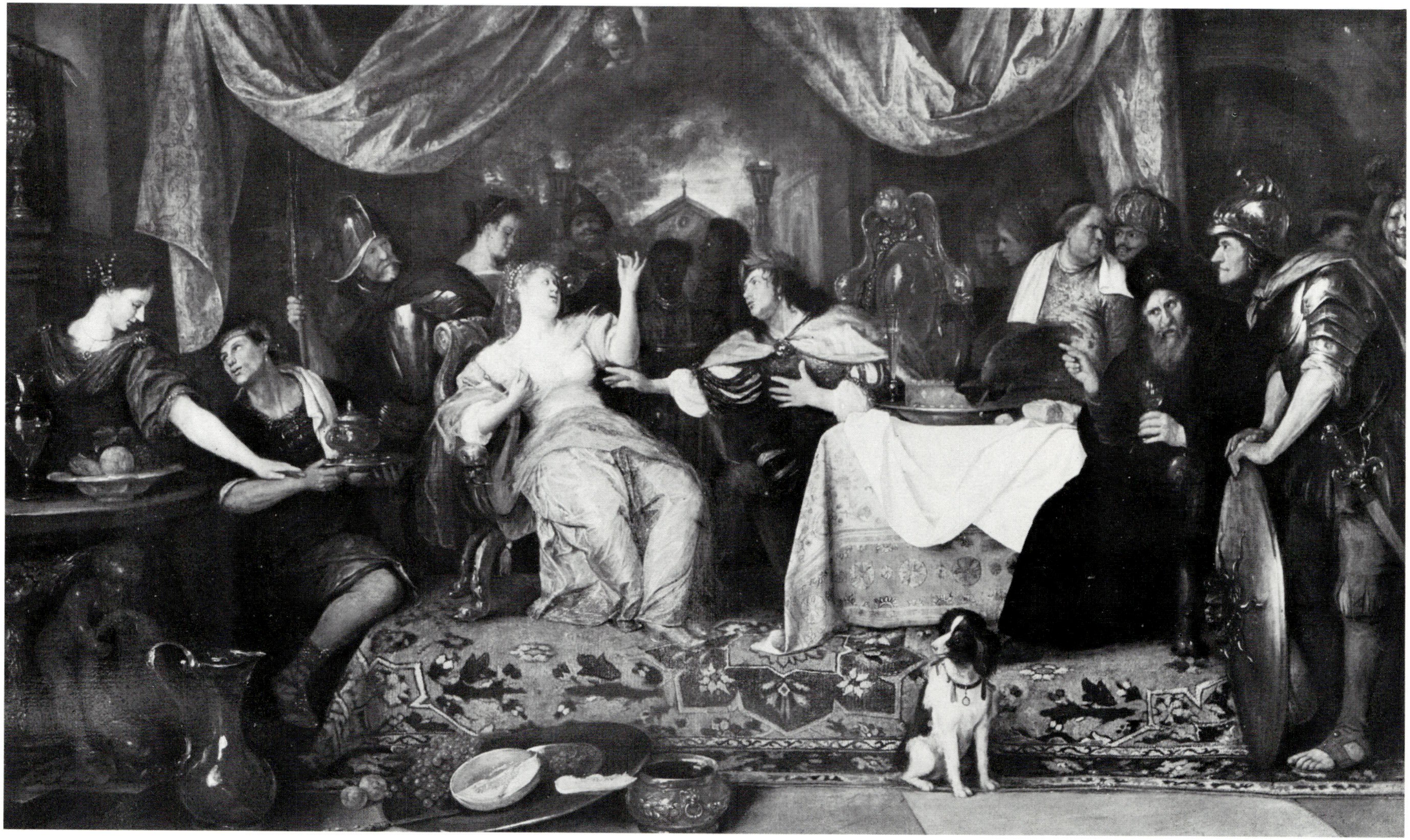

Fig. 60. *Banquet of Antony and Cleopatra* (Cat. 86a/b). Rolzaal, Binnenhof, The Hague (on loan from Dienst voor 's Rijks Verspreide Kunstvoorwerpen).

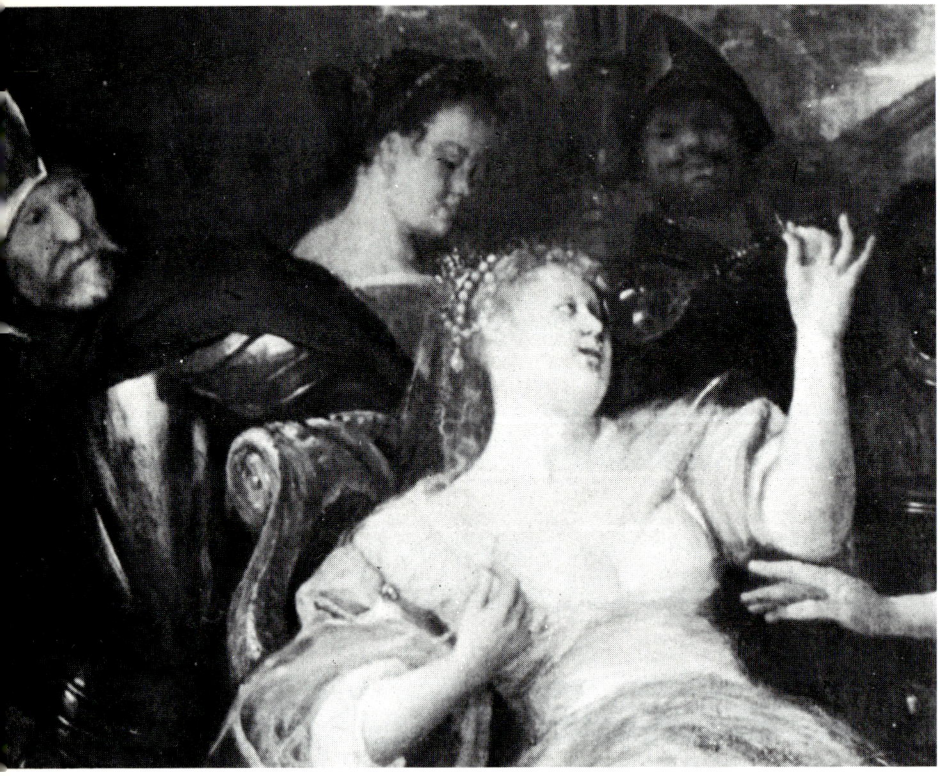

Fig. 60a. Detail, Fig. 60.

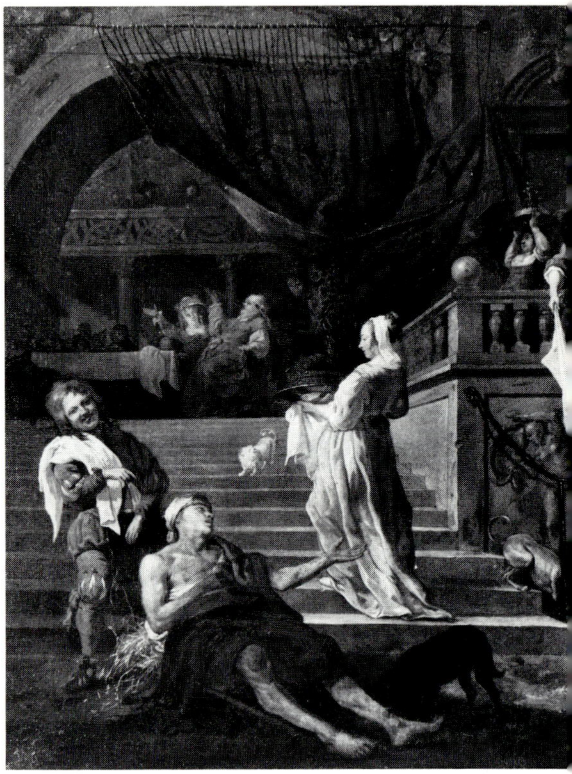

Fig. 61. Knüpfer (?), *The Rich Man and Lazarus*. Musée des Beaux-Arts, Strasbourg.

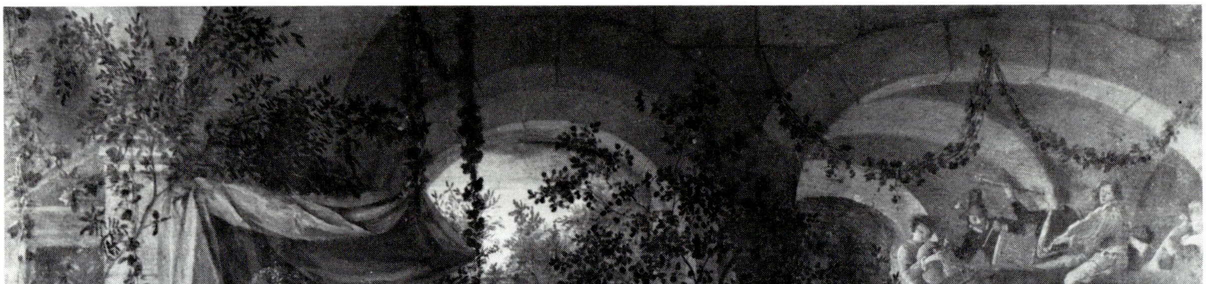

Fig. 62. *The Marriage at Cana* (Cat. 48/49). Sir Alfred Beit collection, Blessington, Ireland.

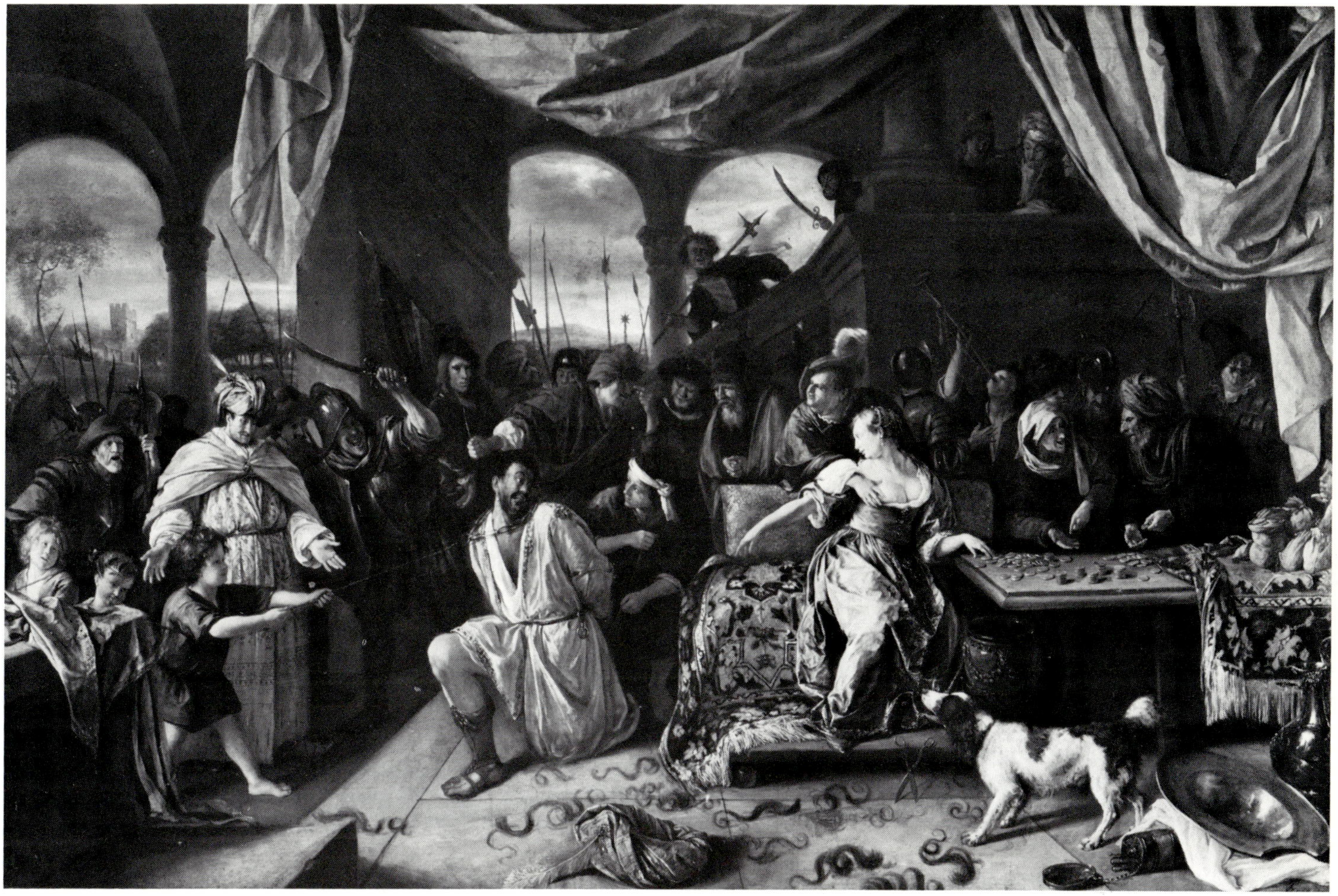

Fig. 63. *Samson Mocked by the Philistines* (Cat. 12/10a). Wallraf-Richartz Museum, Cologne.

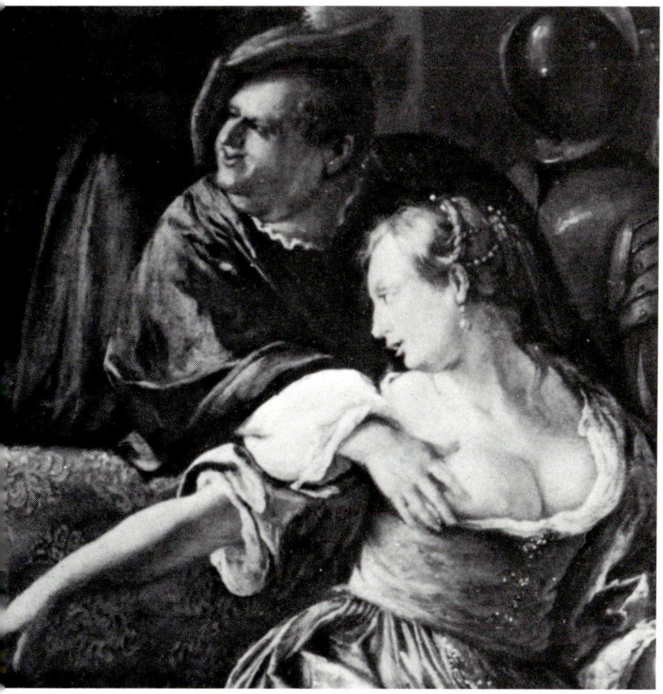

Fig. 63a. Detail, Fig. 63.

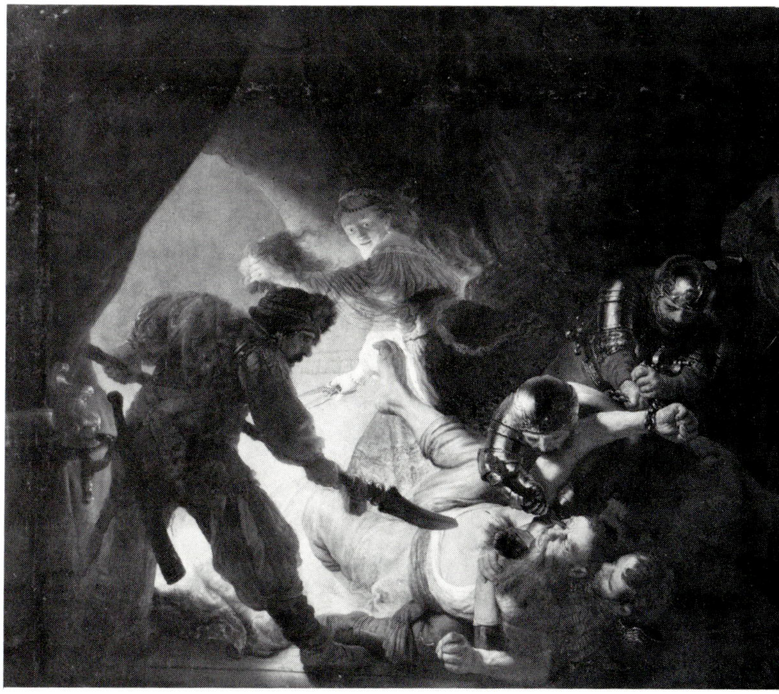

Fig. 64 Rembrandt, *The Blinding of Samson*. Städelsches Kunstinstitut, Frankfurt-am-Main.

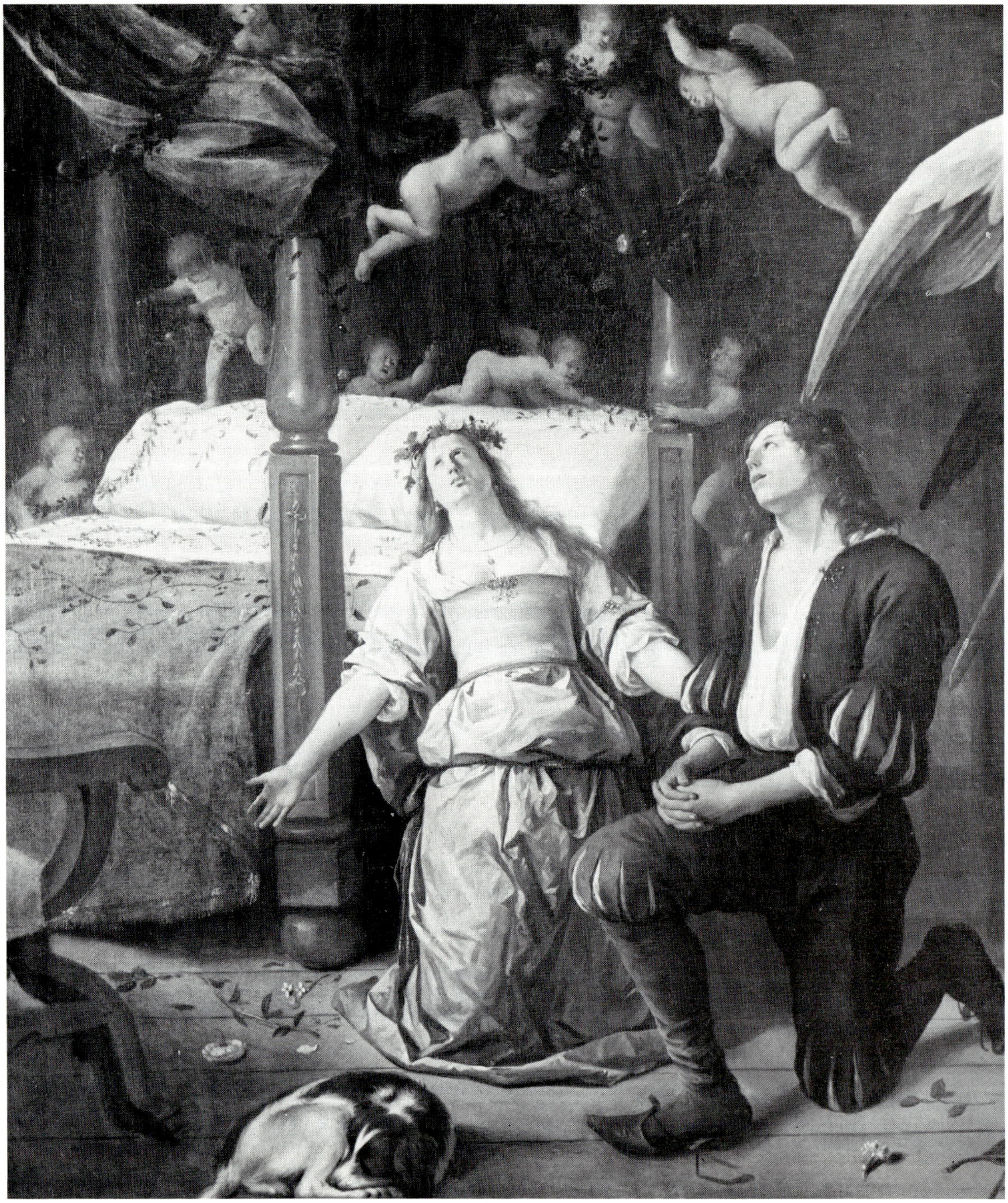

Fig. 65. *The Prayer of Tobias and Sarah* (Cat. 25c). Centraal Museum, Utrecht, on loan from the Dutch Government (Dienst voor 's Rijks Verspreide Kunstvorwerpen, The Hague, 1948).

Fig. 66. *The Marriage of Tobias and Sarah* (Cat. 25a/457). Staatliches Herzog Anton-Ulrich Museum. Brunswick.

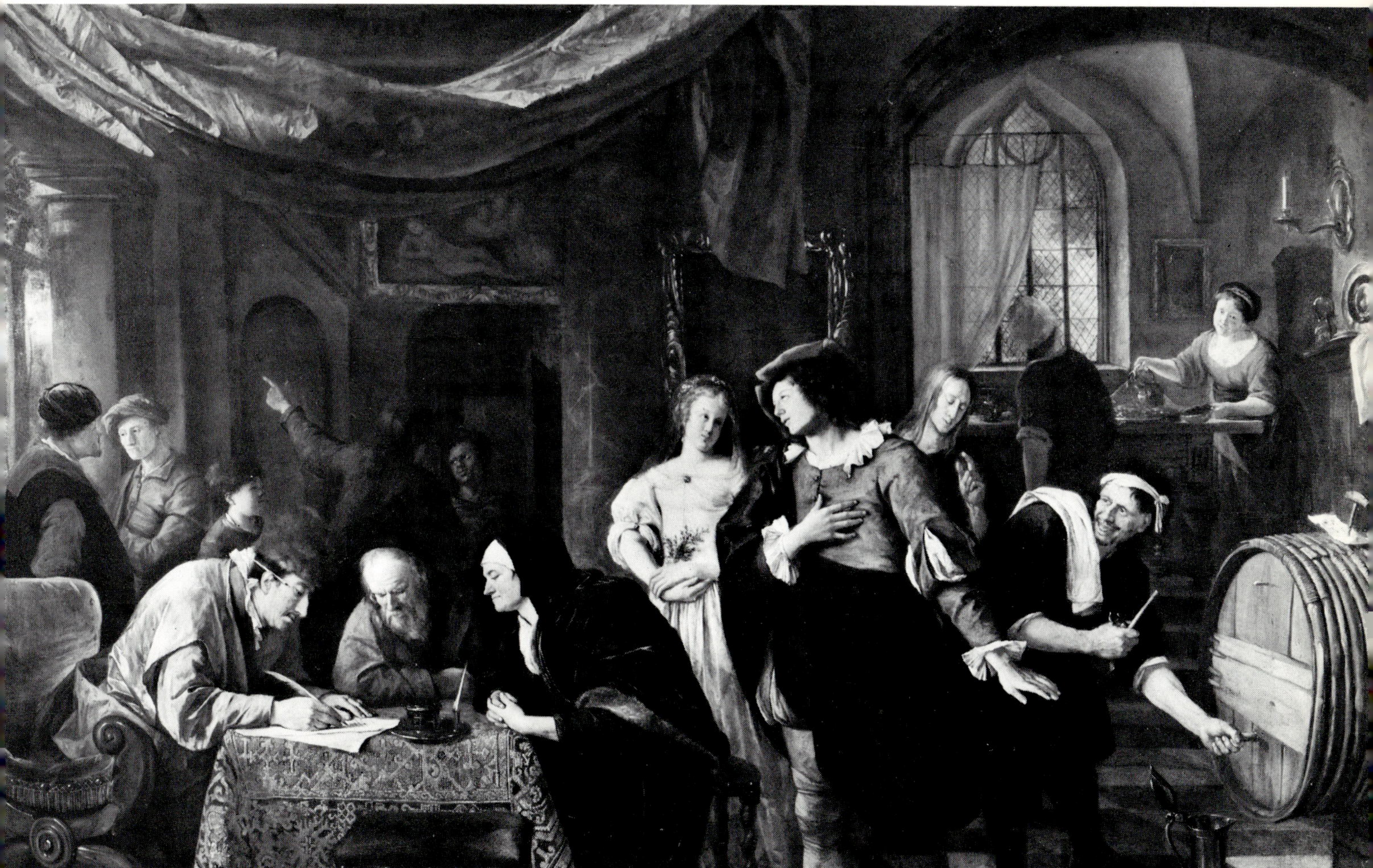

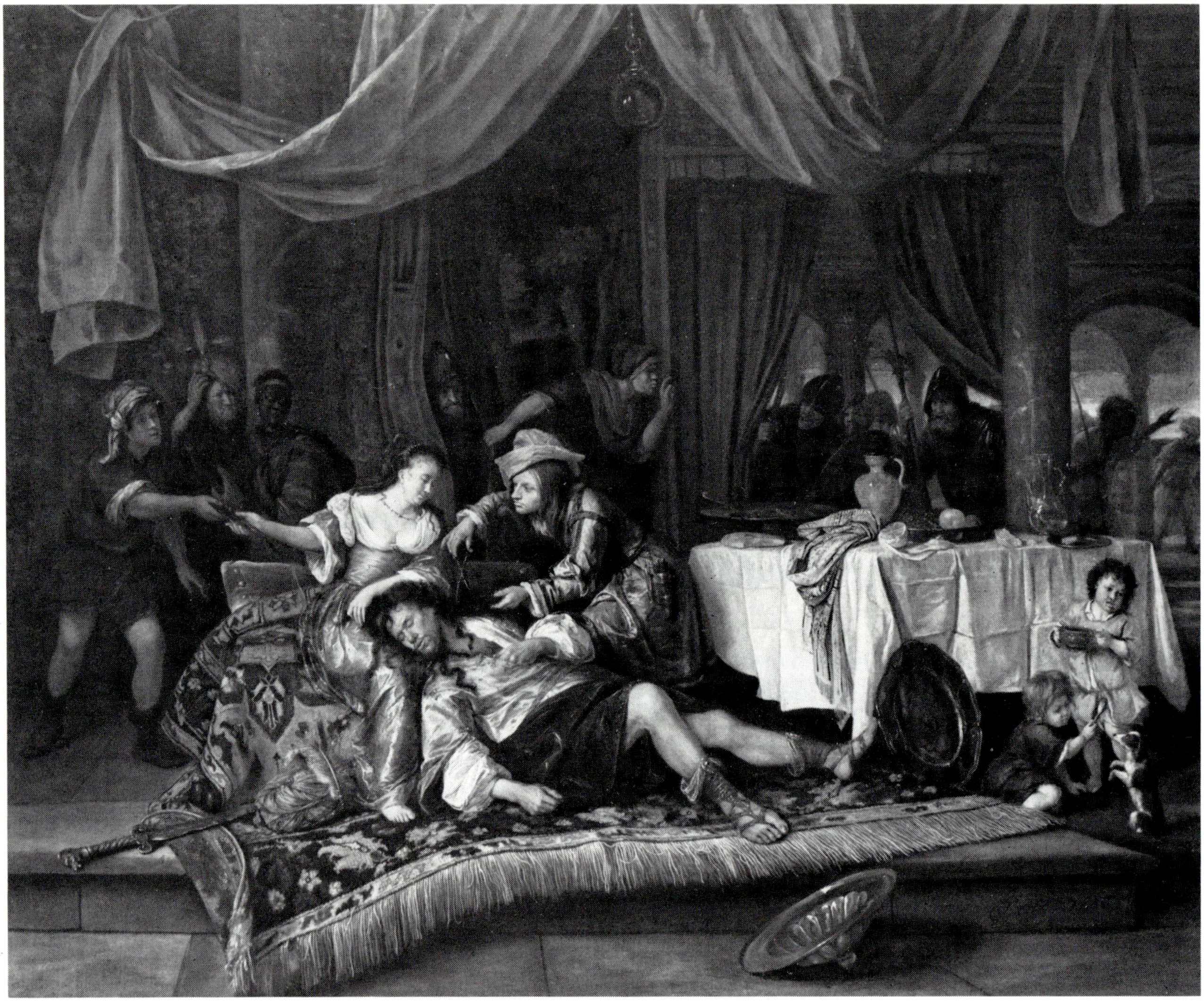

Fig. 67. *Samson and Delilah,* 1668 (Cat. 10). Private collection, The Netherlands.

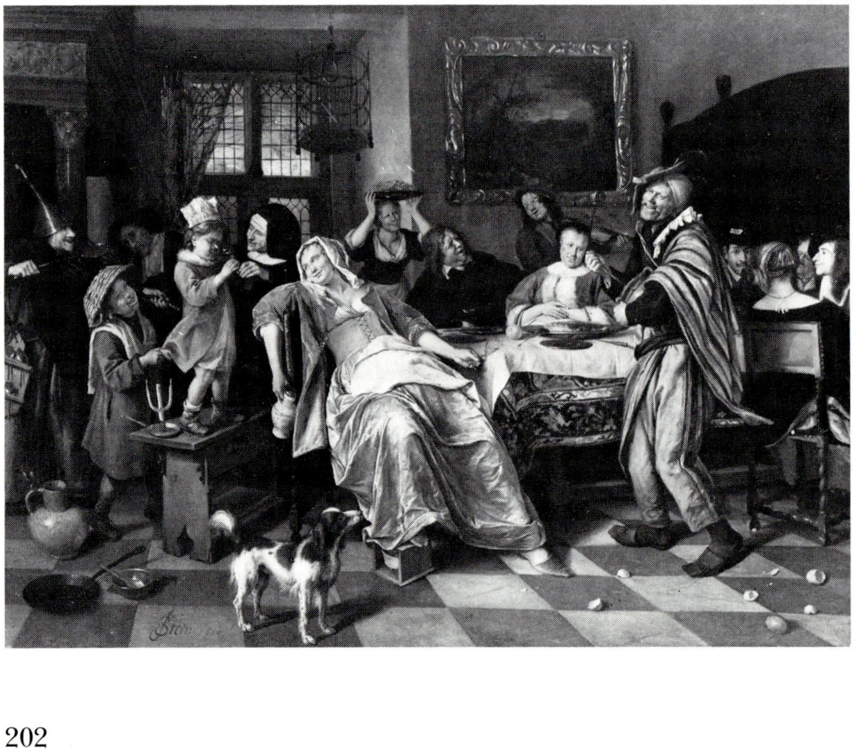

Fig. 68. *Twelfth Night Feast* 1668 (HdG 494). Staatliche Kunstsammlungen, Kassel.

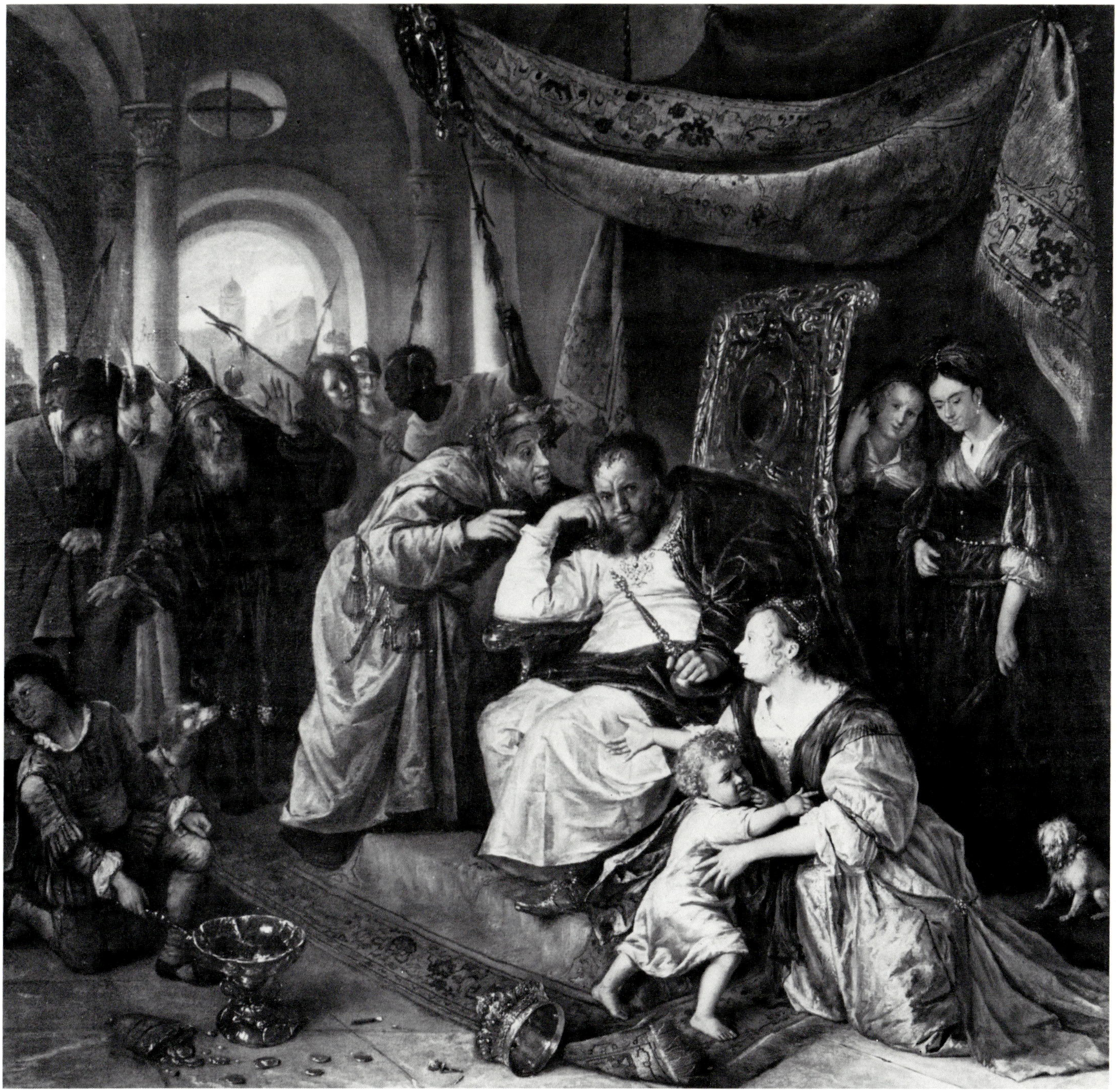

Fig. 69. *The Trial of the Infant Moses* (Cat. 6). Wetzlar collection, Amsterdam.

Fig. 70. *Bathseba Receiving David's Letter* (Cat. 14). Present location unknown.

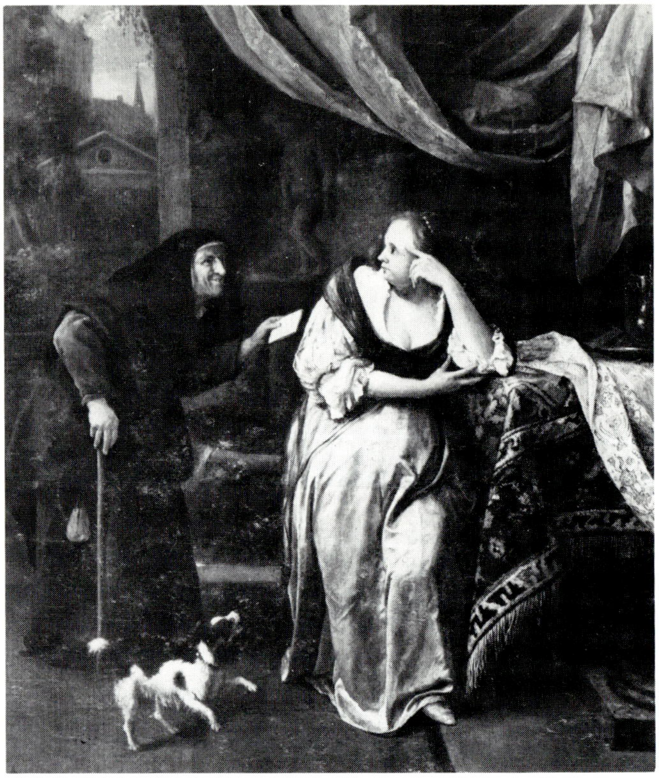

Fig. 71. *Bathseba Receiving David's Letter* (Cat. 14b/348). Virginia Museum of Fine Arts, Richmond, Virginia.

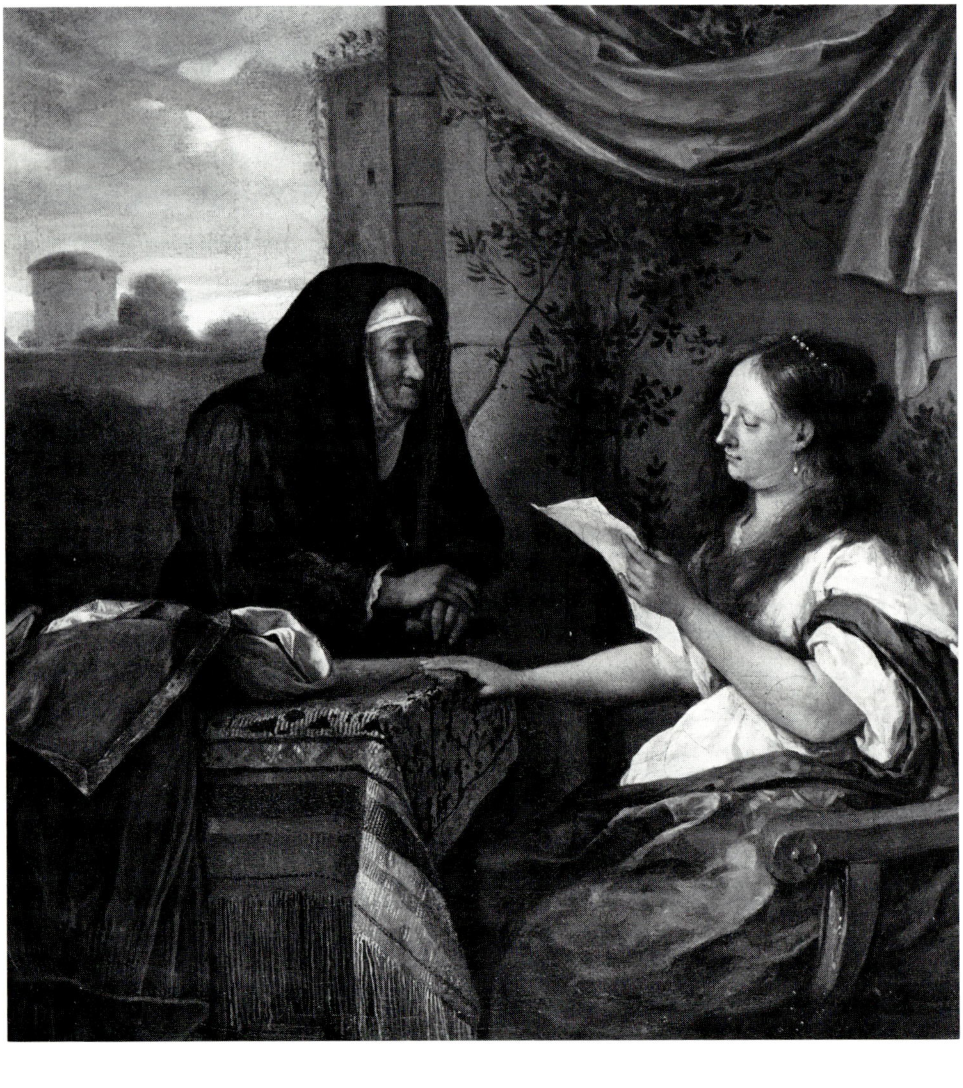

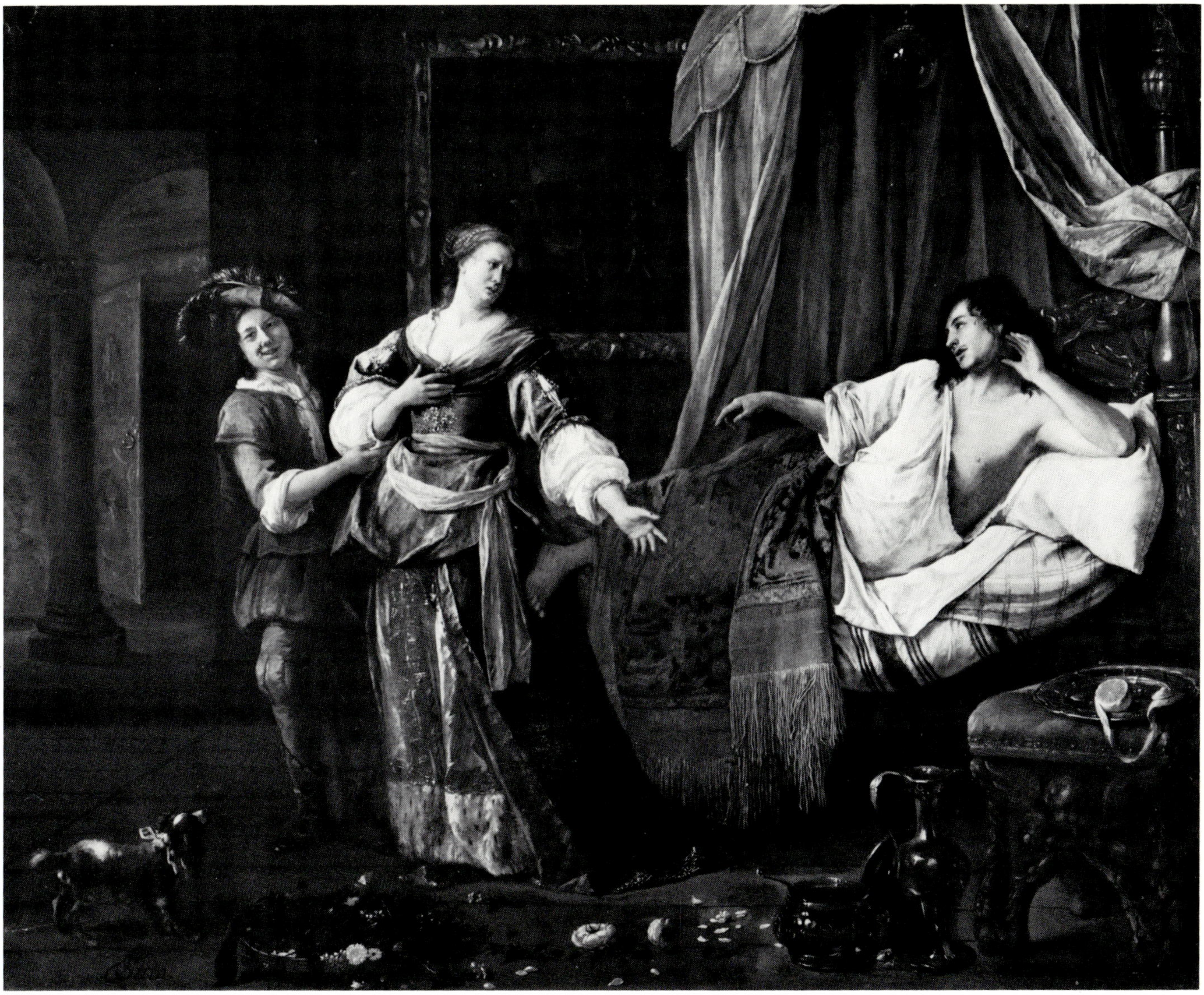

Fig. 72. *Tamar and Amnon* (Cat. 16). Wallraf-Richartz Museum, Cologne.

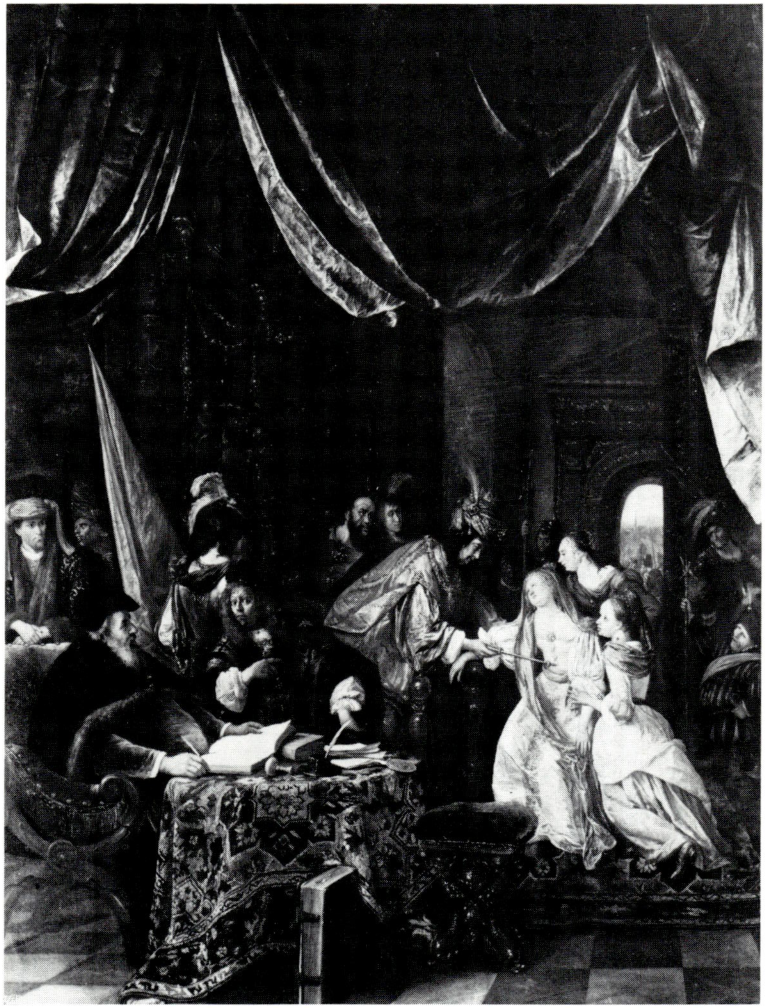

Fig. 73. *Esther Before Ahasuerus* (Cat. 17). The Hermitage, Leningrad.

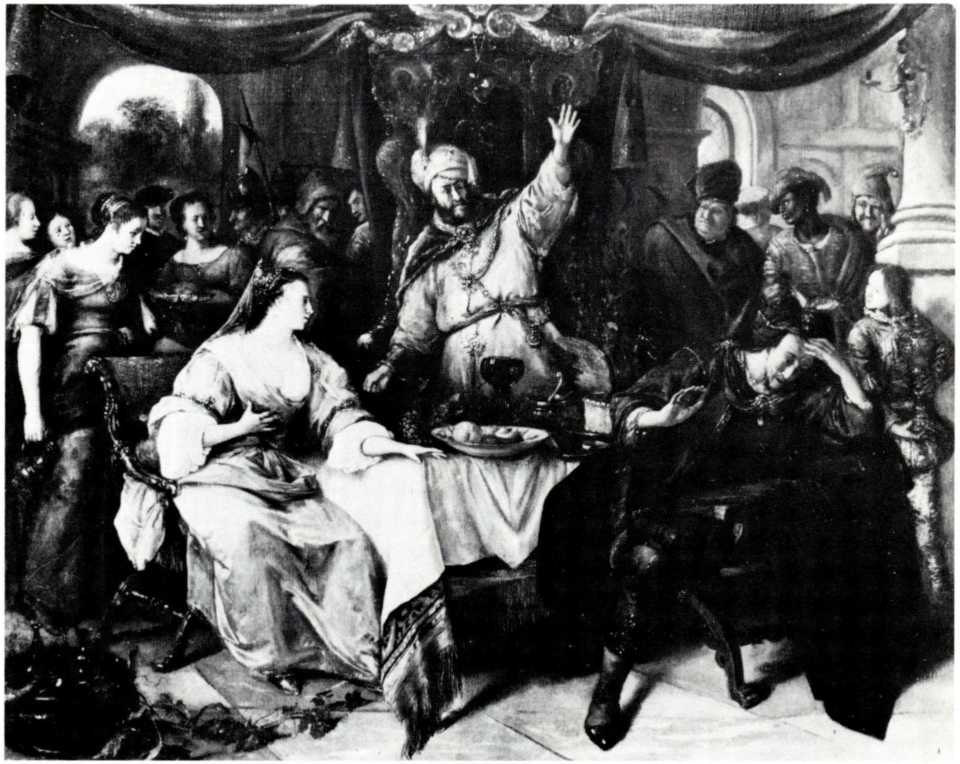

Fig. 75. *The Wrath of Ahasuerus* (Cat. 19). Present location unknown.

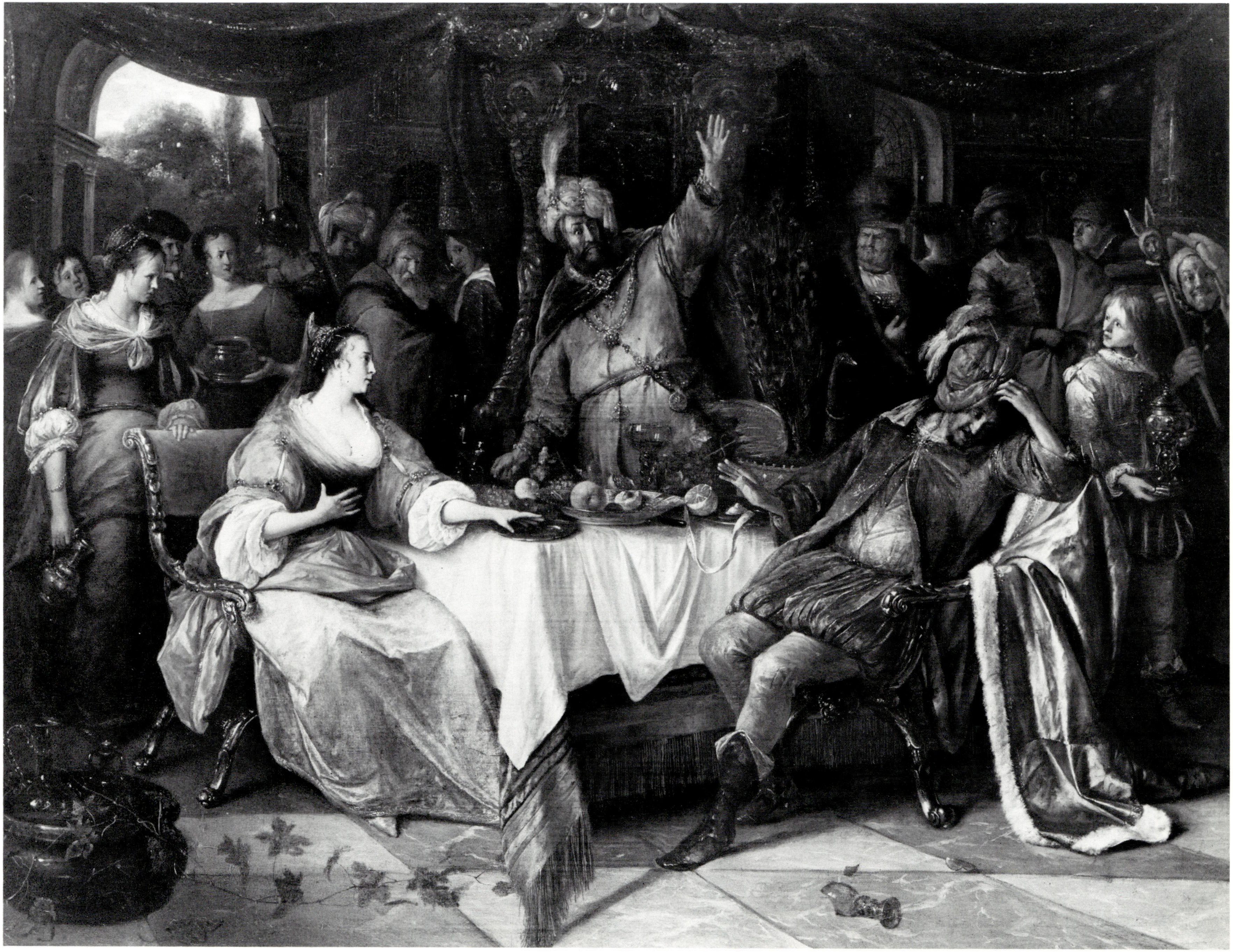

Fig. 74. *The Wrath of Ahasuerus* (Cat. 19a). The Cleveland Museum of Art, John L. Severance Fund.

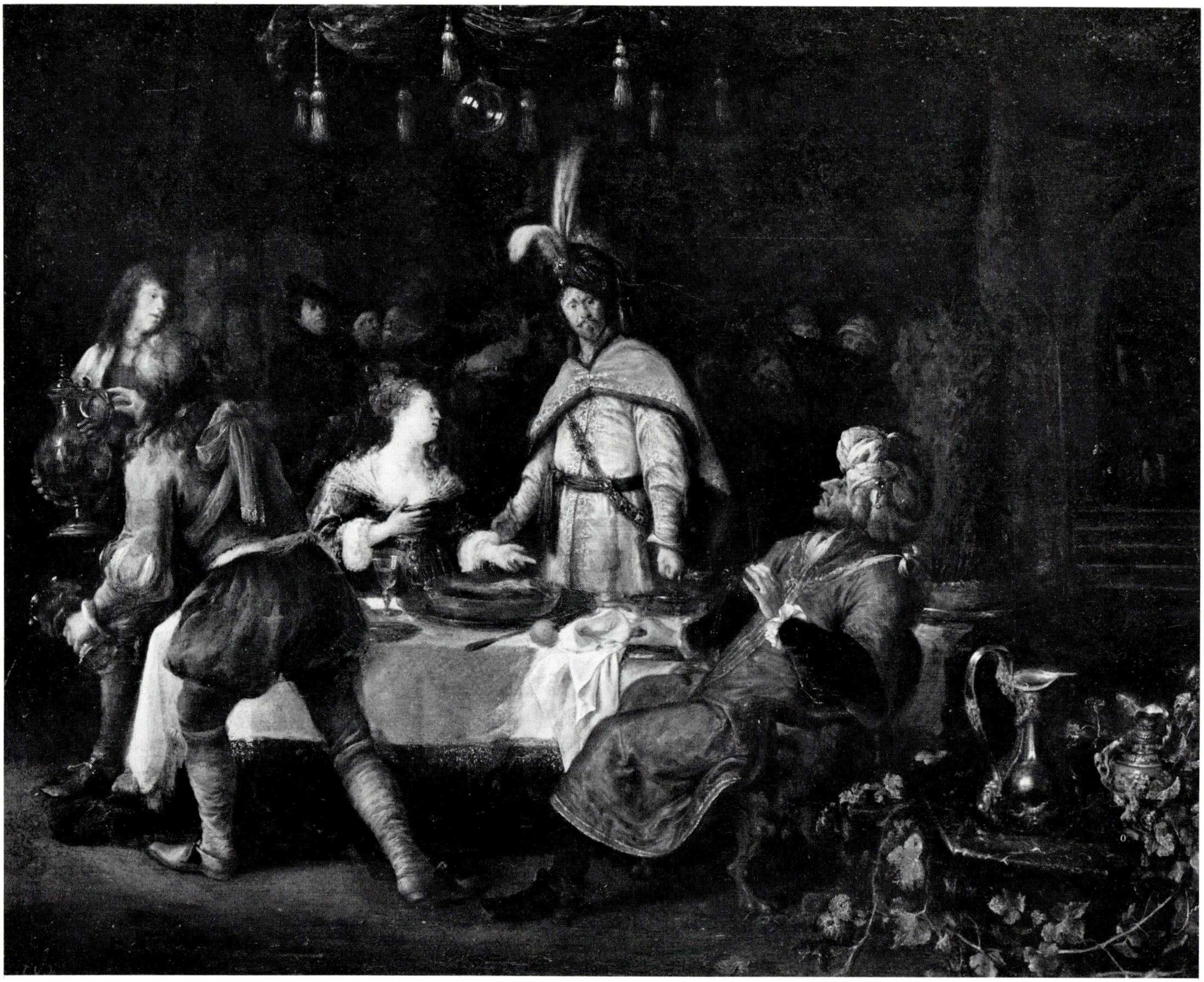

Fig. 76. *The Wrath of Ahasuerus* (Cat. 20). Private collection, England.

Fig. 77. *The Marriage of Tobias and Sarah* (Cat. 25b). Present location unknown.

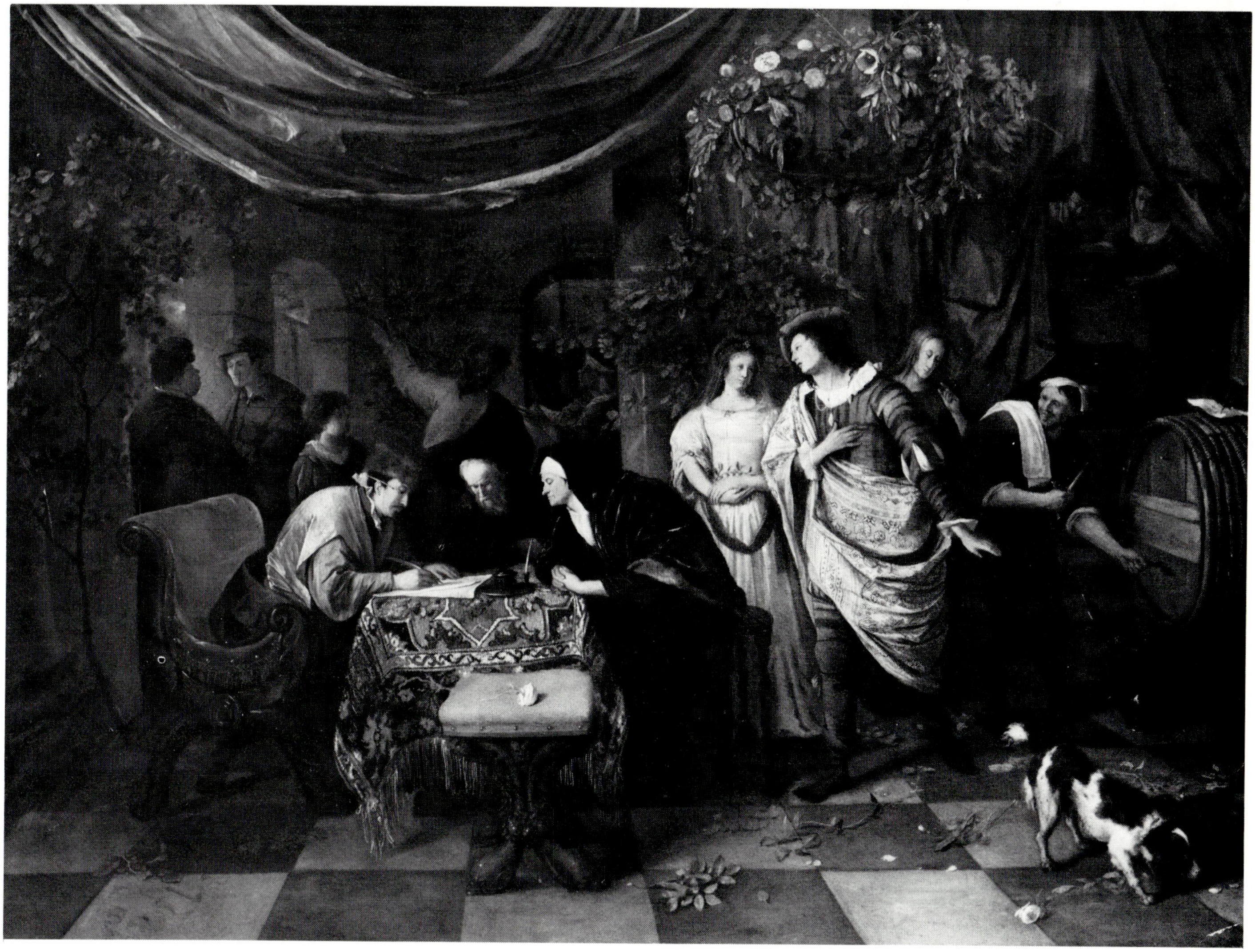

Fig. 78. *The Angel Raphael Casting Out the Devil* (Cat. 25d/69). Museum Bredius, The Hague.

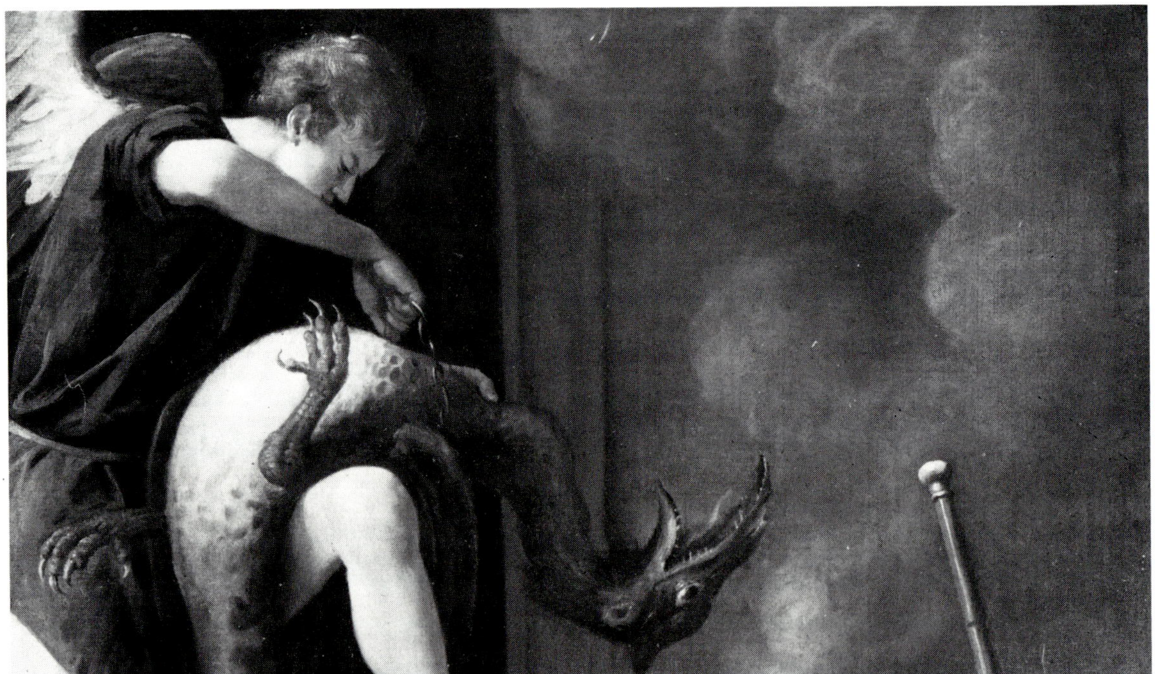

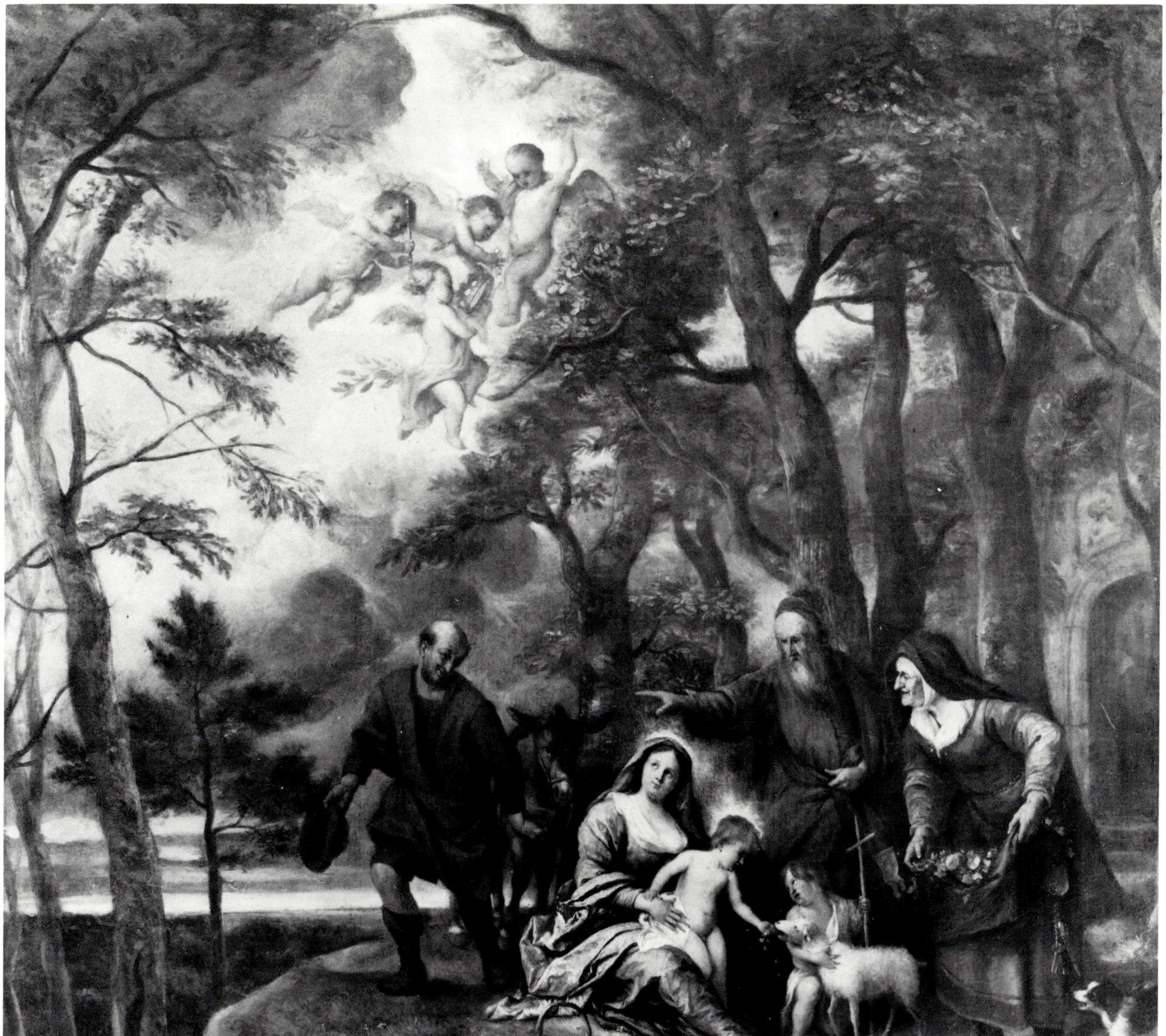

Fig. 79. *The Rest on the Flight to Egypt* (Cat. 39). Dunkirk Museum, Dunkirk.

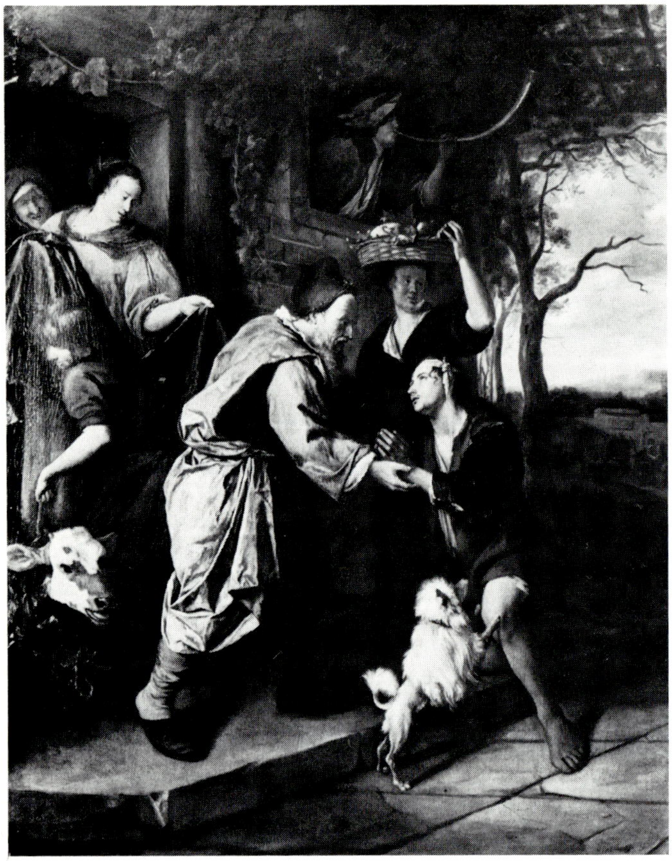

Fig. 80. *The Return of the Prodigal Son* (Cat. 55). Countess Brita Wachmeister, Kulla Gunnarstorp, Sweden.

Fig. 81. *Antiochus and Stratonice* (Cat. 84b/54). Wetzlar collection, Amsterdam.

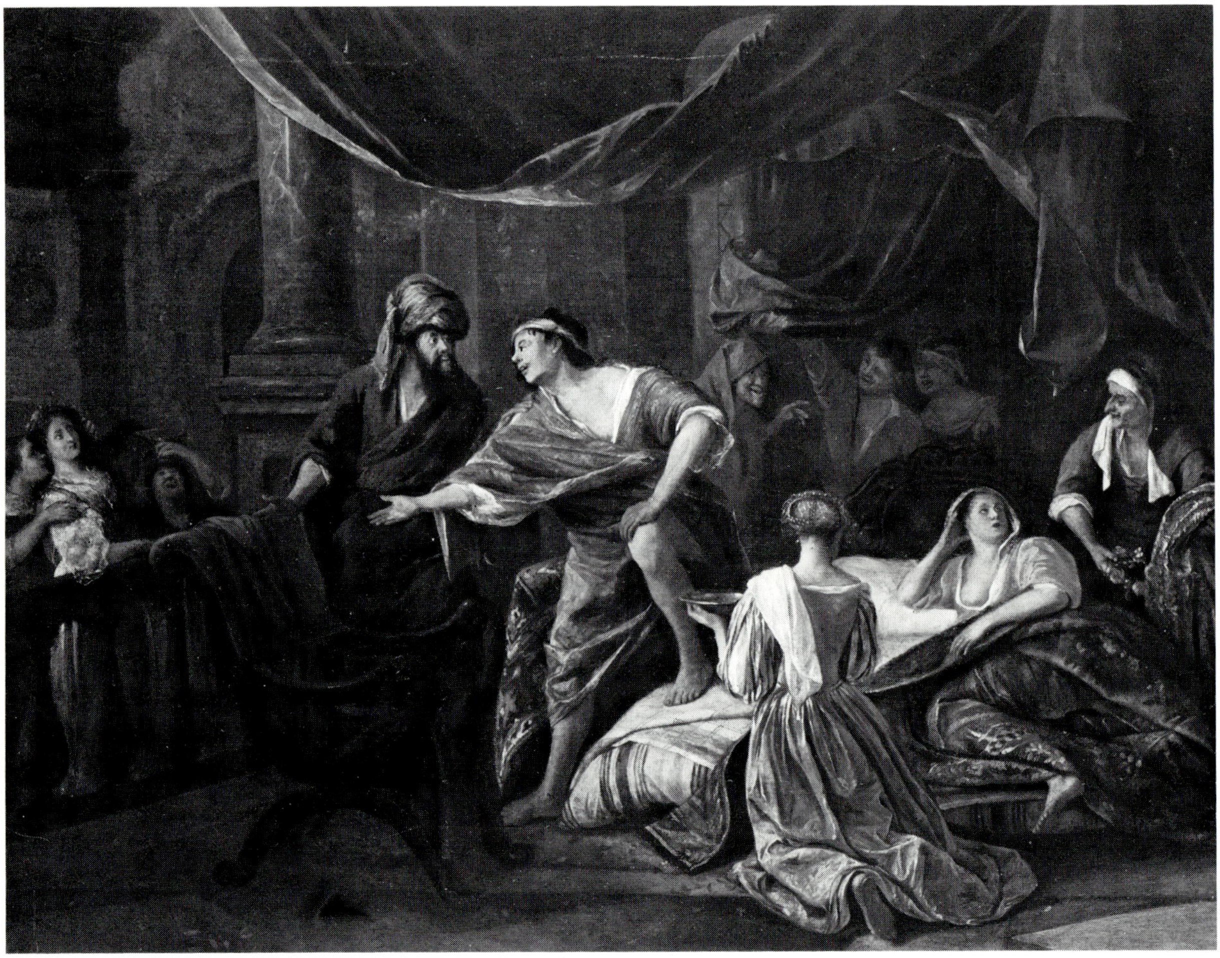

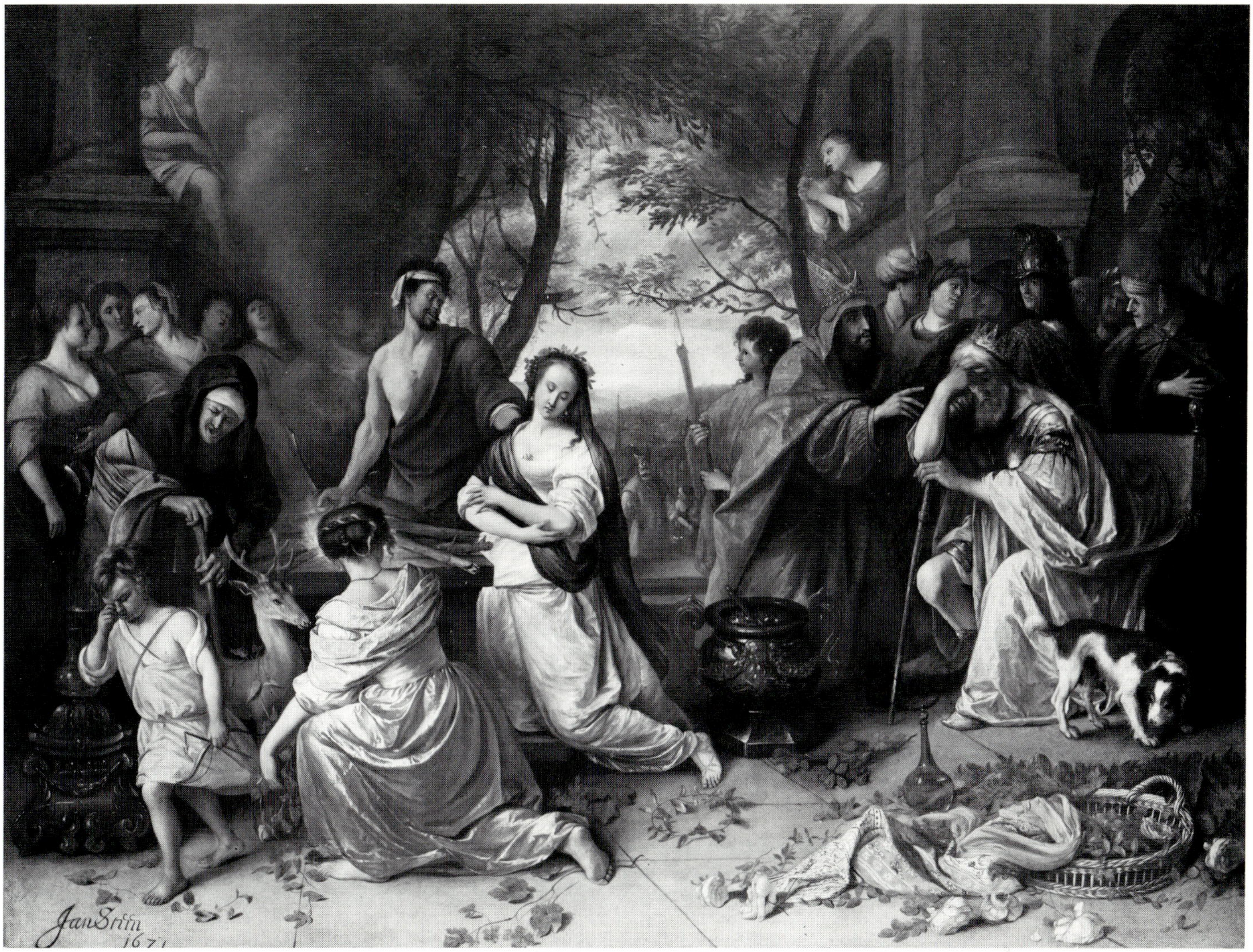

Fig. 82. *The Sacrifice of Iphigenia,* 1671 (Cat. 74). Rijksmuseum, Amsterdam; on loan from the Dutch Government (Dienst voor 's Rijks Verspreide Kunstvoorwerpen, The Hague).

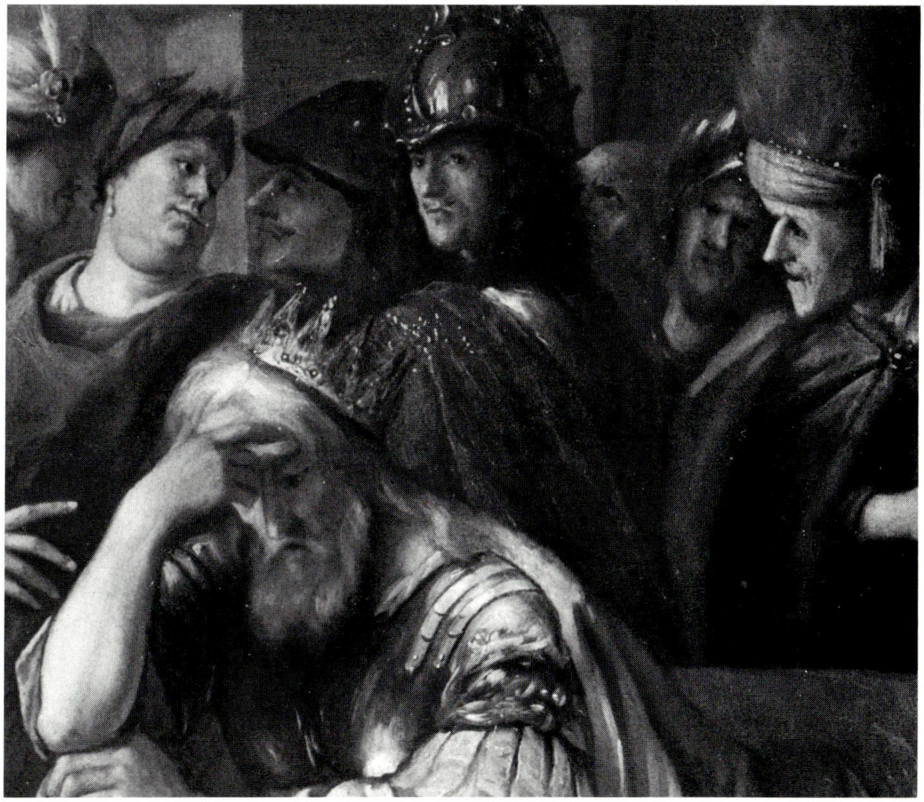

Fig. 82a. Detail, Fig. 82.

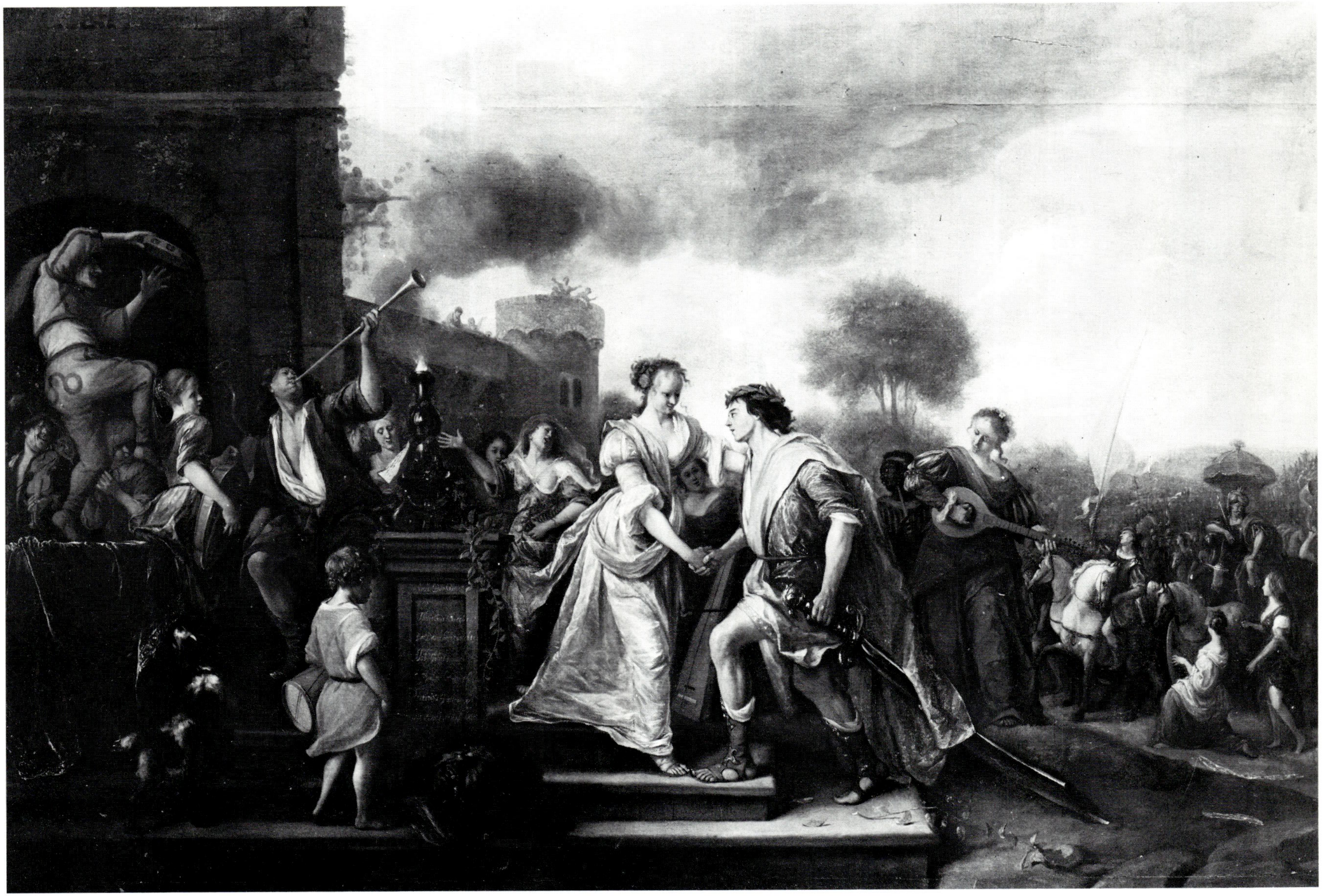

Fig. 83. *David Returning Victorious* (Cat. 13). Kronborg Castle, Elsinore, Denmark; property of Royal Museum of Fine Arts, Copenhagen.

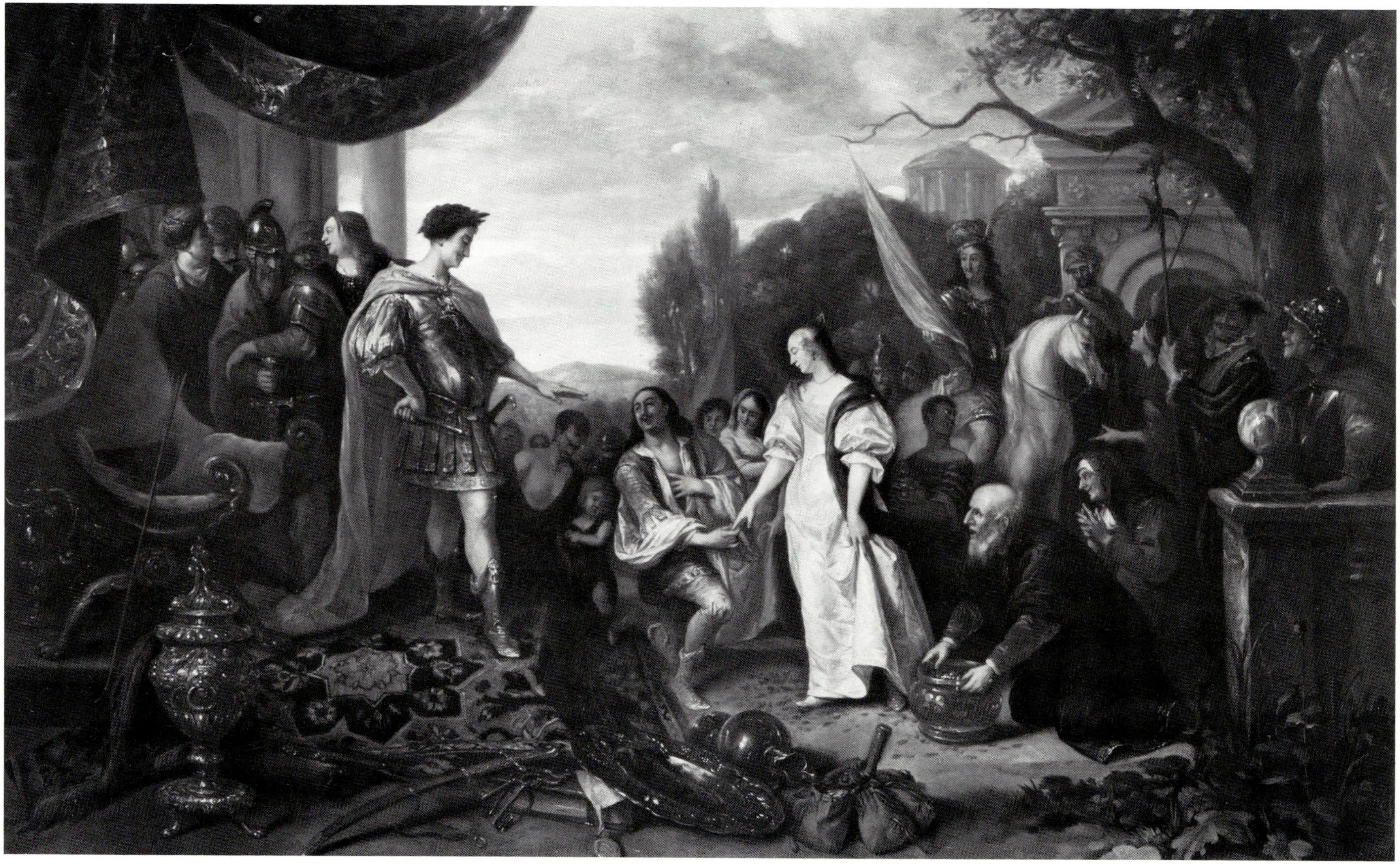

Fig. 84. *The Generosity of Scipio* (Cat. 83). Present location unknown.

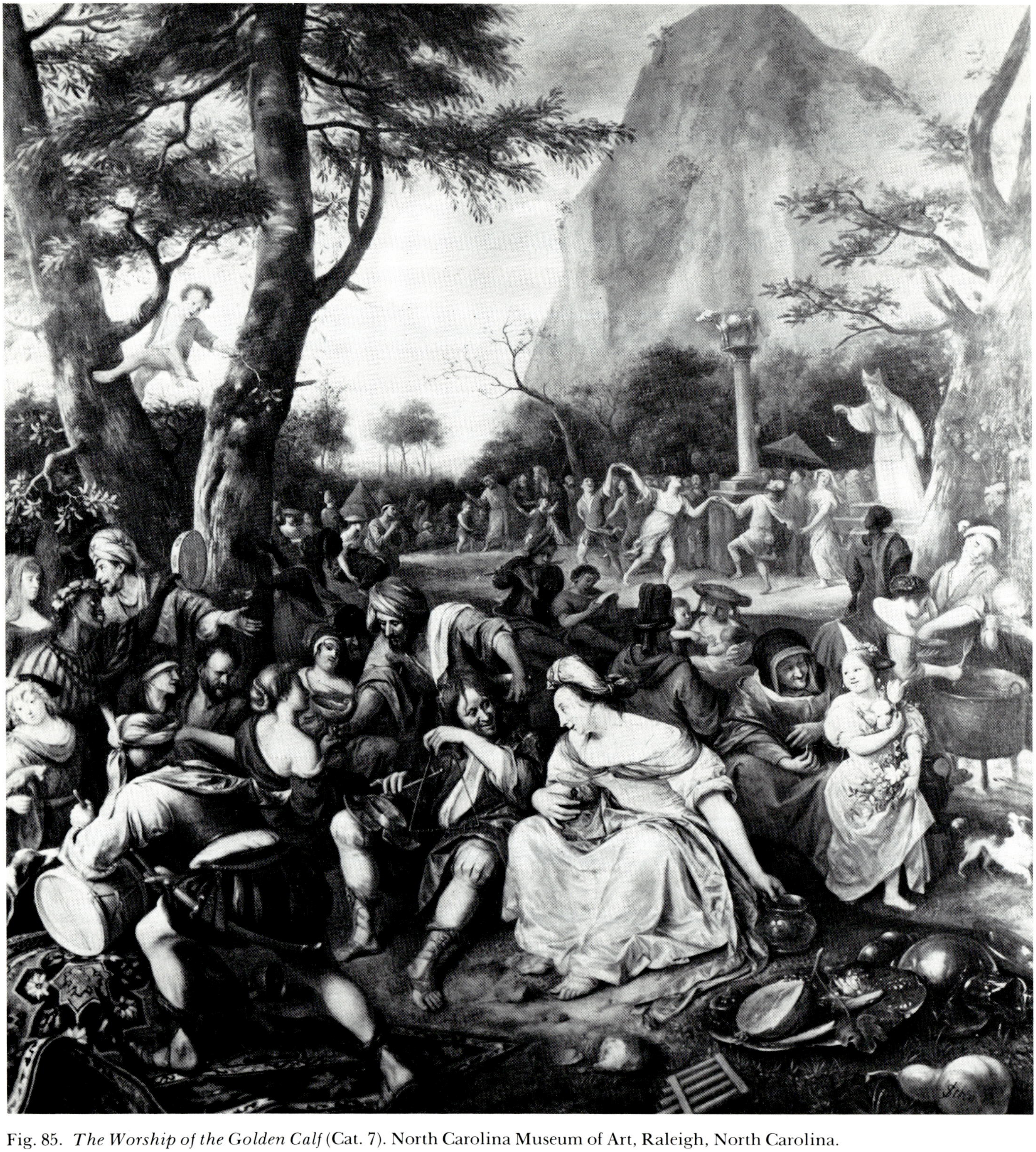

Fig. 85. *The Worship of the Golden Calf* (Cat. 7). North Carolina Museum of Art, Raleigh, North Carolina.

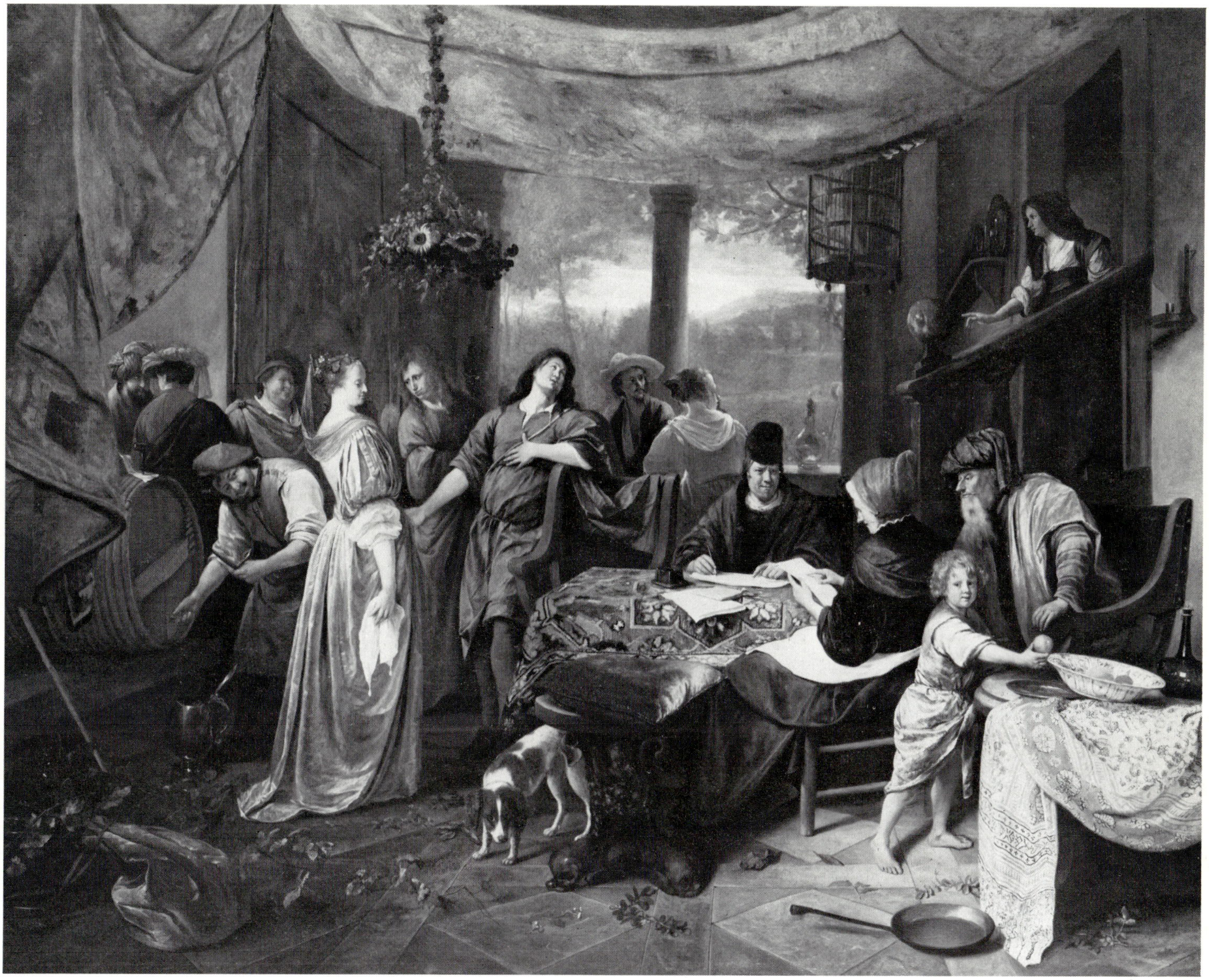

Fig. 86. *The Marriage of Tobias and Sarah* (Cat. 25/487). M. H. de Young Memorial Museum, San Francisco, California.

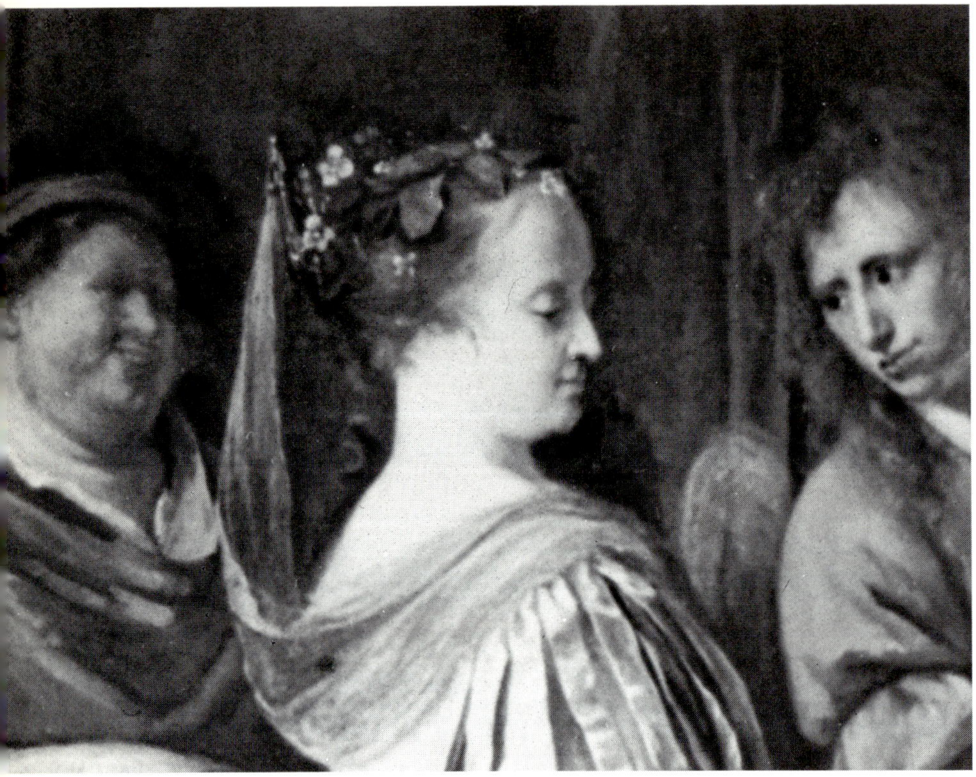

Fig. 86a. Detail, Fig. 86.

Fig. 87. *The Banquet of Antony and Cleopatra* (Cat. 85). S. Nystad, The Hague.

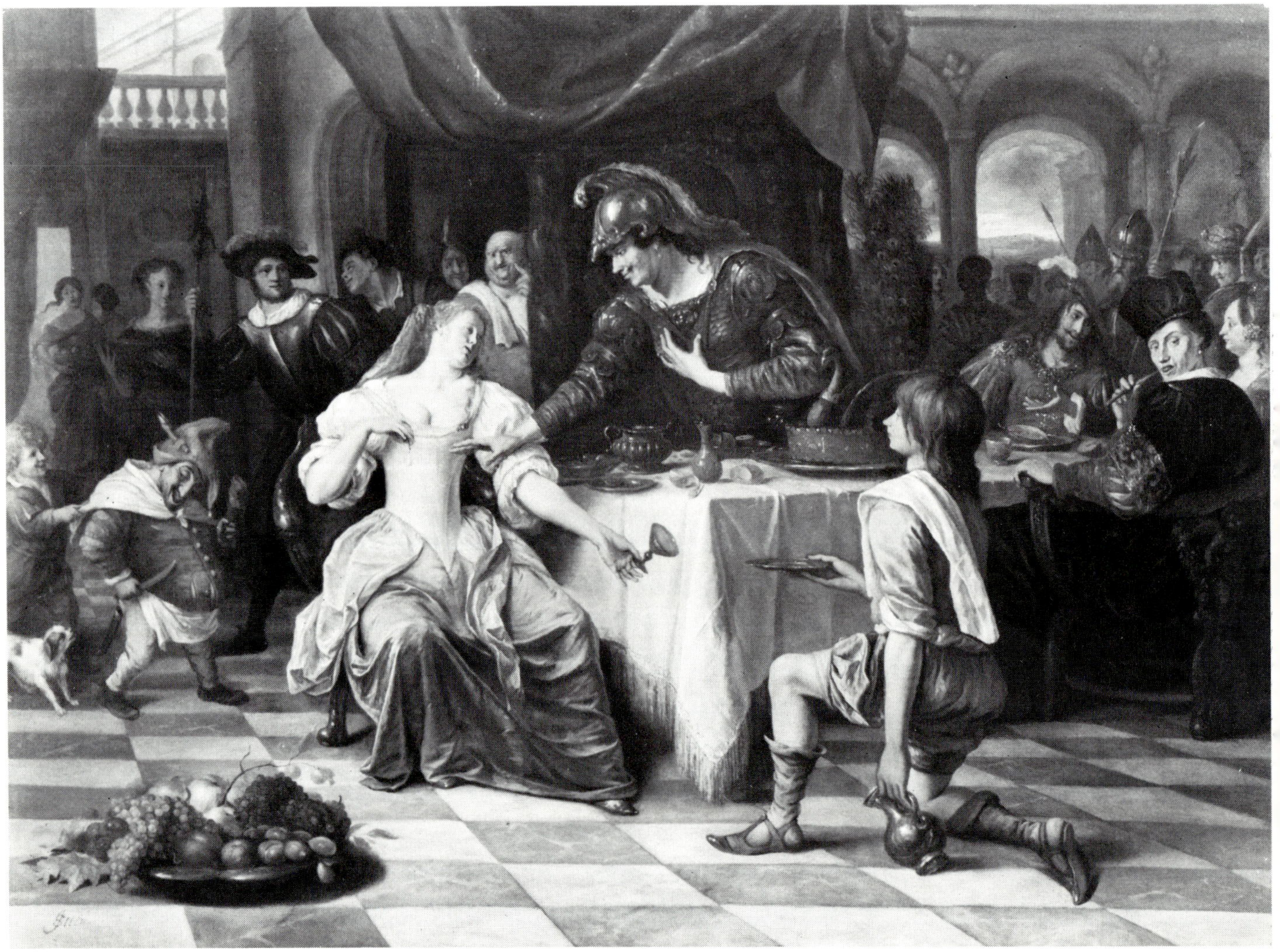

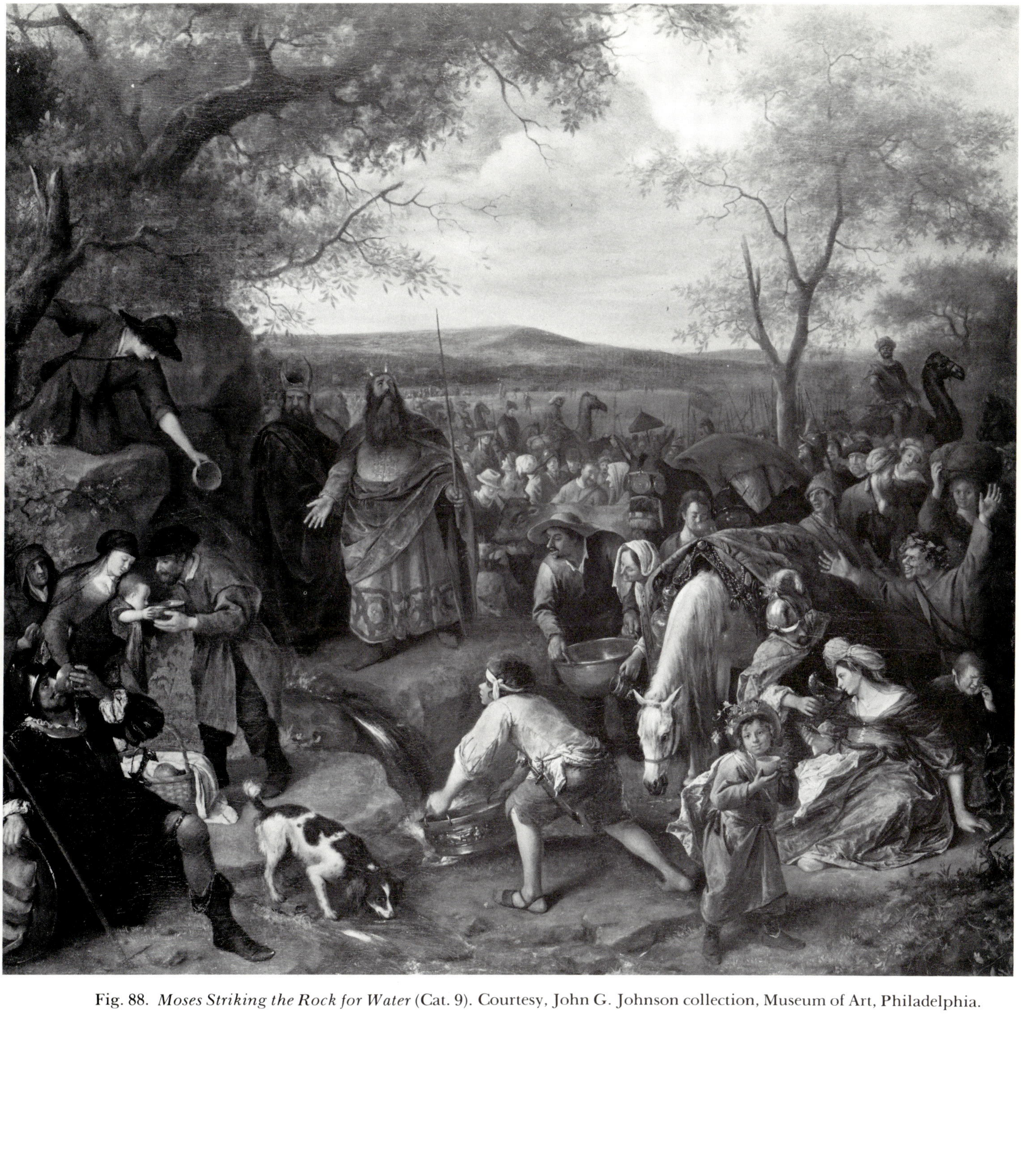

Fig. 88. *Moses Striking the Rock for Water* (Cat. 9). Courtesy, John G. Johnson collection, Museum of Art, Philadelphia.

Fig. 88a. Detail, Fig. 88.

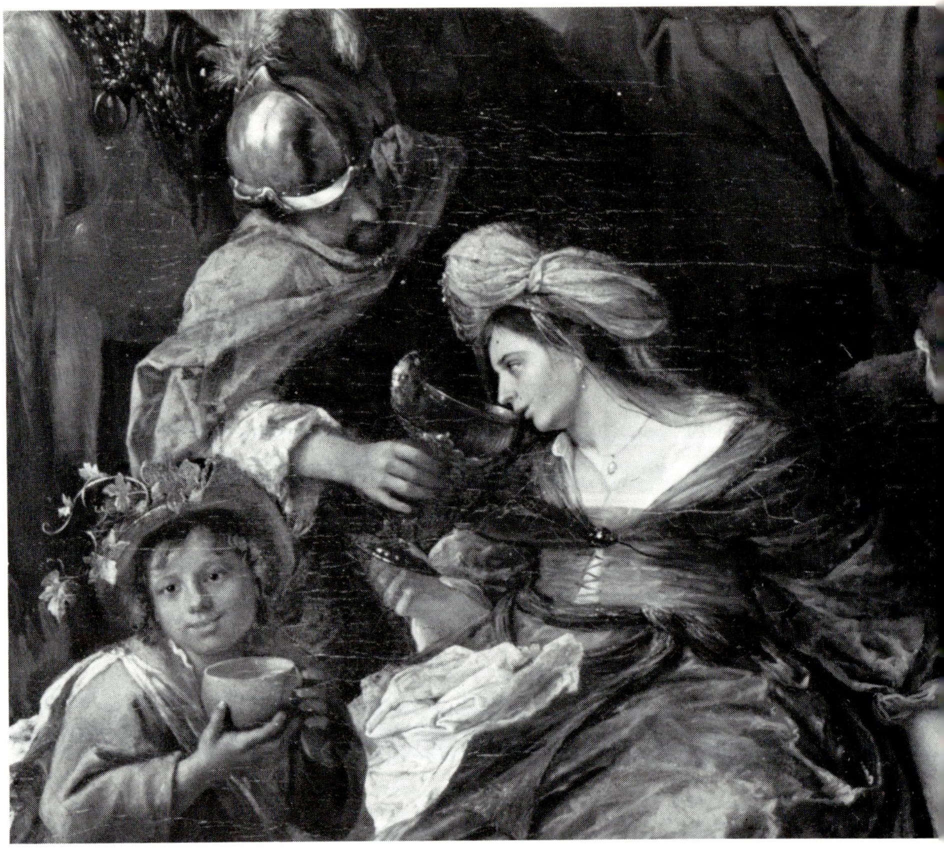

Fig. 89. *Laban Searching for the Idols Hidden by Rachel* (Cat. 4/652a). Stedelijk Museum "De Lakenhal," Leiden.

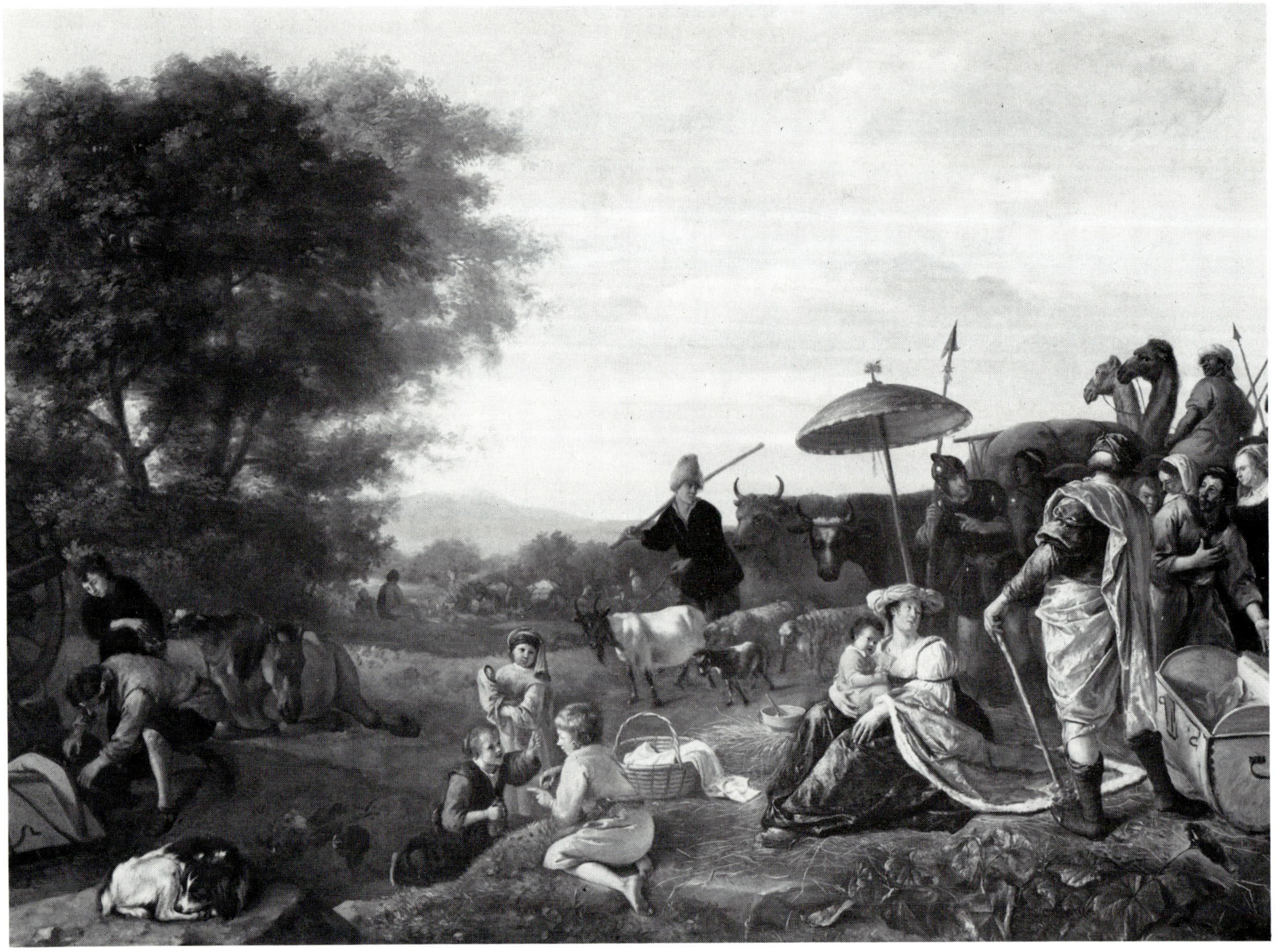

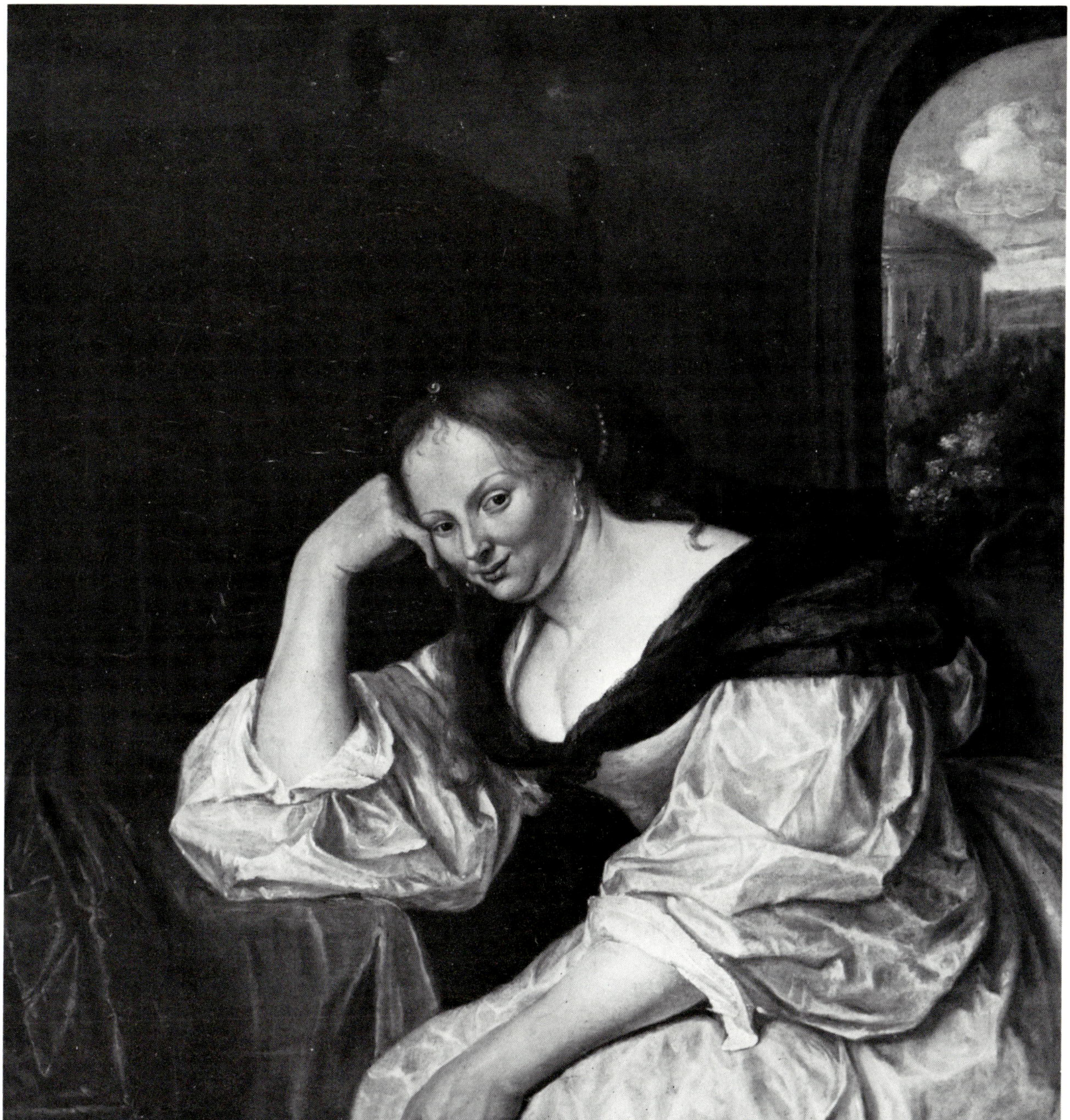

Fig. 90. *Bathseba with David's Letter* (Cat. 14a/814a). Wetzlar collection, Amsterdam.

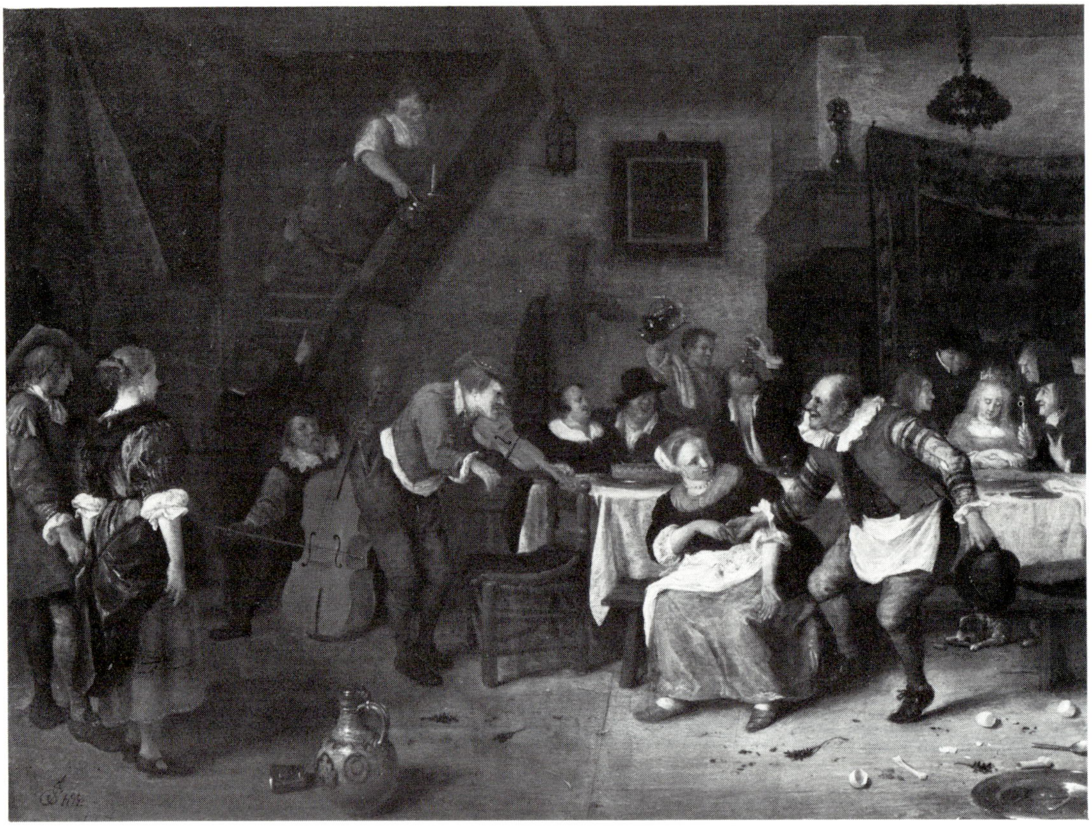

Fig. 91. *The Village Wedding,* 1672 (HdG 454). Rijksmuseum, Amsterdam.

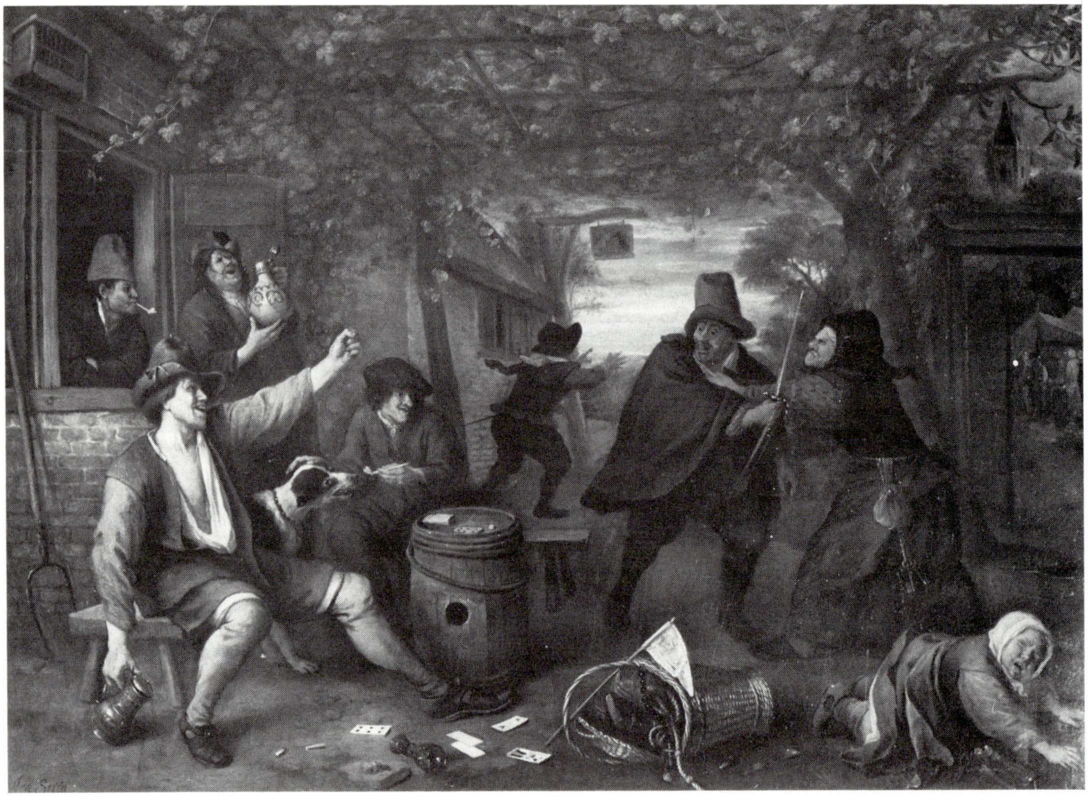

Fig. 92. *Quarrel Over Cards,* 1671 (HdG 774). Gemeentemuseum, Arnhem.

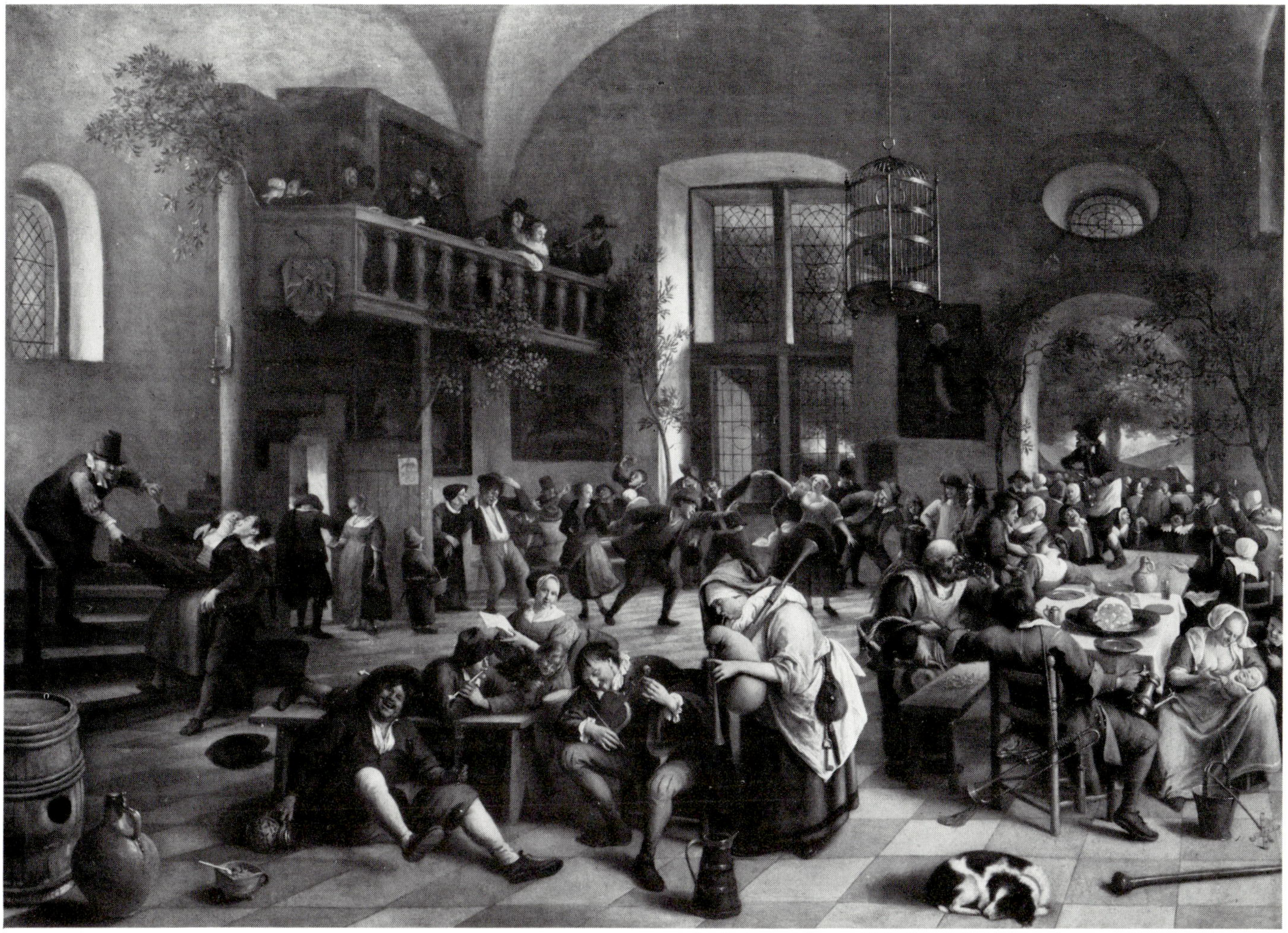

Fig. 93. *Rustic Feast in a Large Tavern,* 1674 (HdG 601). Louvre, Paris.

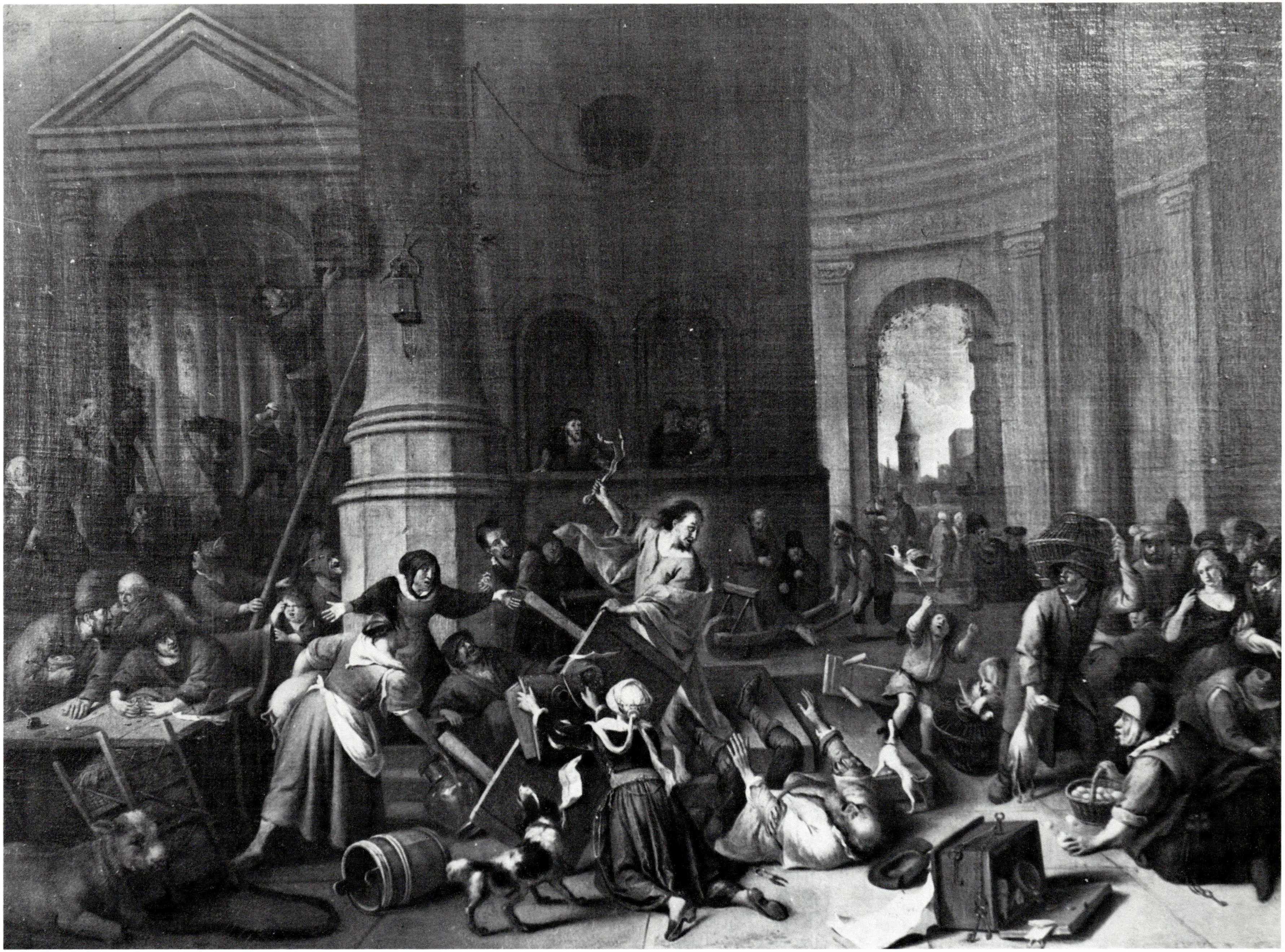

Fig. 94. *The Expulsion from the Temple,* 1675 (Cat. 62). Stedelijk Museum "De Lakenhal," Leiden; on loan from the Dutch Government (Dienst voor 's Rijks Verspreide Kunstvoorwerpen, The Hague).

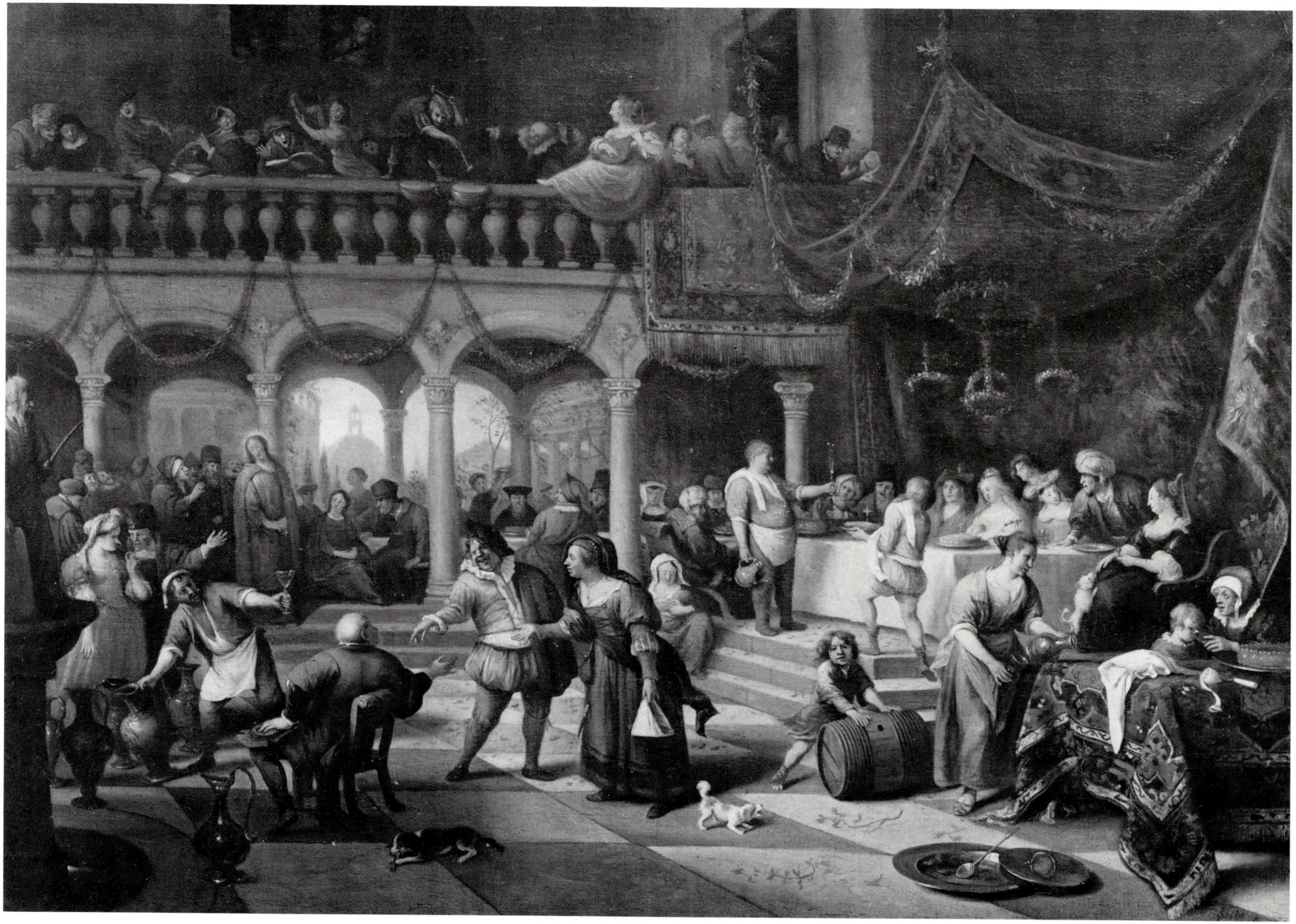

Fig. 95. *The Marriage at Cana,* 1676 (Cat. 50). The Norton Simon Collection, Los Angeles, California.

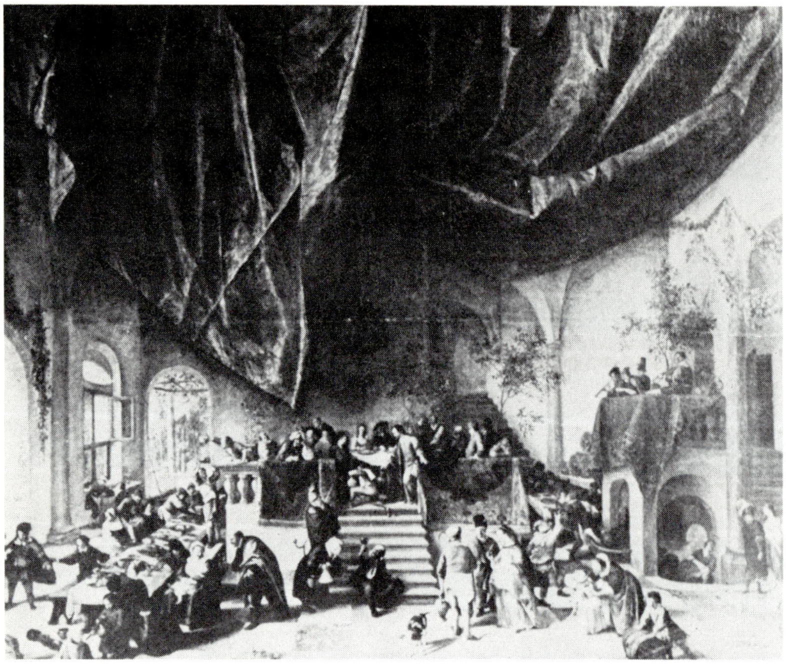

Fig. 96. *The Marriage at Cana* (Cat. 46). Present location unknown.

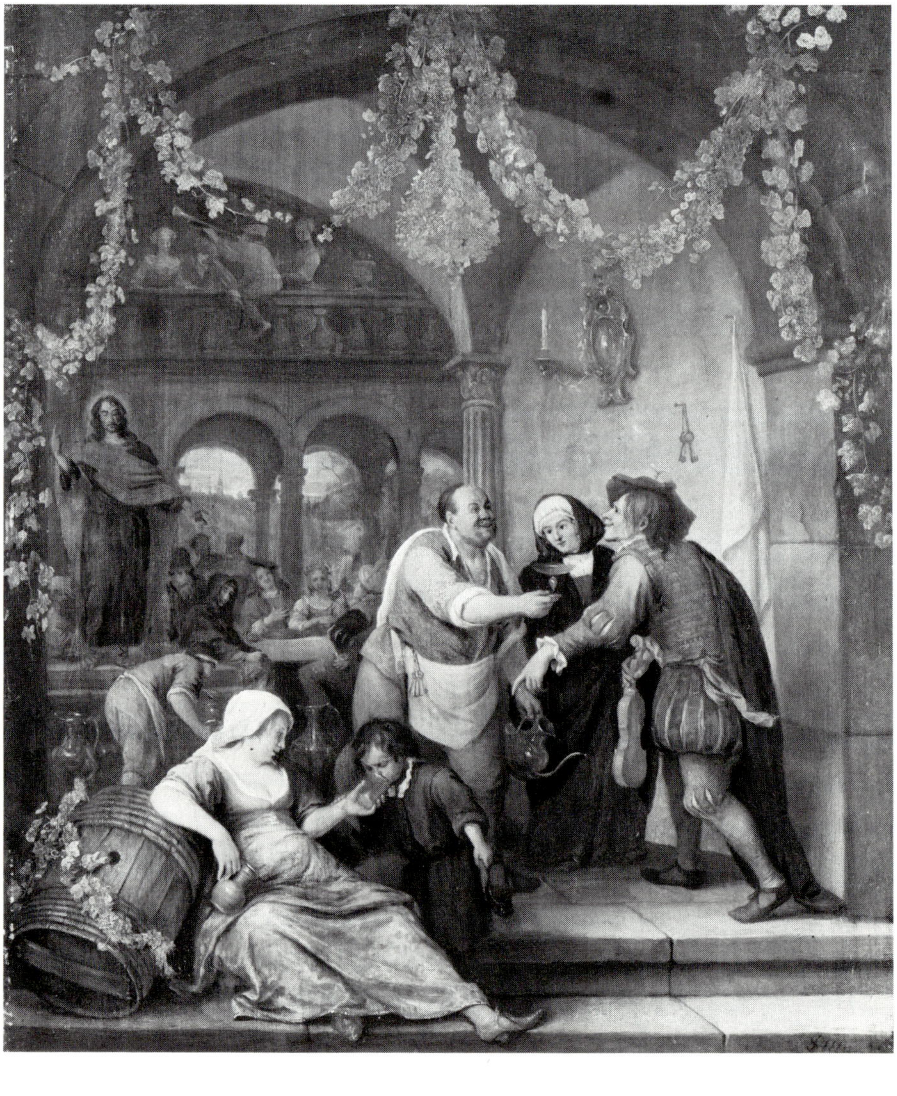

Fig. 97. *The Marriage at Cana* (Cat. 47). Staatliche Kunstsammlungen, Dresden.

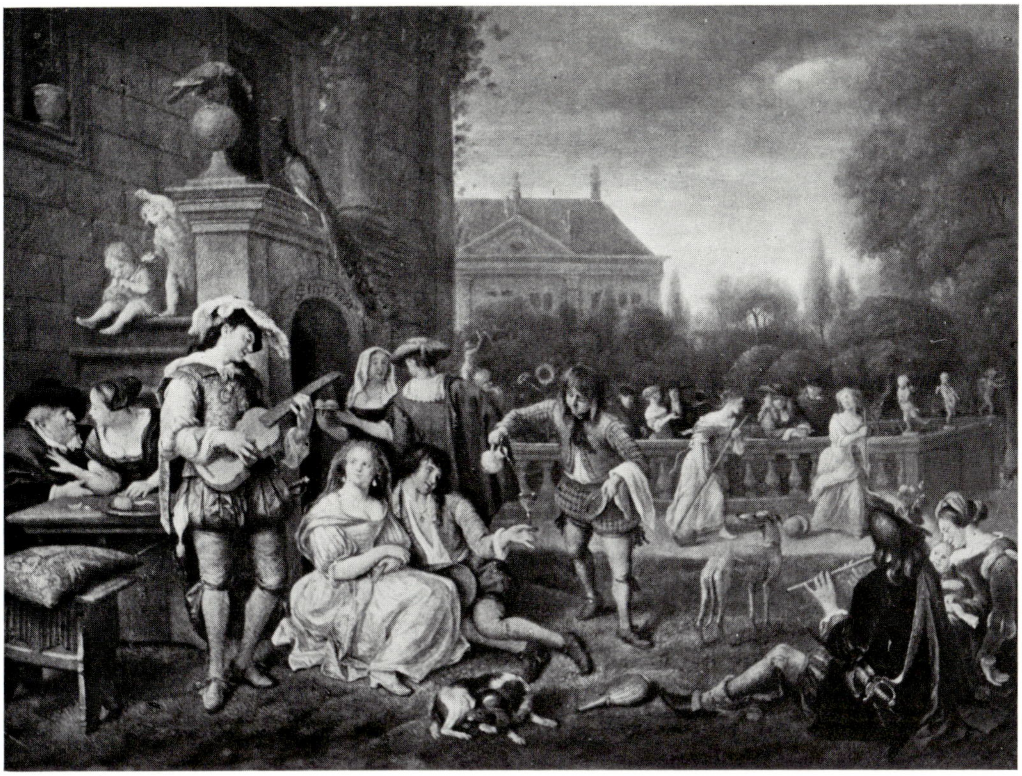

Fig. 98. *The Garden Party*, 1677 (HdG 52/440, Cat. Addendum 13). Private collection, United States.

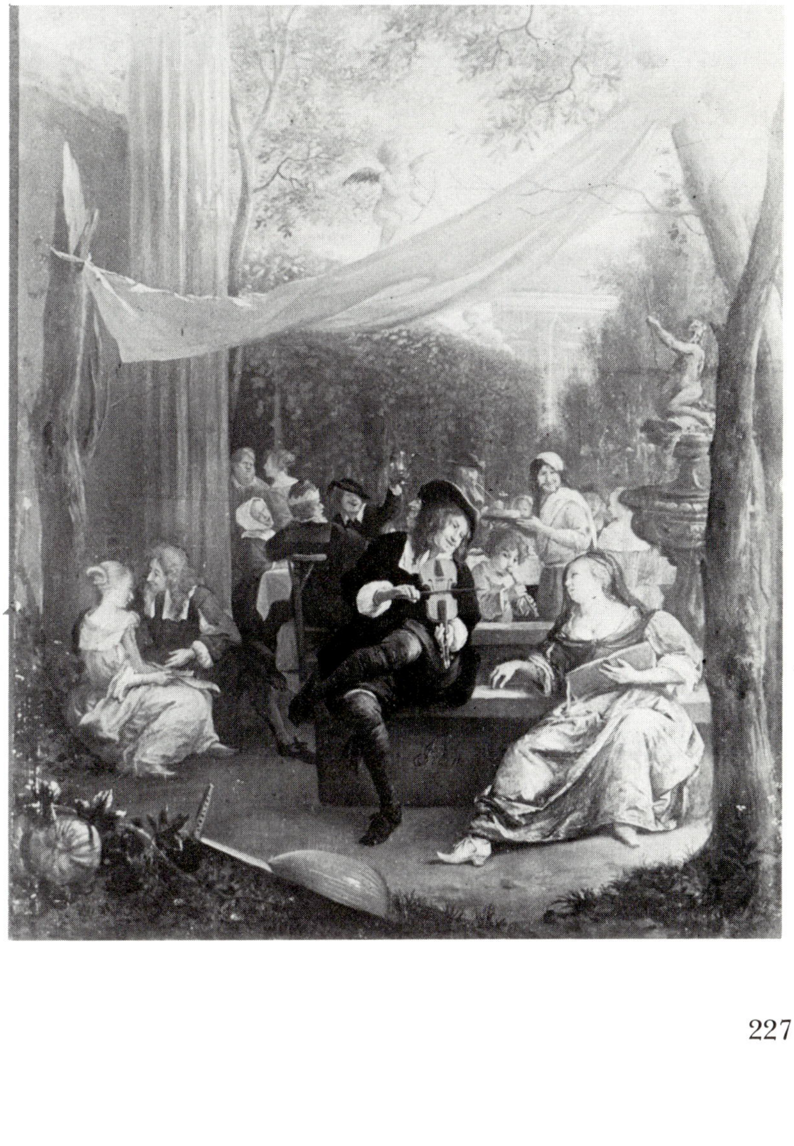

Fig. 99. *The Garden Party* (HdG 416). Hermitage, Leningrad.

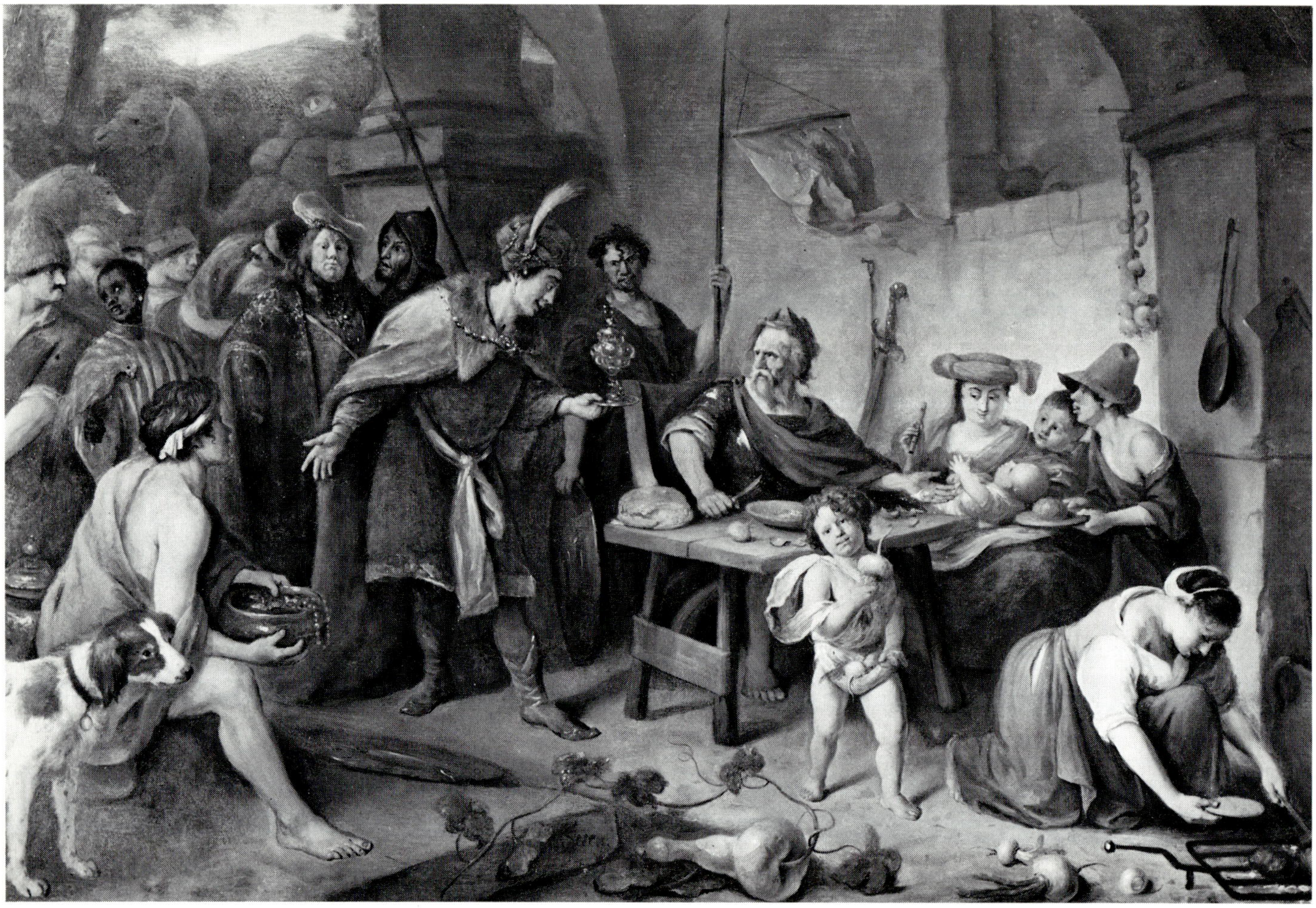

Fig. 100. *Manius Curius Dentatus and the Samnite Ambassadors* (Cat. 84). Present location unknown.

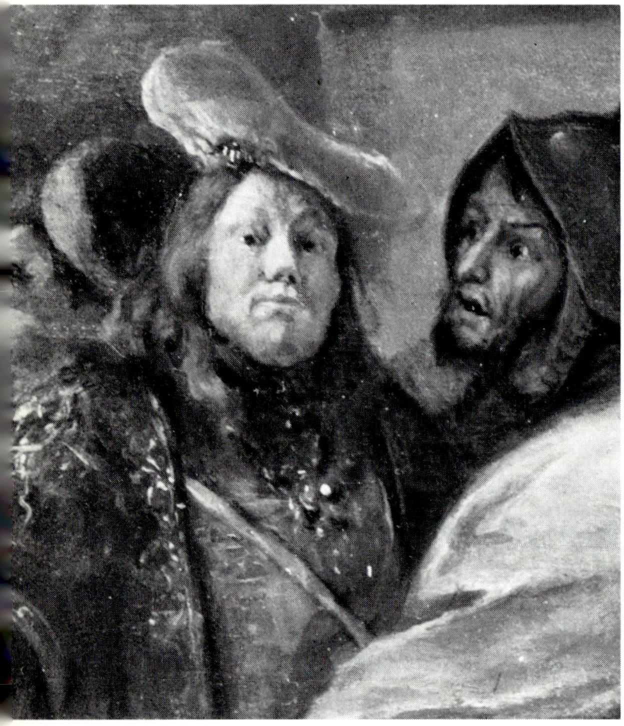

Fig. 100a. Detail, Fig. 100.

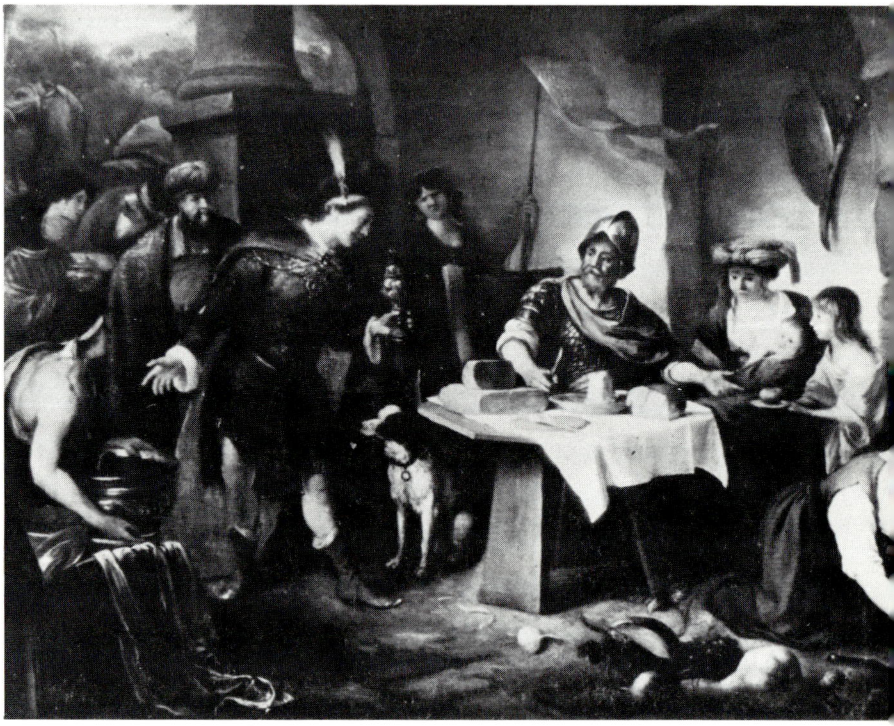

Fig. 101. *Manius Curius Dentatus and the Samnite Ambassadors* (Cat. 84a). Present location unknown.

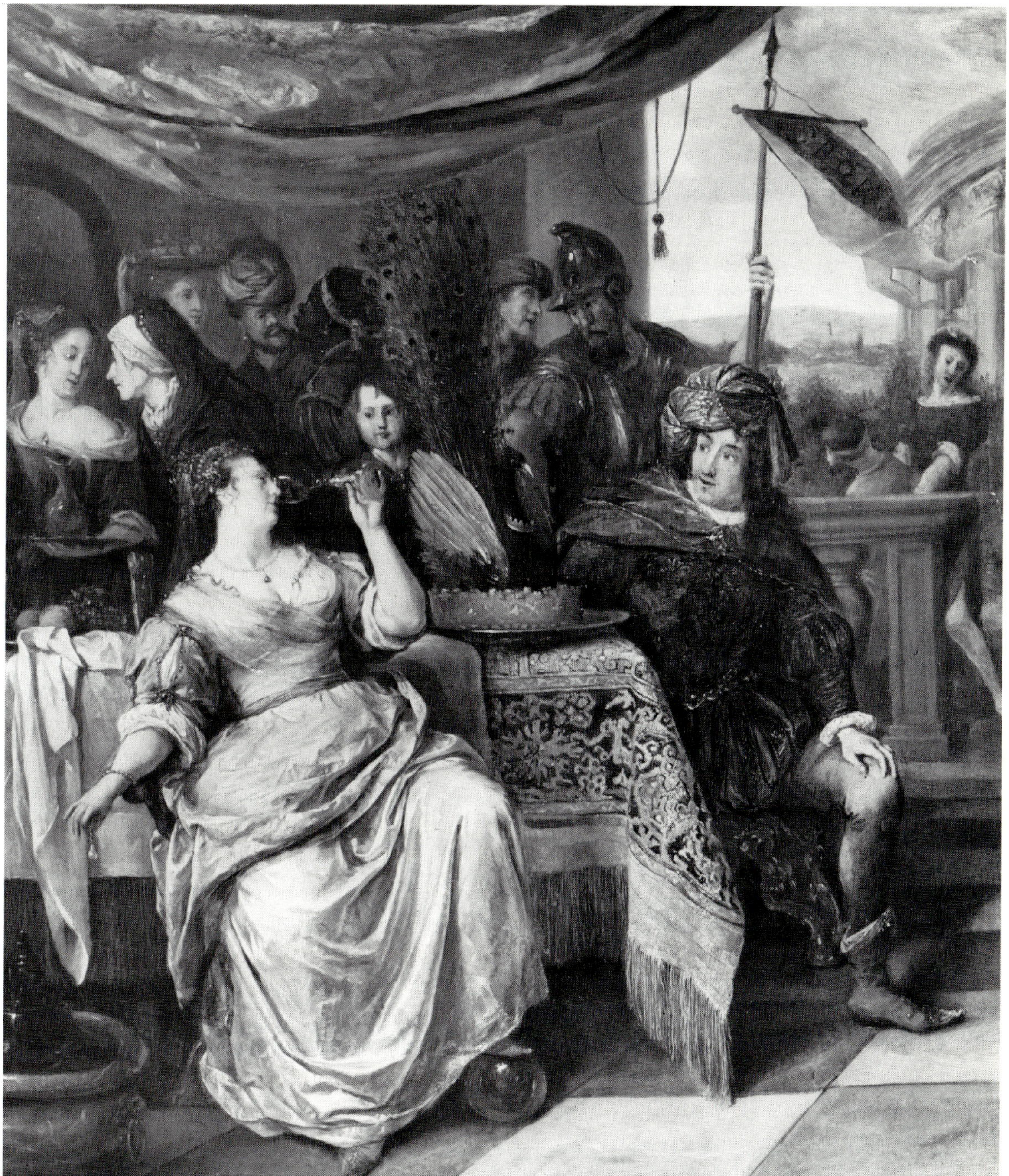

Fig. 102. *The Banquet of Antony and Cleopatra* (Cat. 86c). Private collection, The Netherlands.

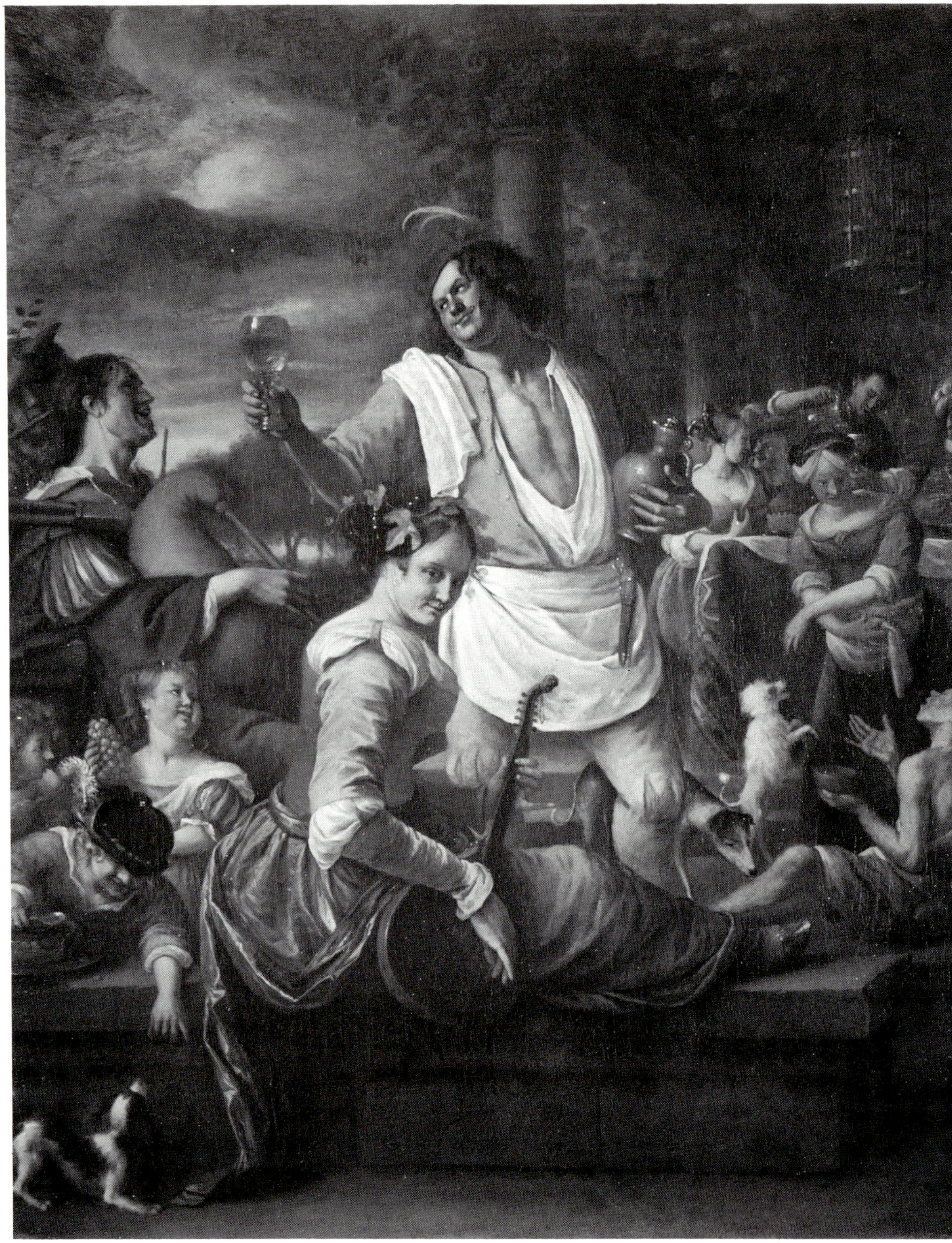

Fig. 103. *The Parable of the Rich Man and Lazarus* (Cat. 58). Private collection, New York.

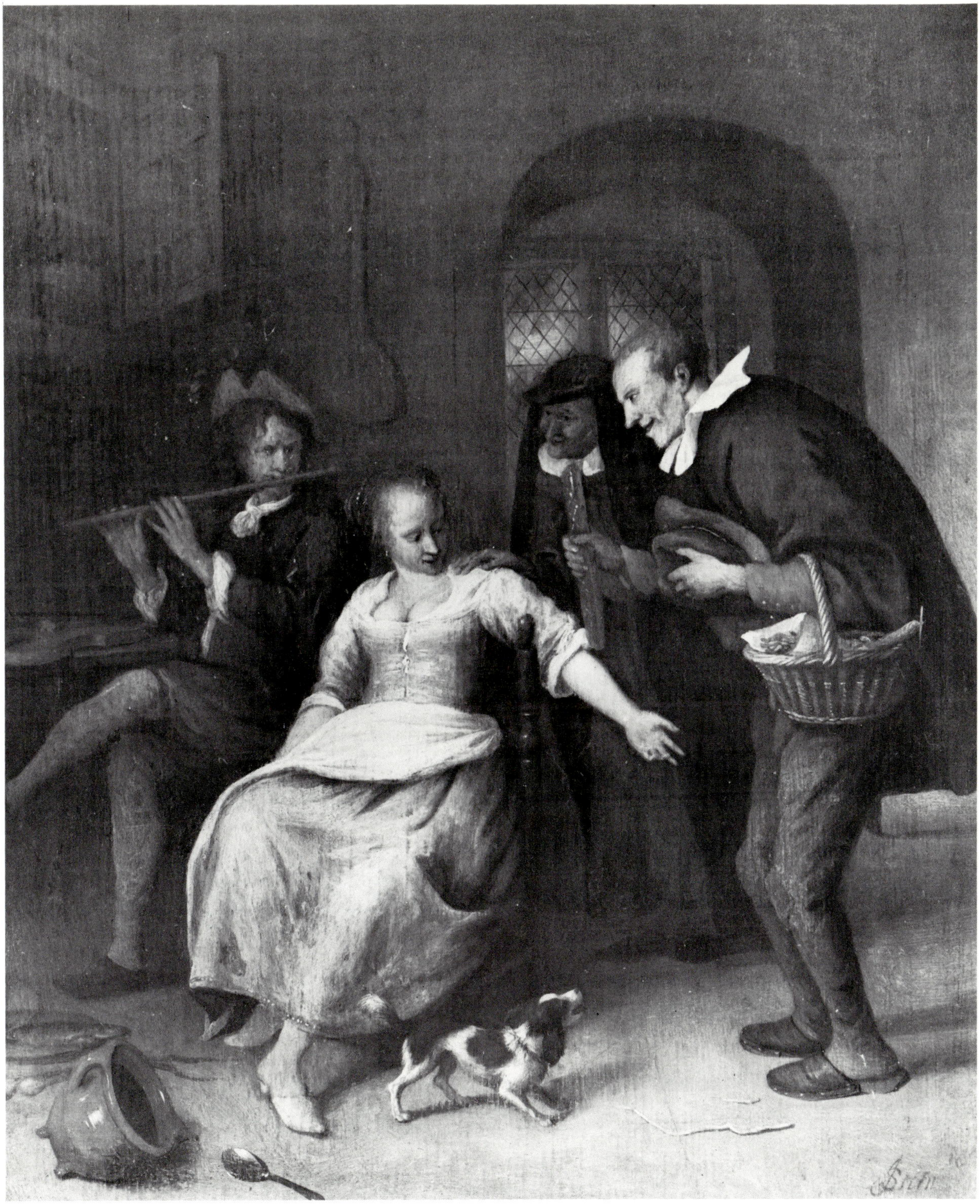

Fig. 104. *The Pastry Seller* (HdG 267). Musée des Beaux-Arts, Rouen.

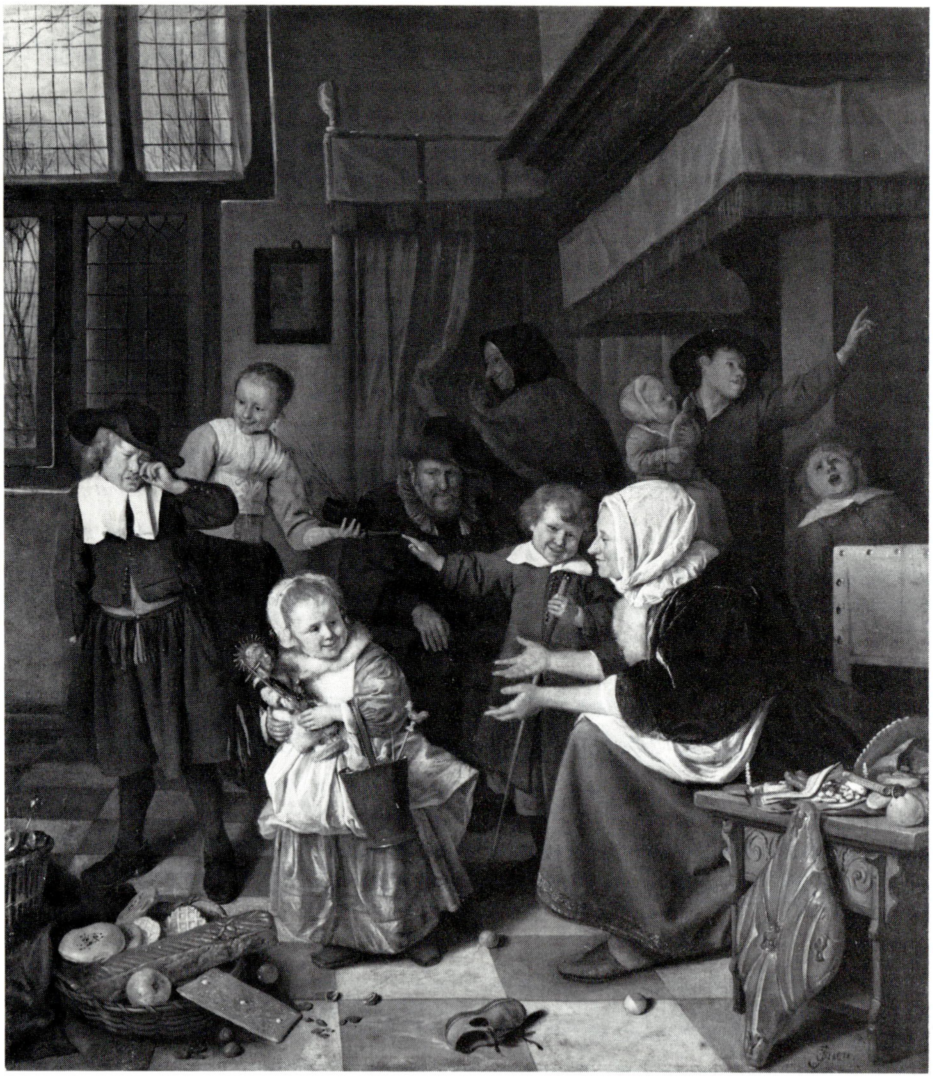

Fig. 105. *St. Nicolaas Day* (HdG 510). Rijksmuseum, Amsterdam.

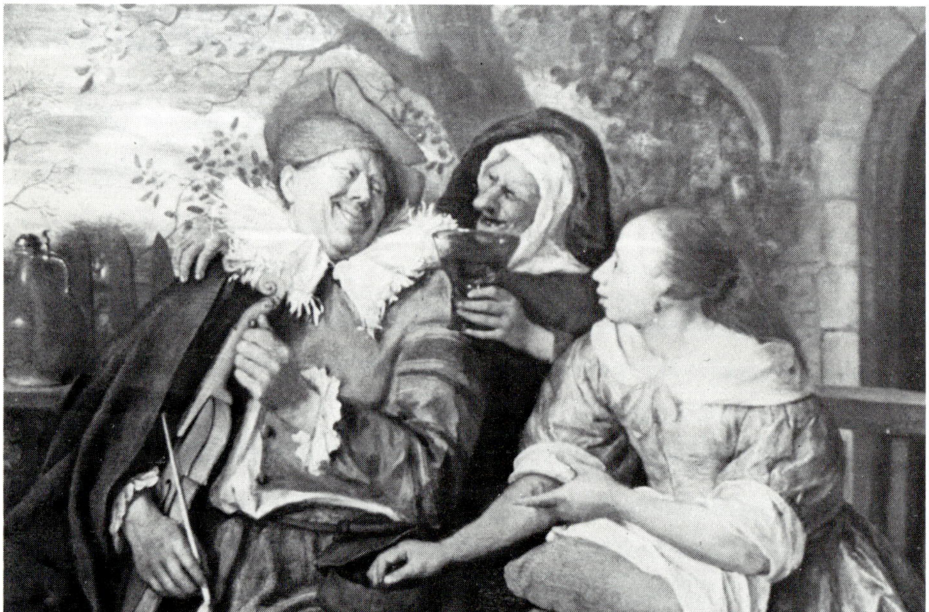

Fig. 106. *The Violinist* (HdG 429a). Formerly Kohn Collection, The Hague

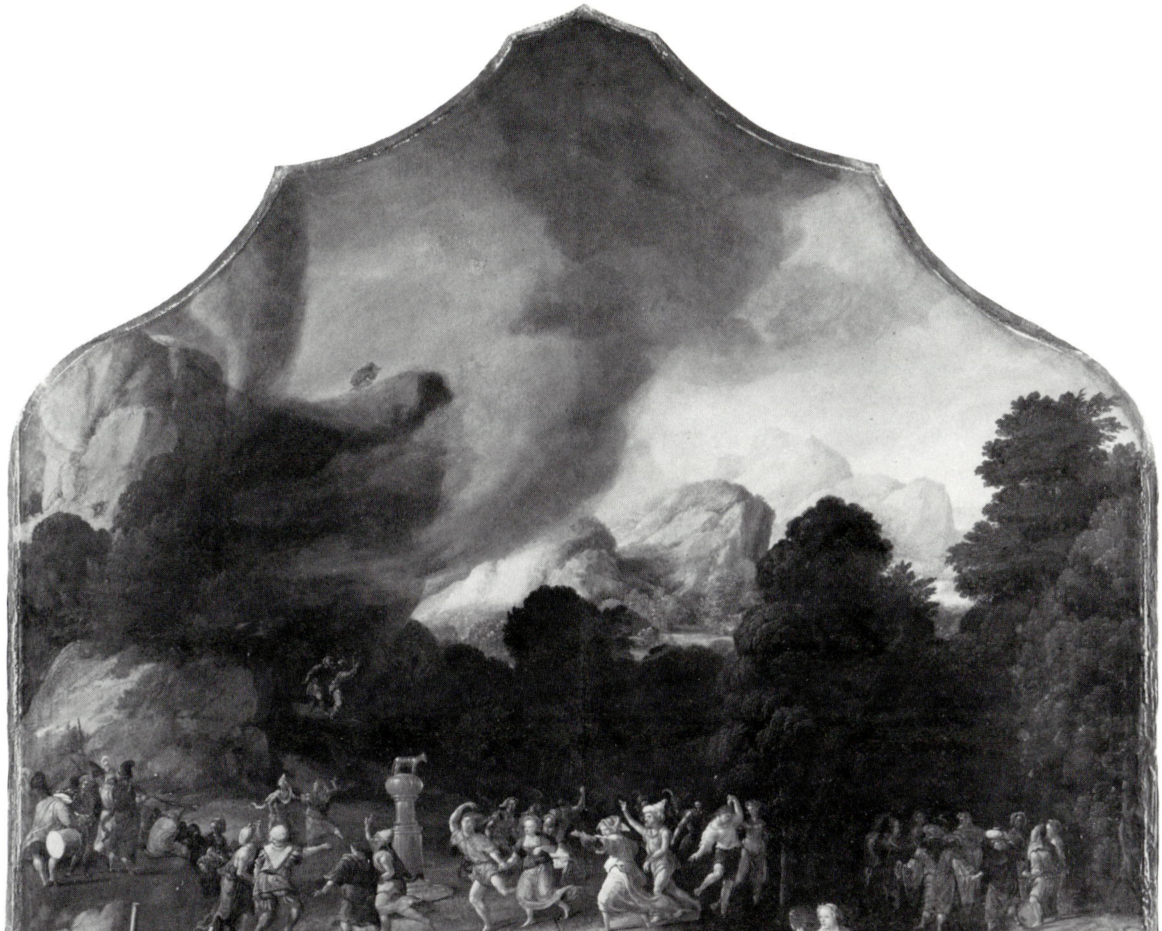

Fig. 107. Van Leyden, *The Worship of the Golden Calf* (central panel). Rijksmuseum, Amsterdam.

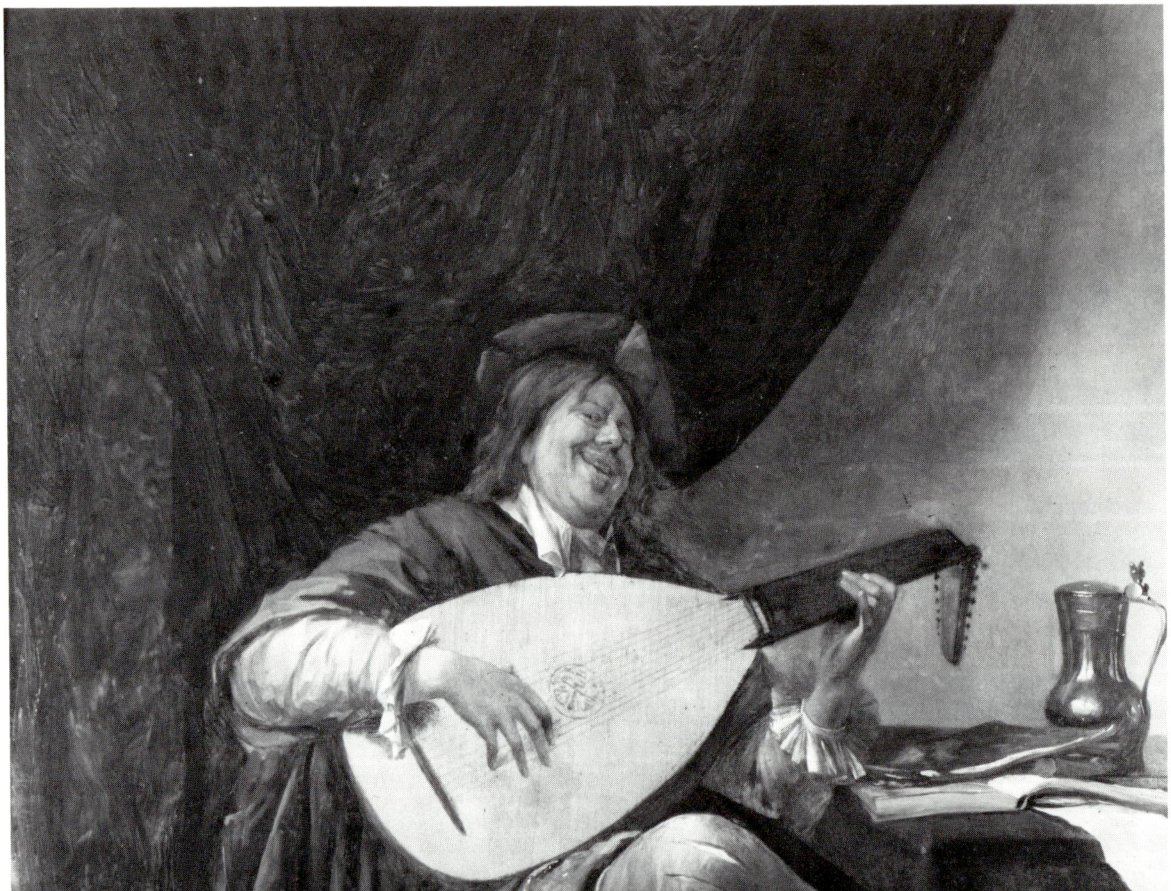

Fig. 108. *Self-Portrait Playing the Lute* (HdG 863). Thyssen collection, Lugano.

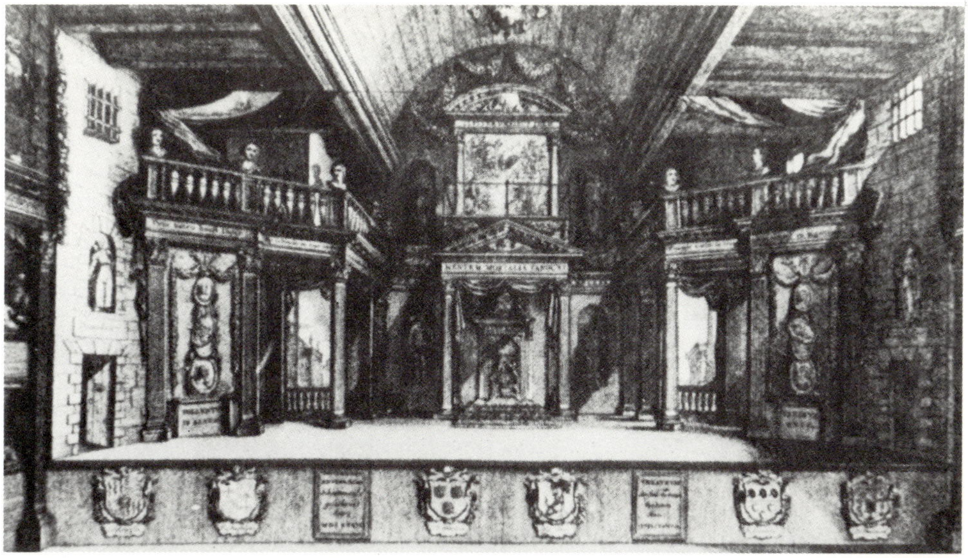

Fig. 109. *Stage of the Amsterdam Schouwburg 1637-1665,* etching.

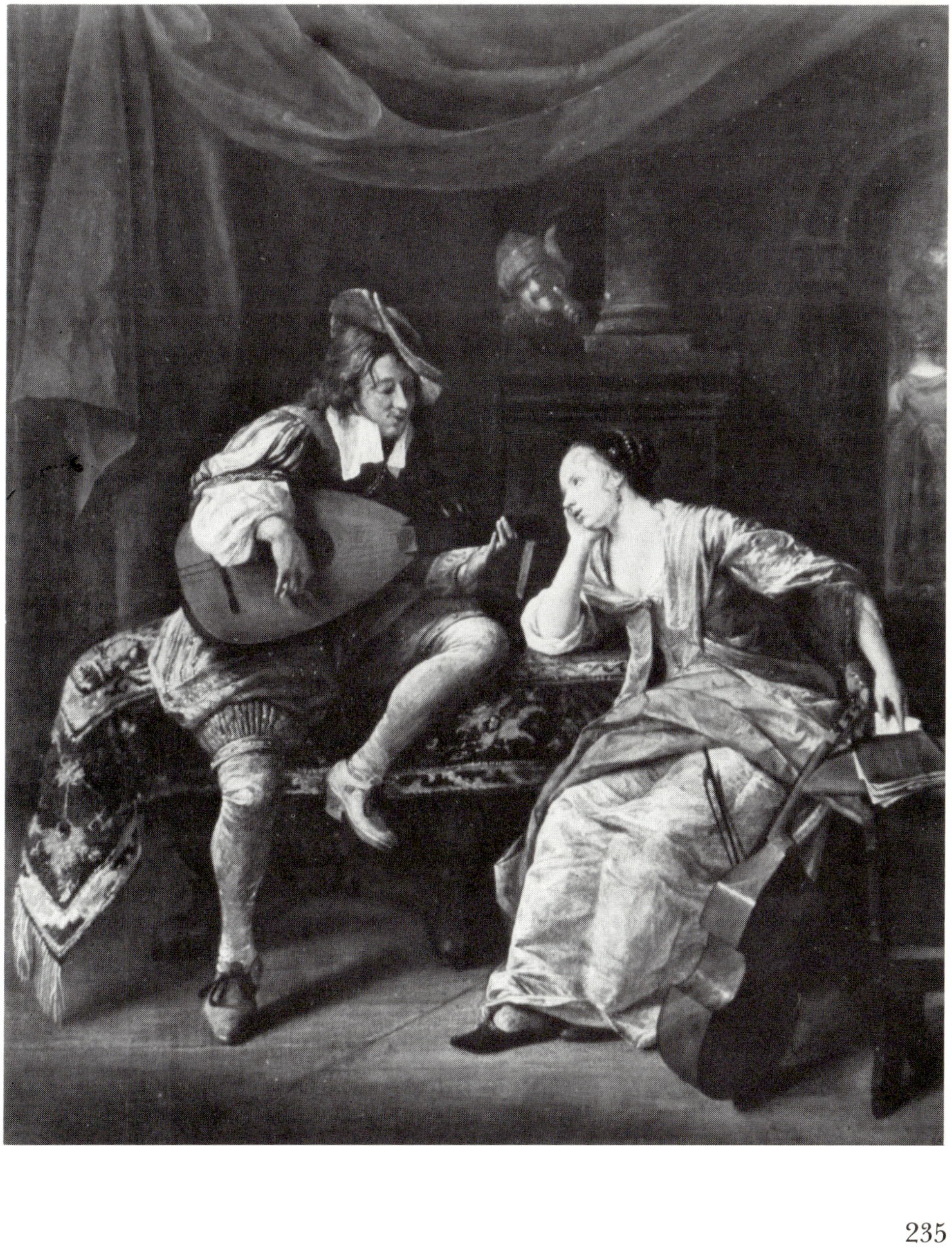

Fig. 110. *Ascanius and Lucilla* (Cat. Addendum 14). Private collection.

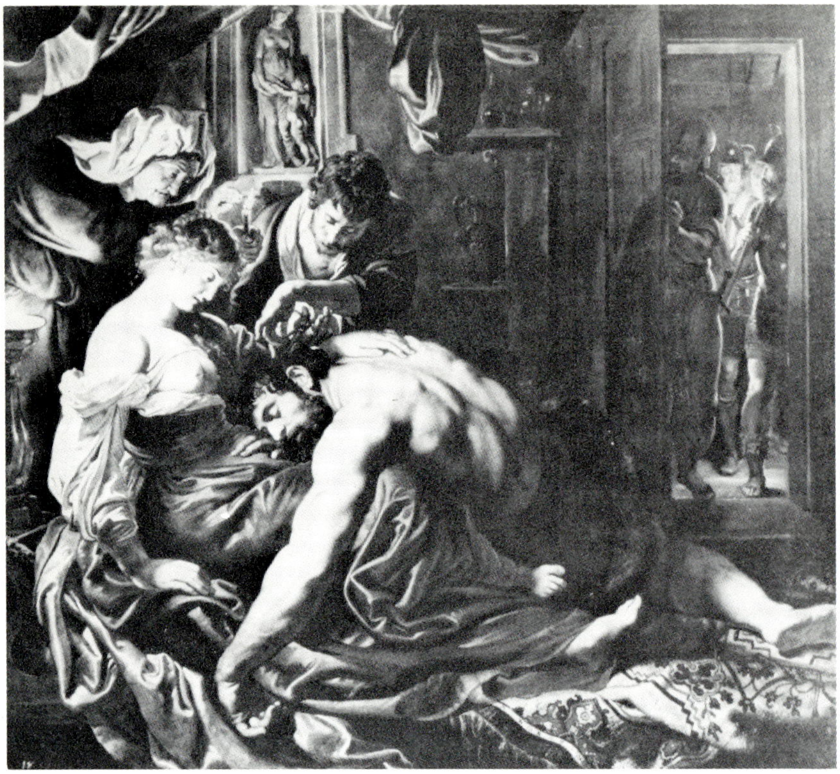

Fig. 111. Rubens, *Samson and Delilah*. Köser collection, Hamburg.

Fig. 112. Van Dyck, *Samson and Delilah*. Dulwich College, Dulwich.

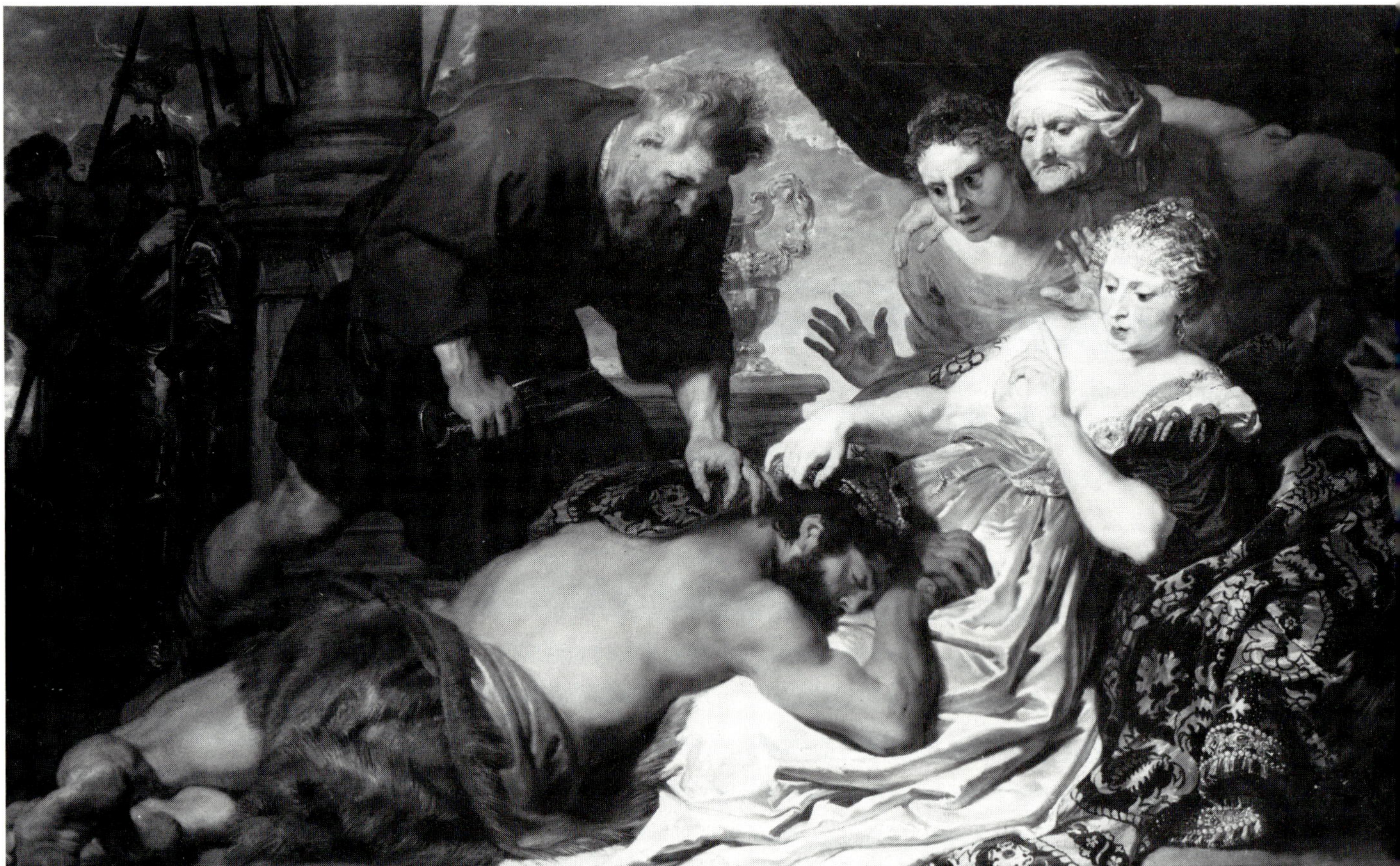

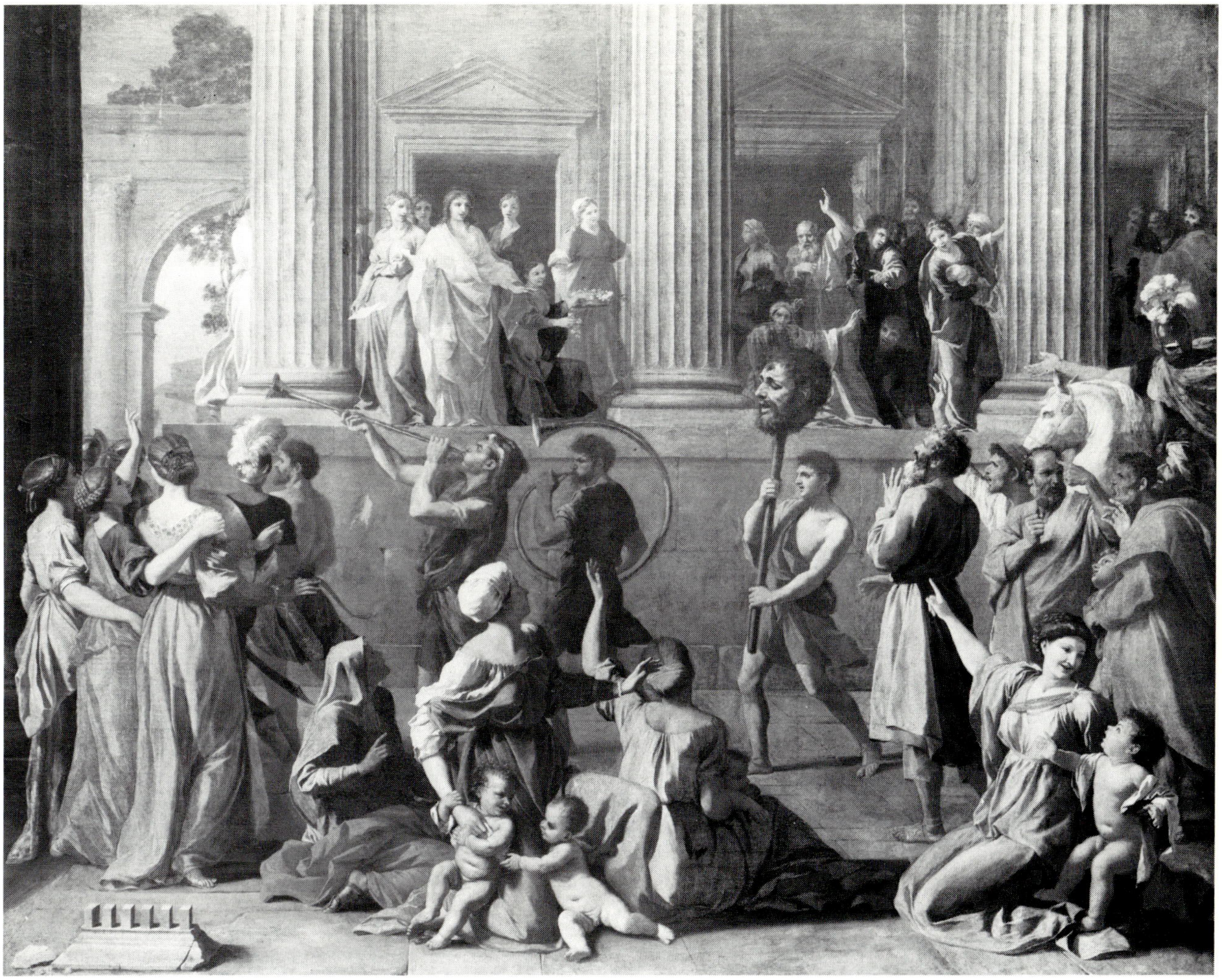

Fig. 113. Poussin, *David Returning Victorious*. Dulwich College, Dulwich.

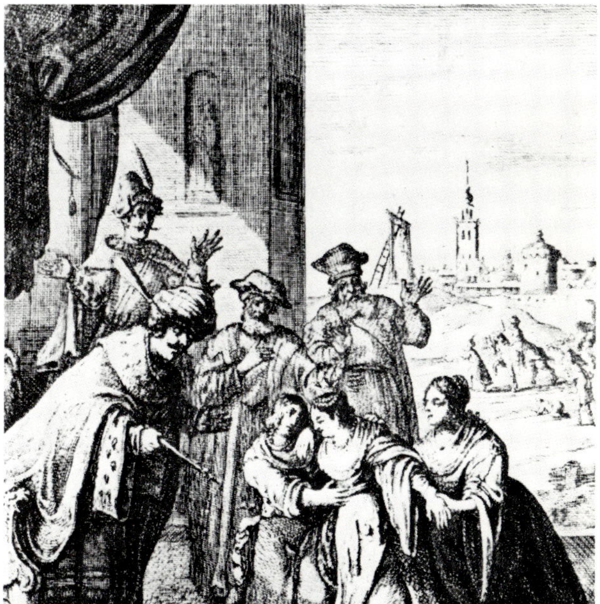

Fig. 114. Quast (?), *Esther Before Ahasuerus*, engraving.

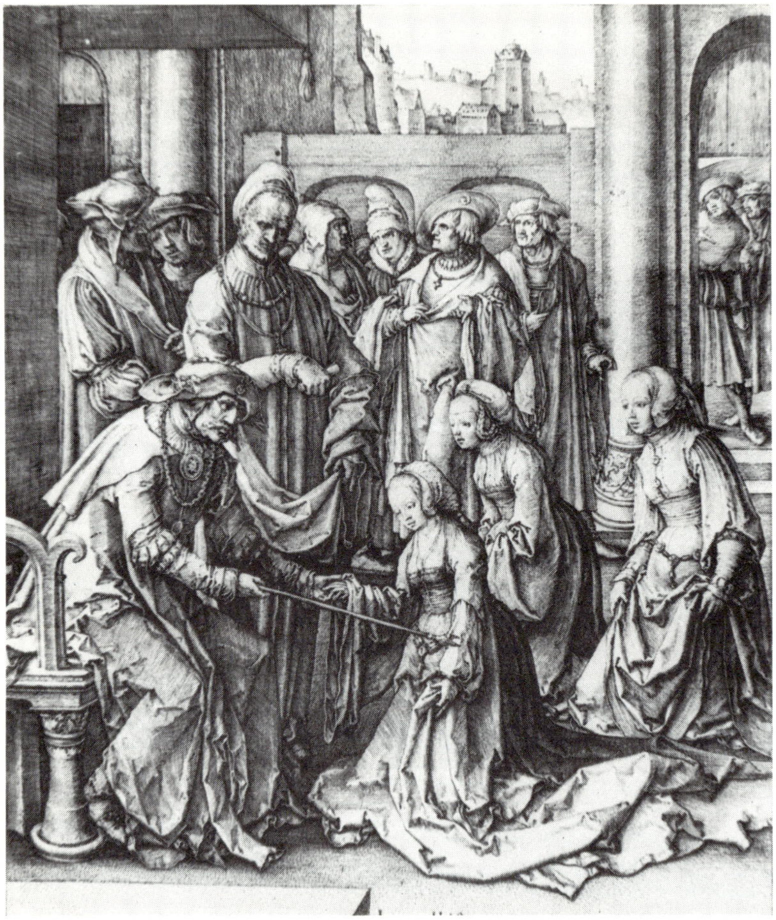

Fig. 115. Van Leyden, *Esther Before Ahasuerus,* engraving, 1618.

Fig. 116. Bol (?), *The Wrath of Ahasuerus.* Wallraf-Richartz Museum, Cologne.

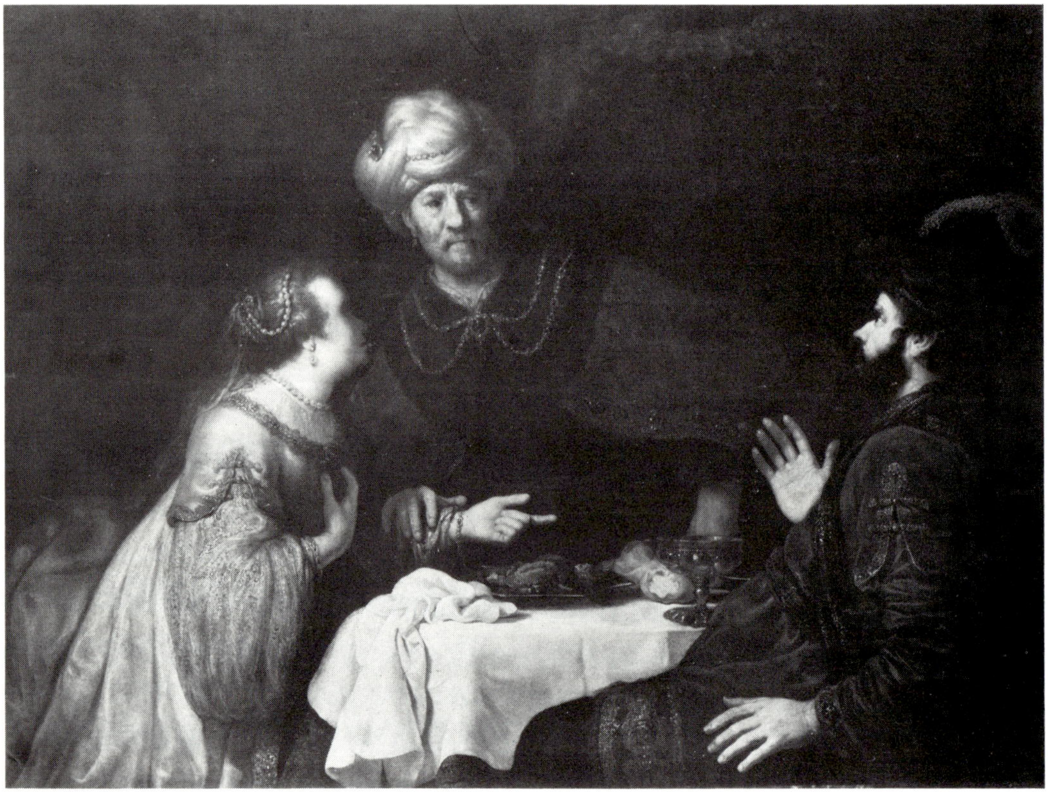

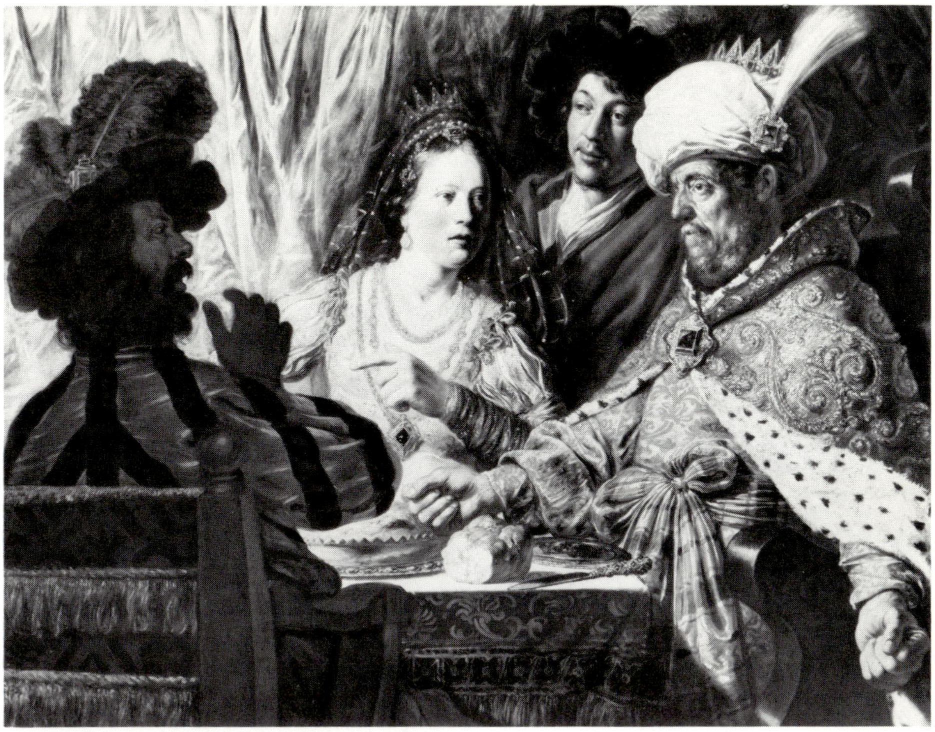

Fig. 117. Rembrandt (?), *The Wrath of Ahasuerus*. Museum of Art, Raleigh, North Carolina.

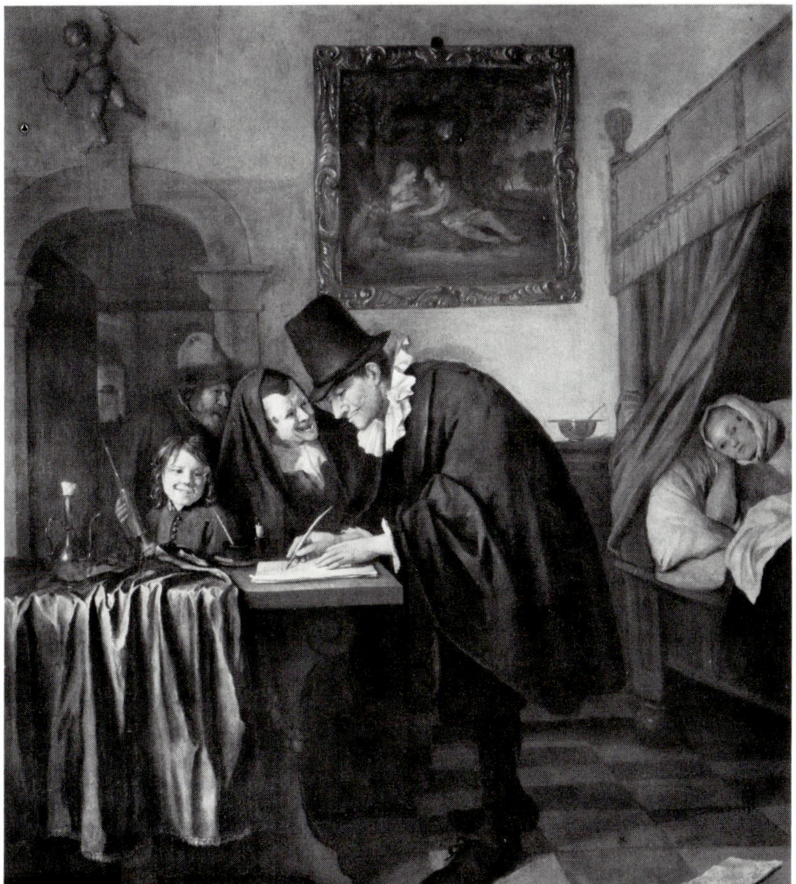

Fig. 118. *The Doctor's Visit* (HdG 136). Willem van der Vorm Foundation, Rotterdam.

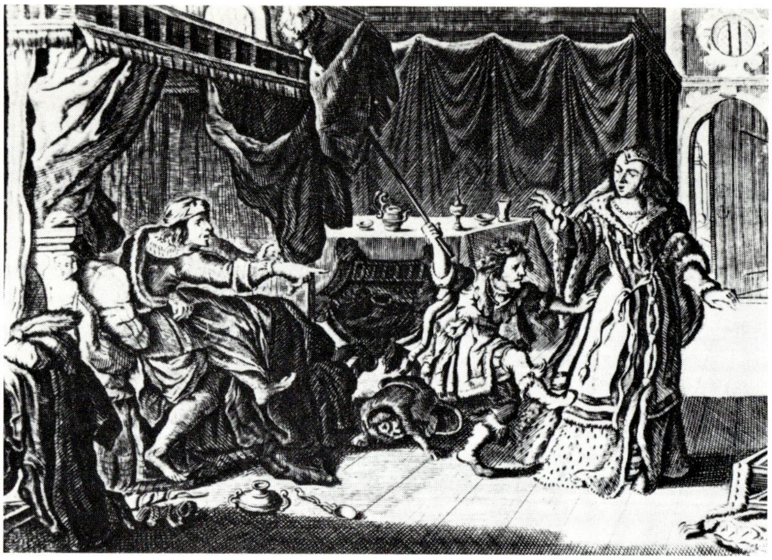

Fig. 119. *Tamar and Amnon,* engraving (from Cats' *Houwelick*).

Fig. 120. *Self-Portrait* (HdG 850). Rijksmuseum, Amsterdam.

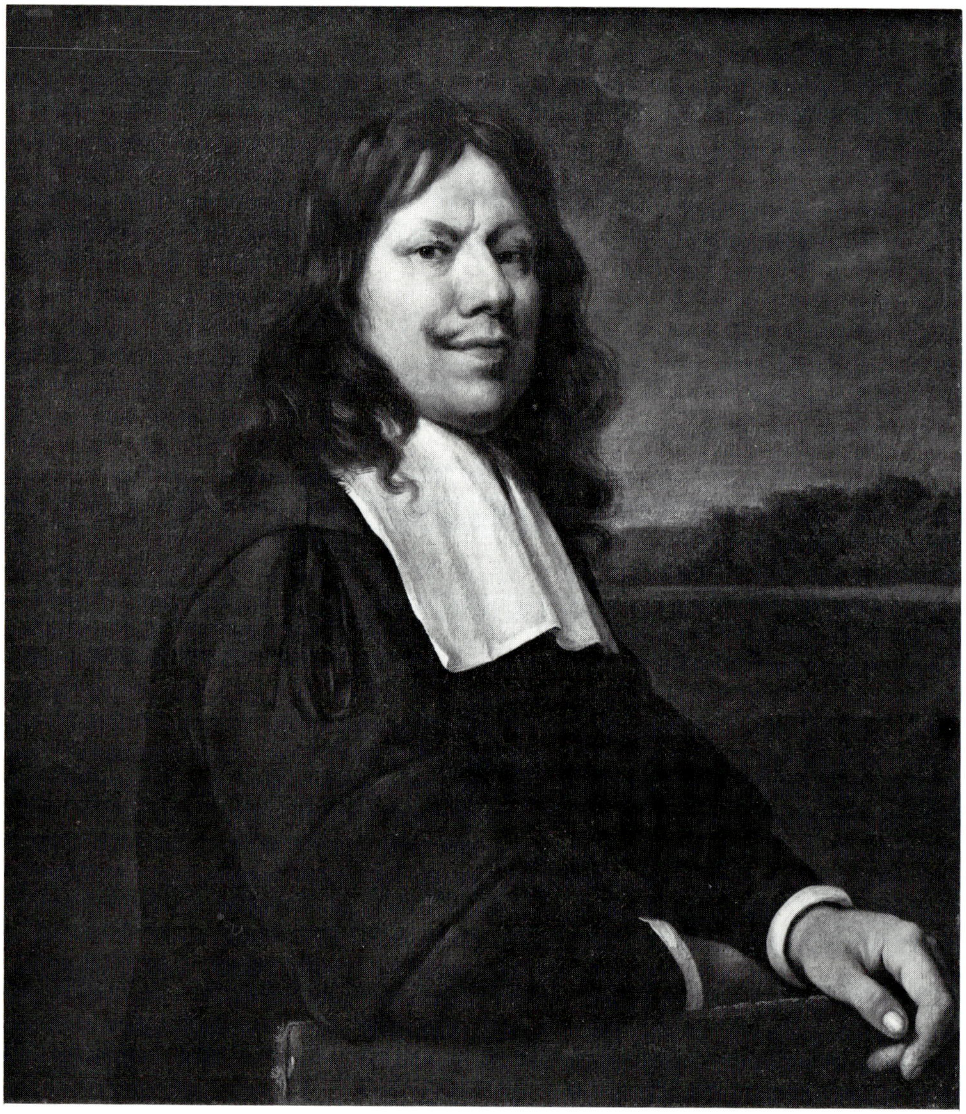

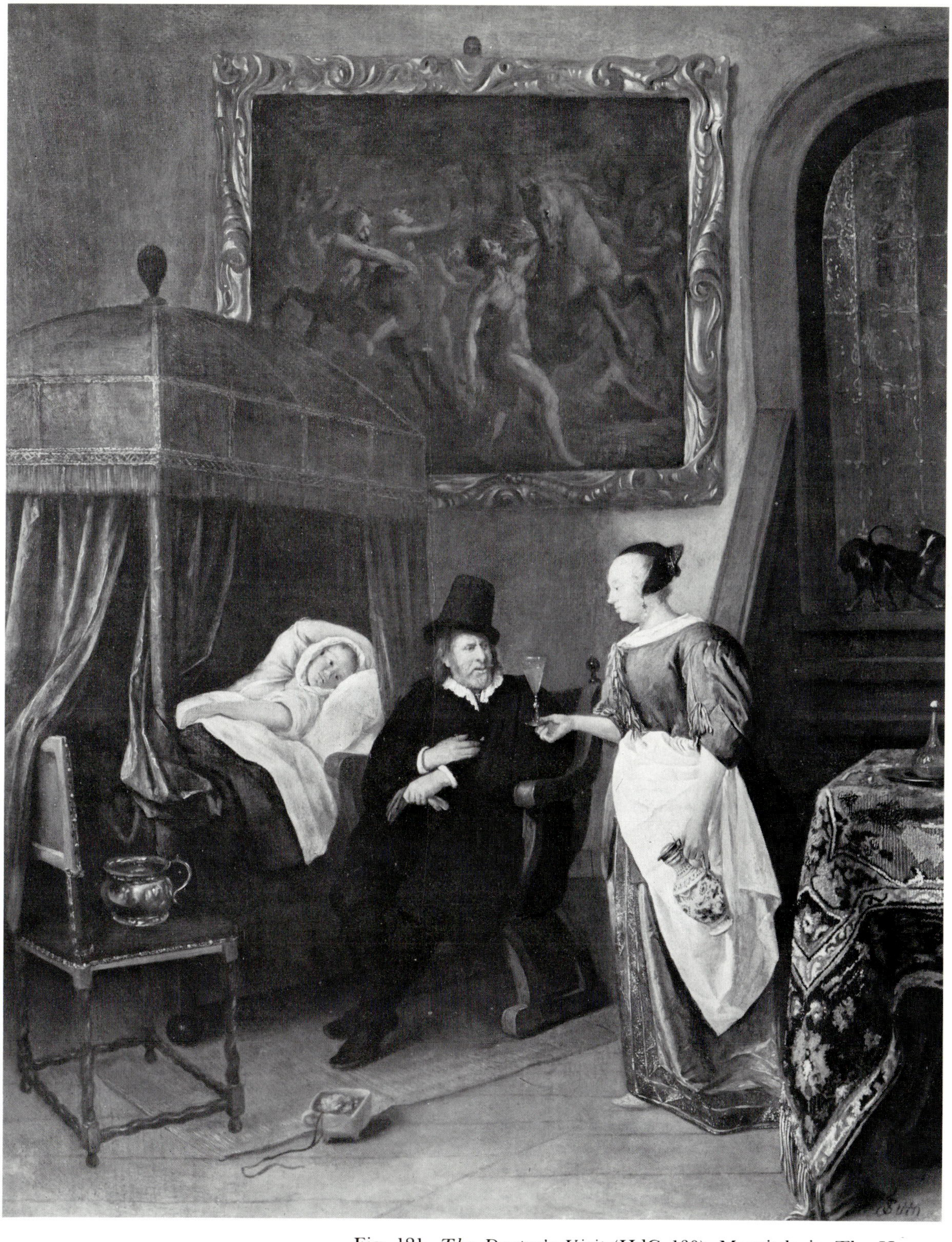

Fig. 121. *The Doctor's Visit* (HdG 130). Mauritshuis, The Hague.

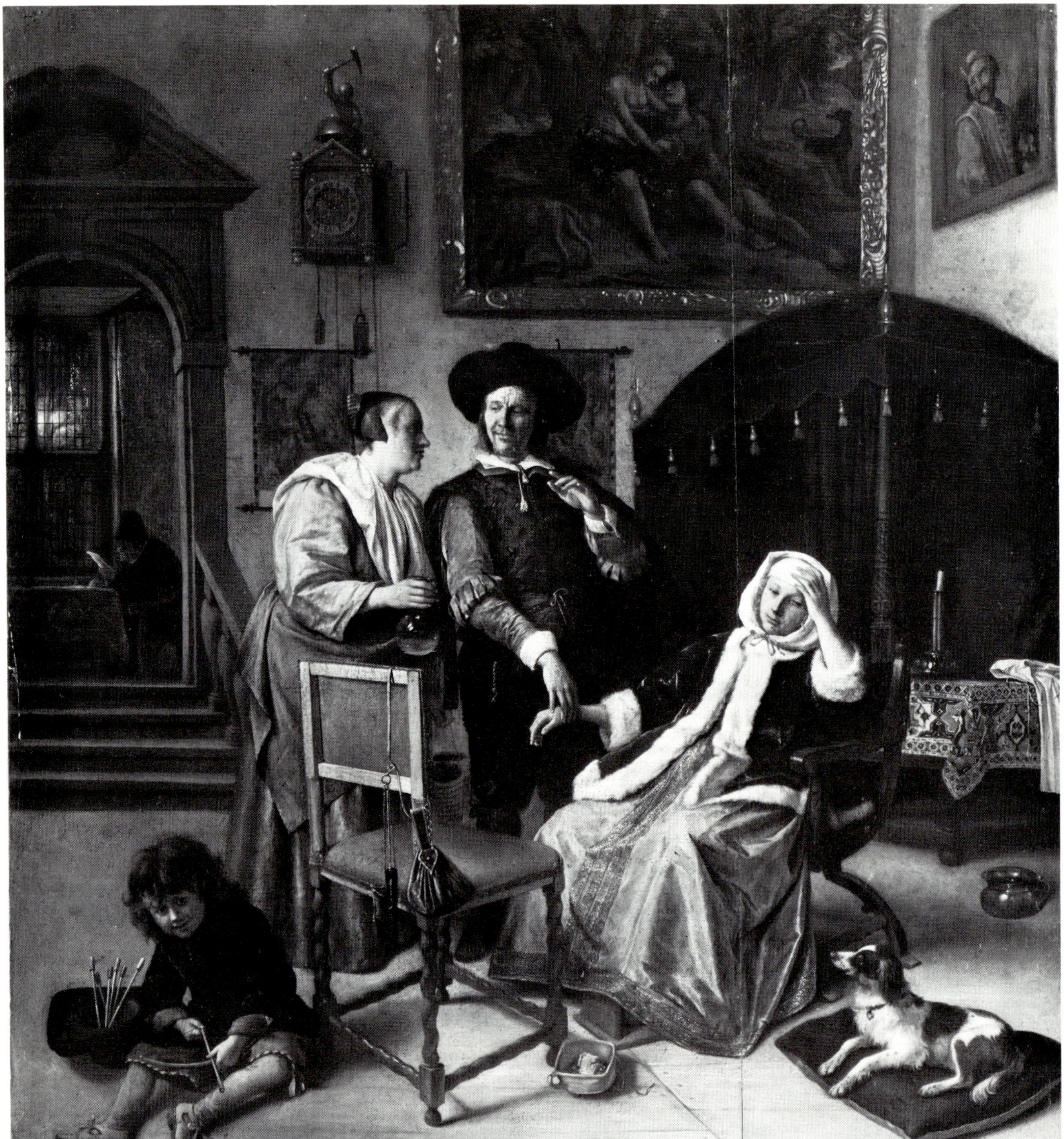

Fig. 122. *The Doctor's Visit* (HdG 137). Wellington collection, Apsley House, London.

Fig. 123. *The Doctor's Visit* (HdG 175). Taft Museum, Cincinnati.

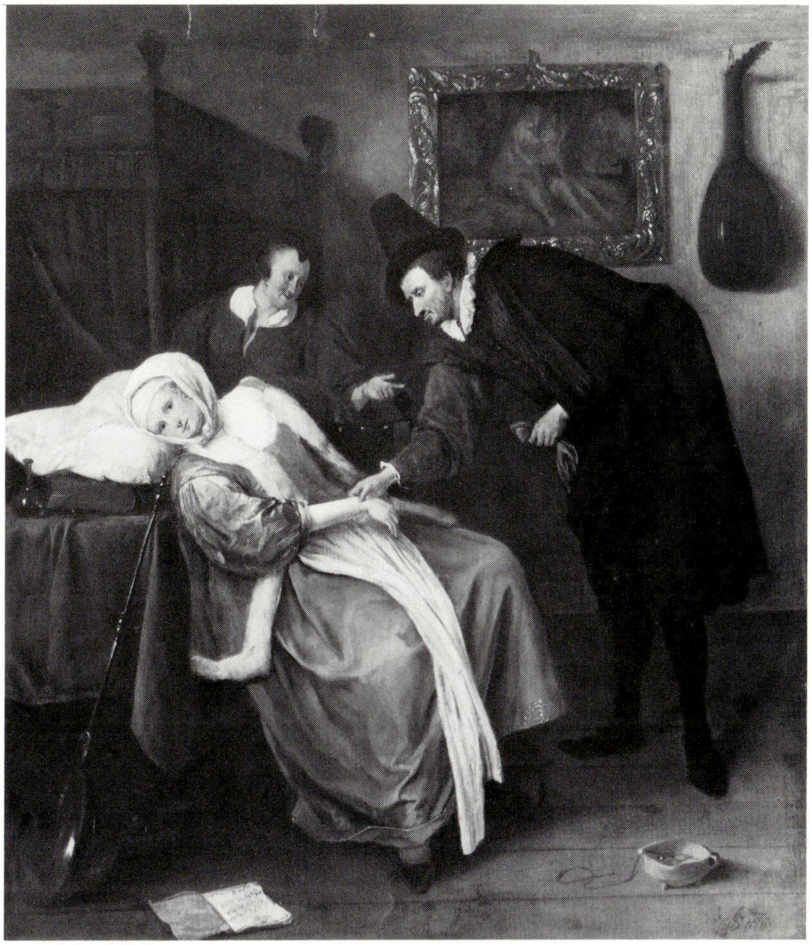

Fig. 124. *The Generosity of Scipio,* oil sketch. Michaelis Gallery, Cape Town.

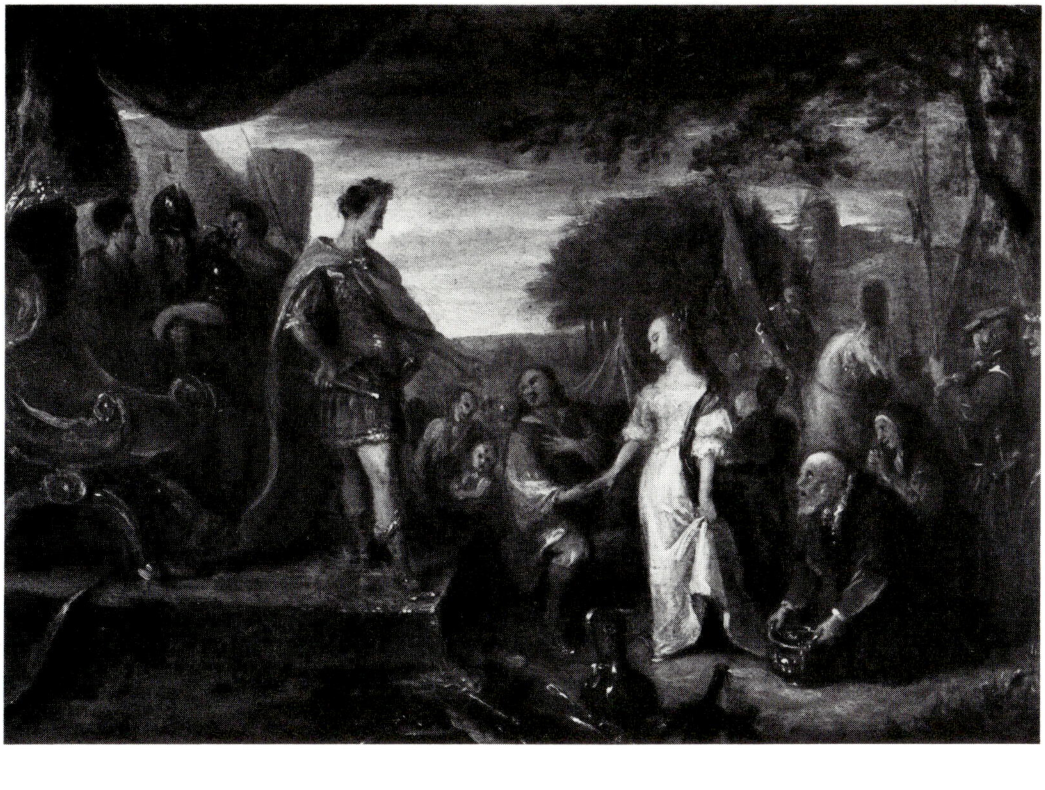

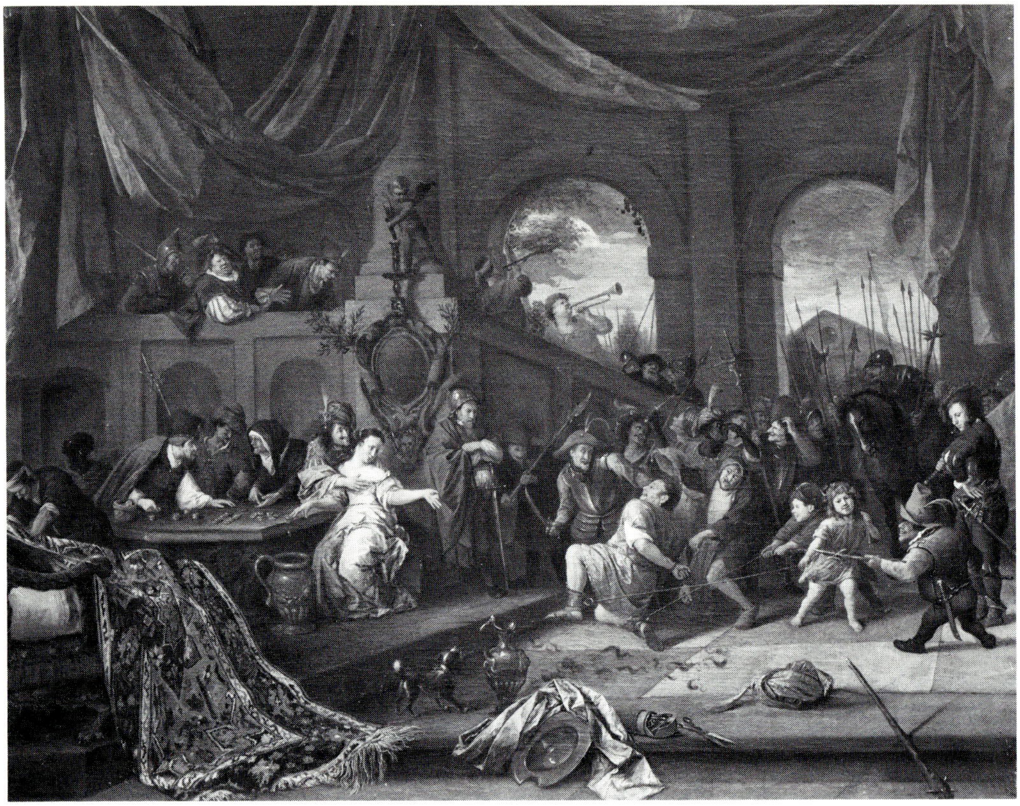

Fig. 125. *Samson Mocked by the Philistines* (Cat. Addendum 1). Musée Royal des Beaux-Arts, Antwerp.

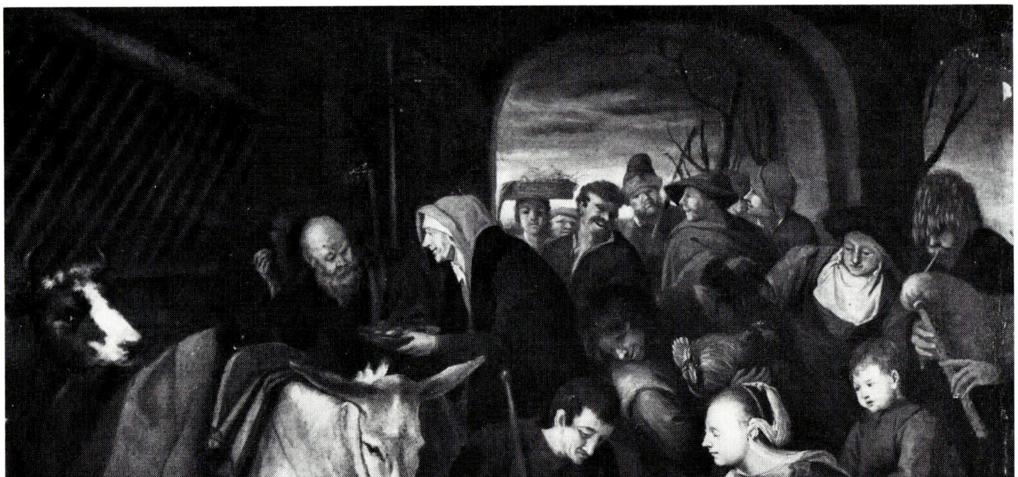

Fig. 126. *The Adoration of the Shepherds* (Cat. Addendum 3). The Wawel State Collection of Art, Cracow, Poland.

Fig. 127. *The Holy Family* (Cat. Addendum 5). Present location unknown.

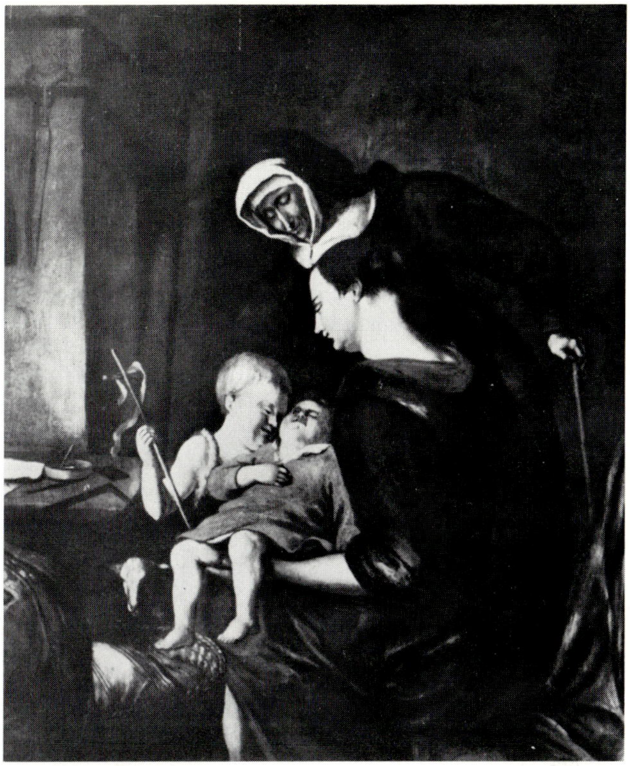

Fig. 128. *Christ in the House of Mary and Martha* (Cat. Addendum 6). Present location unknown.

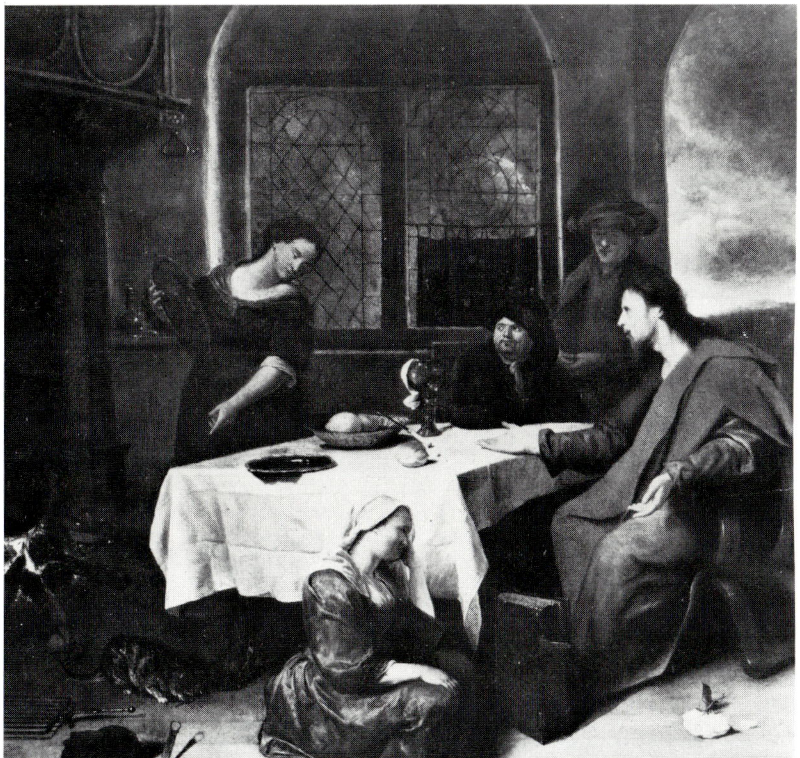

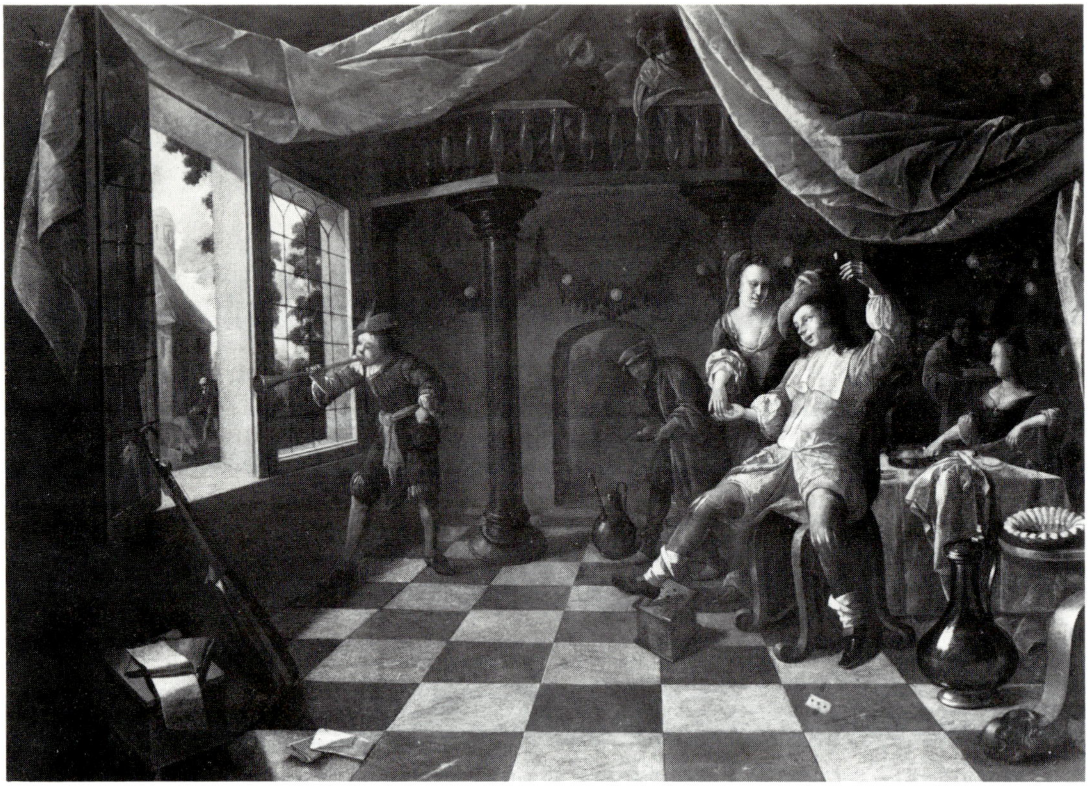

Fig. 129. *The Prodigal Son* (Cat. Addendum 7). Present location unknown.

Fig. 130. *The Prodigal Son* (Cat. Addendum 8). Present location unknown.

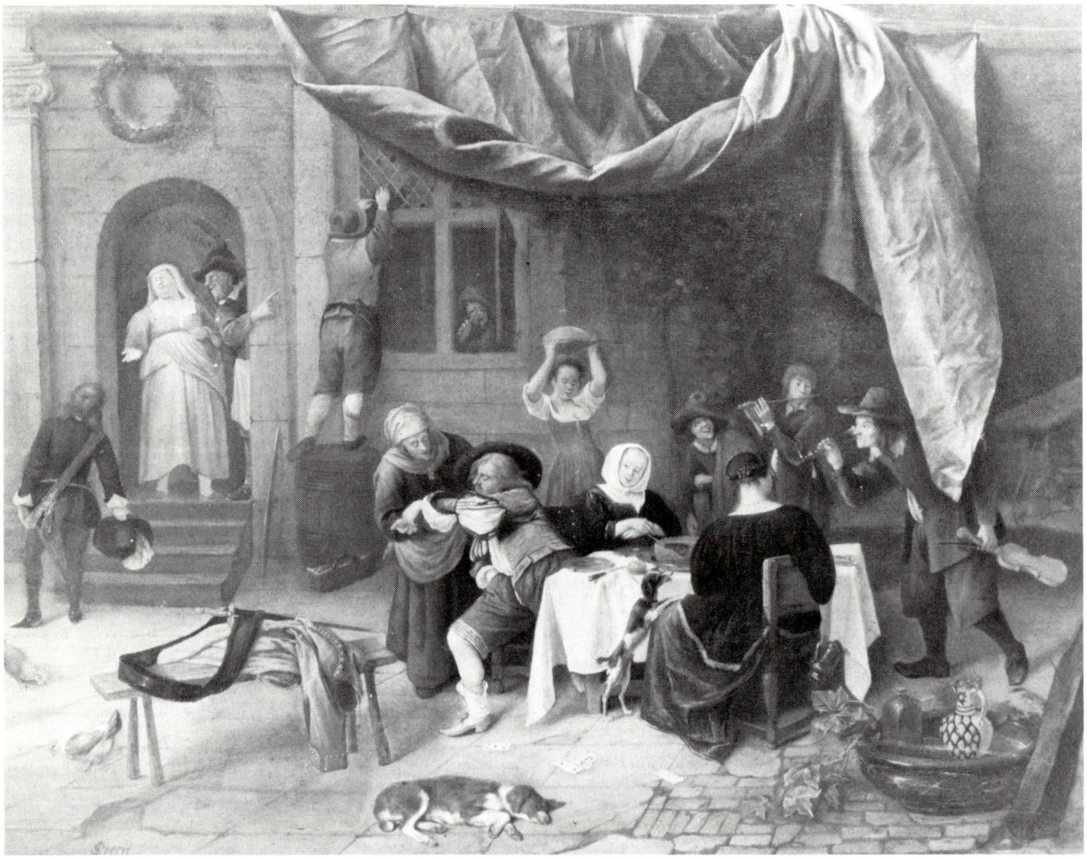

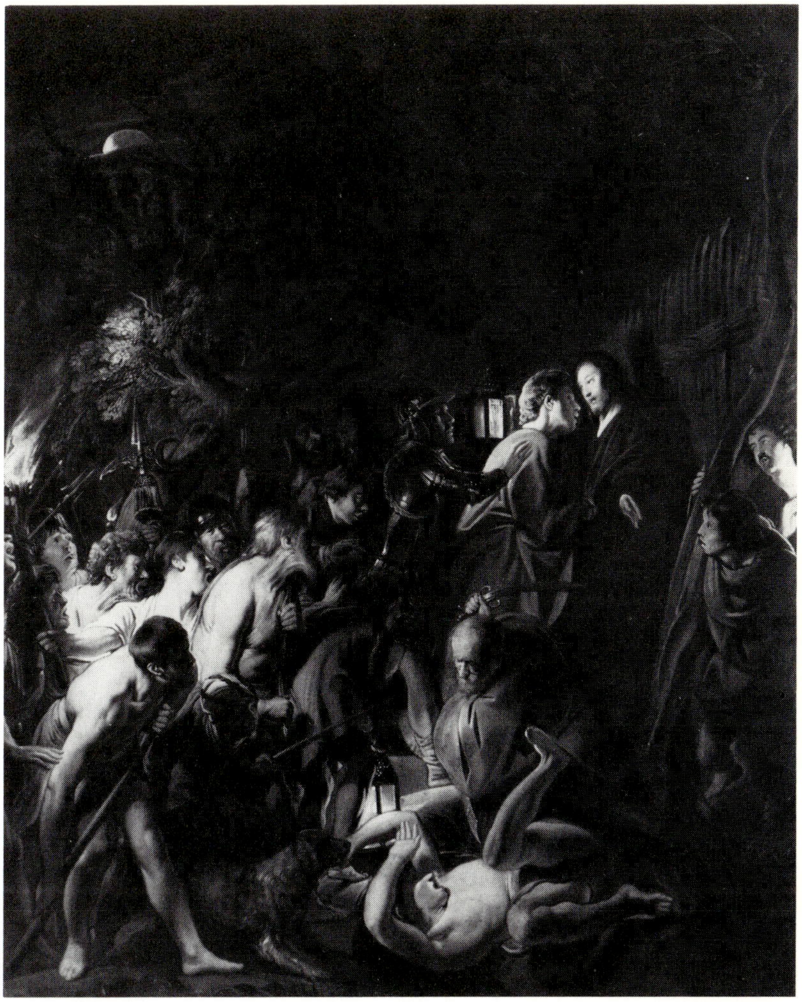

Fig. 131. *The Betrayal of Christ* (Cat. Addendum 10). National Gallery, Prague.

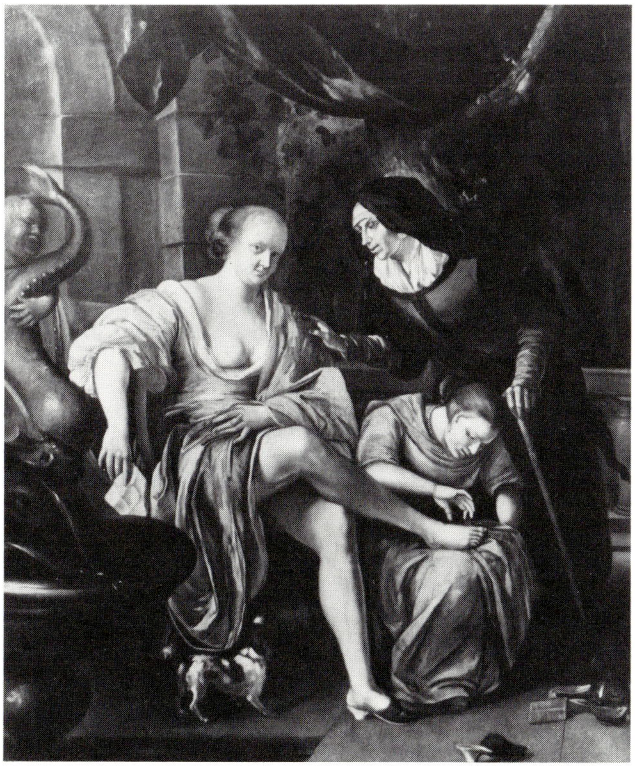

Fig. 132. *Bathseba After the Bath* (Cat. Addendum 12). Museum der Bildenden Künste, Leipzig.

Photographic Credits

AMSTERDAM, Rijksmuseum, Figs. 45, 51, 82, 82a, 91, 105, 107, 120, (Dienst voor Schone Kunsten der Gemeente, 's-Gravenhage) Fig. 37; Wetzlar collection (A. Dingjan, The Hague), 81, 90, Fig. 69; ANTWERP, Musée Royal des Beaux-Arts, Fig. 125; ARNHEM, Gemeentemuseum, Fig. 92; BASEL, Kunstmuseum, Fig. 39; BIRMINGHAM, ENGLAND, The Barber Institute of Fine Arts, University of Birmingham, Fig. 59; BLESSINGTON, IRELAND, Sir Alfred Beit collection, Fig. 62; BOSTON, Courtesy Museum of Fine Arts, Figs. 38, 42; BRUNSWICK, W. GERMANY, Staatliche Herzog Anton-Ulrich Museum, Fig. 66; CAPE TOWN, Michaelis Gallery (Colin Richards), Fig. 124; CASSEL, W. GERMANY, Gemäldegalerie (Staatliche Kunstsammlungen), Figs. 9, 68; CHICAGO, Courtesy of the Art Institute of Chicago, Fig. 55; CINCINNATI, The Taft Museum, Fig. 123; CLEVELAND, The Cleveland Museum of Art, John L. Severance Fund, Fig. 74; COLOGNE, Fritz Lehmann (Courtauld Institute of Art, London), Fig. 57; Stadtmuseum (Rheinisches Bildarchiv), Fig. 116; Wallraf-Richartz Museum (Rheinisches Bildarchiv), Figs. 63, 63a, 72; CONSTANCE, W. GERMANY, Wessenbergische Gemäldegalerie (Jeanine Le Brun), Fig. 48; COPENHAGEN, Royal Museum of Fine Arts, Fig. 83; CRACOW, Wawel State Collection of Art, Fig. 126; DETROIT, Courtesy of the Detroit Institute of Arts, Gift of Mr. & Mrs. Henry Ford II, Fig. 43; DRESDEN, Gemäldegalerie—Alte Meister (Staatliche Kunstsammlungen), Fig. 41, 97; DULWICH, ENGLAND, Dulwich College, Figs. 112, 113; DUNKIRK, Museum (Photographie Bulloz), Fig. 79; FRANKFURT-AM-MAIN, Städelsches Kunstinstitut (U. Edel-Mann FFM), Figs. 26, 27, 64; GLASGOW, Property of Donald Maxwell Macdonald, on show at Pollok House (Annan Photographer), Fig. 40; GOTTINGEN, W. GERMANY, University Museum (Georgia Augusta), Fig. 56; THE HAGUE, Foundation Johan Maurits van Nassau (A. Dingjan), Fig. 32; (Frequin), Fig. 121; Museum Bredius (Gemeente-museum), Fig. 36, (Dienst voor Schone Kunsten der Gemeente, s' Gravenhage), Fig. 78; S. Nystad (A. Dingjan), Fig. 87; Rolzaal, Binnenhof (Dienst voor 's Rijks Verspreide Kunstvoorwerpen), Figs. 60, 94; LEIDEN, Stedelijk Museum "De Lakenhal" (A. Dingjan), Figs. 47, 89; LEIPZIG, Museum der Bildenden Künste, Fig. 132; LEITMERITZ, CZECHOSLOVAKIA, Bishop's Residence, Fig. 28; LIEGE, Musée des Beaux-Arts, Fig. 7; LONDON, Buckingham Palace (Copyright reserved), (A.C. Cooper Ltd), Fig. 33; British Museum (Courtesy of the Trustees), Fig. 21; The National Gallery (Courtesy of the Trustees), Figs. 35, 58;

Wallace Collection (Courtesy of the Trustees), Fig. 54; Wellington Collection, Apsley House (Crown Copyright, Victoria and Albert Museum), Fig. 122; LUGANO—CASTAGNOLA, Thyssen Gallery (Foto Brunel, Lugano), Fig. 108; MUNICH, Alte Pinakothek, Fig. 23; NEW YORK, Elizabeth M. Drey collection (John D. Schiff), Fig. 46; The Metropolitan Museum of Art, Harris Brisbane Dick Fund, 1947, Fig. 49, Rogers Fund, 1917, Fig. 19; PARIS, Louvre, (Service de Documentation Photographique), Fig. 93; PHILADELPHIA, Museum of Art, John G. Johnson Collection, Figs. 10, 18, 88; PRAGUE, National Gallery (Vladimir Fyman), Fig. 131; RALEIGH, North Carolina Museum of Art, Figs. 85, 117; RICHMOND, From the Collection of the Virginia Museum of Fine Arts, Fig. 71; ROTTERDAM, Museum Boymans-van Beuningen, Fig. 25, (A. Frequin), Figs. 17; Museum Boymans-van Beuningen, Willem van der Vorm Collection, Fig. 118; ROUEN, Musée des Beaux-Arts (Lauros-Giraudon), Fig. 104; SAN FRANCISCO, The Fine Arts Museum of San Francisco, Gift of the de Young Museum Society, Figs. 86, 86a; SARASOTA, FLORIDA, John and Mabel Ringling Museum of Art, Fig. 50; SCHWERIN, E. GERMANY, Staatliches Museum, Figs. 8, 11; STRASBOURG, Musée des Beaux-Arts (service de Documentation Photographique), Fig. 61; UTRECHT, Centraal Museum, Figs. 6, 65; VIENNA, Kunsthistorisches Museum, Fig. 24; WARSAW, National Museum, Fig. 31; LOCATION UNKNOWN: (A. Dingjan, The Hague), Fig. 4; (F. C. Cooper, Ltd.), Fig. 52; (Rijksbureau voor Kunsthistorische Documentatie, The Hague), Figs. 12, 16, 30; PRIVATE COLLECTIONS: ENGLAND, (Alan Jacobs, London) Fig. 75, (Kunstverlag Wolfrum, Vienna) Fig. 34; THE NETHERLANDS: (A. Dingjan, The Hague), Figs. 67, 102; (Wim Zeulemaker), Fig. 15.

Bibliography

The Bibliography is divided into two sections: I. Works on Steen himself; II. Works on related subjects. The entries are arranged alphabetically by author.

I. Works on Jan Steen

Alfrink, Bern. "Raphaël, niet Daniël bij Jan Steen," *Oud-Holland,* LIX (1942), 127-28.

Antal, Friedrich. "Concerning Some Jan Steen Pictures in America," *Art in America and Elsewhere,* XIII (1925), 107-16.

Bijleveld, W. J. J. C. "Het Tuinfeest van Jan Steen," *Oud-Holland,* XLIII (1926), 132-35.

Bredius, Abraham. "Een Jan Steen van 1646?" *Oud-Holland,* LXIII (1926), 267-68.

———. *Jan Steen, met Honderd Platten bevattende 101 Afbeeldingen in Photogravure van zijne Beste Werken.* Amsterdam, 1927.

Bremmer, H. P. "Jan Steen, de Aanbidding der Herders," *Die Constgheselllen,* I (1946), 163-66.

de Groot, C. W. *Jan Steen, Beeld en Woord.* Utrecht/Nijmegen, 1952.

de Jonge. *Jan Steen.* (Palet Series.) Amsterdam, n.d. [Also published in *Jan Steen en zijn Tijdgenooten,* Amsterdam, n.d.]

Descamps, J. B. *La vie des peintres flamands, allemands et hollandais.* III, Paris, 1760.

DeVries, Lyckle. "Achttiende-en negentiende-eeuwse auteurs over Jan Steen," *Oud-Holland,* LXXXVII (1973), 227-39.

Fink, August. "Jan Steen's Hochzeit des Tobias," *Zeitschrift für bildende Kunst,* LX (1926/27), 230-33.

———. "Jan Steen die Eheverschreibung," *Atlantis,* XXI (1949), 181-82.

Gerson, Horst. "Landschappen van Jan Steen," *Kunsthistorische Mededelinging,* III (1948), 50-56.

Gudlaugsson, Sturla. *De Komedianten bij Jan Steen en zijn Tijdgenooten.* The Hague, 1945.

Guldener, Hermine van. "De Aanbidding der Herders van J. Steen," *Phoenix,* III (1948), 18-21.

Henkel, M. D. "Jan Steen und der Delfter Vermeer," *Kunstwanderer,* XIV (1931/32), 265-66.

Heppner, Albert. "Heinrich Heine en Jan Steen," *Op de Hoogte,* XXXIII (1936), 317-19.

———. "The Popular Theater of the Rederijkers in the Works of Jan Steen and his Contemporaries," *Journal of the Warburg and Cortauld Institutes,* XXX (1939/40), 22-48.

Hofstede de Groot, C. "Een Altaarstuk van Jan Steen," *De Nederlandsche Spectator,* Feb. 10, 1892, 104-05.

———. *A Catalogue Raisonné of the Works of the Most Eminent Dutch Painters of the Seventeenth Century.* 8 vols. I, London, 1908 (German ed., 1907).

———. "Jan Steen and his Master Nicholaes Knüpfer," *Art in America and Elsewhere,* XVI (1927/28), 249-53.

Holmes, C. J. "Notes on the Chronology of Jan Steen," *Burlington Magazine,* XV (1909), 243-44.

Houbraken, A. *De Groote Schouburgh der Nederlantsche Konstschilders en Schilderessen.* 3 vols. Amsterdam, 1718/21. [New ed., P. T. A. Swillens, 3 vols., Maastricht, 1943/53.]

Kuznetsov, I. V. "Kartiny Iana Stena v Gosudarstvennom ermitazha," *Ezhegodnik,* Akademiia nauk SSSR, Institut istorii iskusstv, 1957, 371-415.

Laurie, A. T. "Jan Steen, Esther, Ahasuerus and Haman," *Bulletin*, Cleveland Museum of Art, LII (1965), 94-100.

Maandblad "Het Kind," IX (1953), 287.

Martin, Willem. "Jan Steen en zijn Kunst op de Tentoonstelling te London," *Onze Kunst*, XI (1909), 141-72.

———. "L'exposition Jan Steen à Londres," *L'art flamand et hollandais*, XII (1909), 130-58.

———. "Studien zu Jan Steen Anlasslich der Ausstellung seiner Werke in London," *Monatshefte für Kunstwissenschaft*, III (1910), 179-89.

———. *Jan Steen, over zijn Leven en Kunst, naar Aanleiding van Jan Steen Tentoonstelling te Leiden.* Leiden, 1926.

———. "Neues über Jan Steen," *Zeitschrift für bildende Kunst*, LXI (1927/28), 325-41.

———. "Jan Steen as a Landscape Painter," *Burlington Magazine*, LXVII (1935), 211-12.

———. "Wrath of Ahasuerus," *Bulletin of the Bachstitz Gallery* (1935), 34-35.

———. *Jan Steen.* Amsterdam, 1954.

Moes, E. W. "Genesis XXXV van Jan Steen," *Oude en Nieuw* (1889), 67-70.

"Recent Important Acquisitions of American Collections," *The Art Quarterly*, XVII (1954), 428-30.

Schmidt-Degener, F. and van Gelder, H. E. *Veertig Meesterwerken van Jan Steen met een Karakteristiek van zijn Kunst.* Amsterdam, 1927. [English ed. trans., G. J. Renier, London, 1927.]

Simon, Kurt. "Jan Steen and Utrecht," *Pantheon*, XXV (1940), 162-65.

Smith, John. *A Catalogue Raisonné of the Works of the Most Eminent Dutch, Flemish, and French Painters. . . .* 5 vols. I, London, 1833; V (Supplement), London, 1842.

Stechow, Wolfgang. "Bermerkungen zu Jan Steens künstlerischer Entwicklung," *Zeitschrift für bildende Kunst*, LXII (1928/29), 173-79.

———. "Jan Steen's Merry Company," *Allen Memorial Art Museum Bulletin*, Oberlin College, Oberlin (Ohio), XV (1953), 90-100.

———. "Jan Steen's Representation of the Marriage in Cana," *Nederlands Kunsthistorisch Jaarboek*, XXIII (1972), 73-83.

Jan Steen Tentoonstelling. (Catalogue) Leiden: Stedlijk Museum "De Lakenhal," 1926.

Jan Steen Tentoonstelling. (Catalogue) The Hague: Mauritshuis, 1958/59.

Trautscholdt, E. "Jan Steen," *Thieme-Becker Kunstlerlexikon*, XXXI (1937), 509-15.

van Gelder, J. G. "Een Vroeg Werk van Jan Steen," *Oud-Holland*, XLIII (1926), 203-20.

van Gils, J. B. F. "J. Steen en de Rederijkers," *Oud-Holland*, LII (1935), 130-33.

———. "J. Steen in den Schouwburg," *Op de Hoogte*, XXXIV (1937), 92-93.

———. "Theseus bij Acheloüs van Jan Steen," *Oud-Holland*, LVII (1940), 145-48.

———. "Jan Steen in den Shouwburg," *Oud-Holland*, LIX (1942), 57-63.

———. "Toch Daniel niet Raphaël," *Oud-Holland*, LIX (1942), 184-86.

van Leeuwen, Frans. "Een Jan Steen, De Aanbidding der Herders in het Rijksmuseum," *De Kroniek van de Vriendenkring van het Rembrandthuis*, XX (1966), 59-64.

van Regteren Altena, J. Q. "Hoe teekende Jan Steen," *Oud-Holland*, LX (1943), 97-117.

van Westrheene, Tobias. *Jan Steen, étude sur l'art en Hollande.* The Hague, 1856.

Welcker, A. "Jan Steen's Samson en Delila," *Oud-Holland*, LIV (1937), 254-62.

Weyerman, Jacob Campo. *De Levens-Beschryving en der Nederlandsche Konst-Schilders en Konst-Schilderessen met een Uytbreyding over de Schilderkonst der Ouden. . .* 4 vols. The Hague, 1729 (I-III); Dordrecht, 1769 (IV).

II. Works on Related Subjects

Bauwen. *La tragedie française et le théatre hollandais au dix-septième siècle.* Amsterdam, 1921.

Bax, Dirk. *Skilders wat Vertel 'n Uitleg van sewe Nederlandse en Vlaamse Sewentiende-eeuse Skilderye in Suid Afrikaanse Museums.* London, Capetown, New York, 1951.

———. *Hollandse en Vlaamse Schilderkunst in Zuid-Afrika.* Amsterdam, 1952.

Benesch, Otto. *The Drawings of Rembrandt.* London, 1954/57. 6 vols.

Bialostoski, Jan, and Wolicki, Michal. *Europäische Malerei in polnischen Sammlungen.* Warsaw, 1957.

Bijbelsche Kunst. (Catalogue) Amsterdam: Rijksmuseum, 1939.

Bille, Clara. *De Tempel der Kunst of Het Kabinet van den Heer Braacamp.* 2 vols. Amsterdam, 1961.

Bode, Wilhelm. *Catalogue of the Collection of Pictures and Bronzes in the Possession of Mr. Otto Breit.* London, 1913.

———. *Catalogue of the Rudolph Kann Collection.* Paris, 1907.

———. *Die Gemälde-Galerie des Herrn Rudolf Kann in Paris.* Paris, 1900.

———. *Die Kunst Sammlungen des Herrn Alfred Beit.* Berlin, 1904.

———. *Die Meister der holländischen und flämischen Malerschulen.* Leipzig, 1917. Ed. E. Plietzsch, Leipzig, 1958.

———. *De Sammlung Oscar Huldschinsky.* Berlin, 1908.

Bredius, Abraham. "Kunstmarkt," *Kunstchronik,* XXIII (1887), 91.

———. *De Leidse Tentoonstelling in 1906.* Leiden, 1906.

———. *Kunstler-Inventare.* The Hague, 1915. 7 vols.

———. "Het Schetsboek van Jacob de Wet," *Oud-Holland,* XXXVII (1919), 215-22.

———. *The Paintings of Rembrandt.* Vienna, 1936.

Bruyn, J. and Emmens, J. A. "The Sunflower Again," *Burlington Magazine,* IC (1957), 96-97.

Buchanan, W. *Memoirs of Painting.* 2 vols. London, 1824.

Bürger-Thoré, W. *Galerie d'Arenberg à Bruxelles avec le catalogue complet de la collection.* Brussels, 1859.

———. *Le Musée de la Hollande.* 2 vols. Paris, 1860.

———. "Le musée d'Anvers (École Hollandais)," *Gazette des Beaux-Arts,* XII (1862), 152-67.

Cats, Jacob. *Alle de Wercken van den Heere.* 2 vols. Amsterdam, 1712.

Chastel, André. "Le tableau dans le tableau," *Akten des 21. Internationalen Kongresses für Kunstgeschichte in Bonn 1964.* I, Berlin (1967), 15-29.

Czarnik, B. *Wystawa Rembrandt-owska w Lejdzie.* Lwów, 1908.

de Bastide, Jean François. *Le temple des arts ou le cabinet de Monsieur Braacamp.* Amsterdam, 1766.

De Jongh, E. "Erotica in Vogelperspectief, De dubbelzinnigheid van een reeks 17de eeuwse genrevoorstellingen," *Simiolus,* III (1968/69), 22-74.

de Saint-Groux, André. "La collection Ch. Sedelmeyer," *Les Arts,* VI (1907), 17-28.

La Decouverte de la Lumière (Catalogue). Bordeaux, 1959.

Fiorillo. *Beschreibung der Gemälde Sammlung der Universität zu Göttingen.* Göttingen, 1805.

———. *Geschichte der Zeichnenden Künste in Deutschland und vereinigten Niederlanden.* 4 vols. Hanover, 1815/20.

Fischel, Oskar. "Art and Theater," *Burlington Magazine,* LXVI (1935), 4-14, 54-67.

Fransen, J. *Les comédiens français en Hollande au XVIIe et XVIIIe siècle.* Paris, 1925.

Freise, Kurt von. "Neue Bilder in holländischen Sammlungen," *Der Cicerone,* IV (1912), 653-63.

Furst, Herbert. "How to Appreciate Art," *Apollo,* XXX (1939), 214-18.

Goetz, Hermann. "Oriental Types and Scenes in Renaissance and Baroque Painting," *Burlington Magazine,* LXXIII (1938), I 50-63; II 105-11.

Granberg, Olaf. *Catalogue of the Wachtmeister Collection.* Stockholm (?), 1886.

———. "Schilderijen in 1651 voor Kaü Gustav Graf von Wrangel te s'Gravenhage Aangekocht," *Oud-Holland,* XXV (1907), 132.

———. *Inventaire Général des Trésors d'Art en Suède.* 3 vols. Stockholm, 1911.

Gudlaugsson, Sturla. *Ikonographische Studien über die holländische Malerei und das Theater des 17. Jahrhunderts.* Wurtzburg, 1938.

———. "Bredero's Lucelle door Eenige Zeventiende Eeuwsche Meesters Uitbeeld," *Nederlandsche Kunsthistorisch Jaarboek,* I (1947), 177-79.

Hamann, Richard. "Hagars Abschied bei Rembrandt und in Rembrandt-Kreise," *Marburger Jahrbuch für Kunstwissenschaft,* VIII-IX (1936), 471-578.

Harderwijk, J. "Brieven," *Kunstkronijk,* XI (1950).

Hartt, Frederick. *Love in Baroque Art.* New York, 1964.

Harvard, Henri. "Les chefs-d'oeuvre de l'école hollandais," *Gazette des Beaux-Arts,* VI (1872), 211-24, 295-311, 372-92.

Haverkorn van Rijsewijk. *Het Museum-Boymans te Rotterdam.* The Hague/Amsterdam, 1909.

Hennus, M. F. "In den Oude-Schilderijen Handel," *Maandblad voor Beeldende Kunsten,* VII (1930), 284.

Hind, Arthur M. *Catalogue of Drawings by Dutch and Flemish Artists in the British Museum.* 2 vols. London, 1915.

Hobson, R. L. "Chinese Porcelain in Dutch Pictures," *Country Life,* LXV (1929), 243–55.

Hofstede de Groot, C. *Arnold Houbraken und seine "Groote Schouburgh"* (Quellenstudien zur holländischen Kunstgeschichte). The Hague, 1893.

Hollstein, F. W. H. *Dutch and Flemish Etchings, Engravings, and Woodcuts.* 14 vols. Amsterdam, n.d.

Jaarverslag, Boymans Museum, Rotterdam, 1912, 6.

Judson, Richard. *Gerrit van Honthorst.* The Hague, 1959.

Kahr, Madlyn. "Delilah," *Art Bulletin,* LIV (1972), 282-99.

———. "Rembrandt and Delilah," *Art Bulletin,* LV (1973), 240-59.

———. "Rembrandt's Esther," *Oud-Holland,* LXXXI (1966) 228–44.

Kernodle, George R. *From Art to Theatre.* Chicago, 1944.

Keyszelitz, Robert. *Der "clavis interpretandi" in der holländischen Malerei des 17. Jahrhunderts.* (Dissertation.) Munich, 1956.

Knipping, B. *De Iconografie van de Contra-Reformatie in de Nederlanden.* 2 vols. Hilversum, 1939/40.

Kunoth-Leifels, E. *Über die Darstellungen der Bathseba im Bade.* Essen, 1962.

Kurzes Verzeichnis der Gemaldesammlung im Herzog Anton-Ulrich-Museum. Brunswick, 1932.

Kuznetsov, I. V. "Nikolaus Knupfer-Biografiia, Eemy i istochniki tvorchestva, Katalog proizvedenii," *Trudy Gosudarstvennogo ermitazha,* VIII, No. 3, n.d., 187–232.

———. "Het werkelijke onderwerpen van de werken van A. Elsheimer en N. Knüpfer bekind onder de naam "Contento of de Jacht naar het Geluk,'" *Oud-Holland,* LXXIX (1964) 229–30.

Lagrante, Leon. "La Galerie de M. le Duc de Morny," *Gazette des Beaux-Arts,* XIV (1863), 300.

Larsen, Erik. "The Duality of Flemish and Dutch Art in the Seventeenth Century," *Akten des 21. Internationalen Kongresses für Kunstgeschichte in Bonn, 1964.* III, Berlin, 1967, 59-65.

Leclercq, Emile. "Collection von den Heche-Baut," *Gazette des Beaux-Arts,* IX (1861), 42–49.

Die Leidener Ausstellung von 1906 zur Erinnerung und Flier des 300-Jahr Geburtstages Rembrandts (ed. Bredius). Leipzig/Haarlem, 1907.

Lilienfeld, Karl. "Kunstschätze in Schweden," *Monatshefte für Kunstwissenschaft,* IV (1911), 50–52.

Lugt, Frits. *Répertoire des catalogues de ventes publiques. 1600–1860.* 2 vols. The Hague, 1953.

Maclaren, Neil. *The Dutch School.* (National Gallery Catalogues.) London, 1960.

Marguillier, A. "La collection de M. Rodolphe Kann," *Les Arts,* II (1903), 24–25.

Martin, Willem. *De Hollandsche Schilderkunst in de Zeventiende Eeuw.* 2 vols. Amsterdam, 1935/36.

———, and Moes, E. W. *Oude Schilder-Kunst in Nederland.* 2 vols. The Hague, 1912.

Michel, E. "La Galerie de M. Rodolphe Kann," *Gazette des Beaux-Arts,* XXV (1901), 385–400, 493–506.

Mirimonde, A. P. "La musique dans les allegories de l'amour," *Gazette des Beaux-Arts,* Series 6, LXVIII (1966), 265–90.

Mündler, O. "Meisterwerke der Braunschweiger Galerie," *Zeitschrift für bildende Kunst,* (1868), 184–94.

Münz, Ludwig. *Rembrandt's Etchings.* 2 vols. London, 1952.

Nicoll, A. *The Development of the Theatre.* New York, 1948.

100 Masterpieces: a selection from pictures by old masters which form or have formed part of the Sedelmayer Collection. (Catalogue.) Paris, 1914.

Pflugk-Hartung, J. von. "Berichte und Mittheilungen aus Sammlungen und Museen (Die Weber'sche Gemäldesammlung)," *Repertorium für Kunstwissenshaft,* VIII (1885), 80–94.

Plietzsch, E. "Gabriel Metsu," *Pantheon,* XXII (1936), 1-13.

Puvelde, L. *Schilderkunst in Toneelvertooningen op het Einde van de Middeleeuwen,* Antwerp, 1912.

Reynolds, Joshua. *Discourses on Art,* ed. Robert R. Wark. San Marino, California, 1959.

Richardson, E. P. "A Late Rembrandt for the Institute," *Bulletin of the Detroit Institute of Arts,* XXXVI (1956/57).

Richter, Jean Paul. *Catalogue of the Collection of the Marquis of Bute.* London, 1884.

Rosand, David. "Theater and Structure in the Art of Paolo Veronese," *Art Bulletin,* LV (1973), 217–39.

Rovenskii, Dimitri. *L'oeuvre gravé des élèves de Rembrandt et des Maîtres qui gravé dans son goüt.* 2 vols. St. Petersburg, 1894.

Rudloff-Hille, Gertrud. *Die Dresdner Gemäldegalerie.* Munich, 1960.

Schlie, Friedrich. *Uber Nikolaus Knüpfer und einige seiner Gemälde, besonders über seine "Jagd nach dem Glück (Sog Contento)" in München und Schwerin.* Schwerin, 1896.

Slive, Seymour. "Notes on the Relationship of Protestantism to Seventeenth Century Dutch Painting," *Art Quarterly,* XIX (1956), 2-15.

Stechow, Wolfgang. "The Love of Antiochus with the Fair Stratonice," *Art Bulletin,* XXVII (1945), 221-37.

Swillens, P. T. A. *Jacob van Campen, Schilder en Bouwmeester, 1595-1657.* Amsterdam, 1961.

Tietze, Hans. *Masterpieces of European Painting in America.* London, 1939.

Treter, M. *Album Wystawy mistrzów dawnych.* Lwów, 1911.

Valentiner, W. R. *Catalogue of a Collection of Paintings and Some Art Objects* (Johnson Collection). 2 vols. Philadelphia, 1914.

——. *Dutch and Flemish Old Masters in the Collection of Dr. C. J. K. van Aalst.* Huis-te-Hoevelaken, Holland, 1939.

——. *Rembrandt des Meisters Handzeichnungen.* "Klassiker der Kunst," XXX. 2 vols. Stuttgart, 1925.

Van der Willigen, A. *Les Artistes de Haarlem.* The Hague, 1870.

Van der Waal, H. *Drie Eeuwen Vaderlandsche Geschied-Uitbeelding. 1500-1800: Een Iconologische Studie.* 2 vols. The Hague, 1952.

Waagen, Gustav Friedrich. *Treasures of Art in Great Britain.* 3 vols. London, 1854. Supplement, London, 1857.

Watson, F. J. B. "The Collection of Sir Alfred Beit," *Connoisseur,* XLV (1961), 156-63, 216-24.

Willnau, Carl von. "Von Elsheimers contento zu Knüpfers contentement," *Zeitschrift für bildende Kunst,* LXV (1931/32), 113-20.

Wood, T. M. *The Max Michaelis Gift to the Union of South Africa—Flemish and Dutch Paintings.* Michaelis Gallery, Capetown; London, 1913.

Worp, J. A. *Geschiedenis van den Amsterdamschen Schouwburg.* Amsterdam, 1920.

*Index**

*Plates are reproduced on pages listed in italics.